AF506094

Business
Mathematics

Business Mathematics

J. Roland Kelley *Tarrant County Junior College*
Jimmy C. McKenzie *Tarrant County Junior College*
Alton W. Evans *Tarrant County Junior College*

Houghton Mifflin Company **Boston**
Dallas   Geneva, Illinois   Hopewell, New Jersey   Palo Alto   London

Printed in the U.S.A.

Library of Congress Catalog Card Number: 80-50973

ISBN: 0-395-30670-1

Contents

Preface

Business Mathematics is an applied math text designed to provide the math background that you will need in other business courses, in your business career, and in your role as an informed consumer. The beginning chapters review the basic fundamentals of mathematics. The next chapters cover various topics in business: marketing, accounting, finance, real estate, insurance, and transportation. These topics include most of the key areas of business activity. The last chapter discusses business statistics.

The material has been arranged in five major parts. Each part is divided into chapters containing two or more learning units. Student performance objectives preceding each chapter provide a study outline of the chapter. An exam designed for self-evaluation is provided at the end of each chapter, providing an opportunity for you to check your comprehension of the material contained in the chapter. After completing the chapter, you should complete the self-evaluation and check your answers against the answer key in Appendix M.

Each learning unit develops a single concept (or closely related concepts). The organization of a learning unit consists of (1) explanations of where, why, and how each concept is used in business, (2) examples illustrating application of the concepts and of problem-solving techniques, and (3) realistic exercise problems of graduated difficulty that enable you to apply the concept to typical business situations. These exercise problems include a variety of word and computational problems that provide valuable training for actual business situations. Answers to the odd-numbered problems are included in Appendix L. This will enable you to receive immediate feedback.

The Appendices also contain information on the metric system, computer number systems, and using the electronic calculator, as well as various tables to be used in conjunction with the text.

Acknowledgments

Many people assisted us in the preparation and publication of this book. Although assuming final responsibility for the material contained in this book, the authors gratefully acknowledge the help of these people.

The authors owe a considerable debt to the following individuals. Ed Jaffe recognized the need for a hard-cover business mathematics book and encouraged the authors to undertake the project. He provided guidance throughout the process of developing the materials for the book. Laverne Dellinger made numerous editorial changes that improved the manuscript. Lorraine Wolf guided the manuscript through the publication process and made numerous suggestions that contributed to the final product.

The authors gratefully acknowledge the help of the following reviewers: David Strong, Prince Georges Community College, Largo, Maryland; Rhosan Strykes, Delta College, University Center, Michigan; William Wright, Mt. Hood Community College, Gresham, Oregon; Clara Nelson, Central Piedmont Community College, Charlotte, North Carolina; and Howard Propes, San Antonio College.

A special thank you is extended the following members of the faculty of Tarrant County Junior College, whose valuable suggestions moved the book toward completion: Jon R. Evans, Assistant Professor, Business Administration; Arthur L. Griffin, Jr., Associate Professor, Business Administration; Gary E. Holt, Associate Professor, Business Administration; John P. Keating, Jr., Assistant Professor, Business Administration; Richard Wakefield, Associate Professor, Business Administration; and John C. Woods, Professor, Business Administration. Also, William D. (Bill) Souder, Forest Hill National Bank, Fort Worth, Texas.

The authors would like to thank the following business firms for their permission to reproduce the several business-related specimens and forms used in this text: NCR Corporation of Dayton, Ohio (Figure 10.1, Common and Preferred Stock Certificates); Odee Company of Dallas, Texas (Figure 11.1, Promissory Note); Forest Hill State Bank of Fort Worth, Texas (Figure 13.2, Disclosure Statement of Loan); and LTV Corporation (Figure 14.1, Corporate Bond).

This book is dedicated to our wives, Beth Evans, Janie McKenzie, and Ann Kelley, in recognition of their encouragement and support during the preparation of the manuscript.

Business Mathematics

PART ONE
A REVIEW OF BASIC ARITHMETIC OPERATIONS

The ability to perform the fundamental operations of arithmetic with reasonable skill is essential to success in many business courses and occupations. The chapters in Part One provide you with the opportunity to review the fundamental operations of arithmetic involving whole numbers, decimals, fractions, and percents. Your primary objective in this review is to improve your speed and accuracy when working problems involving basic arithmetic.

Chapter 1
Whole Numbers and Decimal Numbers

Ray's Van Service used 2,746 gallons of gasoline last month. At a contract rate of $1.899 per gallon, what was the cost of gasoline for the month?

Determining the cost of gasoline for Ray's Van Service involves a basic arithmetic computation. Although most businesses use machines to perform this type of computation, students majoring in business should have a working knowledge of basic arithmetic skills in order to solve this type of problem on their own.

This chapter will provide an opportunity for you to develop and practice basic arithmetic operations involving both whole and decimal numbers. This should prove particularly helpful in the immediate future, since the United States is in the process of converting to the metric system. This change will create an increased emphasis on understanding and working with decimals because all metric measurements are based on decimal values.

This chapter will enable you to:

1. **identify and express a whole or decimal number according to its positional notation (place value)**

2. **perform fundamental operations of arithmetic involving whole and decimal numbers**

3. **round answers to specified degrees of accuracy**

<ol start="4">
<li>demonstrate speed and accuracy when performing fundamental operations involving whole and decimal numbers</li>
<li>use shortcut methods in working multiplication and division problems</li>
<li>perform basic calculations necessary to complete business forms and solve business problems</li>
</ol>

Learning Unit 1.1
Reading and Writing Numbers

Decimal System

Our number system, the *Hindu-Arabic system,* is based on the number 10. It is called the *decimal system,* a term derived from the Latin word *decem,* meaning 10. The decimal system is the base for our measuring system, the *English system,* and the foundation for the *metric system,* the measuring system used by most of the world. An integral part of modern commerce, it is the core of business mathematics.

The decimal system has two distinctive features: digits and positional notation. There are 10 digits, or symbols, in the system. They are of Hindu origin but were borrowed by the Arabic nations as a base for their number system. The 10 digits used are

0, 1, 2, 3, 4, 5, 6, 7, 8, 9

The order of the digits is sequential, which determines the value of each digit. Combinations of the 10 digits are used to form other numbers. The number 10 is a composite of the first two digits. Any number can be written using combinations of the 10 digits. Because all numbers are written using one or more of these 10 digits, the decimal system is said to be of base 10. This means that the decimal system is organized by 10 and some power of 10.

Positional Notation

The key to reading and interpreting the value of a number is the positional notation of the digits in the number in relation to the decimal point. The *decimal* is the starting point and is indicated by a dot (.). As shown in Table 1.1, the whole number is that portion of a number that is located to the left of the decimal point. A decimal number is that portion of a number that is located to the right of the decimal point. Each portion of the number (whole and decimal) is read and its value interpreted according to the size of the digit at each position and place of the digit in relation to the decimal point. For example, in the whole number 3,624, the 4 is in the ones position,

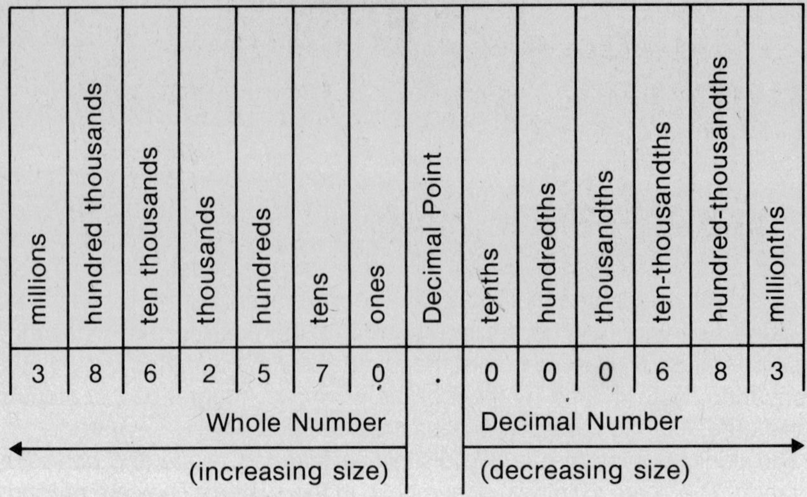

Table 1.1 Positional Notation: Whole Numbers and Decimal Numbers

millions	hundred thousands	ten thousands	thousands	hundreds	tens	ones	Decimal Point	tenths	hundredths	thousandths	ten-thousandths	hundred-thousandths	millionths
3	8	6	2	5	7	0	.	0	0	0	6	8	3

Whole Number — (increasing size) ← | → Decimal Number — (decreasing size)

indicating 4 ones; the 2 is in the tens position, indicating 2 tens; the 6 is in the hundreds position, indicating 6 hundreds; and the 3 is in the thousands position, indicating 3 thousands.

A decimal number is often referred to as a *decimal fraction* because the number is expressed as some integral power of 10 (10, 100, 1000, etc.) and should be read tenth, hundredth, thousandth, etc. For example, in the number .752, the 7 is in the tenth position, indicating 7 tenths; the 5 is in the hundredths position, indicating 5 hundredths; and the 2 is in the thousandths position, indicating 2 thousandths.

In reading a number, the word *and* is used to indicate the separating point between the whole number and the decimal (fractional ending). In writing a number, a hyphen (-) is used in compound numbers less than 100—for example, twenty-six and fifty-eight. Also, numbers of more than three digits are generally written with commas preceding every third digit to the left of the decimal point. This breaks the number into easily read groups of digits, with each group having a name. For example, for the number 100,000,000,000, the first group on the right is the units group; the second, thousands; the third, millions; and the fourth, billions. Thus, the number in Table 1.1 should be written 3,862,570.000683 and is interpreted as three million, eight hundred sixty-two thousand, five hundred seventy, and six hundred eighty-three millionths.

Exercises

Write the following numbers in words.

1.	18	2.	370	3.	4,073
4.	62,152	5.	170,600	6.	1,420,000
7.	39,040,327	8.	1,070,600,000	9.	.03
10.	.765	11.	122.5	12.	76.82
13.	9.00363	14.	146.001	15.	5.000263
16.	1,000.9003				

Express the following numbers using figures.

17. Eight hundred twenty-five

18. Four million ten thousand nine

19. Seven thousand two hundred

20. Two hundred one million thirty thousand

21. Forty-eight thousand two hundred three

22. Seven hundred six thousand

23. One hundred twenty-three and four hundred fifty-six thousandths

24. Nine thousand three and six ten-thousandths

25. Four hundred one and thirty-four hundred-thousandths

26. Fifteen and three hundred fourteen millionths

27. Thirteen thousand two hundred forty and sixty-five thousandths

28. Forty-two and nineteen hundredths

Supply the following information for each number.

29. The number .37 represents ___ tenths ___ hundredths and would be read ________________________________ .

30. The number 1.06 represents ___ ones ___ tenths ___ hundredths and would be read ________________________________ .

31. The number 46.038 represents _4_ tens _6_ ones _0_ tenths _3_ hundredths _8_ thousandths and would be read ________________________________ .

32. The number 146.9261 represents ___ hundreds ___ tens ___ ones ___ tenths ___ hundredths ___ thousandths ___ ten-thousandths and would be read ________________________________ .

33. The number 588.7123 represents ___ hundreds ___ tens ___ ones ___ tenths ___ hundredths ___ thousandths ___ ten-thousandths and would be read ________________________________ .

34. The number 5,423.000056 represents ______ thousands ______ hundreds ___ tens ___ ones ___ tenths ___ hundredths ___ thousandths ___ ten-thousandths ___ hundred-thousandths ___ millionths and would be read ________________________________ .

Learning Unit 1.2
Rounding and Approximations

Exact figures are often not necessary when handling large numbers. It may be sufficient and more desirable to approximate in "round" numbers, that is, to round them to the nearest ten, hundred, thousand, million, or billion. *Rounded numbers* are often more desirable for a number of reasons: the essential facts may be more easily kept in mind if the numbers are rounded; the computation may be easier if the numbers are rounded; and, rounded numbers are valuable in obtaining a rough approximation, either for a preliminary estimate or for a check on computations already made. Rounding is often used to make a quick comparison of figures or to estimate solutions to various problems.

The following steps are used for rounding whole numbers:

1. Determine to which position the number will be rounded.
2. If the digit to the right of the position being rounded is 5 or more, increase the digit in the place being rounded by one. If the digit to the right of the position being rounded is 4 or less, do not change the digit in the position being rounded.
3. Change all digits that are to the right of the place being rounded to zero.

Examples: (a) round 486 to tens
(b) round 9,149 to hundreds
(c) round 78,835 to thousands
(d) round 2,392,552 to millions

Solutions: (a) 490　(b) 9,100　(c) 79,000　(d) 2,000,000

In rounding decimal numbers, use the same rules for rounding whole numbers, with the exception that the discarded digits are not replaced by zeros.

Examples: (a) round 6.9284 to the nearest thousandth
(b) round 6.9284 to the nearest hundredth
(c) round 6.9284 to the nearest tenth
(d) round 6.9284 to the nearest unit

Solutions: (a) 6.928　(b) 6.93　(c) 6.9　(d) 7

Normally, you are to round only the final answer of a problem. When performing approximate computations, retain one more place in the intermediate work and then round the result to the degree of accuracy indicated by the particular situation. In the problems to be worked in this book, decimal answers correct to the nearest hundredth will usually be sufficient. If your final answer is to be rounded to a position other than the hundredth, your instructions will indicate the degree of accuracy required.

Exercises

Round each of the following numbers to the nearest ten, nearest hundred, and nearest thousand.

1. 26,487   2. 193,828   3. 7,143

4. 14,926   5. 1,855

Round each of the following numbers to the nearest thousand, nearest ten thousand, and nearest hundred thousand.

6. 682,554   7. 327,119   8. 774,074

9. 149,666   10. 573,988

Round each of the following numbers to the nearest million.

11. 78,903,667   12. 12,499,999

13. 3,389,221   14. 7,734,231

Round each of the following numbers to the nearest unit, nearest tenth, and nearest hundredth.

15. 76.8279   16. 2.6544   17. 9.4398

18. 3.673   19. 5.432

Round each of the following numbers to the nearest hundredth and nearest thousandth.

20. .64394   21. .39356   22. 7.5423

23. 13.65347   24. .49335

Learning Unit 1.3
Addition and Subtraction of Whole Numbers

Addition

Addition, the combining of two or more numbers into a single quantity, is indicated by a plus sign (+). The numbers being added are called *addends;* the result of the addition is called the *sum.* Addition becomes fairly easy when you use positional notation. A sum is easier to obtain when you align ones with ones, tens with tens, hundreds with hundreds, etc.

Example: Express 719, 934 and 1,345 as a single quantity.

Solution:

$$
\begin{array}{rl}
719 & \text{addend} \\
934 & \text{addend} \\
+\,1{,}345 & \text{addend} \\
\hline
2{,}998 & \text{sum}
\end{array}
$$

One of the most common methods of checking addition is to add in reverse order and compare the resulting sum to the first sum obtained.

Speed and accuracy in addition may be developed by grouping tens. When solving addition problems, combine two or more numbers that add to 10 in the same column. In the units column of the example shown below, the 6 and 4 equal 10, and the 1, 5, and 4 equal 10. In the tens column, the 4 and 4 and the carried 2 equal 10, and the 9 and 1 equal 10.

Example:

$$
\begin{array}{r}
10 = \left[\begin{array}{r} 2 \\ 46 \\ 44 \end{array}\right] = 10 \\
\left[\begin{array}{r} 81 \\ 35 \end{array}\right] = 10 \\
10 = \left[\begin{array}{r} 94 \\ 18 \end{array}\right] \\
\hline
318
\end{array}
$$

Remember to group tens to achieve greater speed and accuracy.

Speed and accuracy in addition may be developed by using subtotals. When adding a long column of numbers, add parts of the column and record the subtotals to the side. To obtain the final sum, add the subtotals.

Example: 876

      100   976   subtotal

      342

      135

      422   899   subtotal

      248

      450

      301   999   subtotal

          2,874 sum

Subtraction

Subtraction, the process of finding the difference between numbers, is indicated by a minus sign ($-$). The *minuend* is the number from which another number is subtracted; the *subtrahend* is the number being subtracted from the minuend; and the result is the *difference.* In the problem $25 - 6 = 19$, the minuend is 25, the subtrahend is 6, and the difference is 19. As in addition, the numbers are aligned so that ones are subtracted from ones, tens are subtracted from tens, etc.

Example: Determine the difference between 922 and 14.

  Solution: 922   minuend

              $-$ 14   subtrahend

              908   difference

When the subtrahend is larger than the minuend, as it is in the ones position in this problem, you must borrow one positional value from the next column to the left (tens). This leaves 1 in the tens position and makes the subtraction problem in the ones column $12 - 4 = 8$.

The simplest method of checking subtraction is to add the difference to the subtrahend and check to see that the sum is equal to the minuend.

Exercises

Express the following numbers as a single quantity.

1. $1,247 + 13,488 + 344$ 2. $907 + 1,326 + 18,945$

3. $17 + 133 + 1,904$ 4. $723 + 1,422 + 1,036$

Add the following numbers using combinations of 10 whenever possible.

5.	29	6.	73	7.	333	8.	448
	86		29		672		621
	31		36		135		381
	+44		+74		899		317
					+216		+495

Add the following numbers by obtaining subtotals and then the final sum.

9.
```
342
734
584  ___ subtotal
521
935
754  ___ subtotal
606
419
197  ___ subtotal
     ___ sum
```

10.
```
924
652
370  ___ subtotal
503
479
830  ___ subtotal
215
146
307  ___ subtotal
     ___ sum
```

11.
```
382
149
661  ___ subtotal
724
382
974  ___ subtotal
506
293
810
421  ___ subtotal
     ___ sum
```

12.
```
140
376
894  ___ subtotal
502
468
249  ___ subtotal
791
610
485
904  ___ subtotal
     ___ sum
```

Determine the difference in each of the following.

13.	397	14.	892	15.	762
	−256		−376		−575

16.	5,488	17.	7,253	18.	3,136
	−3,257		−2,567		−2,749

19.	18,759 − 6,247	20.	39,302 −12,736	21.	41,424 − 7,589
22.	54,521 −12,375	23.	105,624 − 3,731	24.	157,309 − 44,632

Determine the difference in each of the following.

25. $346 - 32$ 26. $9,728 - 539$

27. $8,655 - 364$ 28. $10,233 - 1,145$

29. $29,342 - 18,778$ 30. $16,779 - 7,886$

Find the answer to each of the following.

31. $862 − $427 − $34   32. $605 − $148 − $121

33. $998 + $673 − $186   34. $322 + $298 − $428

35. $1,605 − $413 + $219   36. $1,064 − $872 + $987

37. $6,741 + $692 − $745   38. $3,208 + $570 − $391

Practical Applications

During the week of July 10, the Hampton Manufacturing Company produced the following items. What was the total number of each item produced during this period?

Hampton Manufacturing Company
Manufacturing Report, Week of July 10

	Articles	M	T	W	T	F	Total
39.	Slide Trays	462	347	512	391	427	_______
40.	Slide Files	98	106	113	107	117	_______
41.	Slide Cubes	732	640	756	710	684	_______
42.	Slide Sorters	103	86	108	116	114	_______
43.	Movie Screens	219	273	314	221	306	_______

The Summit Wholesale Company made the following sales during the week of January 4. What were the total weekly sales for each item? What was the amount of sales for each day during the week?

Summit Wholesale Company
Sales Report, Week of January 4

	Model #	M	T	W	T	F	Total
44.	A133	$1,240	$1,765	$1,872	$1,136	$1,307	_______
45.	A137	$ 348	$ 634	$ 506	$ 722	$ 512	_______
46.	A138	$1,866	$1,292	$1,460	$1,756	$1,424	_______
47.	TOTAL	_______	_______	_______	_______	_______	_______

Determine the gross profit on the following sales of lawn and garden equipment by using the formula: SALES − COST OF GOODS SOLD = GROSS PROFIT.

Central Supply Company
Sales Record of Lawn and Garden Equipment
Week Ending July 19

	Item	Sales	Cost	Gross Profit
48.	Spreader	$ 942	$ 567	_______
49.	Auger	$ 168	$ 87	_______
50.	Mower	$6,347	$3,238	_______
51.	Edger	$3,063	$1,607	_______

Learning Unit 1.4
Multiplication and Division of Whole Numbers

Multiplication

Multiplication is a short method of repeat addition, usually indicated by a times sign ($\times$). When we say that $3 \times 4 = 12$, we mean that the sum of three 4s is 12 ($4 + 4 + 4 = 12$). If two or more numbers are multiplied, the result is called the *product,* whereas each of the numbers being multiplied is a *factor* of the product. The first factor is the *multiplicand;* the second factor, the *multiplier.*

Example:

```
 12    multiplicand
× 7    multiplier
 84    product
```

Example:

```
  463      multiplicand
×  25      multiplier
 2315      (463 × 5) partial product
  926      (463 × 2) partial product
11,575     product
```

Multiplication also can be indicated in the following ways:

1. Use of a dot: $3 \cdot 4 = 12$
2. Use of parentheses: $(3)4 = 12$

Division

Division is the process of determining how many times a certain amount is contained in a given value. The original number is called the *dividend;* the number contained in the dividend is called the *divisor;* and the result is called the *quotient.* For example, in the problem $57 \div 19$, you are trying to determine how many groups of 19 are contained in 57. The dividend is 57, the divisor is 19, and the quotient is 3. Division can be indicated in the following ways:

1. Use of the symbol ÷: 57 ÷ 19
2. Use of the diagonal /: 14/7
3. Use of the symbol $\overline{)}$: 7)14

In solving some division problems, the divisor does not go into the dividend an even number of times. For example, 17 ÷ 5 will result in a quotient of 3 (3 × 5 = 15) with 2 left over (3 × 5 = 15 + 2 = 17). The 2 is called the *remainder*.

$$\begin{array}{r} 118 \\ 4\overline{)473} \\ \underline{4} \\ 7 \\ \underline{4} \\ 33 \\ \underline{32} \\ 1 \end{array}$$

Example: divisor 4)473 — 118 quotient, 473 dividend, 1 remainder

Exercises

Complete the following multiplication problems.

1. 4,970 × 31	2. 3,205 × 16	3. 7,614 × 24
4. 5,089 × 76	5. 1,898 × 575	6. 8,924 × 896
7. 2,945 × 854	8. 36,054 × 396	9. 45,806 × 427
10. 74,683 × 787	11. 80,249 × 363	12. 39,625 × 706

Complete the following multiplication problems.

13. 147,892 × 300	14. 532,300 × 160
15. 305,076 × 885	16. 308,207 × 275

Find the answer to each of the following.

17. 372 × 45 − 467	18. 185 × 39 − 512
19. 643 × 762 − 897	20. 459 × 188 − 632

Perform the following division problems. Indicate the amount of the remainder when applicable.

21. 2,488/22

22. 4,605/54

23. 1,876/31

24. 5,647/68

25. 2,672/154

26. 7,083/344

27. 17,396/407

28. 29,107/326

29. 14,252/176

30. 23,931/324

Complete the following division problems.

31. $496 \times \underline{\hspace{1cm}} = 26,784$

32. $721 \times \underline{\hspace{1cm}} = 16,583$

33. $384 \times \underline{\hspace{1cm}} = 29,952$

34. $587 \times \underline{\hspace{1cm}} = 39,916$

35. $\underline{\hspace{1cm}} \times 39 = 30,771$

36. $\underline{\hspace{1cm}} \times 28 = 25,844$

37. $\underline{\hspace{1cm}} \times 63 = 20,601$

38. $\underline{\hspace{1cm}} \times 147 = 56,154$

Practical Applications

39. The Speedy Delivery Service has a truck that gets 14 miles per gallon. The truck holds 48 gallons of gasoline. How many miles can the truck travel on a tank of gasoline?

40. The Silver Specialty Shop ordered 35 food warmers at a cost of $72 each. What was the total cost of all the items?

41. The ABC Nursery Center purchased the following items. (a) What was the total cost of each item? (b) What was the total cost of the order?

Item	Quantity		Unit Price		Total Cost
Walker/Bouncer	6	×	$18	=	(a) $______
Automatic Swing	12	×	$11	=	$______
Cradle	5	×	$29	=	$______
Table and Chair Set	19	×	$28	=	$______
			TOTAL		(b) $______

42. An airplane averages 225 miles per hour. How many hours will it take the plane to fly a distance of 1,575 miles?

43. The North Mall Specialty Shop paid $216 for three dozen monkeypod fruit trays. What was the cost of each item?

44. A group of college students decided to bicycle to the coast during the summer break. The coast is 560 miles from the campus, and they estimate they can average 14 miles per hour. How many cycling hours will the trip take each way?

Learning Unit 1.5
Addition and Subtraction of Decimal Numbers

When performing addition and subtraction of decimal numbers, align the decimal points vertically and then perform the computations.

Example:

$189.46	addend
+ 42.77	addend
$232.23	sum

Example:

$475.18	minuend
− 199.03	subtrahend
$276.15	difference

The decimal numbers being added or subtracted may have a varying number of digits after the decimal point. In this situation, it is still necessary to align the decimal points vertically before performing the computation.

Example:

4.98	addend
17.6	addend
9.201	addend
18.	addend
49.781	sum

Example: 9.036   minuend
          −1.8   subtrahend
          7.236   difference

Exercises

Add the following numbers, rounding all answers to hundredths.

1.		2.		3.	
	1.045		5.081		2.09
	7.231		1.707		1.706
	8.104		6.014		3.1
	5.742		1.624		4.106
	6.208		1.002		3.164
	+1.901		+4.682		+7.772

4.		5.	
	$172.50		4.805
	95.20		13.8
	297.14		.6061
	13.90		17.401
	105.50		22.63
	+ 3.47		+125

6. $1.6 + 34.021 + 11.4 + 176.1 + 98.774 + 33.3967$

7. $14.98 + $788.62 + $590 + $50.38 + $10.49 + $865.07

8. $.5602 + 69.2 + 480 + 4.6405 + 12.209 + 926.44$

9. $36.1 + 9.7763 + 259 + 33.89 + 444.6762 + 1{,}233$

Subtract the following numbers, rounding all answers to hundredths.

10.		11.		12.	
	4.27		$159.06		1.343
	−1.643		− 73.40		−1.279

13.		14.	
	1.002		$99.10
	− .1432		− 73.69

15. $9.1275 − 6.139$ 16. $259.1769 − 93.407$

17. $495.881 − 158.7729$ 18. $1{,}642.34 − 692.366$

Practical Applications

19. Find the sum of .065, 4.1365, 1.01, and .0014 and then subtract the sum of 1.17, .715, 2.006, and .104. Round the answer to the nearest hundredth.

20. If an article sold for $76.47, which is a reduction of $17.26 from the original price, what was the original price?

21. What is the new selling price of a dress if the old selling price was $47.50 and the discount was $12.32?

22. The book value of a company automobile is $2,146.76. The trade-in allowance on a new automobile is $3,400. How much gain did the company realize on the trade-in?

23. A man's suit marked $179.95 was sold for $132. How much was the price reduced?

24. A customer bought three articles priced at $4.98, $6.02, and $5.19. The sales tax is $.81. How much change will the customer receive if she pays with a $20 bill?

25. The ABC Corporation deposited three checks for $87, $11.29, and $762.40, less cash of $200. What was the amount of the deposit?

26. The Central Supply Company deposited three checks for $348.12, $87.25, and $1,482.68, less cash of $226. What was the amount of the deposit?

Learning Unit 1.6
Multiplication and Division of Decimal Numbers

When multiplying decimal numbers, add the number of digits after the decimal point in the multiplicand and multiplier. Place the decimal point in the product an equal number of digits from the right.

Example:

multiplicand	×	multiplier	=	product
1.48	×	5.6	=	8.288
2 digits	+	one digit	=	3 digits

When performing division and the divisor is a decimal number, change the divisor to a whole number, adjust the decimal point in the dividend an equal number of spaces, then complete the division.

Example: Divide 78.921 by 4.06.

Solution: (1) Change the divisor (4.06) to a whole number by moving the decimal point two digits to the right.

$$4.06\overline{)78.921}$$

(2) Move the decimal point in the dividend to the right the same number of digits as you did in the divisor.

$$406\overline{)78.921}$$

(3) Place the decimal point in the quotient directly above the decimal point in the dividend.

$$406\overline{)7892.1}$$

(4) Complete the division problem.

$$
\begin{array}{r}
19.4 \\
406\overline{)7892.1} \\
\underline{406} \\
3832 \\
\underline{3654} \\
1781 \\
\underline{1624} \\
157
\end{array}
$$

If necessary, add zeros to the dividend in order to move the decimal point the correct number of digits.

Example: Divide 76.2 by 4.05.

Solution: 4.05)76.2<u>0</u>

Shortcuts in Multiplication

The multiplication process can be shortened when the multiplier is 10, 100, or 1,000 by moving the decimal to the right.

Examples: $3.69 × 10 = 3.69 = $36.90
$3.69 × 100 = 3.69 = $369.00
$3.69 × 1,000 = 3.690 = $3,690.00

(Moving the decimal in the last example requires adding a zero.)

If the multiplier is a multiple of 10, 100, or 1,000, say 30, multiply by 10 and then multiply by 3.

Example: Multiply $3.69 by 30.

Solution: $3.69 × 10 = $36.90
$36.90 × 3 = $110.70

If the multiplier is 25 or 50, the multiplication process can again be shortened. To multiply by 50, multiply by 100 and then divide by 2. To multiply by 25, multiply by 100 and then divide the answer by 4.

Example: Multiply 284 by 25.

Solution: 284 × 100 = 28,400
28,400 ÷ 4 = 7,100

Shortcuts in Division

The division process can be shortened when the divisor is 10, 100, or 1,000 by moving the decimal point to the left.

Examples: $4,880 ÷ 10 = 488.0 = $488.00
$4,880 ÷ 100 = 48.80 = $48.80
$4.85 ÷ 100 = .04.85 = $.0485   ◄—— add a zero.

If the divisor is a multiple of 10, 100, or 1,000, say 40, divide by 10 and then divide by 4.

Example: Divide 268 by 40.

> **Solution:** $268 \div 10 = 26.8$
> $26.8 \div 4 = 6.7$

If the divisor is 25 or 50, the division process can again be shortened. To divide by 50, divide by 100 and then multiply by 2. To divide by 25, divide by 100 and then multiply by 4.

Example: Divide 284 by 25.

> **Solution:** $284 \div 100 = 2.84$
> $2.84 \times 4 = 11.36$

Exercises

Multiply the following numbers, rounding your answers to hundredths.

1. $\begin{array}{r} 4.02 \\ \times\, 1.17 \\ \hline \end{array}$
2. $\begin{array}{r} 7.09 \\ \times\, .062 \\ \hline \end{array}$
3. $\begin{array}{r} 1.227 \\ \times\quad .61 \\ \hline \end{array}$

4. $\begin{array}{r} 5.162 \\ \times\quad 93 \\ \hline \end{array}$
5. $\begin{array}{r} \$99.08 \\ \times\ 1.304 \\ \hline \end{array}$

6. 34.19×11.93
7. 1.456×1.2

8. $46.93 \times .0761$
9. 76.45×3.75

Divide the following numbers, rounding your answers to hundredths.

10. $2.51\overline{)45.893}$
11. $1.45\overline{)60.14}$
12. $.57\overline{)8.997}$

13. $.229\overline{)34.26}$
14. $1.19\overline{)90.4326}$
15. $\$9.65\overline{)\$1,237}$

16. $8.835 \div 49.87$
17. $.8826 \div 123.1$
18. $10,009 \div 23.71$

Work the following problems using shortcut multiplication.

19. 372×10
20. 7.2×10
21. 9.6×100

22. 86×100	23. $.36 \times 100$	24. $9.8 \times 1,000$
25. 3.6×40	26. 25×100	27. 963×100
28. 92×30	29. 67×20	30. 6.5×50
31. 550×30	32. 162×25	33. 9.55×50
34. 175×40	35. 920×60	36. 24.28×25
37. $.79 \times 2,000$	38. 7.94×50	

Work the following problems using shortcut division. Do not round.

39. $45.9 \div 10$	40. $76 \div 100$	41. $14,654 \div 1,000$
42. $9.21 \div 10$	43. $420 \div 25$	44. $.26 \div 10$
45. $368 \div 100$	46. $.05 \div 100$	47. $768 \div 1,000$
48. $\$7.60 \div 10$	49. $6.2 \div 10$	50. $800 \div 500$
51. $\$160 \div 25$	52. $\$160 \div 100$	53. $3,249 \div 1,000$
54. $280 \div 40$	55. $\$3,420 \div 2,000$	56. $275.1 \div 30$
57. $5.46 \div 100$	58. $17.5 \div 25$	

Practical Applications

59. Ray's Trucking Company used 2,746 gallons of gas last week. At a contract rate of $1.88 per gallon, what was the cost of gasoline?

60. If 14 government bonds cost $17,675, what is the cost per bond?

61. What is the total cost of 768 items if each item costs $.185?

62. A package contains 92 articles that weigh .125 of a pound each. What is the total weight of this package?

63. The market price of a share of stock is $14.875. A broker charges $.15 a share for buying the stock for a customer. What is the total cost of 75 shares of stock?

64. A stock costs $14.875 per share plus brokerage fees of $.15 per share. How many shares of stock can be bought for $1,202?

65. What is the cost of 2 dozen cans of cleaner if the price of the cleaner is 2 cans for 24 cents?

Chapter 1
Self-Evaluation

1. Express the number one hundred twenty-four thousand three hundred fifty-seven in figures.

2. Write 6.5004 in words.

3. Round the following numbers as indicated: 133.1649 to hundredths, 548.2844 to tenths, and 4.2236 to thousandths.

4. Express 3,402 + 18,961 + 340,265 as a single quantity.

5. Determine the difference between 1,742 and 396.

6. The ABC Corporation had 31,482 widgets in stock on the first day of the month. Widget sales during the month were 16,539. How many widgets were in the company's inventory on the last day of the month?

7. A machine cost $103,000 plus $1,542 freight charges, $312 insurance while in transit, and $1,400 installation charges. What was the total cost of the machine?

8. Sales for the Central Wholesale Company for the past month were $463,282. Cost of the merchandise sold was $274,406. What was the gross profit (sales − cost) for the month?

9. Add 34.2567, 122.3, 4.333, and 36.23.

10. Subtract 34.9621 from 244.5.

11. Find the sum of 13.453, 162.3265, and .8132 and then subtract the sum of .354, 15.76, and 8.3647.

12. Divide 53.65 by 3.7.

13. A merchant purchased 23 marble ashtrays for a cost of $6.95 each. What was the total cost of the order?

Chapter 2
Fractions

A *fraction* is one way of expressing a part of a whole unit. The circle in Figure 2.1 is divided into five equal parts. The entire circle represents a whole unit. Each of the five parts represents a portion of the whole unit. Each portion is called a *fractional unit.* One fractional unit of the whole unit is expressed as $\frac{1}{5}$; two units, $\frac{2}{5}$; three units, $\frac{3}{5}$; etc.

Figure 2.1 Relationship of Fractional Unit to Whole

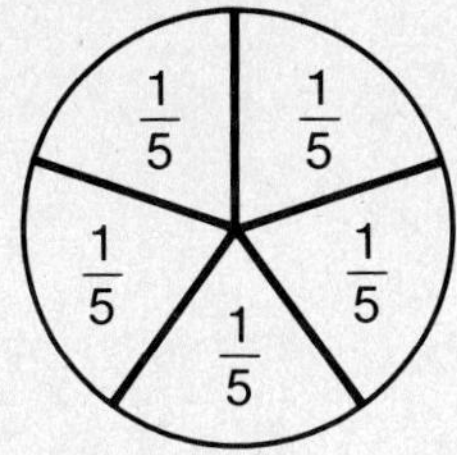

This chapter will provide an opportunity for you to read, interpret, and work problems containing fractions.

This chapter will enable you to:

1.   **identify the parts and types of fractions**

2.   **determine the greatest common divisor**

3. reduce fractions to lowest terms using the greatest common divisor

4. raise fractions to higher terms

5. convert mixed numbers to improper fractions and vice versa

6. convert fractions to decimals and vice versa

7. determine the lowest common denominator using prime factors

8. perform fundamental operations of arithmetic involving fractions

Learning Unit 2.1
Changing the Terms of Fractions

Parts and Types of Fractions

The top number of a fraction is called the *numerator,* and the bottom number is called the *denominator.* The numerator expresses how many parts of the whole are being considered, whereas the denominator expresses how many equal parts the whole unit has been divided into.

Example: $\dfrac{3}{5}$ numerator
denominator

In the fraction $\frac{3}{5}$, the whole unit is divided into five equal parts, and three of those parts are being considered.

When the numerator of a fraction is smaller than the denominator, the fraction is called a *proper fraction.* Examples of proper fractions are $\frac{1}{2}$, $\frac{2}{3}$, $\frac{3}{4}$, and $\frac{4}{5}$. Proper fractions have a value of less than 1. When the numerator is equal to or greater than the denominator, the fraction is called an *improper fraction.* Examples of improper fractions are $\frac{7}{6}$, $\frac{5}{5}$, $\frac{7}{4}$, and $\frac{3}{2}$. Improper fractions have a value equal to or greater than 1.

Changing Terms—Unchanging Value

A fraction is unique in that the terms of a fraction can be changed without changing the value of the fraction. For instance, the fraction $\frac{2}{6}$ may be changed to a higher term as $\frac{4}{12}$ or to a lower term as $\frac{1}{3}$ without changing its value.

Reducing Fractions to Lowest Terms

Because it is often simpler to use fractions in their least complicated form, the smallest possible numbers are usually used to express fractional values. Thus, the fractions $\frac{2}{6}$, $\frac{3}{9}$, and $\frac{4}{12}$ would usually be expressed as $\frac{1}{3}$. To reduce a fraction to lower terms, divide both the numerator and denomi-

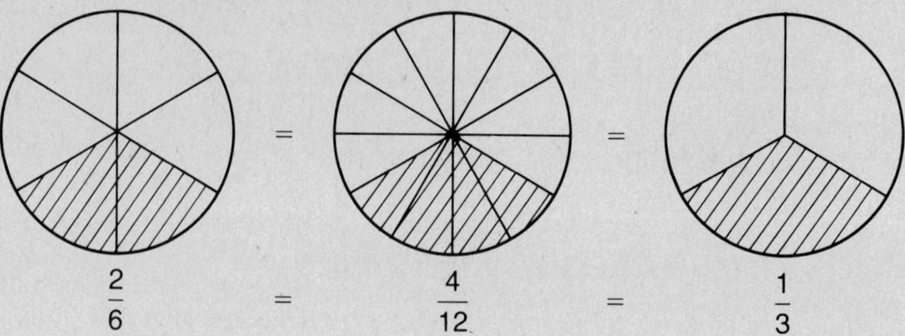

Figure 2.2 Equivalency of Fractions

$$\frac{2}{6} = \frac{4}{12} = \frac{1}{3}$$

nator by a number that will divide evenly (no remainder) into both numbers. When a fraction cannot be further reduced, the fraction is said to be reduced to its *lowest terms. Reducing a fraction to its lowest terms, then, involves dividing both the numerator and denominator by the largest number that will divide evenly into both numbers.* This divisor is called the *greatest common divisor.* In the following example, 4 is the largest number that can be divided evenly into the numerator and denominator and thus is the greatest common divisor.

Example: Reduce $\frac{4}{12}$ to its lowest terms.

Solution: $\dfrac{4 \div 4 = 1}{12 \div 4 = 3}$

$\frac{4}{12}$ reduced to its lowest terms is $\frac{1}{3}$.

Determining the Greatest Common Divisor

In some instances, an examination of the fraction will reveal the greatest common divisor that can be used for reducing that fraction. If you are unable to determine the largest number that divides into the numerator and denominator by examination, use the following procedure to determine the greatest common divisor.

Example: Reduce the fraction $\frac{148}{259}$ to its lowest terms.

Solution: (1) Divide the denominator by the numerator.

$$\begin{array}{r}1\\148\overline{)259}\\148\\\hline 111\end{array}$$

(2) Divide the remainder (111) into the previous divisor (148).

$$\begin{array}{r}1\\148\overline{)259}\\148\ 1\\\hline 111\overline{)148}\\111\\\hline 37\end{array}$$

(3) Continue dividing each remainder into the previous divisor until there is no remainder.

$$\begin{array}{r}1\\148\overline{)259}\\148\ 1\\\hline 111\overline{)148}\\111\ 3\\\hline 37\overline{)111}\\111\end{array}$$

(4) The last divisor is the largest number that will divide into both the numerator and the denominator. Thus,

$$\frac{148 \div 37 = 4}{259 \div 37 = 7}$$

$$\frac{148}{259} = \frac{4}{7}$$

When the final divisor is 1, the fraction cannot be reduced.

Raising Fractions to Higher Terms

Fractions may be changed to higher terms without changing their value. For instance, $\frac{1}{4}$ may be changed to $\frac{2}{8}$ or $\frac{4}{16}$ without altering the original value. Raising fractions to higher terms is simply the reverse of reducing fractions. Instead of dividing both the numerator and denominator by the same number, we *multiply both the numerator and denominator by the same number.*

To determine the multiplier to use, divide the denominator of the fraction presented into the new denominator. Then multiply the numerator and denominator by that number.

Example: Raise $\frac{1}{4}$ to 64ths.

Solution: $64 \div 4 = 16$

$$\frac{1 \times 16 = 16}{4 \times 16 = 64}$$

$$\frac{1}{4} = \frac{16}{64}$$

$\frac{1}{4}$ raised to 64ths is $\frac{16}{64}$.

Exercises

Reduce the following fractions to their lowest terms.

1. $\frac{9}{15}$ 2. $\frac{28}{36}$ 3. $\frac{45}{75}$ 4. $\frac{35}{49}$

5. $\frac{57}{76}$ 6. $\frac{126}{190}$ 7. $\frac{18}{53}$ 8. $\frac{320}{448}$

9. $\frac{210}{546}$ 10. $\frac{265}{477}$ 11. $\frac{315}{560}$ 12. $\frac{528}{716}$

13. $\frac{1221}{1998}$ 14. $\frac{452}{761}$ 15. $\frac{511}{876}$

Raise the following fractions to the higher terms indicated.

16. $\frac{2}{3} = \frac{}{12}$ 17. $\frac{5}{6} = \frac{}{18}$ 18. $\frac{3}{8} = \frac{}{48}$

19. $\frac{7}{9} = \frac{}{63}$ 20. $\frac{4}{9} = \frac{}{81}$ 21. $\frac{5}{12} = \frac{}{156}$

22. $\dfrac{4}{5} = \dfrac{}{135}$ 23. $\dfrac{3}{4} = \dfrac{}{136}$ 24. $\dfrac{12}{21} = \dfrac{}{315}$

25. $\dfrac{3}{10} = \dfrac{}{220}$ 26. $\dfrac{11}{12} = \dfrac{}{516}$ 27. $\dfrac{29}{65} = \dfrac{}{780}$

Raise the denominator of each of the following fractions to 48.

28. $\dfrac{1}{4}$ 29. $\dfrac{3}{8}$ 30. $\dfrac{5}{16}$

31. $\dfrac{19}{24}$ 32. $\dfrac{7}{12}$ 33. $\dfrac{2}{3}$

Learning Unit 2.2
Improper Fractions, Mixed Numbers, and Decimals

Solving problems containing fractions often requires you to change or convert the fraction to a different form. Depending on the type of problem, you may have to convert (1) improper fractions to mixed numbers, (2) mixed numbers to fractions, (3) fractions to decimals, or (4) decimals to fractions.

Converting Improper Fractions to Mixed Numbers

As mentioned in the preceding unit, an *improper fraction* is a fraction that has a numerator equal to or greater than the denominator. Examples of improper fractions are $\frac{6}{6}$ and $\frac{19}{15}$. A *mixed number* is a number containing a whole number and a common fraction. Examples of mixed numbers are $8\frac{2}{3}$ and $14\frac{1}{5}$. *To convert an improper fraction to a whole number or mixed number, divide the numerator by the denominator.*

Example: Change $\dfrac{6}{6}$ to a whole number.

Solution: $6 \div 6 = 1$

$$\dfrac{6}{6} = 1$$

Example: Change $\dfrac{19}{15}$ to a mixed number.

Solution:

$$\begin{array}{r} 1 \\ 15\overline{)19} \\ \underline{15} \\ 4 \quad \text{remainder} \end{array}$$

$$\dfrac{19}{15} = 1\dfrac{4}{15}$$

Converting Mixed Numbers to Improper Fractions

To convert a mixed number to an improper fraction, multiply the denominator of the fraction by the whole number and then add the numerator. The answer is the numerator of the improper fraction. The denominator remains the same.

Example: Convert $8\dfrac{2}{3}$ to an improper fraction.

Solution: $\dfrac{(3 \times 8) + 2}{3} = \dfrac{26}{3}$

$$8\dfrac{2}{3} = \dfrac{26}{3}$$

Example: Convert $14\dfrac{1}{5}$ to an improper fraction.

Solution: $\dfrac{(5 \times 14) + 1}{5} = \dfrac{71}{5}$

$$14\dfrac{1}{5} = \dfrac{71}{5}$$

Converting Fractions to Decimals

To convert a fraction to a decimal, divide the numerator by the denominator. When the denominator does not divide into a numerator evenly, carry the decimal one more place than is required and then round your answer to the appropriate number of digits. If the answer requires rounding to thousandths, carry the decimal to ten-thousandths (four digits) and then round the decimal to thousandths (three digits).

Example: Convert $\frac{1}{4}$ to a decimal.

Solution:

$$
\begin{array}{r}
.25 \\
4\overline{)1.00} \\
\underline{8} \\
20 \\
\underline{20}
\end{array}
$$

$$\frac{1}{4} = .25$$

Example: Convert $\frac{1}{3}$ to a decimal.

Solution:

$$
\begin{array}{r}
.3333 = .333 \\
3\overline{)1.0000}
\end{array}
$$

$$\frac{1}{3} = .333$$

Converting Decimals to Fractions

When converting decimals to fractions, remember that a decimal is really a fraction. The decimal number given becomes the numerator of the fraction. For example, in the decimal number .253, the numerator is 253. The denominator is always 10 or some power of 10, such as 100 or 1,000. In other words, the denominator of a decimal fraction is 1 followed by as many zeros as there are digits after the decimal point in the decimal number.

1 digit: denominator is 10

2 digits: denominator is 100

3 digits: denominator is 1,000

4 digits: denominator is 10,000

The denominator for .253 is 1 followed by three zeros, or 1,000. Thus, .253 converted to a fraction is $\frac{253}{1000}$.

Example: Convert .75 to a fraction.

Solution: $.75 = \frac{75}{100} = \frac{3}{4}$ (reduced to lowest terms)

Example: Convert .593 to a fraction.

Solution: $.593 = \frac{593}{1000}$

Exercises

Convert the following improper fractions to mixed numbers.

1. $\frac{5}{2}$ 2. $\frac{9}{4}$ 3. $\frac{37}{6}$ 4. $\frac{59}{12}$

5. $\frac{69}{4}$ 6. $\frac{117}{8}$ 7. $\frac{97}{30}$ 8. $\frac{210}{25}$

Change the following mixed numbers to improper fractions.

9. $6\frac{1}{2}$ 10. $3\frac{4}{7}$ 11. $6\frac{3}{8}$ 12. $9\frac{7}{16}$

13. $4\frac{11}{12}$ 14. $8\frac{3}{11}$ 15. $14\frac{13}{20}$ 16. $26\frac{19}{24}$

Convert the following fractions or mixed numbers to decimals. Round uneven answers to the nearest thousandth.

17. $\frac{3}{5}$ 18. $12\frac{5}{8}$ 19. $\frac{5}{6}$ 20. $8\frac{7}{12}$

21. $\frac{9}{16}$ 22. $\frac{5}{9}$ 23. $26\frac{29}{40}$ 24. $\frac{41}{250}$

Convert the following decimals to fractions or mixed numbers.

25. 0.7   26. 4.75   27. 0.65   28. 0.875

29. 18.025   30. 0.0025   31. 3.250   32. 4.352

Learning Unit 2.3
Addition and Subtraction of Fractions

Common Denominators and Unlike Denominators

Fractions cannot be added or subtracted unless all fractions in the problem contain the same denominator. The denominator that is used in solving a problem is called the lowest common denominator. The *lowest common denominator* is the smallest nonzero whole number evenly divisible by the denominators of the given fractions. The lowest common denominator may be determined by examining the problem.

Example: Find the lowest common denominator of $\frac{1}{2}$, $\frac{3}{4}$, and $\frac{5}{8}$.

Solution: 8, which is a multiple of both 2 and 4, is the lowest common denominator.

$$\frac{1}{2} = \frac{4}{8}; \quad \frac{3}{4} = \frac{6}{8}; \quad \frac{5}{8} = \frac{5}{8}$$

Finding the Lowest Common Denominator

For more difficult problems, the *prime factor method* may be used to determine the lowest common denominator. A *prime factor* is a number that is evenly divisible only by itself and by 1. Examples of prime factors are 1, 2, 3, 5, 7, 11, 13, 17, etc. Since the prime factor 1 does not reduce the denominators, it is never used when determining the lowest common denominator. Use the following steps in determining the lowest common denominator by the prime factor method.

Example: Find the lowest common denominator of $\frac{2}{3}$, $\frac{9}{16}$, $\frac{7}{15}$, and $\frac{5}{8}$.

Solution: (1) Place all the denominators of the problem in a row.

3   16   15   8

(2) Select a prime factor that will divide into at least *two* of the denominators.

3)3   16   15   8

(3) Divide the prime factor into as many of the denominators as possible. If the prime factor does not divide into a denominator an even number of times, bring the denominator down to the next line.

3)3̶   16   1̶5̶   8
  1   16   5   8

(4) Continue dividing by prime factors until you are no longer able to divide a prime factor into two numbers.

3)3̶   16   1̶5̶   8
2)1   1̶6̶   5   8̶
2)1   8̶   5   4̶
2)1   4̶   5   2̶
  1   2   5   1

(5) Multiply the prime numbers on the left and the numbers remaining in the bottom row to obtain the lowest common denominator.

3)
2)
2)
2)________
  1   2   5   1

3 × 2 × 2 × 2 × 1 × 2 × 5 × 1 = 240

The lowest common denominator for $\frac{2}{3}$, $\frac{9}{16}$, $\frac{7}{15}$, and $\frac{5}{8}$ is 240.

Adding Fractions

When the denominators of the given fractions are alike, the fractions can be added by merely adding the numerators of the given fractions and carrying forward the original denominator.

Example: Find the sum of $\dfrac{1}{4} + \dfrac{2}{4}$.

Solution: $\dfrac{1}{4} + \dfrac{2}{4} = \dfrac{3}{4}$

To add fractions with denominators that are not alike, (1) *determine the lowest common denominator*, (2) *convert all fractions to equivalent fractions containing the lowest common denominator*, and (3) *add the numerators to obtain the sum of the fractions.* The denominator remains the same.

Example: Add $\dfrac{2}{3}$, $\dfrac{9}{16}$, $\dfrac{7}{15}$, and $\dfrac{5}{8}$.

Solution: $\dfrac{2}{3} = \dfrac{160}{240}$, $\dfrac{9}{16} = \dfrac{135}{240}$, $\dfrac{7}{15} = \dfrac{112}{240}$, $\dfrac{5}{8} = \dfrac{150}{240}$

$$\dfrac{160 + 135 + 112 + 150}{240} = \dfrac{557}{240} = 2\dfrac{77}{240}$$

Adding Mixed Numbers

When adding mixed numbers, (1) *determine the lowest common denominator for the fractions*, (2) *convert the fractions to equivalent fractions containing the lowest common denominator*, (3) *add the fractions*, (4) *add the whole numbers*, and (5) *add the sum of the fractions and the sum of the whole numbers.*

Example: Find the sum of $5\dfrac{1}{4}$, $4\dfrac{1}{2}$, $17\dfrac{1}{3}$, and $6\dfrac{5}{6}$.

Solution: The lowest common denominator is 12.

$$5\dfrac{1}{4} = 5\dfrac{3}{12} \qquad\qquad 4\dfrac{1}{2} = 4\dfrac{6}{12}$$

$$17\dfrac{1}{3} = 17\dfrac{4}{12} \qquad\qquad 6\dfrac{5}{6} = 6\dfrac{10}{12}$$

$$\dfrac{3 + 6 + 4 + 10}{12} = \dfrac{23}{12} = 1\dfrac{11}{12}$$

$$5 + 4 + 17 + 6 = 32$$

$$32 + 1\dfrac{11}{12} = 33\dfrac{11}{12}$$

Subtracting Fractions

To subtract fractions with denominators that are alike, subtract the numerators and carry forward the original denominator.

Example: Find the difference between $\dfrac{63}{67}$ and $\dfrac{61}{67}$.

Solution: $\dfrac{63}{67} - \dfrac{61}{67} = \dfrac{2}{67}$

To subtract fractions with denominators that are not alike, (1) determine the lowest common denominator, (2) convert all fractions to equivalent fractions containing the lowest common denominator, and (3) subtract the numerators. The common denominator remains the same.

Example: Find the difference between $\dfrac{5}{6}$ and $\dfrac{3}{4}$.

Solution: The lowest common denominator is 12.

$$\frac{5}{6} = \frac{10}{12}, \quad \frac{3}{4} = \frac{9}{12}$$

$$\frac{10 - 9}{12} = \frac{1}{12}$$

Subtracting Mixed Numbers

When subtracting mixed numbers, (1) determine the lowest common denominator, (2) convert the fractions to equivalent fractions containing the lowest common denominator, and (3) subtract the fractions and the whole numbers in the minuend and the subtrahend to obtain the difference. Sometimes it is necessary to borrow from the whole number in the minuend and enlarge the fractional portion in the minuend in order to complete the subtraction process.

Example: Find the difference between $31\dfrac{1}{4}$ and $18\dfrac{5}{6}$.

Solution: The lowest common denominator is 12.

$$31\frac{1}{4} = 31\frac{3}{12} = 30\frac{15}{12}$$

$$-18\frac{5}{6} = -18\frac{10}{12}$$

(Since $\frac{10}{12}$ cannot be subtracted from $\frac{3}{12}$, it was necessary to borrow 1, or $\frac{12}{12}$, and increase $\frac{3}{12}$ to $\frac{15}{12}$.)

$$30\frac{15}{12} - 18\frac{10}{12} = 12\frac{5}{12}$$

Exercises

Solve the following problems using the lowest common denominator.

1. $\dfrac{3}{5} + \dfrac{4}{10} + \dfrac{1}{2}$

2. $6\dfrac{2}{9} + \dfrac{2}{3} + 1\dfrac{1}{5}$

3. $7\dfrac{3}{4} + 18\dfrac{7}{10} + 4\dfrac{1}{2}$

4. $11\dfrac{4}{9} + \dfrac{5}{18} + 8\dfrac{3}{4}$

5. $\dfrac{5}{8} + 3\dfrac{7}{9} + 2\dfrac{5}{6}$

6. $17\dfrac{3}{5} + 6\dfrac{1}{8} + 12\dfrac{4}{7}$

7. $\dfrac{7}{10} - \dfrac{1}{5}$

8. $3\dfrac{11}{12} - 2\dfrac{2}{3}$

9. $43\dfrac{1}{4} - 17\dfrac{3}{15}$

10. $9\dfrac{7}{12} - 6\dfrac{1}{3}$

11. $5\dfrac{1}{9} - 3\dfrac{1}{10}$

12. $\dfrac{13}{18} - \dfrac{1}{12}$

13. $\dfrac{5}{9} + \dfrac{1}{3} + \dfrac{1}{2} + \dfrac{8}{15}$

14. $\dfrac{2}{3} - \dfrac{7}{12} - \dfrac{2}{5} + \dfrac{5}{6}$

15. $\dfrac{1}{9} + \dfrac{2}{3} - \dfrac{2}{5} - \dfrac{1}{4}$

16. $\dfrac{5}{6} - \dfrac{1}{3} + \dfrac{3}{4} - \dfrac{3}{5}$

17. $19\frac{2}{3} - 4\frac{1}{2} - 7\frac{1}{5}$

18. $26\frac{7}{12} - 18\frac{2}{3} + 3\frac{5}{6}$

Practical Applications

19. In order to install the plumbing for a building, Mr. Grainger needs the following lengths of $\frac{1}{2}$-inch copper tubing: $46\frac{1}{2}$ feet, $13\frac{2}{3}$ feet, $7\frac{3}{8}$ feet, 9 feet and $1\frac{5}{8}$ feet. How many total feet of copper tubing does he need?

20. Flight 94 requires $4\frac{1}{4}$ hours to fly from Houston to New York, while Flight 88 requires only $2\frac{5}{6}$ hours. How many hours' difference is there between the two flights?

21. On Monday morning, the underground storage tank at Jones, Inc., contained $246\frac{1}{2}$ gallons of gasoline. During the week, the following four delivery trucks were filled: Truck 101, $19\frac{1}{8}$ gallons; Truck 102, $21\frac{1}{4}$ gallons; Truck 105, $17\frac{7}{10}$ gallons; Truck 107, $24\frac{1}{2}$ gallons. How many gallons remain in the tank?

22. How much did the price of a share of utilities stock fall during the past week if Monday's price was $109\frac{1}{16}$ and Friday's price was $86\frac{7}{8}$?

Learning Unit 2.4
Multiplication and Division of Fractions

Cancellation

Before beginning the actual process of multiplication or division of fractions, a great deal of time and effort can be saved by *cancellation.* Cancellation is the process of dividing any numerator and denominator by the same number. This reduces the numerators and denominators to smaller numbers, simplifying the multiplication or division process.

Example: Reduce $\dfrac{28}{64}$ by cancellation.

Solution: $\dfrac{28 \div 4}{64 \div 4} = \dfrac{7}{16}$

Multiplication

To multiply two or more fractions, (1) cancel wherever possible, (2) multiply the numerators to obtain the numerator of the new fraction, and (3) multiply the denominators to obtain the denominator of the new fraction.

Example: Multiply $\dfrac{1}{2}$ by $\dfrac{4}{5}$.

Solution: $\dfrac{1}{\underset{1}{\cancel{2}}} \times \dfrac{\overset{2}{\cancel{4}}}{5} = \dfrac{1 \times 2}{1 \times 5} = \dfrac{2}{5}$

Example: Multiply $\dfrac{3}{8}, \dfrac{7}{9}$, and $\dfrac{9}{14}$.

Solution: $\dfrac{3}{8} \times \dfrac{\overset{1}{\cancel{7}}}{\underset{1}{\cancel{9}}} \times \dfrac{\overset{1}{\cancel{9}}}{\underset{2}{\cancel{14}}} = \dfrac{3 \times 1 \times 1}{8 \times 1 \times 2} = \dfrac{3}{16}$

When multiplying mixed numbers, convert the numbers to improper fractions, cancel, and then multiply.

Example: Multiply $12\dfrac{1}{2}$ by $3\dfrac{1}{5}$.

Solution: $12\dfrac{1}{2} \times 3\dfrac{1}{5} = \dfrac{\overset{5}{\cancel{25}}}{\underset{1}{\cancel{2}}} \times \dfrac{\overset{8}{\cancel{16}}}{\underset{1}{\cancel{5}}} = \dfrac{40}{1} = 40$

Division

Dividing fractions is basically the same as multiplying, except that in division the second fraction must be *inverted,* or turned upside down (the numerator becomes the denominator and the denominator becomes the numerator). An inverted fraction is called the *reciprocal*. Thus, *to divide fractions, (1) invert the second fraction (use the reciprocal), (2) cancel whenever possible, (3) multiply the numerators, and (4) multiply the denominators.*

Example: Divide $\dfrac{3}{4}$ by $\dfrac{9}{16}$.

Solution: $\dfrac{3}{4} \div \dfrac{9}{16} = \dfrac{3}{4} \times \dfrac{16}{9} = \dfrac{\overset{1}{\cancel{3}}}{\underset{1}{\cancel{4}}} \times \dfrac{\overset{4}{\cancel{16}}}{\underset{3}{\cancel{9}}} = \dfrac{1 \times 4}{1 \times 3} = \dfrac{4}{3} = 1\dfrac{1}{3}$

Example: Divide $\dfrac{5}{6}$ by $\dfrac{7}{8}$ by $\dfrac{7}{9}$.

Solution: $\dfrac{5}{6} \div \dfrac{7}{8} \div \dfrac{7}{9} = \dfrac{5}{6} \times \dfrac{8}{7} \times \dfrac{9}{7} = \dfrac{5}{\underset{3}{\cancel{6}}} \times \dfrac{\overset{4}{\cancel{8}}}{7} \times \dfrac{\overset{3}{\cancel{9}}}{7} = \dfrac{60}{49} = 1\dfrac{11}{49}$

When dividing mixed numbers, (1) convert the mixed numbers to improper fractions, (2) invert the second fraction, (3) cancel, and (4) multiply.

Example: Divide $40\dfrac{1}{2}$ by $2\dfrac{1}{4}$.

Solution: $40\dfrac{1}{2} \div 2\dfrac{1}{4} = \dfrac{81}{2} \div \dfrac{9}{4} = \dfrac{\overset{9}{\cancel{81}}}{\underset{1}{\cancel{2}}} \times \dfrac{\overset{2}{\cancel{4}}}{\underset{1}{\cancel{9}}} = \dfrac{9 \times 2}{1 \times 1} = \dfrac{18}{1} = 18$

Exercises

Solve the following problems.

1. $\dfrac{1}{2} \times \dfrac{4}{9}$ 2. $\dfrac{1}{6} \times \dfrac{3}{8}$

3. $\dfrac{5}{16} \times \dfrac{8}{9} \times \dfrac{6}{7}$

4. $\dfrac{9}{32} \times \dfrac{17}{21} \times \dfrac{11}{15}$

5. $7 \times 5\dfrac{1}{6}$

6. $2\dfrac{3}{8} \times 4\dfrac{1}{7}$

7. $17\dfrac{1}{5} \times 2\dfrac{2}{3}$

8. $1\dfrac{3}{5} \times 3\dfrac{1}{4} \times 1\dfrac{1}{15}$

9. $\dfrac{1}{4} \times \dfrac{4}{9} \times \dfrac{5}{16} \times \dfrac{4}{15}$

10. $8 \times 4\dfrac{1}{3} \times 2\dfrac{2}{5}$

11. $\dfrac{5}{8} \div \dfrac{11}{16}$

12. $\dfrac{1}{6} \div \dfrac{11}{15}$

13. $\dfrac{3}{5} \div \dfrac{4}{5}$

14. $18 \div \dfrac{2}{3}$

15. $4\dfrac{5}{8} \div 9\dfrac{1}{2}$

16. $16\dfrac{1}{2} \div 14$

17. $8\dfrac{2}{3} \div \dfrac{4}{9} \div 6$

18. $15\dfrac{2}{3} \div 3\dfrac{3}{4} \div \dfrac{1}{8}$

19. $17\dfrac{5}{8} \div 16\dfrac{5}{12}$

20. $9\dfrac{7}{8} \div 9\dfrac{1}{4}$

Practical Applications

21. Judy Hunt plans to deposit $\frac{1}{12}$ of her $696 salary in a savings account this month. How much is the deposit?

22. A damaged article sold for $36, which was $\frac{3}{5}$ of its original cost. What did the article originally cost?

23. Rust, Smith, and Towns entered into a partnership with the following income division ratio: Rust, $\frac{1}{3}$ of the profits; Smith, $\frac{1}{4}$ of the profits; and Towns, the remaining profits. How much did each partner receive if the profits were $55,440?

24. Michelle Cross invested $268 of her savings in stock. If this represents $\frac{3}{5}$ of the balance in her savings account, what was the original balance?

25. What is the square footage of a room measuring $12\frac{3}{8}$ by $9\frac{1}{6}$ feet?

26. A carpet remnant, $\frac{7}{12}$ of a square yard, sells for $2.87. At this rate, what is the cost of a square yard?

Chapter 2
Self-Evaluation

1. Reduce the following fraction to its lowest terms.

$$\frac{52}{78}$$

2. Raise the denominator of $\frac{1}{4}$ to 36.

3. Find the missing numerator in the following problem.

$$\frac{3}{8} = \frac{?}{24}$$

4. Convert the following improper fraction to a mixed number.

$$\frac{39}{4}$$

5. Convert the following mixed number to an improper fraction.

$$7\frac{1}{4}$$

6. Convert the following fraction to a decimal number.

$$\frac{1}{4}$$

7. Convert the following decimal to a fraction.

.75

8. $\dfrac{3}{8} + \dfrac{1}{6} + \dfrac{3}{4}$

9. $\dfrac{3}{4} - \dfrac{1}{3}$

10. $\dfrac{2}{3} \times \dfrac{5}{6} \times \dfrac{3}{5}$

11. $5\dfrac{1}{3} \div 2\dfrac{1}{4}$

12. A stock is quoted at $12\frac{3}{8}$ per share. What is the cost of 15 shares?

13. A seed dealer purchased 84 pounds of grass seed and divided it into $\frac{3}{4}$-pound packages for resale. How many packages were available for resale?

Chapter 3
Percents

Fractions, decimals, and percents represent three ways of expressing a number. However, percents make it easier to compare numbers that appear to be quite different at first glance. For instance, relative difference in size or value between the fractions $\frac{1}{3}$ and $\frac{13}{40}$ is not readily apparent in fractional form; however, once changed to percents, the difference in value can be easily compared: $33\frac{1}{3}\%$ and $32\frac{1}{2}\%$, respectively.

Understanding percents is vital to problem-solving success in any field of business, because it is an important tool for summarizing and comparing business data and information. Business reports relating to the current year's sales, profits, losses, expenses, etc., are more meaningful when compared to the previous year's figures. Dollar differences can be quite difficult to analyze; however, percent amounts for increases and decreases are quite easily measured.

This chapter will provide an opportunity for you to become better acquainted with the use of percents and will show you how to convert percents to decimals and fractions in order to solve business problems.

This chapter will enable you to:

1. **convert a percent to a decimal or a fraction and vice versa**

2. **solve an equation with one unknown variable**

3. **find the part when the rate and base are known**

4. **find the base when the part and rate are known**

5. **find the rate when the part and base are known**

Learning Unit 3.1
Converting Decimals, Fractions, and Percents

Chapter 2 demonstrated how to convert fractions to decimals and decimals to fractions in solving specific types of problems. Since it is often more convenient in business to express fractions and decimals as percents, you must also know how to convert fractions and decimals to percents. Before a percentage of any number can be found arithmetically, percents first must be changed to either fractional or decimal form.

Meaning of Percent

Working with percents will be easier if you remember that *percent means hundredths.* Even the percent sign itself can be seen to contain a 1 and two zeros (% = 100). By simply remembering this rule, you can easily write the number twenty-five hundredths as:

$$\text{a fraction: } \frac{25}{100}$$

a decimal: .25

a percent: 25%

Changing Decimals to Percents

Just as percent means hundredths, so does *hundredths mean percent.* In any given decimal, the hundredths place of the decimal indicates the whole percents between 1% and 99%. *To change a decimal to a percent, (1) move the decimal point two places to the right and (2) add a percent sign.* Add zeros when necessary to hold the place position.

Example: Change .4, .25, .183, .054, and 1.3 to percents.

Solution: .4 = .40 = 40%

$$.25 = .25 = 25\%$$
$$.183 = .183 = 18.3\%$$
$$.054 = .054 = 5.4\%$$
$$1.3 = 1.30 = 130\%$$

Changing Percents to Decimals

To change a percent to a decimal, reverse the above procedure: (1) *remove the percent sign and* (2) *move the decimal point two places to the left.* Add zeros when necessary to hold the place position.

Example: Change .5%, 25%, 15.7%, and 6.07% to decimals.

Solution: $.5\% = 00.5 = .005$

$25\% = 25. = .25$

$15.7\% = 15.7 = .157$

$6.07\% = 06.07 = .0607$

Changing Fractions to Percents

To change a fraction to a percent, (1) *convert the fraction to a decimal by dividing the numerator by the denominator,* (2) *move the decimal point two places to the right, and* (3) *add a percent sign.* Add zeros when necessary to hold the place position.

Example: Change $\dfrac{1}{4}, \dfrac{3}{8}, \dfrac{19}{100},$ and $1\dfrac{1}{2}$ to percents.

Solution: $\dfrac{1}{4} = 1 \div 4 = .25 = .25 = 25\%$

$\dfrac{3}{8} = 3 \div 8 = .375 = .375 = 37.5\%$

$\dfrac{19}{100} = 19 \div 100 = .19 = .19 = 19\%$

$1\dfrac{1}{2} = \dfrac{3}{2} = 3 \div 2 = 1.5 = 1.50 = 150\%$

Changing Percents to Fractions

To change a percent to a fraction, (1) remove the percent sign, (2) move the decimal point two places to the left, (3) change the decimal to a fraction by placing the number over a denominator of 100, and (4) reduce the resulting fraction to lowest terms. Add zeros when necessary to hold the place position.

Example: Change 25%, $12\frac{1}{2}$%, 125%, and $\frac{1}{4}$% to fractions.

Solution: $25\% = 25. = .25 = \dfrac{25}{100} = \dfrac{1}{4}$

$$12\frac{1}{2}\% = 12.\frac{1}{2} = .12\frac{1}{2} = \frac{12\frac{1}{2}}{100} = \frac{25}{2} \div \frac{100}{1} = \frac{25}{2} \times \frac{1}{100} = \frac{1}{8}$$

$$125\% = 125. = 1.25 = 1\frac{25}{100} = 1\frac{1}{4}$$

$$\frac{1}{4}\% = 00.\frac{1}{4} = .00\frac{1}{4} = \frac{\frac{1}{4}}{100} = \frac{1}{4} \div \frac{100}{1} = \frac{1}{4} \times \frac{1}{100} = \frac{1}{400}$$

An alternate method of converting a fractional percent to a decimal is to change the fraction to a decimal before removing the percent sign.

Example: Change $\frac{1}{4}$ to a percent.

Solution: $\dfrac{1}{4}\% = .25\% = 00.25 = .0025 = \dfrac{25}{10,000} = \dfrac{1}{400}$

Changing Whole Numbers to Percents

To change a whole number to a percent, (1) locate the decimal point, which is always to the right of the last digit in a whole number, (2) move the decimal point two places to the right, and (3) add a percent sign. Add zeros to hold the place position.

Example: Change 1, 29, and 335 to percents.

Solution: $1 = 1.00 = 100\%$

$$29 = 29.00 = 2{,}900\%$$

$$335 = 335.00 = 33{,}500\%$$

Aliquot Parts

An *aliquot part* is an *equal part* of some number. For instance, an aliquot part of 100 is any number that will divide evenly into 100. Equal parts of $1.00 and 100% are used frequently in business when buying, selling, or pricing merchandise. It is easier to compute the price of 16 items at 25¢ each by multiplying the aliquot part (25¢ $= \frac{1}{4}$ of a dollar) by 16 ($\frac{1}{4} \times \frac{16}{1}$) than it is to compute it by multiplying the number itself (.25) by 16 (.25 $\times$ 16). In addition, the use of aliquot parts permits a rapid conversion of percents into fractions.

An *aliquot fraction* is a fraction in which the numerator is an aliquot part of the base—the denominator. An aliquot fraction will always reduce to a fraction with 1 as the numerator.

Example: Is 25 an aliquot part of 100?

Solution: $\dfrac{25}{100} = \dfrac{1}{4}$ (25 is an equal part of 100.)

Table 3.1 Commonly Used Conversions of Aliquot Parts of 100%

$\frac{1}{2} = .50 = 50\%$	$\frac{1}{9} = .11\frac{1}{9} = 11\frac{1}{9}\%$
$\frac{1}{3} = .33\frac{1}{3} = 33\frac{1}{3}\%$	$\frac{1}{10} = .10 = 10\%$
$\frac{1}{4} = .25 = 25\%$	$\frac{1}{12} = .08\frac{1}{3} = 8\frac{1}{3}\%$
$\frac{1}{5} = .20 = 20\%$	$\frac{1}{16} = .06\frac{1}{4} = 6\frac{1}{4}\%$
$\frac{1}{6} = .16\frac{2}{3} = 16\frac{2}{3}\%$	$\frac{1}{20} = .05 = 5\%$
$\frac{1}{8} = .12\frac{1}{2} = 12\frac{1}{2}\%$	

Conversion List

Certain percents occur frequently in business because they are equivalent to certain fractions, making computations simpler. Table 3.1 on page 55 shows a listing of conversions of frequently used aliquot parts of 100%. (This list can also be used to find aliquot parts of $1.00.)

Exercises

Change the following percents to decimals.

1. 3%	2. 7%	3. 36%	4. 45%
5. 27.3%	6. 58.9%	7. 14.06%	8. 72.99%
9. $13\frac{1}{2}\%$	10. $27\frac{1}{2}\%$	11. $26\frac{1}{4}\%$	12. $18\frac{3}{4}\%$
13. $\frac{1}{2}\%$	14. $\frac{1}{4}\%$	15. 197%	16. 305%
17. 96.32%	18. 54.08%	19. 273.7%	20. 406.84%

Change the following numbers to percents.

21. .04	22. .35	23. 5.2	24. 17
25. .022	26. $.12\frac{1}{2}$	27. 9	28. 1.3052
29. $.33\frac{1}{3}$	30. $.008\frac{1}{4}$	31. $\frac{1}{5}$	32. 2
33. .4206	34. 6.003	35. $5\frac{1}{4}$	36. 2.14
37. 37	38. .892	39. 13.26	40. 3.702

Change the following percents to fractions or mixed numbers.

41. 10%	42. 375%	43. $1\frac{1}{7}\%$	44. 72.5%
45. 216.2%	46. .4%	47. 16%	48. 36.8%

49. .75%   50. .362%   51. 25%   52. 143%

53. $\dfrac{1}{5}$%   54. 24%   55. $2\dfrac{1}{4}$%   56. 225%

57. 50%   58. $\dfrac{1}{8}$%   59. .5%   60. 304%

Change the following fractions or mixed numbers to percents.

61. $\dfrac{1}{3}$ 62. $3\dfrac{1}{4}$ 63. $\dfrac{1}{5}$ 64. $\dfrac{3}{4}$

65. $17\dfrac{1}{10}$ 66. $\dfrac{1}{6}$ 67. $\dfrac{7}{8}$ 68. $\dfrac{3}{8}$

69. $5\dfrac{7}{10}$ 70. $1\dfrac{3}{20}$ 71. $2\dfrac{5}{8}$ 72. $1\dfrac{3}{8}$

73. $1\dfrac{1}{16}$ 74. $\dfrac{4}{5}$ 75. $\dfrac{3}{4}$ 76. $\dfrac{13}{25}$

77. $18\dfrac{1}{5}$ 78. $\dfrac{1}{10}$ 79. $\dfrac{1}{8}$ 80. $\dfrac{3}{5}$

Determine the missing numbers.

	Fraction	Decimal	Percent
81.	$\dfrac{1}{2}$	__________	__________
82.	__________	.25	__________
83.	$\dfrac{1}{5}$	__________	__________
84.	__________	__________	30%
85.	__________	2.45	__________
86.	__________	__________	75%

87. $2\frac{3}{4}$ _________ _________

88. _________ 36.4 _________

89. _________ _________ 15.5%

90. $\frac{5}{8}$ _________ _________

Compute the total cost for each of the following articles using the aliquot parts of a dollar.

91. 80 ft. of wire at \$.06$\frac{1}{4}$ per foot

92. 1,500 washers at \$.05 each

93. 420 bolts at \$.14$\frac{2}{7}$ each

94. 810 candy bars at \$.11$\frac{1}{9}$ each

95. 600 $\frac{1}{2}''$ PVC couplers at \$.16$\frac{2}{3}$ each

Learning Unit 3.2
Solving Equations

The material in Learning Unit 3.2 is presented primarily to aid in solving problems similar to those in Learning Unit 3.3.

Definition and Components of Equation

An *equation* is a mathematical expression of the equality of two quantities. In an equation, the right-hand quantity is separated from the left-hand quantity by an equal sign to show that one side is equal to the other. Each side is made up of numbers called constants or variables or combinations of constants and variables. A *constant* is a number whose value is known and does not change from problem to problem. A *variable* is a number whose value or quantity is unknown, is represented by a letter of the alphabet, and changes from problem to problem. In the equation $30 = a + 10$, 30 and 10 are constants and a is a variable. When constants and variables are multiplied together on one side of the equation, the constant is then referred to as a *coefficient*. In the equation $15 = 3 \times B$ (or $15 = 3B$), 15 is a constant, B is a variable, and 3 is a coefficient.

Solving an Equation

The object in solving any equation containing a variable is to find what value of the variable will make one side equal to the other. Finding the value of the unknown quantity is basically accomplished by isolating the variable on one side of the equation and the constants on the other side. The isolation process involves (1) determining which arithmetic operation—addition, subtraction, multiplication, or division—is taking place on the variable's side of the equation and (2) performing the *opposite* arithmetic process on *both* sides of the equation. The opposite process for addition is subtraction; the opposite process for multiplication is division; and vice versa. Remember that the equality of the equation is not disturbed as long as the *same operation* is performed with the *same number* on *both sides* of the equation.

Example: Solve for C: $C + 7 = 14$.

Solution: In order to isolate the variable C on one side of the equation, we must remove the 7. The equation operation is addition. The opposite arithmetic operation is subtraction. Therefore, we must subtract 7 from both sides.

$$C + 7 = 14$$
$$C + 7 - 7 = 14 - 7$$
$$C = 7$$

Example: Solve for M: $M - 4 = 7$.

Solution: The equation operation is subtraction. The opposite arithmetic operation is addition. To isolate M, we must add 4 to both sides.

$$M - 4 = 7$$
$$M - 4 + 4 = 7 + 4$$
$$M = 11$$

Example: Solve for A: $3A = 15$.

Solution: The equation operation is multiplication. The opposite arithmetic operation is division. To isolate A we must divide both sides by 3.

$$3A = 15$$
$$\frac{3A}{3} = \frac{15}{3}$$
$$A = 5$$

Example: Solve for x: $\dfrac{x}{5} = 4$.

Solution: The equation operation is division. The opposite arithmetic operation is multiplication. To isolate x, we must multiply both sides by 5.

$$\frac{x}{5} = 4$$
$$\frac{x}{5} \cdot \frac{5}{1} = 4 \cdot 5$$
$$x = 20$$

Exercises

Solve for the variable in each of the following equations.

1. $a + 7 = 21$
2. $c - 3 = 7$
3. $\dfrac{b}{3} = 3$

4. $4c = 12$
5. $\dfrac{2}{a} = 7$
6. $7 - b = 3$

7. $4 + c = 11$
8. $8m = 32$
9. $r + 2 = 7$

10. $\dfrac{a}{21} = 3$
11. $b - 3 = 17$
12. $6c = 3$

13. $5a = 7$
14. $y - 9 = 1$
15. $x + \dfrac{1}{2} = \dfrac{2}{3}$

16. $.25c = 3$ 17. $\dfrac{b}{\frac{1}{2}} = 7$ 18. $a - .17 = 3.2$

19. $3\frac{1}{2}x = 7$ 20. $\dfrac{a}{.2} = 6$

Learning Unit 3.3
Finding Part, Base, and Rate

Percentage Formula

One of the most valuable tools in solving business problems is known as the *percentage formula: Part = Base × Rate,* or $P = B \times R$. The percentage formula can be used to solve business problems involving interest, discounts, commissions, retail pricing policies, taxes, comparison data on sales, expenses, profits, and much more. For example, if the interest rate and the amount of money borrowed are known, the entire year's interest can be computed by using this formula. In fact, all problems that involve the use of the percent are some variation of this basic equation.

Components of Percentage Formula

The three components of the percentage formula are the part[1] (P), the base (B), and the rate (R). The *base* is the whole amount and always represents 100%. It is the central unit to which everything else refers and is the quantity one calculates a part or percentage of. The *part* is simply a part of the whole and is the product of the base and the rate. The *rate* is some percent or fraction of the base. It is the relationship of the part and the base expressed as a percent. Rate expressed as a percent must be converted to a decimal or a fraction in working a problem. However, as an answer, rate should always be expressed as a percent.

[1] P is often referred to as "percentage"; however, since R (rate) is always expressed as a percent (%), the term P will be defined as "part" throughout this discussion in order to avoid confusion in differentiating between P and R.

Example: A real estate broker sold a house for $50,000. The broker earned 6% commission on the sale. The amount of commission received by the broker was $3,000. Which of these items is the base, the rate, the part?

Solution: The base is $50,000. The rate is 6%. The part is $3,000.

In many business situations, only two of the components (base, part, or rate) are known, and it is necessary to determine the missing item. If any two of the percentage formula variables are known, the third variable can be found by algebraically changing the basic percentage formula. Before the formula can be changed, however, it is necessary to identify the two variables that are *known* and the one that is *unknown*.

Identifying the Unknown Variable

To identify the unknown variable, use the following sentence format:

_________ is _________% of _________.

When this sentence format is read as *something* is *some* % of *something else,* the blanks can be labeled as follows:

_________ is _________% of _________.
    P R B

When the problem is changed to this sentence format,

R: The rate can always be identified by a percent sign (%) or the word *percent.*

B: The base follows the word *of* when the problem is read.

P: Since the part is a portion of the whole, part is always expressed in the same terms as the base. The part can be identified by elimination once the base has been identified.

The word *is* is the written version of an equal sign, and the word *of* indicates a multiplication process; therefore, _____________ is _____________ % of
                                                                P R

_____________ is basically the percentage formula in words:
      B

$$P = R \times B \text{ (or } P = B \times R)$$

Once the known and unknown variables are identified, the value of the unknown variable can be found by using the appropriate variation of the percentage formula.

Finding the Part

When the base and rate are known, *multiply the base by the rate to determine the part.*

$$Part = Base \times Rate \text{ or}$$
$$P = B \times R$$

Example: What is 10% of 100?

Solution: $\underbrace{\quad ? \quad}_{P}$ is $\underbrace{\quad 10 \quad}_{R}$ % of $\underbrace{\quad 100 \quad}_{B}$.

P = unknown; use the formula for P and solve.

$$P = B \times R$$
$$P = 100 \times .10$$
$$P = 10$$

Finding the Base

When the part and rate are known, *divide the part by the rate to determine the base.* Using the basic percentage formula, the base is isolated by dividing both sides of the equation by rate.

$$P = B \times R$$

$$\frac{P}{R} = \frac{B \times \overset{1}{\cancel{R}}}{\underset{1}{\cancel{R}}}$$

$$\frac{P}{R} = B \text{ or } B = \frac{P}{R}$$

$$Base = \frac{Part}{Rate}$$

Example: 21 is 20% of what number?

Solution: $\underbrace{\quad 21 \quad}_{P}$ is $\underbrace{\quad 20 \quad}_{R}$ % of $\underbrace{\quad ? \quad}_{B}$.

B = unknown; use the formula for B and solve.

$$B = \frac{P}{R} \qquad B = \frac{21}{.20} \qquad B = 105$$

Finding the Rate

When the part and the base are known, *divide the part by the base to determine the rate.* Using the basic percentage formula, the rate is isolated by dividing both sides of the equation by the base.

$$P = B \times R$$

$$\frac{P}{B} = \frac{\overset{1}{\cancel{B}} \times R}{\underset{1}{\cancel{B}}}$$

$$\frac{P}{B} = R \text{ or } R = \frac{P}{B}$$

$$Rate = \frac{Part}{Base}$$

Example: What percent of 70 is 14?

Solution: $\underset{P}{\underline{\quad 14 \quad}}$ is $\underset{R}{\underline{\quad ? \quad}}$ % of $\underset{B}{\underline{\quad 70 \quad}}$.

R = unknown; use the formula for R and solve.

$$R = \frac{P}{B}$$

$$R = \frac{\overset{2}{\cancel{14}}}{\underset{10}{\cancel{70}}}$$

$$R = \frac{2}{10}$$

$$R = 20\%$$

Formula Shortcut

An easy way to remember the three variations of the percentage formula is presented in Figure 3.1. Cover up the variable for which a formula is needed. The correct formula is that part of Figure 3.1 that is left uncovered.

Figure 3.1 Calculating Part, Base, and Rate

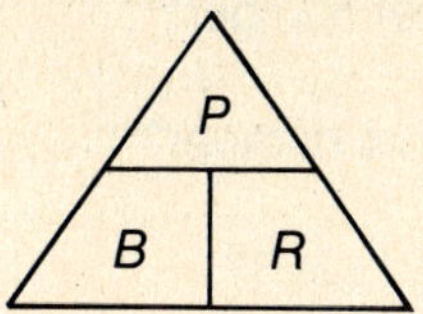

If P is unknown: $P =$ $P = B \times R$

If B is unknown: $B =$ $B = \dfrac{P}{R}$

If R is unknown: $R =$ $R = \dfrac{P}{B}$

Exercises

Solve the following.

1. 20% of 72 is what number?

2. 15% of 15 is what number?

3. $\frac{1}{2}$% of 7 is what number?

4. What percent of 9 is 3?

5. What percent of 36 is 9?

6. What percent of 6 is 9?

7. 8% of what number is 20?

8. $33\frac{1}{3}$% of what number is 17?

9. 50% of what number is 50?

10. 16% of 10 is what number?

11. $16\frac{2}{3}\%$ of 36 is what number?

12. What percent of 12 is 3?

13. What percent of 35 is 7?

14. 5% of what number is 25?

15. 12% of what number is 144?

Practical Applications

16. The Southwest Wholesale Company has an annual payroll of $304,265. The company is considering a 7% across-the-board pay increase. What additional amount will the company have to provide in its budget for the next year if the raise is granted?

17. Mathville, a thriving suburban community, charges real estate developers 20% of the cost of road construction in new residential developments. What was the total cost of road building in a development if the city billed the developer $42,000?

18. The landlord of an apartment complex increases the rent 15%. One of the tenants has been paying $275 monthly rent.
    (a) How much additional rent will the tenant be required to pay?
    (b) How much total rent will the tenant be required to pay following the increase?

19. A community college recently awarded 156 associate degrees. A survey showed that 61% of the graduates intended to enroll at a senior college. How many of the graduates intend to enroll at a senior college?

20. The state sales tax is 5%. How much tax is collected on a $21.40 sale?

21. James made a 10% deposit on two reserved seat tickets for a tennis tournament. His deposit was $11.00.
    (a)   What was the total cost of the two tickets?
    (b)   What is the remaining balance for the tickets?

22. If 442 of the 613 employees of a company participate in an optional retirement plan, what percent of the company's workers participate?

23. A student paid $150 on a debt. This payment was 20% of the debt. What was the total debt?

24. A theater building is valued at $420,000 and is insured for $336,000. What percent of the total value is insured?

25. A salesperson is paid a commission of 3% on the first $30,000 of sales and 5% on sales in excess of this amount. How much commission will the salesperson earn on sales of $43,254?

26. The enrollment at a college last semester was 6,200. The enrollment dropped 7% this semester. What is this semester's enrollment?

27. Frank was earning $150 per week before receiving a 4% raise. How much does he earn following the raise?

28. A merchant ordered 18 shirts. The order was checked by the shipping and receiving department upon receipt and only 15 shirts were found in the carton. What percent of the shirts was missing?

29. Jim Jakes earned a $40 commission on the sale of a color television set. What was the selling price if the commission was 5%?

30. Forty students are enrolled in a business math class. Roll is checked and 35 students are present. What percent of the class is absent?

31. A small manufacturing company has two departments: production and accounting. The production department occupies 75% of the total square footage of the plant. Since overhead expenses are shared on a proportionate basis, how much of a $10,000 monthly overhead expense should be charged to the production department?

32. Jones's Department Store received a shipment of shoes only to find that 7 pairs were missing. If there should have been 25 pairs of shoes, what percent of the order was missing?

33. An invoice for $285 was received on February 27. When the shipment arrived, $50 worth of goods were found to be damaged and were returned to the seller. What was the percent of goods returned?

34. Mary Williams donated $350 to her church last year. If this represents 60% of her donations, what was her total contribution?

35. Last year, an investment earned $172, which represented a 7% return on the investment. How much was invested?

36. Paul's Print Shop spent $1,575 last year for advertising. This year it plans to spend 110% of last year's amount. How much will be spent for advertising this year?

37. A college teacher has a net monthly income of $1,078. After deducting all housing expenses (mortgage and utilities), the balance is $553. What is the percent of income spent on housing?

38. A house that cost $51,000 eighteen months ago is valued at $60,000 today. By what percent has the house appreciated in value?

39. A salesman earned $17,500 last year working on a 5% commission rate. How much merchandise did he sell last year?

40. Edward Sims spends 38% of his $225 weekly pay for food. How much money does he spend for food?

Chapter 3
Self-Evaluation

1. Change the following percent to a decimal number.

   29%

2. Change the following decimal number to a percent.

   .355

3. Change the following percent to a fraction.

   25%

4. Change the following mixed number to a percent.

   $3\frac{1}{5}$

5. What is 3% of $120.00?

6. What percent of 240 is 60?

7. The interest on a one-year 6% loan is $72. What is the amount of the loan?

8. A business math class with 25 students was given an exam. Five of the students earned an A on the exam. What percent of the students earned an A on the exam?

9. A textbook in the college bookstore is marked $12.65. The state sales tax is 5%. What is the total cost of the book?

10. A local factory produced 3,400 football helmets during the past month. The quality control department rejected 68 of the helmets as defective. What percent of the helmets was rejected?

11. A salesperson was paid a commission of 5% on sales of $52,000 during the previous month. How much commission did the salesperson receive for the month?

12. A home is insured for $60,000, which is 90% of the value of the home. What is the value of the home?

13. Solve for the unknown: $3B = 12$.

14. Solve for the unknown: $B - 7 = 10$.

15. If 1″ bolts cost $6\frac{1}{4}$ cents each, how much will a buyer spend for 320 bolts? (Use aliquots.)

PART TWO
THE MATHEMATICS OF MARKETING

A businessperson must be able to determine the
cost of merchandise available for sale and the selling
price that must be obtained in order to cover
expenses and make a satisfactory profit. The chapters
in this part of the text will introduce you to the
mathematical processes required to make these
determinations.

Chapter 4
Trade Pricing

Businesses rarely manufacture the items that they sell to the general public. They usually buy those items from a manufacturer or wholesaler. The trade price is the price that a business pays for the goods it sells.

In most trade sales, businesses do not pay the full price at which an item is offered to the public for sale. They often receive some type of commercial discount, which must be considered in finding the amount a business must actually pay for the good. Therefore, it is important that a businessperson understand the types and terms of commercial discounts and be able to apply them in calculating trade prices.

This chapter will provide an opportunity for you to become more familiar with two of the most common commercial discounts—trade discounts and cash discounts. In addition, you will become acquainted with the process of figuring partial payments.

This chapter will enable you to:

1.   **explain the role of trade and cash discounts in business**

2.   **define the terms *trade discount, list price, trade price, net decimal equivalent, single discount equivalent, trade credit* and *cash discount***

3.   **calculate the amount of a single or chain (series) discount**

4.   **determine the trade price of a catalog item if a trade discount is allowed**

5.   **compute cash discounts and the amount due on an invoice**

6.   **compute the balance due when a partial payment is made on an account in which a cash discount is allowed**

Learning Unit 4.1
Trade Discounts

Definition and Purpose of Trade Discounts

Manufacturers and wholesalers publish catalogs containing descriptions and prices of their products. The catalog price, which is usually the suggested retail price, is known as the *list price*. Customers may be granted a *trade discount* or deduction from the list, or catalog, price. The trade discount is expressed as a percent (%) of the list price and is deducted from the list price to determine the *trade price (net price),* or cost of the item to the customer. The trade discount may consist of a single discount or a series of discounts based on various factors such as order date (to promote sales during a slack period), quantity, or frequency of purchase.

One of the main uses of trade discounts is to communicate price changes in an economical manner. Instead of going to the expense of publishing a new catalog each time prices change, businesses usually mail a printed sheet to customers stating the new discounts that are to be taken on the prices quoted in the catalog. When prices rise, a discount is reduced or dropped. When prices go down, a discount is increased or added.

In addition to facilitating price changes, trade discounts are also used to provide incentive for large-quantity purchases, to attract desirable accounts, to meet the competition, or to grant more attractive or appropriate rates to different buyer groups, such as wholesalers, dealers, or retailers.

Trade discounts apply only to the costs of merchandise; the full amount must be paid for the costs of freight, insurance, or other charges.

Computing Trade Prices Using a Single Trade Discount

Application of Single Discount to List Price. One method of computing the trade price when a single trade discount is allowed is to compute the trade discount and then subtract it from the list price, according to the following formulas:

(1)   Trade discount = List Price × Discount Rate[1]
(2)   Trade Price = List Price − Trade Discount

[1]The trade discount formula is a form of the basic percentage formula ($P = B \times R$), as discussed in Chapter 3, where P = Trade Discount, B = List Price, and R = Discount

Example: The list price of a lawn mower is $80 and the trade discount
is 35%. What is the trade price?

Solution: (1) $80   list price
                   $\times$ .35   rate of discount
                   ———
                   400

                   240
                   ———
                   $28.00   trade discount

   (2) $80   list price
        $-$ 28   trade discount
        ———
        $52   trade price

Notice that the 35% trade discount was converted to a decimal in the
solution shown above. Problems with certain discount percents, such as
$16\frac{2}{3}\%$ $(\frac{1}{6})$ or 20% $(\frac{1}{5})$, may be easier to solve by using the fractional form of
the discount percent. (See Chapter 2 for a list of commonly used percents
and their fractional equivalents.)

Example: The list price of a TV set is $579, and the trade discount is
$33\frac{1}{3}\%$. What is the trade price?

Solution: $33\frac{1}{3}\% = \dfrac{33\frac{1}{3}}{100} = \dfrac{1}{3}$

$\$579 \times \dfrac{1}{3} = \$193$ trade discount

$\$579 - \$193 = \$386$ trade price

Percent Paid. Since the percent of discount indicates what percent of
the list price is *not* paid by the buyer, it follows that the percent of discount
subtracted from 100% (the whole list price) will indicate what percent of the
list price *is paid.* Thus,

if 100% (Whole List Price) = % Discount + % Paid, then

% Paid = 100% $-$ % Discount

(footnote 1, continued)
Rate. All the variations of the basic percentage formula can be applied here. Thus, by alge-
braically changing the trade discount formula, we can find the list price, List Price = Trade
Discount $\div$ Discount Rate; or the discount rate, Discount Rate = Trade Discount $\div$ List
Price.

The *percent paid* is the complement of the discount percent; that is, it is the number that when added to the given discount percent will equal the whole, or 100%.

By using the complement (percent paid), the trade price of an item allowed a single discount can be computed in one step:

$$\text{Trade Price} = \text{List Price} \times \% \text{ Paid}^2$$

Example: The list price of a sunlamp is $149, and the trade discount is 45%. What is the trade price?

Solution:
$$
\begin{array}{ll}
\$149 & \text{list price} \\
\times\ .55 & \text{complement of 45\% (100\% } - \text{ 45\%)} \\
\hline
745 & \\
745 & \\
\hline
\$81.95 & \text{trade price}
\end{array}
$$

Computing Trade Prices Using a Chain (Series) Discount

Often, two or more successive trade discounts are quoted on the same goods: for instance, 20%, 10%, 5% (often written 20/10/5) might be one seller's discount terms for a particular item. Such a multiple discount is known as a *chain,* or *series, discount.* Ordinarily, the largest discount is expressed first.

Application of Discount Series. One method of computing the trade price when a chain discount is allowed is by directly applying each discount against the list price. When using this method, each discount must be taken separately, although the order in which the discounts are taken will not affect the final result. The first discount is computed on the basis of the list price and is subtracted from the list price. Each succeeding discount is computed on the basis of the balance remaining after the preceding discount has been deducted and is then subtracted from that balance. Under this method, the amount remaining after the last discount has been subtracted is the trade price. The trade discount can then be found by subtracting the trade price from the list price.

---

[2]The percent paid formula is also a form of the basic percentage formula ($P = B \times R$), as explained in Chapter 3, where P = Trade Price, B = List Price, and R = % Paid. All of the variations of the basic percentage formula are applicable here. Thus, by algebraically changing the percent paid formula, we can find the list price, List Price = Trade Price ÷ % Paid; or the percent paid, % Paid = Trade Price ÷ List Price.

Example: The list price of a bedroom suite is $900 and the trade discount is 20%, 20%, and 10%. How much is the trade discount and what is the trade price?

Solution:

$900.00	list price
− 180.00	first discount (20% of $900)
$720.00	net amount after first discount
− 144.00	second discount (20% of $720)
$576.00	net amount after second discount
− 57.60	third discount (10% of $576)
$518.40	trade price
$900.00	list price
− 518.40	trade price
$381.60	trade discount

Notice that it is incorrect to add the series of discounts and apply this combined percent to the list price. In other words, a 20%, 20%, 10% chain discount is not equivalent to a 50% discount on the list price. (The "combined percent" of a chain discount can be computed only by finding the single discount equivalent, according to the procedure described below.)

Percent Paid. The percent paid method (Trade Price = List Price × % Paid) that was explained above for single trade discounts can also be applied to series discounts by using the *net decimal equivalent of the percent paid.* This value may be found by multiplying together the complements of each of the discount percents in the series. Thus, to find the trade price when a series of discounts is allowed:

1. Determine the complements of the series.
2. Multiply the complements to determine percent paid.
3. Multiply the net decimal equivalent of the percent paid by the list price.

Example: Find the trade price of a stereo that lists for $440 when the trade discount is 30/20/10.

Solution: (1) 100% − 30% = 70% = .7   complement of 30%
100% − 20% = 80% = .8   complement of 20%
100% − 10% = 90% = .9   complement of 10%

(2) .7 × .8 × .9 = .504   net decimal equivalent of percent paid

(3) $440 × .504 = $221.76   trade price

Single Discount Equivalent. Sometimes it is convenient to find the *single discount equivalent* of a series of discounts, especially when several items on the same invoice are subject to the same chain discount or when a business wants to compare costs. To compute the single discount equivalent:

1. Determine the complements of the series.
2. Multiply the complements to determine the net decimal equivalent of the percent paid.
3. Subtract the net decimal equivalent of the percent paid from 1.00 (100%).

(Remember to convert the answer to a percent by moving the decimal point two digits to the right and adding the percent sign, as indicated in Chapter 2.)

Example: Find the single discount equivalent for a 30%, 20%, 10% chain discount.

Solution: (1) 100% − 30% = 70% = .7 complement of 30%
100% − 20% = 80% = .8 complement of 20%
100% − 10% = 90% = .9 complement of 10%

(2) .7 × .8 × .9 = .504 percent paid

(3) 1.00 − .504 = .496 = 49.6% single discount
equivalent

Exercises

Find the percent paid and the trade price (single trade discounts).

	List Price	Discount Rate	Percent Paid	Trade Price
1.	$ 90.00	43%	__________	__________
2.	$786.00	30%	__________	__________
3.	$650.00	24%	__________	__________
4.	$647.00	46%	__________	__________
5.	$936.00	$33\frac{1}{3}$%	__________	__________
6.	$ 6.36	$16\frac{2}{3}$%	__________	__________
7.	$ 36.24	32%	__________	__________
8.	$ 95.44	41%	__________	__________
9.	$ 48.48	$12\frac{1}{2}$%	__________	__________
10.	$ 33.93	$33\frac{1}{3}$%	__________	__________

Find the net decimal equivalent and the trade price (chain discounts).

	List Price	Chain Discount	Net Decimal Equivalent	Trade Price
11.	$192.40	25%, 20%	_______________	_________
12.	$ 72.30	20%, 10%	_______________	_________
13.	$196.00	30%, 10%, 10%	_______________	_________
14.	$ 45.20	35%, 20%, 5%	_______________	_________
15.	$114.10	20%, 20%, 10%	_______________	_________
16.	$221.80	20%, 10%, 10%	_______________	_________

Find the single discount equal to each of the following chain discounts.

	Chain Discount	Single Discount Equivalent
17.	20%, 10%	_______________
18.	30%, 20%	_______________
19.	30%, 10%, 10%	_______________
20.	25%, 20%, 10%	_______________
21.	40%, 5%, 5%	_______________
22.	35%, 10%, 5%	_______________

Which of each set of chain discounts will result in the lower net price?

23.	30/10 or 20/20	_________
24.	33/15 or 25/20	_________
25.	20/15/10 or 25/20	_________
26.	15/10/5 or 20/10	_________

Practical Applications

27. Ace Electronics Company recently purchased a shipment of mobile CB radios from a wholesaler. Each unit had a list price of $299.95 with a trade discount of 30%. Find the trade price for each unit.

28. Reed Supply Company sells portable heaters at discounts of 30%, 10%, and 10%. The heaters list for $37.99. What is the trade price of the heaters?

29. Ferm's Furniture Company buys desks from a furniture wholesaler. The desks list for $319.95 with a trade discount of 30% and 20%.
(a) What is the trade price?
(b) If the freight charges are $14.79, what is the billing price?

30. A dining room set with a list price of $1,640 is subject to a chain discount of 45% and 20%.
(a) What is the trade price?
(b) If the freight charges are $53.20, what is the billing price?

31. The list price of a bookcase is $278 and the trade discount is 30%, 20%, and 10%.
(a) What is the trade price?
(b) What is the trade discount?

32. Southwest Wholesale Company lists executive desks for $730 and allows its customers a trade discount of 40% and 20%.
(a) What is the trade discount?
(b) What is the trade price?

33. What is the net cost of five dozen men's ties if the list price is $96 per dozen subject to a 30/10/10 chain discount?

34. The XYZ Manufacturing Company has a list price of $39.95 for electric edgers. A chain discount of 15/15/10 is offered to wholesalers while a 20/15 trade discount is offered retailers.
(a) What is the trade price for wholesalers?
(b) What is the trade price for retailers?

35. The A & J Stone Company has a list price of $29.95 for marble bookends and offers a trade discount of 30/10/5. The Specialty Wholesale Company markets the same item with a list price of $28.95 subject to a chain discount of 20/20/10.
(a) Which company has the lower trade price?
(b) How much is saved by taking advantage of the lower price?

36. The list price of a toy table and chair set is $34.95. What is the net cost to a customer who is granted a trade discount of 10/5/5?

Learning Unit 4.2
Cash Discounts

A common form of business debt is trade (or mercantile) credit. *Trade credit* is short-term credit extended by a supplier to a buyer in conjunction with the purchase of goods for ultimate resale. Most retailers do not pay cash for merchandise they purchase for resale. Instead, they purchase on account (on credit). As a result, manufacturers and wholesalers allow retailers a cash discount to encourage prompt payment. A *cash discount* is a reduction from the net amount of an invoice, but it may be deducted only if the account is paid within a specified amount of time. Like trade discounts, cash discounts can be taken only on the net cost of goods, not on freight or other charges.

The invoice or monthly statement contains the *terms of sale,* which specify the cash discount rate, if any, and the time period within which the invoice must be paid. In some situations, the terms involve no credit. For instance, when the terms are C.B.D. (cash before delivery), the buyer must pay for the goods before the supplier will ship them. When the invoice indicates C.O.D. (cash on delivery), the supplier will ship the goods, but the buyer must pay for them before taking possession from the carrier. When the terms are R.O.G. (receipt of goods), the buyer must pay immediately; no discount is offered and there is no extra time in which to pay.

Determining Payment Date

Some companies quote credit terms that do not include a cash discount but that do allow the buyer extra time in which to pay. For instance, credit terms of net/30 allow the buyer to pay for the merchandise within 30 days of the date shown on the invoice. In this situation, the last day of the credit period is calculated as follows:

1. Subtract the invoice date from the number of days in the month of the invoice.
2. Add as many full months as possible without exceeding the number of days in the credit period.
3. Total the number of days in these months.
4. Subtract the number of days obtained in step 3 from the number of days in the credit period.

Note that, when determining the last day of a credit period, the *exact* number of days is used. For instance the term n/90 means exactly 90 days, not three months.

Example: When is payment due on a n/90 sale if the invoice is dated March 20?

Solution: (1)   31   days in March
           −20   invoice date
           11   days of credit in March
    (2)   +30   days in April
           +31   days in May
    (3)   72   total
    (4)   90   days in credit period
           −72   total from step 3
           18   due date in June

You may find the "knuckle method" useful for verifying the number of days in each month. Figure 4.1 illustrates this method.

Determining Amount of Payment

Cash discounts vary considerably among industries. Ordinary credit terms allow a cash discount if the invoice is paid within 10 to 20 days of the date of the invoice and require payment in full in 30 to 90 days. Credit terms of 2/10, n/30 (read as "two ten, net thirty") are typical. These terms mean that:

1. a discount of two percent may be taken if the invoice is paid within 10 days of the invoice date
2. from the eleventh to the thirtieth day, the net amount (the price after trade discounts) is due
3. after 30 days, the account is overdue

Example: Find the amount of discount and amount of payment for an invoice for $158 dated January 10, terms 2/10, n/30 if it is paid on January 20.

Solution: $158 × .02 = $3.16   amount of discount
          $158 − $3.16 = $154.84   amount of payment

When only the amount of payment is to be computed, you may use the complement of the discount rate to find the answer in a single step.

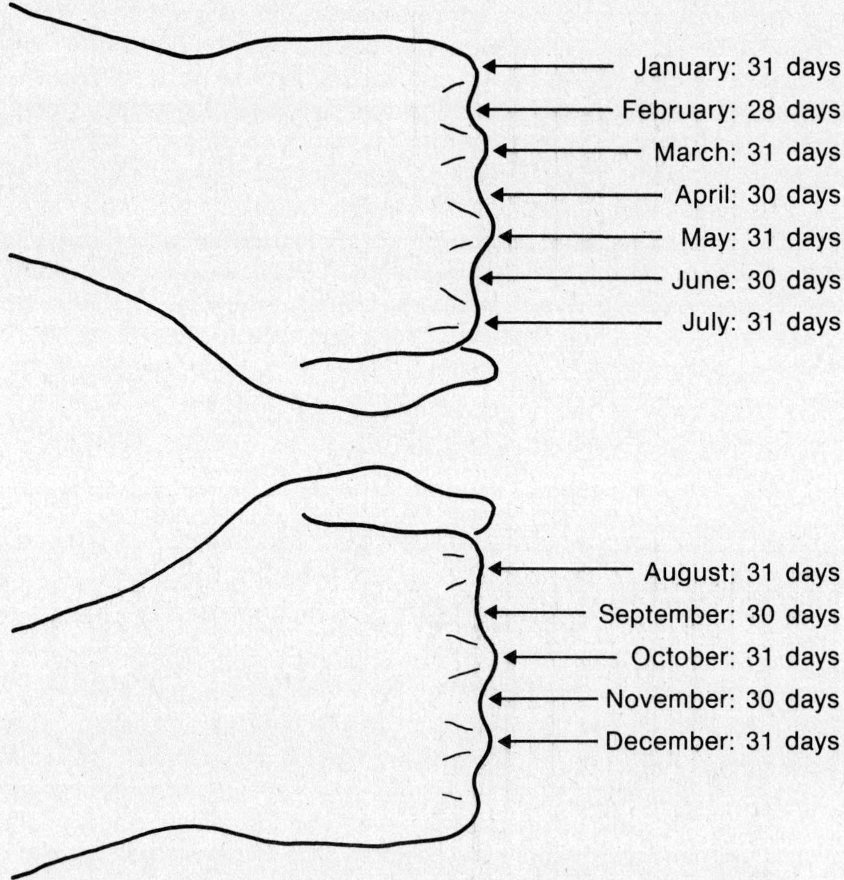

* 29 days in leap years. Any year evenly divisible by four is a leap year. 1980, 1984, and 1988 are leap years.

Example: The amount of an invoice is $504 and the credit terms are 2/10, n/30. What is the amount of payment needed to clear the debt within the discount period?

Solution: $504 × .98 = $493.92

Credit Terms: R.O.G., E.O.M., and Extra Dating

Credit terms are expressed in a variety of other ways. When the buyer is a distance away from the point of shipment, the terms may be 2/10, n/30, *R.O.G.* (receipt of goods), which indicate that the discount period begins on the day the merchandise arrives (rather than on the date of the invoice as in ordinary dating). Thus, the cash discount is allowed if payment is made within ten days of receipt of the goods. This arrangement provides the buyer an opportunity to inspect the goods before paying for them.

Some companies use monthly billing with terms 2/10, *E.O.M.* (end of month). Under these terms, the buyer may deduct 2% if payment is made by the tenth of the month following the invoice date. For instance, if the invoice were dated for May, a cash discount would be allowed on all purchases made during May if payment were made before June 10.

Some companies allow additional time for the buyer to take advantage of a cash discount. This practice is known as extra dating. For example, a cash discount expressed as "2/10-30 Extra" or "2/10-30 X" means that the buyer is allowed a 2% cash discount if the invoice is paid within 10 days plus 30, or a total of 40 days from the invoice date. Extra dating is sometimes used to encourage earlier ordering of seasonal merchandise.

Merchandise Returns

If part of the merchandise has been returned, the amount of the return must be deducted before determining the amount of the cash discount.

Example: The Southpark Stereo Center purchased merchandise in the amount of $946.14, terms 2/10, n/30. Goods in the amount of $26.14 were defective and returned. What is the amount of cash discount and payment if the invoice is paid within the discount period?

Solution:

$946.14	invoice amount
− 26.14	returned merchandise
$920.00	amount subject to the cash discount
− 18.40	cash discount ($920 × .02)
$901.60	amount due

Transportation Charges

The term *F.O.B.* (free on board) is used on sales contracts to indicate who (buyer and/or seller) is responsible for transportation charges. The term "F.O.B. destination" indicates that the seller will pay all shipping charges to the buyer's place of business. Sometimes, the F.O.B. point is a location other than the buyer's place of business and the buyer must pay the transportation charges from that location. For instance, if the sales terms on an invoice originating in New York are "F.O.B. Chicago" and the destination is Denver, the seller pays shipping charges to Chicago, while the buyer must pay from Chicago to Denver. Finally, the term "F.O.B. shipping point" means that the buyer must pay all transportation charges.

Although the buyer may be responsible for the transportation charges, it may be more convenient for the seller to pay the charges and add this amount to the invoice. When this occurs, the cash discount applies only to the merchandise and not to any transportation charges included in the invoice.

Note that transportation charges must be deducted from the invoice before any cash discount may be taken. However, after the cash discount is taken, the transportation charges must be added to the resulting amount to determine the total amount due on the invoice.

Example: The Bluebonnet Medical Supplies Company received an invoice for $864.22, including transportation charges of $24.22, with terms 2/10, n/60, F.O.B. shipping point. If the invoice is paid within the discount period, what is the amount of cash discount and the amount of the payment?

Solution:

$864.22	invoice amount
− 24.22	transportation charges
$840.00	amount subject to the cash discount
− 16.80	cash discount ($840 × .02)
$823.20	
+ 24.22	transportation charges
$847.42	amount due

Importance of Cash Discounts

From the buyer's standpoint, it is important to take advantage of all available cash discounts even though it may be necessary to borrow the money to make payment.

Example: What is the amount of savings effected by borrowing the money to pay an invoice in the amount of $450, terms 2/10, n/30, within the discount period? The money can be borrowed from a local bank for $2.94 (12% annual interest).

Solution: $9.00 cash discount ($450 × .02)
$\underline{-\ 2.94}$ interest for 20 days, at an annual rate of 12%
      on $441 ($450 − $9)
$6.06 savings effected by borrowing to take the
      cash discount

Notice that the period of the loan is for 20 days, the portion of the credit period remaining after subtracting the discount period (30 − 10). Notice also that the amount of money borrowed is $441, which is the amount of the payment if the invoice is paid within the discount period.

Partial Payments

If a company does not have sufficient cash to pay the invoice in full during the discount period, a partial payment may be forwarded to the supplier. This will enable the buyer to take advantage of the discount, but only on the portion of the amount paid within the discount period. The portion of the bill paid after the discount period (the amount outstanding) must be paid in full.

The amount credited to the total amount of the invoice by the partial payment is found by dividing the amount of the payment by the complement of the rate of cash discount. The amount outstanding after the partial payment is found by subtracting the amount of credit from the total amount of the invoice.

Example: The Central Shoe Store purchased merchandise in the amount of $286.24. The invoice terms are 2/10, n/60. A partial payment of $125 is forwarded within the discount period. How much credit will the firm receive? What amount is still outstanding?

Solution: 100% − 2% = 98%, or .98   complement of the discount
                    rate
$125 ÷ .98 = $127.55   amount of credit received
$286.24 − $127.55 = $158.69   amount still outstanding

Exercises

Find the amount of cash discount and payment due for the following invoices.

	Invoice Amount	Invoice Date	Terms	Date Goods Received	Date Invoice Paid	Payment
1.	$378.56	Oct. 13	2/10, n/30		Oct. 23	_______
2.	$762.18	June 5	1/10, n/30		June 15	_______
3.	$613.42	July 27	3/20, n/60		Aug. 15	_______
4.	$ 77.98	Dec. 24	2/20, n/90		Jan. 12	_______
5.	$946.34	April 7	n/30		May 23	_______
6.	$422.61	Jan. 6	2/10, E.O.M.		Feb. 5	_______
7.	$806.52	Sept. 27	2/10, R.O.G.	Sept. 30	Oct. 7	_______
8.	$235.10	Nov. 11	n/60		Jan. 10	_______
9.	$ 86.48	Aug. 19	1/10, E.O.M.		Sept. 5	_______
10.	$316.98	May 3	2/10, R.O.G.	May 11	May 21	_______
11.	$189.23	June 8	C.O.D.	June 19	June 19	_______
12.	$544.55	Oct. 26	2/10—30 X		Dec. 4	_______

Find the last day of the discount period and credit period for each of the following.

	Invoice Date	Terms	Last Day of Discount Period	Last Day of Credit Period
13.	October 2	2/10, n/30	_____________	_____________
14.	August 7	3/10, n/60	_____________	_____________
15.	April 25	1/15, n/30	_____________	_____________
16.	June 28	2/15, n/60	_____________	_____________
17.	March 21	2/10, n/90	_____________	_____________
18.	May 26	1/15, n/90	_____________	_____________

Find the cash discount and amount of payment for the following invoices.

	Invoice Amount	Returned Goods	Freight Charges	Terms	Cash Discount	Payment
19.	$197.10	$20.00	$ 7.10	2/10, n/30	_______	_______
20.	$246.17	$30.00	$ 6.17	2/10, n/60	_______	_______
21.	$625.00	$15.00	$10.00	4/10, E.O.M.	_______	_______
22.	$574.00	$35.00	$19.00	3/10, E.O.M.	_______	_______

Figure the cash discount and amount of payment for the following invoices.

	Invoice Date	Invoice Amount	Terms	Returned Goods	Date of Payment	Cash Discount	Payment
23.	May 19	$346.24	3/30, n/90	$26.24	June 18	________	________
24.	Sept. 23	$912.42	2/15, n/45	$42.42	Oct. 8	________	________
25.	June 23	$462.00	2/10, n/30	None	July 3	________	________
26.	Aug. 18	$335.00	3/15, n/60	None	Sept. 2	________	________

Find the credit for the following partial payments made during the cash discount period and determine the amount outstanding after the partial payment.

	Invoice Amount	Terms	Partial Payment	Credit	Amount Outstanding
27.	$ 322.40	2/10, n/30	$ 150.00	________	________
28.	$ 454.35	3/10, n/60	$ 225.00	________	________
29.	$ 918.10	1/10, n/30	$ 430.00	________	________
30.	$1,256.90	2/15, n/90	$ 860.00	________	________
31.	$ 399.87	3/10, n/90	$ 175.00	________	________
32.	$1,989.76	2/10, E.O.M.	$1,000.00	________	________

Practical Applications

33. Jane Oldham, a student at Clearview College, manages a gift shop near the campus. She is planning to expand the store's merchandise to include several additional items, including a crystal cannister. The supplier of the cannister has a list price of $16.95 subject to a trade discount of 55%. What is the trade price of the cannister? What is the net cost of the item if the terms are 2/10, net 30 days and payment is made within the discount period?

34. When is payment due on an invoice dated June 14 with terms n/60?

35. When is payment due on an invoice dated September 24 with terms n/90?

36. The Contemporary Apparel Company received an invoice for $368 dated March 16. The invoice terms are 3/10, n/30. On what date does

the credit period end? On what date does the discount period end? What is the amount of cash discount if the invoice is paid within the discount period?

37. The Universal Electric Company received an invoice for $274 dated October 18. The invoice terms are 2/5, n/30. On what date does the credit period end? On what date does the discount period end? If the invoice is paid on October 28, how much is due? If the invoice is paid on October 21, how much is due?

38. What is the total payment due on an invoice for $299.67 if the terms are 2/20, n/60 and the bill is paid within 20 days?

39. Exacto Services received an invoice dated September 3 for $264.22. The terms were 1/20, n/60. The merchandise was inspected, and $24.12 worth of defective merchandise was returned. The invoice includes transportation charges of $10.10. If payment is made on September 23, what is the amount owed?

40. AAA Auto Center received an invoice dated June 15 for $146.82 that included transportation charges of $18.74. The terms were 2/10, n/30. If payment was made on June 25, what was the amount paid?

41. The Jones Discount Company received an invoice dated July 9, terms 2/10, n/30, R.O.G. The goods were received July 16. What is the last date on which the discount may be taken? On what date does the credit period expire?

42. The Learning Resources Company received an invoice for $940, terms 2/15, n/60. How much cash discount is allowed? If money is borrowed to take advantage of the cash discount, how many days would the loan involve, assuming that the payment of the invoice is to be made on the 15th day following the date on the invoice?

43. The J. Jones Company received an invoice dated April 11 in the amount of $310. The invoice terms are 2/10, n/30. The company does not expect to have sufficient cash to pay the invoice on May 11. Should the company consider borrowing the money to pay the invoice before May 11? How many days would the loan involve? How much money will the company save by borrowing the money if the interest on the loan is $1.35?

44. Marketing Specialists, Inc., received an invoice in the amount of $964.28, terms 2/10, n/30, dated June 13. The company sent a $550 partial payment on June 23. What amount of credit will Marketing Specialists receive for the partial payment?

45. A partial payment of $150 was made on a $327 invoice within the discount period. The invoice terms were 3/10, n/30. How much credit was received for the partial payment? How much was still outstanding?

Chapter 4
Self-Evaluation

1. What is the trade price of an item listed in a catalog for $649 subject to a trade discount of 27%?

2. What is the trade price of an item listed in a catalog for $55.80 subject to a trade discount of 38%?

3. Is a 20%, 10% chain discount better for the buyer than a 15%, 15% chain discount?

4. Is a 30%, 20%, 10% chain discount better for the buyer than a 20%, 20%, 20% chain discount?

5. The list price of a catalog item is $164 subject to a trade discount of 20%, 10%, 10%. What are the single discount equivalent and the trade price of the item?

6. The list price of a catalog item is $204.60 subject to a trade discount of 15%, 10%. What are the single discount equivalent and the trade price of the item?

7. An invoice in the amount of $327.60 is subject to terms of 2/20, n/60. If paid within the discount period, what are the cash discount and amount of payment?

8. An invoice in the amount of $144.76 is subject to terms of 2/10, n/60. If paid within the discount period, what are the cash discount and amount of payment due?

9. An invoice in the amount of $186.50 including freight charges of $6.50 is subject to terms of 4/10, n/60. Defective goods in the amount of $20 were returned. What are the cash discount and amount of payment due if the invoice is paid within the discount period?

10. An invoice in the amount of $860.40 including freight charges of $10.40 is subject to terms of 3/10, E.O.M. Defective goods in the amount of $40 were returned. What are the cash discount and amount of payment due if the invoice is paid within the discount period?

11. An invoice in the amount of $891.60 is subject to terms of 2/15, n/60. Determine the credit for a partial payment of $450 made within the discount period. What is the outstanding balance after the partial payment is made?

Chapter 5
Retail Pricing

All merchants must merchandise efficiently to survive. Merchants must provide goods of the right type, quality, and price, in quantities that match demand. The goods must be available at the time customers are ready to inspect and buy and at the places in the store where customers expect to find the goods.

One of the most critical aspects of the merchant's job is pricing goods for retail sale. The merchant must establish a retail price that will cover the cost of the merchandise and the cost of doing business and that will provide a reasonable profit. If the price is too low, a reasonable profit may not be earned. However, if the price is too high, sales may be lost to the merchant's competition. Therefore, it is important that businesspeople thoroughly understand the factors and methods involved in determining retail prices and be able to apply them.

This chapter will provide an opportunity for you to become better acquainted with the elements of retail pricing.

This chapter will enable you to:

1. **identify the elements of retail pricing as the cost of merchandise, retail price, and markon expressed as a dollar amount or as a percent**

2. **calculate markon as a percent of cost or retail price**

3. **determine the retail price, cost of merchandise, or markon percent on cost or retail price when only two of these items are known**

4. calculate markon and retail price for perishable and seasonal products

5. calculate markup and markdown as dollar amounts and as percents

6. calculate the new retail price when markup or markdown percent figures and the original retail price are known

7. convert markon percentage from cost to retail and vice versa

8. calculate off-retail percentage

Learning Unit 5.1
Markon Based on Cost and Retail

Elements of Retail Pricing

There are three main elements of retail pricing: the cost of the merchandise (C), the retail price (R), and the markon (M). Markon is the difference between the cost and the retail price and must cover (1) the expenses incurred in selling the merchandise, and (2) a reasonable profit. Markon may be expressed as (1) a dollar amount (M), (2) a percent of cost (C%), or (3) a percent of retail price (R%). The terms *markon* and *markup* are often used interchangeably; however, *markup* is better used to refer to an increase in price after the original price has been determined (see further discussion of markup in Learning Unit 5.3).

Formulas for Calculating Retail Price, Cost, and Markon

There are three formulas that we will be using in calculating retail price, cost, and markon. By using one or a combination of these formulas, almost any retail pricing problem can be solved.

A. *Retail Price = Cost + Dollar Markon, or R = C + M*

B. *Dollar Markon = Cost × Markon Expressed as Percent of Cost, or M = C × C%*[1]

C. *Dollar Markon = Retail Price × Markon Expressed as Percent of Retail Price, or M = R × R%*

---

[1]When calculating markon using either Formula B or C, the percentage formula relationships studied in Chapter 3 may be applied directly. For example, in Formula B, where $M = C \times C\%$,

$$M = \text{part}$$
$$C = \text{base}$$
$$C\% = \text{rate}$$

Figure 5.1 Markon Symbols and Formulas

Markon Symbols

R = retail price
C = cost
M = dollar markon
$C\%$ = markon expressed as % of cost
$R\%$ = markon expressed as % of retail

Markon Formulas

Basic Percentage Formulas

Dollar Amount (Formula A) and Variations	*Percent of Cost (Formula B) and Variations*	*Percent of Retail (Formula C) and Variations*
$R = C + M$	$C\% = M \div C$	$R\% = M \div R$
$C = R - M$	$C = M \div C\%$	$R = M \div R\%$
$M = R - C$	$M = C \times C\%$	$M = R \times R\%$

The markon symbols and formulas (including their algebraic variations) are summarized in Figure 5.1.

Formula A ($R = C + M$) is the basic selling price formula: selling price equals cost plus markon. By algebraically changing the formula, we can also find markon expressed in dollar amount ($M = R - C$) or cost ($C = R - M$).

Example: A jacket that was purchased by a retailer for $45 has a dollar markon of $18. What is the retail price of the jacket?

Solution: $R = C + M$
$R = \$45 + \$18$
$R = \$63$

Example: A jacket that retails for $63 has a dollar markon of $18. What was the cost of the jacket?

Solution: $C = R - M$
$C = \$63 - \$18$
$C = \$45$

Example: A jacket that was purchased by a retailer for $45 retails for $63. What is the dollar markon?

Solution: $M = R - C$
$M = \$63 - \$45$
$M = \$18$

Note that each of the variables in this formula may be expressed as a dollar and cent value *or* as a percent of some known or unknown amount. For example, R may be $100 in a particular problem, or it may be the unknown value to be solved for. When R is unknown, remember that we still know that the value of R equals 100%R, and, as we shall see in later examples, we can also use this value in the formula. Similarly, when C is unknown, it can be expressed as 100%C in the formula to solve a pricing problem.

Formulas B and C can be used to find dollar markon (M) when markon is expressed as a percent. By using an algebraic variation, we can use Formula B ($M = C \times C\%$) to find markon expressed as a percent of cost ($C\% = M \div C$) and to find cost ($C = M \div C\%$). Similarly, by changing Formula C ($M = R \times R\%$), we can find markon expressed as a percent of the retail price ($R\% = M \div R$) and can find the retail price ($R = M \div R\%$). Formula B and its variations are used to solve problems in which markon is based on cost, while Formula C and its variations are used to solve problems in which markon is based on retail price. Frequently, retail pricing problems will require using either Formula B or C to convert percent markon to dollar markon and then using the found dollar markon in the basic pricing formula. Conversely, some problems will require using Formula A to find a value to be used in Formula B or C. Examples showing the use of these formulas are given in the following section.

Markon Based on Cost

Markon may be calculated on the basis of retail cost. This cost method is used mostly by smaller retail businesses. Since cost figures are readily available and are easy to work with, cost is a convenient base to use for determining and expressing markon information.

Merchants using markon based on cost must be able to compute the retail price, the cost, and the markon percent (and dollar amount) when only two of these factors are known. These problems can be solved by using Formula B ($M = C \times C\%$) or a combination of this formula and the basic pricing formula ($R = C + M$).

Calculating the Retail Price When the Cost and the Markon Based on Cost Are Known

A very convenient pricing policy is *cost-plus*, under which a predetermined percentage of the cost of an item is added to its cost to arrive at a selling price. *To find the selling price, add the dollar markon and the cost* (Formula A). (Dollar markon was found by multiplying retail cost by markon percent, using Formula B.)

Example: A store purchased a jacket for $45. The markon was 40% of cost. What is the retail price of the jacket?

Solution:
$$M = C \times C\%$$
$$M = \$45 \times .40$$
$$M = \$18$$

$$R = C + M$$
$$R = \$45 + \$18$$
$$R = \$63$$

An alternate method for solving the same problem is as follows:

$$R = C + M$$
$$R = 100\%C + 40\%C \quad (C = \text{Cost} = 100\%C; M = \text{Markon} = 40\%C)$$
$$R = 140\%C \quad \text{(Combine similar variables)}$$
$$R = 1.4 \times \$45 \quad \text{(Substitute the dollar value for } C)$$
$$R = \$63$$

Calculating the Percent of Markon on Cost When the Cost and Retail Price Are Known

To achieve maximum profits, different markon percents may be applied to each line of merchandise. *To find the percent of markon on cost, divide the dollar markon by the dollar cost* (Formula B). (Dollar markon was found by subtracting retail cost from retail price, using Formula A.)

Example: A jacket that costs $45 retails for $63. What is the percent markon on cost?

Solution:

$R = C + M$ $\qquad\qquad$ $M = C \times C\%$

$R - C = M$ (Isolate M) $\qquad$ $M \div C = C\%$ (Isolate $C\%$)

$\$63 - \$45 = M$ $\qquad\qquad$ $\$18 \div \$45 = C\%$

$\$18 = M$ $\qquad\qquad\qquad$ $40\% = C\%$

Calculating the Cost When the Retail Price and the Markon Based on Cost Are Known

When retailers know how much buyers are willing to pay for an item and the required markon percent necessary to make a profit, they must be able to determine how much they can afford to pay for that item when they stock their stores. To find the cost, use Formula A, with cost expressed as 100% of itself (100%C) and markon expressed as the given percent of cost.

Example: A merchant plans to sell jackets at $63 after a 40% markon based on cost. What is the most the merchant can pay the wholesaler for jackets to be sold at this price?

Solution:

$R = C + M$

$\$63 = 100\%C + 40\%C$ ($C =$ Cost $= 100\%C$;

$\qquad\qquad\qquad\qquad\qquad\quad$ $M =$ Markon $= 40\%C$)

$\$63 = 140\%C$ (Combine similar variables)

$\$63 \div 1.4 = C$ (Isolate C)

$\$45 = C$

Markon Based on Retail Price

Most large retail businesses base markon on the retail selling price. The retail method is generally accepted as the more desirable basis for calculating markon since so many business expenses are calculated as a percent of net sales. Salespersons' commissions are based on sales, as are sales taxes, inventory values, advertising expenditures, etc.

Merchants using markon based on retail price must be able to compute the retail price, cost, and markon percent (and dollar amount) when only two of these factors are known. These problems can be solved by using Formula C ($M = R \times R\%$) or a combination of this formula and the basic pricing formula ($R = C + M$).

Calculating the Cost When the Retail Price and the Markon Based on Retail Are Known

When a company adds a new product to its existing product line, the retail price may be predetermined by previous pricing policies on related products or by the new product's competition. If a markon policy based on retail is in effect, as in this situation, retailers can determine how much they can afford to pay for the new product. To find the cost, *subtract dollar markon from retail price* (Formula A). (Dollar markon was found by multiplying the retail price by the retail markon percent, using Formula C.)

Example: A jacket that retails for $63 has a markon of 28.57% of retail. What is the cost of the jacket?

Solution: $M = R \times R\%$
$M = \$63 \times 28.57\%$
$M = \$63 \times .2857$
$M = \$18$

$R = C + M$
$R - M = C$ (Isolate C)
$\$63 - \$18 = C$
$\$45 = C$

An alternate method for solving the same problem is as follows:

$R = C + M$ (R = Retail Cost = 100%R; M = 28.57%R)
$100\%R = C + 28.57\%R$ (Values—percents—can be substituted)
$100\%R - 28.57\%R = C$ (Similar variables are combined through the isolation of C)
$71.43\%R = C$
$.7143 \times \$63 = C$ (Substitute the dollar value for R)
$\$45 = C$

Calculating the Percent of Markon Based on Retail When the Cost and Retail Price Are Known

To find the percent of markon based on retail, *divide the dollar markon by the dollar retail price* (Formula C). (Dollar markon was found by subtracting cost from retail price, using Formula A.)

Example: A jacket that cost $45 is sold for $63. What is the percent of markon based on the retail selling price?

Solution: $R = C + M$
$R - C = M$ (Isolate M)
$\$63 - \$45 = M$
$\$18 = M$

$M = R \times R\%$
$M \div R = R\%$ (Isolate $R\%$)
$\$18 \div \$63 = R\%$ (Substitute dollar values for
M and R)

$28.57\% = R\%$

Calculating the Retail Price When the Cost and the Percent Markon Based on Retail Are Known

If a pricing policy using markon based on retail has been established by a merchant on a store-wide basis, new product prices can be computed by knowing the cost of the product and the percent markon based on the retail price. To find the retail price, use Formula A, with retail price expressed as 100% of itself (100% R) and markon expressed as the given percent of cost.

Example: A store maintains a pricing policy of 28.57% markon on the retail price. What will a jacket sell for if its cost is $45?

Solution: $R = C + M$ (R = Retail Cost = 100%R; M = 28.57%R)
$100\%R = C + 28.57\%R$ (Substitute percents)
$100\%R - 28.57\%R = C$
$71.43\%R = C$ (Combine similar variables by isolating C)
$71.43\%R = \$45$ (Substitute the dollar value for C)
$R = \$45 \div .7143$ (Isolate R through division)
$R = \$63$

Figure 5.2 illustrates the relationships of markon formulas.

Cost-to-Retail and Retail-to-Cost Conversions

Any markon percentage can be converted from cost to retail or from retail to cost by using one of the following formulas:

Percent markon based on cost =

$$\frac{\% \text{ markon based on retail}}{100\% - \% \text{ markon based on retail}} \times 100\%$$

Percent markon based on retail =

$$\frac{\% \text{ markon based on cost}}{100\% + \% \text{ markon based on cost}} \times 100\%$$

Exercises

Determine the retail price for the following clocks.

	Item	C	M	R
1.	Triple Chime Mantel Clock	$123	$82	_______
2.	8-Day Chime Clock	$ 96	$64	_______
3.	Westminster Chime Clock	$114	$76	_______
4.	Pendulum Chime Clock	$ 39	$26	_______

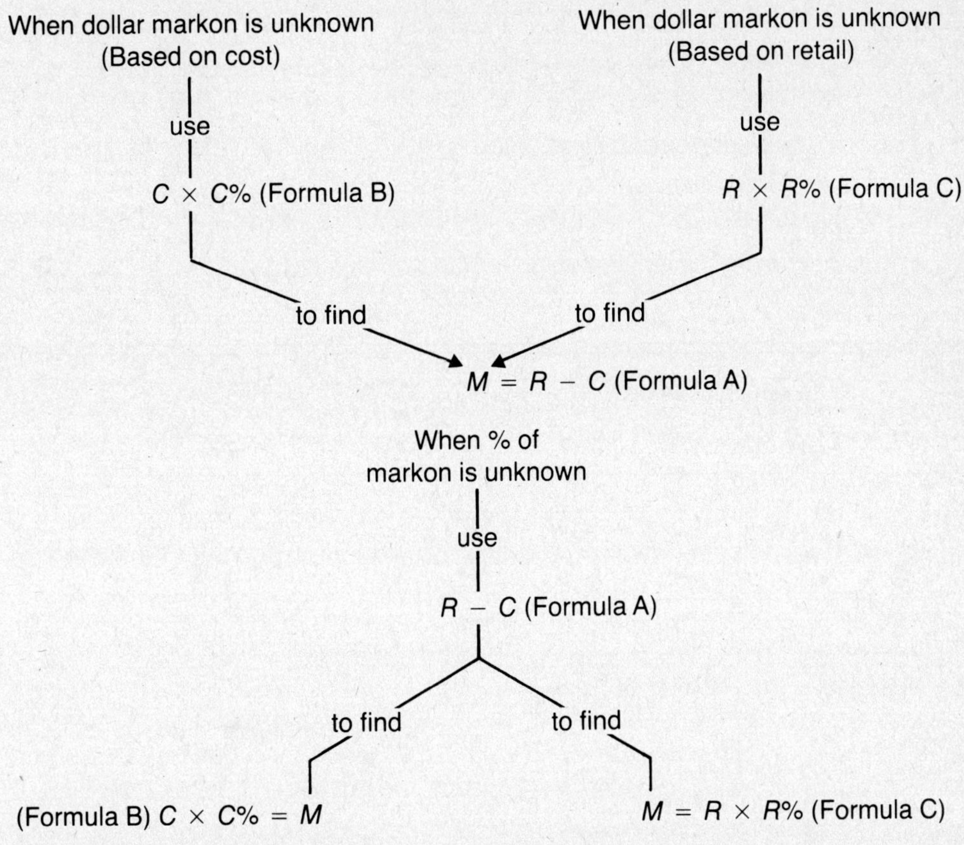

Figure 5.2 Relationships of Markon Formulas
When dollar markon is unknown (Based on cost)
use
C × C% (Formula B)
to find
When dollar markon is unknown (Based on retail)
use
R × R% (Formula C)
to find
M = R − C (Formula A)
When % of markon is unknown
use
R − C (Formula A)
to find
to find
(Formula B) C × C% = M
M = R × R% (Formula C)

Determine the cost of the following clocks.

	Item	R	M	C
5.	Triple Chime Mantel Clock	$205	$82	_______
6.	8-Day Chime Clock	$160	$64	_______
7.	Westminster Chime Clock	$190	$76	_______
8.	Pendulum Chime Clock	$ 65	$26	_______

Determine the dollar markon for the following clocks.

	Item	C	R	M
9.	Triple Chime Mantel Clock	$123	$205	_______
10.	8-Day Chime Clock	$ 96	$160	_______
11.	Westminster Chime Clock	$114	$190	_______
12.	Pendulum Chime Clock	$ 39	$ 65	_______

Determine the retail price of the following items found in a housewares department. The department uses markon based on cost.

	Item	C	C%	R
13.	Pewter Bud Vase	$ 9.90	50%	_______
14.	Pewter Napkin Rings	$ 8.90	50%	_______
15.	Chrome Tray	$ 6.92	46%	_______
16.	Chrome Casserole	$14.33	46%	_______
17.	Crystal Cannister	$24.90	37%	_______
18.	Crystal Cake Plate	$13.96	37%	_______

Determine the cost of the following items found in a specialty shop. The store uses markon based on cost.

	Item	R	C%	C
19.	Music Box	$22.84	53%	_______
20.	Perfume Tray	$10.63	64%	_______
21.	Valet	$ 9.96	50%	_______
22.	Valet/Seat	$29.86	59%	_______
23.	Car Vacuum	$ 8.97	22%	_______
24.	Ice Bucket	$11.46	33%	_______

Determine the markon percent on cost for the following items found in a gift shop. (Round to the nearest hundredth of a percent.) The store uses markon based on cost.

	Item	C	R	M	C%
25.	Pipe	$11.80	$17.23	________	________
26.	Turkish Water Pipe	$12.60	$18.40	________	________
27.	Men's Umbrella	$10.90	$14.72	________	________
28.	Women's Umbrella	$11.20	$15.12	________	________
29.	Manicure Set	$15.60	$19.50	________	________
30.	French Purse	$14.00	$17.50	________	________

Determine the retail price of the following items found in a housewares department. The store uses markon based on retail selling price.

	Item	C	R%	R
31.	Pewter Bud Vase	$ 9.90	50%	________
32.	Pewter Napkin Rings	$ 8.90	50%	________
33.	Chrome Casserole	$14.33	46%	________
34.	Crystal Cannister	$14.90	37%	________
35.	Crystal Cake Plate	$13.96	37%	________
36.	Silver Goblets	$22.40	48%	________

Determine the cost of the following items found in a specialty shop. The store uses markon based on retail selling price.

	Item	R	R%	C
37.	Music Box	$22.84	53%	________
38.	Perfume Tray	$10.63	64%	________
39.	Valet	$ 9.96	50%	________
40.	Peanut Machine	$14.74	53%	________
41.	Car Vacuum	$ 8.97	22%	________
42.	Ice Bucket	$11.46	33%	________

Determine the dollar markon and the markon percent on retail for the following items found in a gift shop. (Round to the nearest hundredth of a percent.) The store uses markon based on retail.

	Item	C	R	M	R%
43.	Pipe	$11.80	$17.23	_______	_______
44.	Turkish Water Pipe	$12.60	$18.40	_______	_______
45.	Man's Umbrella	$10.90	$14.72	_______	_______
46.	Woman's Umbrella	$11.20	$15.12	_______	_______
47.	Manicure Set	$15.60	$19.50	_______	_______
48.	French Purse	$14.00	$17.50	_______	_______

Practical Applications

49. A buyer purchased some shirts at $9.50 each. What retail price must the store charge for the shirts to obtain a markon of 46% on cost?

50. A buyer purchased a group of men's suits at $67.50 each. The markon percent on cost in the department is 45%. What retail price should the buyer establish for the suits?

51. A buyer purchased some dresses at $126 per dozen and priced them to retail for $14.99 each. What is the markon percent on cost?

52. A retailer sells a video game for $49.95. The dollar markon on each game is $22.15. What is the percent of markon on retail?

53. A merchant purchased some ties at $3.75 each. What retail price must the store charge for the ties to obtain a markon of 31.5% on retail?

54. A shoe shop bought a new line of women's shoes at $12 a pair. If the shop maintains a 40% markon based on retail, for what price will the shoes retail?

55. A small dress shop plans to sell casual dresses for $38 after a 25% markon based on cost. What was the cost price for these dresses?

56. Jim's Jeans, Inc. sells a special line of jeans for $18. If Jim uses a 30% markon based on cost, how much did he pay for these jeans?

57. Richard Wilson's brother runs a used-furniture store. A chair that sells for $35 will have a markon of 20% of the retail price. What did this chair cost?

58. Larry's Boot Company sells shoes that have a 38% markon based on the retail price. Determine the cost of a pair of shoes that sells for $42.

59. An umbrella costs $4.50 and sells for $8. What is the percent of markon based on the retail price?

60. Calculate the percent markon based on cost for a pair of gloves that cost $3 and sold for $9.

61. Jerry's Place maintains a 35% markon based on the retail price. What will a shirt sell for if its cost is $10?

62. The current cost for a heavy-duty wheelbarrow is $42.50. With a markon based on retail of 28%, at what price will the wheelbarrow retail?

Learning Unit 5.2
Markon on Seasonal or Perishable Goods

Many businesses sell products that have either a very short life or a limited selling season. Retailers of perishable items, such as fresh produce, bakery goods, or flowers, and retailers of items that are style-dated, such as clothing, automobiles, and appliances, know that they will not be able to sell all of their product at full price. Some products may have to be reduced; other products may have to be thrown away.

In pricing this type of product, prices must be high enough so that those products that sell at the regular price will offset the lower prices of the reduced items and the gross profit needed to stay in business will be maintained.

Calculating the Selling Price on Perishable Merchandise

Experienced businesspersons can very closely approximate the amount of their merchandise they will be able to sell. Knowing how much they will sell enables fresh-produce dealers, for example, to determine a price that will allow for spoilage and that will return the necessary profit.

The basic procedure for computing the selling price on perishable merchandise is:

1. Determine the cost of the entire purchase.
2. Determine the total selling price of the entire purchase.
3. Determine the amount of merchandise that is expected to sell.
4. Divide the total selling price by the amount of merchandise expected to be sold to obtain the per-item or per-pound price.

Example: A supermarket manager bought 200 pounds of tomatoes at 25 cents per pound. Records show that, for various reasons, 12% of the tomatoes will not be sold. At what price per pound must the tomatoes be priced in order to maintain a 40% mark-on based on cost?

Solution: $\text{Cost} = 200 \times \$.25 = \$50$

$R = C + M$

$R = 100\%C + 40\%C \quad (C = 100\%C;\ M = 40\%C)$

$R = 140\%C \quad$ (Combine similar variables)

$R = 1.40 \times \$50 \quad$ (Substitute \$50 for C)

$R = \$70 \quad$ Retail price of 200 pounds of tomatoes

The supermarket manager must make \$70 from the sale of the tomatoes to maintain a 40% markon based on cost. Twelve percent, or 24 pounds, are expected to spoil or otherwise not be sold; therefore, the \$70 must be made on the sale of 176 pounds of tomatoes. The price per pound of tomatoes can be determined by dividing the total income necessary by the number of pounds to be sold:

Price per pound $= \$70 \div 176$

Price per pound $= \$.40$ (rounded to whole cents)

Calculating the Retail Price on Seasonal Merchandise That Will Later Be Marked Down

Experienced retailers also know that some seasonal merchandise will have to be reduced in price toward the end of the selling season as demand for the product diminishes. This fact must be kept in mind when the original selling price is established.

Example: Jill's Dress Shop purchased a new line of women's swimwear. Jill knows that 20% of the line will have to be reduced 50% in order to clear out the stock by the end of the season. She bought 100 swimsuit combinations at a cost of $10 each. If Jill maintains a markon based on cost of 40%, what price will she have to charge for the swimwear?

Solution: Cost $= 100 \times \$10 = \$1{,}000$

$M = C \times C\%$

$M = \$1{,}000 \times 40\%$

$M = \$1{,}000 \times .40$

$M = \$400$

$R = C + M$

$R = \$1{,}000 + \$400$

$R = \$1{,}400$ (Total retail sales price for 100 suits)

Jill must make $1,400 from the sale of the 100 swimsuits in order to maintain the 40% markon based on cost. Eighty suits will be sold at full price and 20%, or 20 suits, will be sold after a 50% reduction (or at half price). The full retail price for the 80 suits is determined as follows:

Let $p = $ the full retail price

$80p + 20(p \div 2) = \$1{,}400$

$80p + 10p = \$1{,}400$ ($20p \div 2 = 10p \div 1 = 10p$)

$90p = \$1{,}400$ (Combine similar terms)

$p = \$1{,}400 \div 90$ (Isolate p)

$p = \$15.56$ (Full retail price rounded to whole cents)

Exercises

Determine the selling price per pound of fresh lake trout necessary to maintain a 40% markon based on cost.

	Pounds Purchased	Price Paid per Pound	Spoilage Rate
1.	50	$1.06	20%
2.	125	$1.58	10%
3.	150	$1.28	15%
4.	500	$1.87	30%

Determine the selling price per pair for skis necessary to maintain a 40% markon based on cost.

	Pairs Purchased	Price Paid per Pair	Stock to Be Sold at Full Price	End-of-Season Price Reduction
5.	30	$42	90%	50%
6.	75	$68	85%	50%
7.	90	$99	65%	50%
8.	175	$15	95%	10%

Practical Applications

9. A grocery purchased ten boxes of bananas at $4 per box. Each box contains 40 pounds of bananas. Experience indicates that 10% of the bananas will probably not be sold. What price per pound should be charged in order to make 25% on cost for the entire purchase?

10. A produce department maintains a 40% markon based on cost for oranges. Of an order for 300 pounds of oranges, it is expected that 8% will not be sold. What should be the retail price per pound of oranges if the total cost is $60?

11. Bell Florists bought 50 potted plants for Mother's Day at $3.50 each. Bell did not expect to sell 10% of the plants. What price must Bell charge per plant to make 30% markon based on the retail price?

12. John's Donut Shop paid an average of $10 for materials and ingredients to make 18 dozen donuts. If two dozen donuts are not expected to be sold, what price must be charged per donut in order to maintain a 40% markon based on retail?

13. Al's Tie Shop carries a markon on cost of 50%. A special shipment of 60 novelty ties cost $6 each. Al plans to sell 15% of these ties at a special clearance price of half the regular retail price at the end of the summer. At what price will the ties sell at full price?

14. A supermarket bought 2,000 ten-ounce packages of medium-sized candy Easter eggs at $.30 per bag. Experience shows that 20% of these will be sold for $.10 per bag after the holiday. If the store wants to maintain a 40% markon on retail, what will they charge for one package of candy eggs?

15. A local fast-food establishment purchases frozen, precut potatoes to sell as french fries. Joe Torres, owner, pays $1 per pound for the potatoes, which he sells in four-ounce (precooked weight) servings. Since fries are cooked in two-pound batches—one two-pound container cooks while a second container is thawing—the maximum quantity of french fries that would not be sold on an average day would be four pounds. Also, on an average day, two gallons of cooking oil will be used to cook the fries at a total per-day cost of $5.25.

    Joe maintains a 100% markon based on cost for his french fries. If an average daily purchase of potatoes amounts to 50 pounds, how much does Joe charge for one serving of french fries?

16. Each week on Tuesday, Anthony's Pizza Place sells "all the pizza you can eat" for lunch. Records indicate that normally 60 large-sized pizzas are needed to meet the lunch demand. Anthony offers a wide selection during the buffet and calculates his *average* ingredient cost per pizza to be $1.90 and his customer count to be approximately 50.

    How much does Anthony have to charge each person if he prepares 10% more pizza than he expects to be eaten on a normal day and if he maintains a 60% markon based on cost?

Learning Unit 5.3
Markup and Markdown

Definitions and Uses

Once an original selling price has been established by using the formula $R = C + M$, that retail price may have to be increased (a *markup*) or decreased (a *markdown*).

A merchant may decide to increase the original price because of increased distribution costs or increased product demand or because the original low price was an introductory offer. On the other hand, a merchant may decide to decrease the original price to sell discontinued merchandise, to promote seasonal items, to meet a competitor's lower price, or to sell slow-moving inventory.

Markup/Markdown Formulas

Dollar markup/markdown. Markups and markdowns may be expressed as dollar amounts or as percents. The *dollar amount* of markup and markdown is related to the relationship between the original retail price and the new retail price and can be found by applying the following formulas:

$$\text{Dollar Markup} = \text{New Retail Price} - \text{Original Retail Price, or}$$
$$\text{Dollar Markup} = NRP - ORP$$

$$\text{Dollar Markdown} = \text{Original Retail Price} - \text{New Retail Price, or}$$
$$\text{Dollar Markdown} = ORP - NRP$$

Example A: A shirt was marked down from $20 to $15 for a special sale. What was the amount of the markdown?

Solution A:

ORP	$20
NRP	− 15
Difference	$ 5 markdown

Example B: The price of a shirt was marked up from $15 to $20 due to a shortage in wool. What was the amount of the markup?

Solution B: *NRP* $20

ORP   − 15

Difference $ 5   markup

Percent markup/markdown. The *percent* of markup and markdown is based on the new retail price and can be found by applying the following formulas:

$$Percent\ Markup = \frac{Dollar\ Markup}{New\ Retail\ Price}$$

$$Percent\ Markdown = \frac{Dollar\ Markdown}{New\ Retail\ Price}$$

Example: Calculate the percent of markdown in Example A above.

Solution: $\dfrac{Amount\ of\ Markdown}{NRP} = \dfrac{\$5}{\$15} = 33\frac{1}{3}\%$ markdown

Example: Calculate the percent of markup in Example B above.

Solution: $\dfrac{Amount\ of\ Markup}{NRP} = \dfrac{\$5}{\$20} = 25\%$ markup

Calculating NRP When the Percent Markdown and ORP Are Known

To find the new retail price when the percent *markdown* and the original retail price are known, solve the percentage formula $R = P \div B$, where R is the percent markdown, P is the dollar amount of the markdown (expressed as a percent of the new retail price), and B is the new retail price (expressed as original price minus dollar markdown).

Example: A merchant is planning a storewide clearance sale. All merchandise will have a $33\frac{1}{3}\%$ markdown. What will be the sale price on a group of dress shirts that previously sold for $10.40 each?

Solution: P = amount of markdown = $33\frac{1}{3}\%B$ (% markdown is expressed as a % of new retail price)

B = $10.40 − $33\frac{1}{3}\%B$ (original price minus $33\frac{1}{3}\%$ of new retail price)

R = $33\frac{1}{3}\%$ (percent markdown)

$$R = \frac{P}{B}$$

$$33\frac{1}{3}\% = \frac{33\frac{1}{3}\%B}{\$10.40 - 33\frac{1}{3}\%B}$$

$$\frac{1}{3} = \frac{\frac{1}{3}B}{\$10.40 - \frac{1}{3}B} \qquad \text{(Change percents to common fractions)}$$

$$\$10.40 - \frac{1}{3}B = 3 \times \frac{1}{3}B \qquad \text{(Cross multiply}^2\text{)}$$

$$\$10.40 = \frac{4}{3}B \qquad \text{(Combine variables)}$$

$$\frac{\$10.40}{\frac{4}{3}} = B \qquad \text{(Isolate } B\text{)}$$

$$\$7.80 = B \qquad \text{(New retail price)}$$

[2]Cross multiplication is a simple algebraic process beginning with two fractions that are equal to one another and contain only one variable: $\frac{1}{2} = \frac{3}{x}$. The numerator of one fraction is multiplied by the denominator of the second fraction with the product being placed on one side of the equal sign. The product of the remaining numerator and denominator is placed on the opposite side of the equation. The equation is then solved for the unknown value:

$$\frac{1}{2} = \frac{3}{x}$$
$$1 \cdot x = 2 \cdot 3$$
$$x = 6$$

Calculating NRP When the Percent Markup and the ORP Are Known

To find the new retail price when the percent *markup* and the original retail price are known, solve the percentage formula $R = P \div B$, where R is the percent markup, P is the dollar amount of the markup (expressed as a percent of the new retail price), and B is the new retail price (expressed as the original price plus dollar markup).

Example: Due to increased costs in labor and an industrywide shortage of raw materials, a furniture store owner finds it necessary to mark up all wooden merchandise in his store by 25%. What will be the new price for a hat rack that previously sold for $7.80?

Solution: P = amount of markup = 25%B (% markup is expressed as a % of the new retail price)

B = \$7.80 + 25%B (original price plus 25% of new retail price)

R = 25% (percent markup)

$$R = \frac{P}{B}$$

$$25\% = \frac{25\%B}{\$7.80 + 25\%B}$$

$$\frac{1}{4} = \frac{\frac{1}{4}B}{\$7.80 + \frac{1}{4}B} \qquad \text{(Change percents to common fractions)}$$

$$\$7.80 + \frac{1}{4}B = 4 \cdot \frac{1}{4}B \qquad \text{(Cross multiply)}$$

$$\$7.80 + \frac{1}{4}B = \frac{4}{4}B$$

$$\$7.80 = \frac{3}{4}B \qquad \text{(Combine variables)}$$

$$\frac{\$7.80}{\frac{3}{4}} = B \qquad \text{(Isolate } B\text{)}$$

$$\$10.40 = B \qquad \text{(New retail price)}$$

Off-Retail Percentages

Percent markup and percent markdown figures are for internal uses and should not be confused with price change percentages that are advertised to the public. Public promotions of reduced prices expressed as percents, for example, are frequently called "off-retail percentages" because the reduction in price is always based on the *original retail price.* (You will remember from the preceding discussion that markup and markdown are based on the *new retail price.*)

Example: A shirt was reduced from $20 to $15 for a special sale. What was the off-retail percent?

Solution:

Original Price	$20
New Price	-15
Difference	$ 5 reduction

$$\frac{\text{Reduction}}{\text{Original Price}} = \frac{\$5}{\$20} = 25\% \quad \text{off-retail percentage}$$

Exercises

Determine the amount of markup *and* the percent of markup from the following information:

1. Original price $10; new price $15.

2. Original price $15; new price $20.

3. Original price $30; new price $36.

4. Original price $12; new price $18.

5. Original price $20; new price $40.

6. Original price $18; new price $24.

7. Original price $6; new price $10.

8. Original price $14; new price $16.

9. Original price $20; new price $32.

10. Original price $.30; new price $.50.

Determine the amount of markdown *and* the percent of markdown for the following:

11.   Original price $.25; new price $.20.

12.   Original price $30; new price $20.

13.   Original price $20; new price $16.

14.   Original price $12; new price $9.

15.   Original price $10; new price $5.

16.   Original price $9; new price $8.

17.   Original price $21; new price $14.

18.   Original price $18; new price $15.

19.   Original price $7; new price $5.

20.   Original price $.28; new price $.24.

Determine the new retail price for the following when the percent markdown and the original retail price are known.

	% Markdown	*Original Retail Price*	*New Retail Price*
21.	50%	$45	_______
22.	$33\frac{1}{3}$%	$12	_______
23.	40%	$14	_______
24.	25%	$25	_______

Determine the new retail price for the following when the percent markup and the original retail price are known

	% Markup	*Original Retail Price*	*New Retail Price*
25.	$33\frac{1}{3}$%	$ 6	_______
26.	40%	$ 12	_______
27.	50%	$ 25	_______
28.	25%	$.15	_______

Practical Applications

29. A pair of shoes that originally sold for $25 now sells for $40. What is the amount and percent of markup?

30. A small gasoline-saving automobile originally sold for $3,500 but now sells for $5,000. What is the percent of markup?

31. Due to decreased demand, the price of handmade clocks dropped from $125 to $75. What was the amount of the markdown and the percent markdown?

32. In order to sell some slow-moving merchandise, the price was lowered from $8 to $5. What was the percent markdown?

33. A department store had 11 vacuum cleaners in stock at a retail price of $124.95 each. The buyer marked them down 28% for a special sale. What was the sale price and the dollar markdown?

34. A battery-powered butane lighter retailing for $39.95 was marked down $33\frac{1}{3}$%. What is the new retail price?

35. All dresses in Kim's were marked up 30%. What is the new selling price for a gown that originally sold for $50?

36. Jim's Stereo recently increased prices 20% based on the new retail price. What is the new retail price for a speaker that originally sold for $35?

Chapter 5
Self-Evaluation

1. Determine the retail price if the cost is $30 and the markon is $15.

2. Determine the cost if the markon is $12 and the retail price is $40.

3. Determine the retail price if the cost is $10 and the markon expressed as a percent of cost is 30%.

4. Determine the cost if the markon expressed as a percent of cost is 50% and the retail price is $18.

5. Calculate the retail price if the markon expressed as a percent of the retail price is 40% and the cost is $20.

6. Find the retail price if the markon expressed as a percent of cost is 25% and the markon is $10.

7. A produce manager bought 300 pounds of peaches at 20 cents per pound. Last year's experience shows that 30% of the peaches will not be sold. At what price per pound must the peaches be sold in order to receive a 50% markon based on cost?

8. A small tie shop knows that it will have to reduce prices by 25% on 40% of its stock of novelty bow ties in order to sell all of them. If 80 bow ties were purchased at a cost of $2.50 each, what price must be charged in order to maintain a 30% markon based on cost?

9. Calculate the amount and percent of markup if the NRP is $25 and the ORP was $20.

10. Calculate the amount and percent of markdown if the NRP is $15 and the ORP was $20.

PART THREE
THE MATHEMATICS OF ACCOUNTING

The primary responsibility of an accounting
department is to accumulate, sort, summarize, report,
and interpret financial information. This information is
used by management as the basis for business
decisions. Your career as a manager will be enhanced
by an increased understanding of the financial
information and reports furnished by accounting
personnel.

Chapter 6
Payroll Accounting

One of the largest expenditures for most organizations is employee compensation and related payroll expenses. The payroll department of a business is expected to accurately and promptly calculate the compensation due each employee after the close of each payroll period. Obviously, a knowledge of payroll accounting is needed by the manager and employees of the payroll department. Less obvious is the fact that managers of other departments throughout a company need to understand payroll accounting in order to answer the questions of employees and periodically resolve payroll disputes. This chapter will provide the opportunity for you to become acquainted with some of the compensation methods used in business and the various types of payroll deductions.

This chapter will enable you to:

1. **calculate employee compensation for salaries and wages, overtime pay, piece-rate pay, and commission**

2. **determine the amount of withholding for federal income tax by using the appropriate table**

3. **determine the amount of withholding for social security (FICA) tax**

4. **calculate total payroll deductions**

5. **determine net pay**

6. **complete and verify a payroll register**

Learning Unit 6.1
Compensation Methods

Employee compensation for services rendered an employer may take the form of salaries, wages, overtime pay, piece-rate pay, and commissions.

Salaries and Wages

The term *salary* is used when an employee's earnings are a fixed payment at regular intervals for services other than manual or mechanical labor. A salary is commonly expressed as a monthly or annual rate. The term *wage* is used when an employee's earnings are for performing skilled or unskilled labor. Wages are usually expressed as an hourly rate.

The classified section of a daily newspaper provides many examples of job opportunities in which the compensation is on a salary or wage basis. Salaries can be paid on any basis agreeable to the employer and employee, subject to some legal limitations. The most common payroll periods for salaries are weekly (52 times a year), biweekly (26 times a year), semimonthly (24 times a year), and monthly (12 times a year).

To compute the earnings of employees paid on a salary basis, divide the annual income by the appropriate payroll factor. In some situations, the amount of annual income will be given in the problem. In other situations, it may be necessary to first determine the annual salary before computing the salary for a particular payroll period.

Example: Reba earns an annual salary of $18,000. If paid on a monthly basis, how much does she earn each month?

Solution: $18,000 ÷ 12 = $1,500 monthly salary

Example: Dave earns a weekly salary of $220. If paid on a semimonthly basis, how much does he earn each pay period?

Solution: $220 × 52 = $11,440 annual salary
$11,440 ÷ 24 = $476.67 semimonthly salary

To compute the earnings of employees paid on an hourly rate basis, multiply the number of hours worked by the hourly rate.

Example: Randy is paid $3.10 per hour. How much did he earn in a
week in which he worked 36 hours?

Solution: $3.10 × 36 = $111.60 earnings for the week

Overtime

The Fair Labor Standards Act of 1938 has several provisions governing
worker compensation. Employees covered by this law must be paid one
and one-half times the hourly rate for time worked in excess of 40 hours in
a week.

To compute weekly earnings with overtime for hourly rate employees:

1. Determine the *overtime rate* per hour (regular hourly rate × 1.5)
   and *overtime hours* (total hours worked − 40).
2. Determine regular pay (regular hourly rate × 40).
3. Determine overtime pay (overtime rate × overtime hours).
4. Add regular pay and overtime pay.

Overtime can also be paid for all hours over eight worked in any single
day. The overtime rate is one and one-half times the normal hourly rate.

Example: Dominick was employed as a fry-cook at a local fish and chips
restaurant. He earned $5.40 an hour and received time and
a half for all hours over eight worked in any one day. Find his
gross pay for the week if he worked the following schedule
of hours: Tuesday–9.5, Wednesday–7, Thursday–8, Friday
and Saturday–10 each.

Solution:

Hours		Regular		Overtime
9.5	=	8	+	1.5
7	=	7	+	0
8	=	8	+	0
10	=	8	+	2
10	=	8	+	2
44.5	=	39	+	5.5

$$1.5 × \$5.40 = \$\ \ 8.10 \text{ overtime pay per hour}$$

39	× $5.40 =	$210.60	regular pay
5.5	× $8.10 =	$ 44.55	overtime pay
44.5		$255.15	gross pay

Example: Larry earns $3.80 per hour plus time and a half for any hours worked in excess of 40. How much did he earn in a week in which he worked 46 hours?

Solution: 1.5 × $3.80 = $5.70 overtime rate per hour

40 hours × $3.80 = $152.00 regular pay
6 hours × $5.70 = 34.20 overtime pay
46 hours $186.20 weekly earnings

Some nonsupervisory salaried personnel are subject to the Fair Labor Standards Act and must be paid extra for overtime. The overtime rate is also one and one-half times the calculated regular hourly rate.

Weekly earnings with overtime for salaried employees is computed the same as for hourly rate employees, except that the hourly rate must first be determined (weekly salary ÷ 40 hours).

Example: An administrative secretary receives a $200 salary for a 40-hour week. Calculate the gross pay if she worked 48 hours.

Solution: $200 ÷ 40 hours = $5.00 regular hourly rate

1.5 × $5.00 = $7.50 overtime rate per hour

40 hours × $5.00 = $200 regular pay
8 hours × $7.50 = 60 overtime pay
48 hours   = $260 gross pay

Piece Rate

In some manufacturing operations, employees are paid according to the number of units produced rather than according to hours worked. The term *piece rate* indicates that an employee's earnings are based on the number of units produced.

To compute the earnings of employees paid on a piece-rate basis, multiply the number of units produced by the piece rate.

Example: Jane is paid $5.25 for each weed trimmer assembled. How much did she earn in a week in which she assembled 36 units?

Solution: $5.25 × 36 = $189 earnings for the week

There are many variations of piece-rate pay. One variation that is commonly used is to pay an hourly wage rate plus a piece-rate bonus for units produced beyond a minimum number (quota).

To compute the earnings of employees paid on a combined hourly rate and piece-rate bonus basis:

1. Determine the number of units above quota.
2. Determine regular pay (hourly rate × 40 [or hours worked]).
3. Determine piece-rate bonus (piece rate × units above quota).
4. Add regular pay and piece-rate bonus.

Example: The Richland Company pays assemblers $4.50 per hour plus $3.00 for each unit over 30 per week. What are the weekly earnings of an employee who worked 40 hours and assembled 48 units?

Solution: 48 units − 30 units = 18 units for piece-rate bonus

$4.50 × 40 = $180 hourly earnings
$3.00 × 18 = $ 54 piece-rate bonus
$234 total earnings for the week

Commission

A commission is similar to piece-rate earnings in that the employee is paid on the basis of his or her productivity. A commission is a percent of the income generated for the business by the employee. Although commission plans vary from company to company, there are three basic types of plans: (1) straight commission, (2) graduated commission, and (3) base salary plus commission.

A *straight commission* plan provides for a fixed percent for all net sales (that is, after any returns and discounts) made by the employee. The employee's earnings are based entirely on sales productivity.

To compute commission, multiply the net sales by the fixed commission percent rate.[1]

---

[1]Here we have another business formula based on the basic percentage formula: Part = Base × Rate (see Chapter 3). In this case, B = net sales, R = percent of net sales, and P = commission.

Example: Martha, a real estate agent, receives a 2% commission on all sales. How much commission will she receive for selling a $47,000 residence?

Solution: $47,000 × .02 = $940 commission

A *graduated commission* plan provides for a different rate on various levels of sales.

Example: Bill, an auto parts representative, receives a commission of 2% on the first $10,000 of sales, 3% on the next $10,000, and 4% on sales over $20,000. How much commission will he receive for a month in which his sales were $25,000?

Solution: $10,000 × .02 = $200
$10,000 × .03 = $300
$ 5,000 × .04 = $200
$700 total commission

A commission plan involving a *base salary plus commission* is designed to provide the employee a minimum salary plus the incentive to achieve a high volume of sales.

Example: Jenny, a sales representative for a home products manufacturer, receives a base salary of $600 per month plus a 1% commission on all sales. How much did she earn in a month in which her sales were $46,000?

Solution: $ 600 base salary
$ 460 commission ($46,000 × .01)
$1,060 earnings for the month

Exercises

Find the earnings for each of the following pay periods.

	Salary	Pay Period	Earnings
1.	$15,000/year	monthly	________
2.	$18,240/year	monthly	________
3.	$17,680/year	weekly	________
4.	$21,600/year	biweekly	________
5.	$ 1,520/month	biweekly	________

Find the earnings for each of the following pay periods. The normal work week is 40 hours with time and a half for overtime.

	Hourly Wage	*Hours Worked*	*Earnings*
6.	$7.20	42	_______
7.	$6.80	44	_______
8.	$3.65	45	_______
9.	$4.80	$52\frac{1}{2}$	_______
10.	$8.14	35	_______

Find the earnings for each of the following pay periods. The company pays $2.80 an hour plus $4.00 for each trimmer assembled.

	Hours Worked	*Units Assembled*	*Earnings*
11.	40	32	_______
12.	40	28	_______
13.	36	26	_______
14.	40	41	_______
15.	18	11	_______

Find the earnings for each of the following pay periods.

	Sales	*Commission*	*Earnings*
16.	$ 3,600	12%	_______
17.	$ 3,900	9%	_______
18.	$18,500	5% on first $10,000, 6% on remainder	_______
19.	$23,920	4% on first $10,000 5% on second $10,000 8% on remainder	_______
20.	$ 7,465	$400 salary 10% on all sales over $5,000	_______
21.	$28,750	4% on first $10,000 $4\frac{1}{2}$% on next $5,000 5% on next $5,000 $5\frac{3}{4}$% on next $5,000 $6\frac{1}{4}$% on all sales over $25,000	_______

Practical Applications

22. Joan, a recent accounting graduate, has been offered a position with an annual salary of $15,500. The company pays all employees on a biweekly basis. How much salary will she earn each pay period?

23. A machinist earns $7.48 per hour plus time and a half for overtime after 40 hours a week. How much did he earn during a week in which he worked 42 hours?

24. A cosmetics salesperson in a drugstore is paid $2.95 an hour plus a commission of $\frac{1}{2}$% on all sales. How much did she earn during a 40-hour week in which her cosmetics sales were $3,200?

25. The ABC Corporation employs sales representatives on a graduated commission basis: 2% on the first $45,000 of sales and $2\frac{1}{2}$% on sales in excess of $45,000. Alice had sales of $72,000 during the previous month. How much commission did she earn for the month?

26. J. Smith earns a salary of $160 for a regular 40-hour week. If she worked 47 hours last week and is eligible for overtime at time and a half after 40 hours, what were her gross earnings?

27. Mary Wiseman, an executive secretary, receives a $200 salary for a 35-hour work week and time and a half for overtime after 35 hours. What will be her gross pay if she works 42 hours during one week?

28. Maxine Fields cooks hamburgers for a living. She earns time and a half for all hours over eight worked in any one day. What would be Maxine's gross earnings if, at an hourly rate of $4.50, she worked the following schedule of hours last week: Monday–8.5, Tuesday–9, Wednesday–sick, Thursday–6, Friday–9, and Saturday–10? (Round your answer to the nearest penny.)

29. Jesse Martinez works for a general contractor at $7.80 an hour plus overtime at the rate of one and one-half times the regular rate for all hours over eight worked in any one day. Jesse worked the following hours one week: 8, 10, 11, 9, and 9.5. What was his gross pay for the week?

30. A local grocery wholesaler pays sales representatives a commission on all net sales. Warren Wilson had gross sales of $750,000 during the month of October. Warren also had $7,855.50 worth of merchandise returned and gave discounts (trade and cash) totaling $150,000. What was his gross pay if his commission was $\frac{1}{2}$%? (Round your answer to the nearest penny.)

Learning Unit 6.2
Payroll Deductions

Types of Deductions

Some payroll deductions are voluntary; others are required. Voluntary deductions may include premiums for group health and life insurance, retirement plans, savings bonds, credit union deposits or payments, and union dues. Required payroll deductions traditionally include the federal income tax and the FICA tax.

Federal Income Tax

Employers are required to withhold the proper percent of an employee's earnings each pay period for federal income tax purposes. As soon as a new employee is hired, the employee fills out a Form W-4, the *Employee's Withholding Allowance Certificate*. Payroll personnel refer to this form to obtain information on the employee's marital status and total number of dependents or allowances. One tax allowance (or exemption) is given for the employee and for each person legally supported by the employee. The amount to be withheld may be determined by using (1) a wage bracket tax table or (2) the percentage method. Information about each of these two methods is contained in *Circular E—Employers' Tax Guide,* which is available from the Internal Revenue Service.

The *Tax Guide* contains wage bracket tax tables for weekly, biweekly, semimonthly, monthly, and daily or miscellaneous pay periods. Different tables are provided for married and single taxpayers. Portions of the tables for married and single taxpayers on a weekly payroll are shown in Tables 6.1 and 6.2 on pp. 132–33 and 134–35. Portions of monthly payroll tables for both taxpayer groups are shown in Tables 6.3 and 6.4 on pp. 136–37 and 138–39.

The amount to be withheld by an employer is based on four factors: (1) payroll period, (2) marital status, (3) earnings, and (4) number of exemptions.

To determine the amount of income tax withholding using the wage bracket tax tables:

1. Refer to the appropriate tax table.
2. Move down the column marked "And the wages are—At least" to the proper line.
3. Follow that line across to the column for the number of allowances claimed by the employee.

Table 6.1. Wage Bracket Table—MARRIED Persons— WEEKLY Payroll Period

And the wages are—		And the number of withholding allowances claimed is—										
At least	But less than	0	1	2	3	4	5	6	7	8	9	10 or more
		The amount of income tax to be withheld shall be—										
$300	$310	$47.50	$43.00	$39.00	$34.90	$30.90	$26.90	$23.40	$19.90	$16.50	$13.00	$10.00
310	320	49.90	45.30	41.10	37.00	33.00	28.90	25.20	21.70	18.30	14.80	11.50
320	330	52.30	47.70	43.20	39.10	35.10	31.00	27.00	23.50	20.10	16.60	13.20
330	340	54.70	50.10	45.50	41.20	37.20	33.10	29.10	25.30	21.90	18.40	15.00
340	350	57.10	52.50	47.90	43.30	39.30	35.20	31.20	27.20	23.70	20.20	16.80
350	360	59.50	54.90	50.30	45.70	41.40	37.30	33.30	29.30	25.50	22.00	18.60
360	370	61.90	57.30	52.70	48.10	43.50	39.40	35.40	31.40	27.30	23.80	20.40
370	380	64.60	59.70	55.10	50.50	45.90	41.50	37.50	33.50	29.40	25.60	22.20
380	390	67.40	62.10	57.50	52.90	48.30	43.70	39.60	35.60	31.50	27.50	24.00
390	400	70.20	64.80	59.90	55.30	50.70	46.10	41.70	37.70	33.60	29.60	25.80
400	410	73.00	67.60	62.30	57.70	53.10	48.50	43.80	39.80	35.70	31.70	27.60
410	420	75.80	70.40	65.00	60.10	55.50	50.90	46.20	41.90	37.80	33.80	29.70
420	430	78.60	73.20	67.80	62.50	57.90	53.30	48.60	44.00	39.90	35.90	31.80
430	440	81.40	76.00	70.60	65.20	60.30	55.70	51.00	46.40	42.00	38.00	33.90
440	450	84.20	78.80	73.40	68.00	62.70	58.10	53.40	48.80	44.20	40.10	36.00
450	460	87.00	81.60	76.20	70.80	65.40	60.50	55.80	51.20	46.60	42.20	38.10
460	470	90.20	84.40	79.00	73.60	68.20	62.90	58.20	53.60	49.00	44.40	40.20
470	480	93.40	87.30	81.80	76.40	71.00	65.60	60.60	56.00	51.40	46.80	42.30
480	490	96.60	90.50	84.60	79.20	73.80	68.40	63.10	58.40	53.80	49.20	44.60
490	500	99.80	93.70	87.50	82.00	76.60	71.20	65.90	60.80	56.20	51.60	47.00
500	510	103.00	96.90	90.70	84.80	79.40	74.00	68.70	63.30	58.60	54.00	49.40
510	520	106.20	100.10	93.90	87.70	82.20	76.80	71.50	66.10	61.00	56.40	51.80
520	530	109.40	103.30	97.10	90.90	85.00	79.60	74.30	68.90	63.50	58.80	54.20
530	540	112.60	106.50	100.30	94.10	88.00	82.40	77.10	71.70	66.30	61.20	56.60
540	550	115.80	109.70	103.50	97.30	91.20	85.20	79.90	74.50	69.10	63.70	59.00

550	560	119.00	112.90	106.70	100.50	94.40	88.20	82.70	77.30	71.90	66.50	61.40
560	570	122.70	116.10	109.90	103.70	97.60	91.40	85.50	80.10	74.70	69.30	63.90
570	580	126.40	119.30	113.10	106.90	100.80	94.60	88.50	82.90	77.50	72.10	66.70
580	590	130.10	123.00	116.30	110.10	104.00	97.80	91.70	85.70	80.30	74.90	69.50
590	600	133.80	126.70	119.50	113.30	107.20	101.00	94.90	88.70	83.10	77.70	72.30
600	610	137.50	130.40	123.20	116.50	110.40	104.20	98.10	91.90	85.90	80.50	75.10
610	620	141.20	134.10	126.90	119.80	113.60	107.40	101.30	95.10	89.00	83.30	77.90
620	630	144.90	137.80	130.60	123.50	116.80	110.60	104.50	98.30	92.20	86.10	80.70
630	640	148.60	141.50	134.30	127.20	120.10	113.80	107.70	101.50	95.40	89.20	83.50
640	650	152.30	145.20	138.00	130.90	123.80	117.00	110.90	104.70	98.60	92.40	86.30
650	660	156.00	148.90	141.70	134.60	127.50	120.40	114.10	107.90	101.80	95.60	89.50
660	670	159.70	152.60	145.40	138.30	131.20	124.10	117.30	111.10	105.00	98.80	92.70
670	680	163.40	156.30	149.10	142.00	134.90	127.80	120.70	114.30	108.20	102.00	95.90
680	690	167.10	160.00	152.80	145.70	138.60	131.50	124.40	117.50	111.40	105.20	99.10
690	700	170.80	163.70	156.50	149.40	142.30	135.20	128.10	121.00	114.60	108.40	102.30
700	710	174.50	167.40	160.20	153.10	146.00	138.90	131.80	124.70	117.80	111.60	105.50
710	720	178.20	171.10	163.90	156.80	149.70	142.60	135.50	128.40	121.20	114.80	108.70
720	730	181.90	174.80	167.60	160.50	153.40	146.30	139.20	132.10	124.90	118.00	111.90
730	740	185.60	178.50	171.30	164.20	157.10	150.00	142.90	135.80	128.60	121.50	115.10
740	750	189.30	182.20	175.00	167.90	160.80	153.70	146.60	139.50	132.30	125.20	118.30
750	760	193.00	185.90	178.70	171.60	164.50	157.40	150.30	143.20	136.00	128.90	121.80
760	770	196.70	189.60	182.40	175.30	168.20	161.10	154.00	146.90	139.70	132.60	125.50
770	780	200.40	193.30	186.10	179.00	171.90	164.80	157.70	150.60	143.40	136.30	129.20
780	790	204.10	197.00	189.80	182.70	175.60	168.50	161.40	154.30	147.10	140.00	132.90
790	800	207.80	200.70	193.50	186.40	179.30	172.20	165.10	158.00	150.80	143.70	136.60
800	810	211.50	204.40	197.20	190.10	183.00	175.90	168.80	161.70	154.50	147.40	140.30
810	820	215.20	208.10	200.90	193.80	186.70	179.60	172.50	165.40	158.20	151.10	144.00
820	830	218.90	211.80	204.60	197.50	190.40	183.30	176.20	169.10	161.90	154.80	147.70
830	840	222.60	215.50	208.30	201.20	194.10	187.00	179.90	172.80	165.60	158.50	151.40
840	850	226.30	219.20	212.00	204.90	197.80	190.70	183.60	176.50	169.30	162.20	155.10

37 percent of the excess over $850 plus—

| $850 and over | | 228.10 | 221.00 | 213.90 | 206.80 | 199.70 | 192.50 | 185.40 | 178.30 | 171.20 | 164.10 | 157.00 |

Table 6.2. Wage Bracket Table—SINGLE Persons— WEEKLY Payroll Period

And the wages are—		And the number of withholding allowances claimed is—										
At least	But less than	0	1	2	3	4	5	6	7	8	9	10 or more
		The amount of income tax to be withheld shall be—										
$135	$140	$19.00	$15.30	$11.80	$8.40	$5.00	$2.10	$0	$0	$0	$0	$0
140	145	20.00	16.20	12.70	9.30	5.80	2.90	0	0	0	0	0
145	150	21.10	17.10	13.60	10.20	6.70	3.60	.70	0	0	0	0
150	160	22.60	18.60	15.00	11.50	8.10	4.70	1.80	0	0	0	0
160	170	24.70	20.70	16.80	13.30	9.90	6.40	3.30	.50	0	0	0
170	180	26.80	22.80	18.80	15.10	11.70	8.20	4.80	2.00	0	0	0
180	190	28.90	24.90	20.90	16.90	13.50	10.00	6.50	3.50	.60	0	0
190	200	31.00	27.00	23.00	18.90	15.30	11.80	8.30	5.00	2.10	0	0
200	210	33.60	29.10	25.10	21.00	17.10	13.60	10.10	6.70	3.60	.70	0
210	220	36.20	31.20	27.20	23.10	19.10	15.40	11.90	8.50	5.10	2.20	0
220	230	38.80	33.80	29.30	25.20	21.20	17.20	13.70	10.30	6.80	3.70	.80
230	240	41.40	36.40	31.40	27.30	23.30	19.20	15.50	12.10	8.60	5.20	2.30
240	250	44.00	39.00	34.00	29.40	25.40	21.30	17.30	13.90	10.40	6.90	3.80
250	260	46.60	41.60	36.60	31.60	27.50	23.40	19.40	15.70	12.20	8.70	5.30
260	270	49.20	44.20	39.20	34.20	29.60	25.50	21.50	17.50	14.00	10.50	7.10
270	280	51.80	46.80	41.80	36.80	31.80	27.60	23.60	19.60	15.80	12.30	8.90
280	290	54.80	49.40	44.40	39.40	34.40	29.70	25.70	21.70	17.60	14.10	10.70
290	300	57.80	52.10	47.00	42.00	37.00	32.00	27.80	23.80	19.70	15.90	12.50
300	310	60.80	55.10	49.60	44.60	39.60	34.60	29.90	25.90	21.80	17.80	14.30
310	320	63.80	58.10	52.30	47.20	42.20	37.20	32.20	28.00	23.90	19.90	16.10
320	330	66.80	61.10	55.30	49.80	44.80	39.80	34.80	30.10	26.00	22.00	17.90
330	340	70.00	64.10	58.30	52.50	47.40	42.40	37.40	32.40	28.10	24.10	20.00
340	350	73.40	67.10	61.30	55.50	50.00	45.00	40.00	35.00	30.20	26.20	22.10
350	360	76.80	70.30	64.30	58.50	52.80	47.60	42.60	37.60	32.60	28.30	24.20
360	370	80.20	73.70	67.30	61.50	55.80	50.20	45.20	40.20	35.20	30.40	26.30

370	380	83.60	77.10	70.50	64.50	58.80	53.00	47.80	42.80	37.80	32.80	28.40
380	390	87.00	80.50	73.90	67.50	61.80	56.00	50.40	45.40	40.40	35.40	30.50
390	400	90.40	83.90	77.30	70.80	64.80	59.00	53.20	48.00	43.00	38.00	33.00
400	410	93.80	87.30	80.70	74.20	67.80	62.00	56.20	50.60	45.60	40.60	35.60
410	420	97.20	90.70	84.10	77.60	71.10	65.00	59.20	53.50	48.20	43.20	38.20
420	430	100.60	94.10	87.50	81.00	74.50	68.00	62.20	56.50	50.80	45.80	40.80
430	440	104.10	97.50	90.90	84.40	77.90	71.30	65.20	59.50	53.70	48.40	43.40
440	450	108.00	100.90	94.30	87.80	81.30	74.70	68.20	62.50	56.70	51.00	46.00
450	460	111.90	104.40	97.70	91.20	84.70	78.10	71.60	65.50	59.70	53.90	48.60
460	470	115.80	108.30	101.10	94.60	88.10	81.50	75.00	68.50	62.70	56.90	51.20
470	480	119.70	112.20	104.70	98.00	91.50	84.90	78.40	71.80	65.70	59.90	54.20
480	490	123.60	116.10	108.60	101.40	94.90	88.30	81.80	75.20	68.70	62.90	57.20
490	500	127.50	120.00	112.50	105.00	98.30	91.70	85.20	78.60	72.10	65.90	60.20
500	510	131.40	123.90	116.40	108.90	101.70	95.10	88.60	82.00	75.50	69.00	63.20
510	520	135.30	127.80	120.30	112.80	105.30	98.50	92.00	85.40	78.90	72.40	66.20
520	530	139.20	131.70	124.20	116.70	109.20	101.90	95.40	88.80	82.30	75.80	69.20
530	540	143.10	135.60	128.10	120.60	113.10	105.60	98.80	92.20	85.70	79.20	72.60
540	550	147.00	139.50	132.00	124.50	117.00	109.50	102.20	95.60	89.10	82.60	76.00
550	560	150.90	143.40	135.90	128.40	120.90	113.40	105.90	99.00	92.50	86.00	79.40
560	570	154.80	147.30	139.80	132.30	124.80	117.30	109.80	102.40	95.90	89.40	82.80
570	580	158.70	151.20	143.70	136.20	128.70	121.20	113.70	106.20	99.30	92.80	86.20
580	590	162.60	155.10	147.60	140.10	132.60	125.10	117.60	110.10	102.70	96.20	89.60
590	600	166.50	159.00	151.50	144.00	136.50	129.00	121.50	114.00	106.50	99.60	93.00
600	610	170.40	162.90	155.40	147.90	140.40	132.90	125.40	117.90	110.40	103.00	96.40
610	620	174.30	166.80	159.30	151.80	144.30	136.80	129.30	121.80	114.30	106.80	99.80
620	630	178.20	170.70	163.20	155.70	148.20	140.70	133.20	125.70	118.20	110.70	103.20
630	640	182.10	174.60	167.10	159.60	152.10	144.60	137.10	129.60	122.10	114.60	107.10
640	650	186.00	178.50	171.00	163.50	156.00	148.50	141.00	133.50	126.00	118.50	111.00
650	660	189.90	182.40	174.90	167.40	159.90	152.40	144.90	137.40	129.90	122.40	114.90
660	670	193.80	186.30	178.80	171.30	163.80	156.30	148.80	141.30	133.80	126.30	118.80
						39 percent of the excess over $670 plus—						
$670 and over		195.80	188.30	180.80	173.30	165.80	158.30	150.80	143.30	135.80	128.30	120.80

Table 6.3. Wage Bracket Table—MARRIED Persons— MONTHLY Payroll Period

| And the wages are— | | And the number of withholding allowances claimed is— | | | | | | | | | | |
At least	But less than	0	1	2	3	4	5	6	7	8	9	10 or more
		The amount of income tax to be withheld shall be—										
$1,360	$1,400	$220.00	$200.00	$181.10	$163.60	$146.10	$128.60	$111.90	$96.90	$81.90	$66.90	$52.00
1,400	1,440	229.60	209.60	189.60	172.00	154.50	137.00	119.50	104.10	89.10	74.10	59.10
1,440	1,480	239.20	219.20	199.20	180.40	162.90	145.40	127.90	111.30	96.30	81.30	66.30
1,480	1,520	248.80	228.80	208.80	188.80	171.30	153.80	136.30	118.80	103.50	88.50	73.50
1,520	1,560	258.40	238.40	218.40	198.40	179.70	162.20	144.70	127.20	110.70	95.70	80.70
1,560	1,600	268.00	248.00	228.00	208.00	188.10	170.60	153.10	135.60	118.10	102.90	87.90
1,600	1,640	278.40	257.60	237.60	217.60	197.60	179.00	161.50	144.00	126.50	110.10	95.10
1,640	1,680	289.60	267.20	247.20	227.20	207.20	187.40	169.90	152.40	134.90	117.40	102.30
1,680	1,720	300.80	277.40	256.80	236.80	216.80	196.80	178.30	160.80	143.30	125.80	109.50
1,720	1,760	312.00	288.60	266.40	246.40	226.40	206.40	186.70	169.20	151.70	134.20	116.70
1,760	1,800	323.20	299.80	276.50	256.00	236.00	216.00	196.00	177.60	160.10	142.60	125.10
1,800	1,840	334.40	311.00	287.70	265.60	245.60	225.60	205.60	186.00	168.50	151.00	133.50
1,840	1,880	345.60	322.20	298.90	275.60	255.20	235.20	215.20	195.20	176.90	159.40	141.90
1,880	1,920	356.80	333.40	310.10	286.80	264.80	244.80	224.80	204.80	185.30	167.80	150.30
1,920	1,960	368.00	344.60	321.30	298.00	274.60	254.40	234.40	214.40	194.40	176.20	158.70
1,960	2,000	379.70	355.80	332.50	309.20	285.80	264.00	244.00	224.00	204.00	184.60	167.10
2,000	2,040	392.50	367.00	343.70	320.40	297.00	273.70	253.60	233.60	213.60	193.60	175.50
2,040	2,080	405.30	378.60	354.90	331.60	308.20	284.90	263.20	243.20	223.20	203.20	183.90
2,080	2,120	418.10	391.40	366.10	342.80	319.40	296.10	272.80	252.80	232.80	212.80	192.80
2,120	2,160	430.90	404.20	377.60	354.00	330.60	307.30	284.00	262.40	242.40	222.40	202.40
2,160	2,200	443.70	417.00	390.40	365.20	341.80	318.50	295.20	272.00	252.00	232.00	212.00
2,200	2,240	456.50	429.80	403.20	376.50	353.00	329.70	306.40	283.00	261.60	241.60	221.60
2,240	2,280	469.30	442.60	416.00	389.30	364.20	340.90	317.60	294.20	271.20	251.20	231.20
2,280	2,320	482.10	455.40	428.80	402.10	375.40	352.10	328.80	305.40	282.10	260.80	240.80
2,320	2,360	494.90	468.20	441.60	414.90	388.20	363.30	340.00	316.60	293.30	270.40	250.40

2,360	2,400	507.70	481.00	454.40	427.70	401.00	374.50	351.20	327.80	304.50	281.20	260.00
2,400	2,440	521.10	493.80	467.20	440.50	413.80	387.20	362.40	339.00	315.70	292.40	269.60
2,440	2,480	535.90	506.60	480.00	453.30	426.60	400.00	373.60	350.20	326.90	303.60	280.20
2,480	2,520	550.70	519.80	492.80	466.10	439.40	412.80	386.10	361.40	338.10	314.80	291.40
2,520	2,560	565.50	534.60	505.60	478.90	452.20	425.60	398.90	372.60	349.30	326.00	302.60
2,560	2,600	580.30	549.40	518.60	491.70	465.00	438.40	411.70	385.00	360.50	337.20	313.80
2,600	2,640	595.10	564.20	533.40	504.50	477.80	451.20	424.50	397.80	371.70	348.40	325.00
2,640	2,680	609.90	579.00	548.20	517.40	490.60	464.00	437.30	410.60	384.00	359.60	336.20
2,680	2,720	624.70	593.80	563.00	532.20	503.40	476.80	450.10	423.40	396.80	370.80	347.40
2,720	2,760	639.50	608.60	577.80	547.00	516.20	489.60	462.90	436.20	409.60	382.90	358.60
2,760	2,800	654.30	623.40	592.60	561.80	530.90	502.40	475.70	449.00	422.40	395.70	369.80
2,800	2,840	669.10	638.20	607.40	576.60	545.70	515.20	488.50	461.80	435.20	408.50	381.80
2,840	2,880	683.90	653.00	622.20	591.40	560.50	529.70	501.30	474.60	448.00	421.30	394.60
2,880	2,920	698.70	667.80	637.00	606.20	575.30	544.50	514.10	487.40	460.80	434.10	407.40
2,920	2,960	713.50	682.60	651.80	621.00	590.10	559.30	528.50	500.20	473.60	446.90	420.20
2,960	3,000	728.30	697.40	666.60	635.80	604.90	574.10	543.30	513.00	486.40	459.70	433.00
3,000	3,040	743.10	712.20	681.40	650.60	619.70	588.90	558.10	527.20	499.20	472.50	445.80
3,040	3,080	757.90	727.00	696.20	665.40	634.50	603.70	572.90	542.00	512.00	485.30	458.60
3,080	3,120	772.70	741.80	711.00	680.20	649.30	618.50	587.70	556.80	526.00	498.10	471.40
3,120	3,160	787.50	756.60	725.80	695.00	664.10	633.30	602.50	571.60	540.80	510.90	484.20
3,160	3,200	802.30	771.40	740.60	709.80	678.90	648.10	617.30	586.40	555.60	524.80	497.00
3,200	3,240	817.10	786.20	755.40	724.60	693.70	662.90	632.10	601.20	570.40	539.60	509.80
3,240	3,280	831.90	801.00	770.20	739.40	708.50	677.70	646.90	616.00	585.20	554.40	523.50
3,280	3,320	846.70	815.80	785.00	754.20	723.30	692.50	661.70	630.80	600.00	569.20	538.30
3,320	3,360	861.50	830.60	799.80	769.00	738.10	707.30	676.50	645.60	614.80	584.00	553.10
3,360	3,400	876.30	845.40	814.60	783.80	752.90	722.10	691.30	660.40	629.60	598.80	567.90
3,400	3,440	891.10	860.20	829.40	798.60	767.70	736.90	706.10	675.20	644.40	613.60	582.70
3,440	3,480	905.90	875.00	844.20	813.40	782.50	751.70	720.90	690.00	659.20	628.40	597.50
3,480	3,520	920.70	889.80	859.00	828.20	797.30	766.50	735.70	704.80	674.00	643.20	612.30
3,520	3,560	935.50	904.60	873.80	843.00	812.10	781.30	750.50	719.60	688.80	658.00	627.10

37 percent of the excess over $3,560 plus—

$3,560 and over		942.90	912.00	881.20	850.40	819.50	788.70	757.90	727.00	696.20	665.40	634.50

Table 6.4. Wage Bracket Table—SINGLE Persons—MONTHLY Payroll Period

| And the wages are— | | And the number of withholding allowances claimed is— | | | | | | | | | | |
At least	But less than	0	1	2	3	4	5	6	7	8	9	10 or more
		The amount of income tax to be withheld shall be—										
$580	$600	$80.90	$65.20	$50.20	$35.20	$20.80	$8.30	$0	$0	$0	$0	$0
600	640	87.20	70.60	55.60	40.60	25.60	12.80	.30	0	0	0	0
640	680	95.60	78.10	62.80	47.80	32.80	18.80	6.30	0	0	0	0
680	720	104.00	86.50	70.00	55.00	40.00	25.00	12.30	0	0	0	0
720	760	112.40	94.90	77.40	62.20	47.20	32.20	18.30	5.80	0	0	0
760	800	120.80	103.30	85.80	69.40	54.40	39.40	24.40	11.80	0	0	0
800	840	129.20	111.70	94.20	76.70	61.60	46.60	31.60	17.80	5.30	0	0
840	880	138.10	120.10	102.60	85.10	68.80	53.80	38.80	23.80	11.30	0	0
880	920	148.50	128.50	111.00	93.50	76.00	61.00	46.00	31.00	17.30	4.80	0
920	960	158.90	137.20	119.40	101.90	84.40	68.20	53.20	38.20	23.30	10.80	0
960	1,000	169.30	147.60	127.80	110.30	92.80	75.40	60.40	45.40	30.40	16.80	4.30
1,000	1,040	179.70	158.00	136.40	118.70	101.20	83.70	67.60	52.60	37.60	22.80	10.30
1,040	1,080	190.10	168.40	146.80	127.10	109.60	92.10	74.80	59.80	44.80	29.80	16.30
1,080	1,120	200.50	178.80	157.20	135.50	118.00	100.50	83.00	67.00	52.00	37.00	22.30
1,120	1,160	210.90	189.20	167.60	145.90	126.40	108.90	91.40	74.20	59.20	44.20	29.20
1,160	1,200	221.30	199.60	178.00	156.30	134.80	117.30	99.80	82.30	66.40	51.40	36.40
1,200	1,240	233.20	210.00	188.40	166.70	145.00	125.70	108.20	90.70	73.60	58.60	43.60
1,240	1,280	245.20	220.40	198.80	177.10	155.40	134.10	116.60	99.10	81.60	65.80	50.80
1,280	1,320	257.20	232.20	209.20	187.50	165.80	144.20	125.00	107.50	90.00	73.00	58.00
1,320	1,360	269.20	244.20	219.60	197.90	176.20	154.60	133.40	115.90	98.40	80.90	65.20
1,360	1,400	281.20	256.20	231.20	208.30	186.60	165.00	143.30	124.30	106.80	89.30	72.40
1,400	1,440	293.20	268.20	243.20	218.70	197.00	175.40	153.70	132.70	115.20	97.70	80.20
1,440	1,480	306.20	280.20	255.20	230.20	207.40	185.80	164.10	142.40	123.60	106.10	88.60
1,480	1,520	319.80	292.20	267.20	242.20	217.80	196.20	174.50	152.80	132.00	114.50	97.00
1,520	1,560	333.40	305.10	279.20	254.20	229.20	206.60	184.90	163.20	141.60	122.90	105.40

1,560	1,600	347.00	318.70	291.20	266.20	241.20	217.00	195.30	173.60	152.00	131.30	113.80
1,600	1,640	360.60	332.30	304.00	278.20	253.20	228.20	205.70	184.00	162.40	140.70	122.20
1,640	1,680	374.20	345.90	317.60	290.20	265.20	240.20	216.10	194.40	172.80	151.10	130.60
1,680	1,720	387.80	359.50	331.20	302.80	277.20	252.20	227.20	204.80	183.20	161.50	139.80
1,720	1,760	401.40	373.10	344.80	316.40	289.20	264.20	239.20	215.20	193.60	171.90	150.20
1,760	1,800	415.00	386.70	358.40	330.00	301.70	276.20	251.20	226.20	204.00	182.30	160.60
1,800	1,840	428.60	400.30	372.00	343.60	315.30	288.20	263.20	238.20	214.40	192.70	171.00
1,840	1,880	442.20	413.90	385.60	357.20	328.90	300.60	275.20	250.20	225.20	203.10	181.40
1,880	1,920	457.10	427.50	399.20	370.80	342.50	314.20	287.20	262.20	237.20	213.50	191.80
1,920	1,960	472.70	441.10	412.80	384.40	356.10	327.80	299.40	274.20	249.20	224.20	202.20
1,960	2,000	488.30	455.80	426.40	398.00	369.70	341.40	313.00	286.20	261.20	236.20	212.60
2,000	2,040	503.90	471.40	440.00	411.60	383.30	355.00	326.60	298.30	273.20	248.20	223.20
2,040	2,080	519.50	487.00	454.50	425.20	396.90	368.60	340.20	311.90	285.20	260.20	235.20
2,080	2,120	535.10	502.60	470.10	438.80	410.50	382.20	353.80	325.50	297.20	272.20	247.20
2,120	2,160	550.70	518.20	485.70	453.20	424.10	395.80	367.40	339.10	310.80	284.20	259.20
2,160	2,200	566.30	533.80	501.30	468.80	437.70	409.40	381.00	352.70	324.40	296.20	271.20
2,200	2,240	581.90	549.40	516.90	484.40	451.90	423.00	394.60	366.30	338.00	309.60	283.20
2,240	2,280	597.50	565.00	532.50	500.00	467.50	436.60	408.20	379.90	351.60	323.20	295.20
2,280	2,320	613.10	580.60	548.10	515.60	483.10	450.60	421.80	393.50	365.20	336.80	308.50
2,320	2,360	628.70	596.20	563.70	531.20	498.70	466.20	435.40	407.10	378.80	350.40	322.10
2,360	2,400	644.30	611.80	579.30	546.80	514.30	481.80	449.30	420.70	392.40	364.00	335.70
2,400	2,440	659.90	627.40	594.90	562.40	529.90	497.40	464.90	434.30	406.00	377.60	349.30
2,440	2,480	675.50	643.00	610.50	578.00	545.50	513.00	480.50	448.00	419.60	391.20	362.90
2,480	2,520	691.10	658.60	626.10	593.60	561.10	528.60	496.10	463.60	433.20	404.80	376.50
2,520	2,560	706.70	674.20	641.70	609.20	576.70	544.20	511.70	479.20	446.80	418.40	390.10
2,560	2,600	722.30	689.80	657.30	624.80	592.30	559.80	527.30	494.80	462.30	432.00	403.70
2,600	2,640	737.90	705.40	672.90	640.40	607.90	575.40	542.90	510.40	477.90	445.60	417.30
2,640	2,680	753.50	721.00	688.50	656.00	623.50	591.00	558.50	526.00	493.50	461.00	430.90
2,680	2,720	769.10	736.60	704.10	671.60	639.10	606.60	574.10	541.60	509.10	476.60	444.50
2,720	2,760	784.70	752.20	719.70	687.20	654.70	622.20	589.70	557.20	524.70	492.20	459.70
						39 percent of the excess over $2,760 plus—						
$2,760 and over		792.50	760.00	727.50	695.00	662.50	630.00	597.50	565.00	532.50	500.00	467.50

Example: A married taxpayer with four withholding allowances (including the taxpayer) earned $328.40 during the past week. What amount should the employer withhold from the employee's wage payment for income taxes?

Solution: Use the wage bracket table for married persons—weekly payroll (Table 6.1). Move down the left column to the point at which the wages are at least $320 but less than $330, and move across to the column for four allowances. The answer is $35.10.

Employers who prefer not to use the wage bracket tax tables in computing the amount of income tax to withhold can make a percentage computation based on the data in Table 6.5 and the appropriate rate table. The *Tax Guide* provides rate tables for weekly, biweekly, semimonthly, monthly, quarterly, semiannual, annual, and daily or miscellaneous payroll periods. Rate tables for weekly and monthly payroll periods are shown in Tables 6.6 and 6.7.

To determine the amount to withhold for income taxes using the percentage method:

1. Determine the total withholding allowance (dollar value for one withholding allowance × number of allowances claimed by the employee; see Table 6.5).
2. Determine the amount of taxable income (employee's wages − total withholding allowance).
3. Determine the amount to be withheld from the appropriate rate table (Table 6.6 or 6.7).

Table 6.5. Percentage Method— Withholding Allowance Table

Payroll period	One withholding allowance
Weekly	$19.23
Biweekly	38.46
Semimonthly	41.66
Monthly	83.33
Quarterly	250.00
Semiannually	500.00
Annually	1,000.00
Daily or miscellaneous (each day of the payroll period)	2.74

Table 6.6. Percentage Method of Withholding— Weekly Payroll Period

(a) SINGLE person—including head of household:

If the amount of wages is: | The amount of income tax to be withheld shall be:

Not over $27 0

Over—	But not over—		of excess over—
$27	—$63	15%	—$27
$63	—$131	$5.40 plus 18%	—$63
$131	—$196	$17.64 plus 21%	—$131
$196	—$273	$31.29 plus 26%	—$196
$273	—$331	$51.31 plus 30%	—$273
$331	—$433	$68.71 plus 34%	—$331
$433		$103.39 plus 39%	—$433

(b) MARRIED person—

If the amount of wages is: | The amount of income tax to be withheld shall be:

Not over $46 0

Over—	But not over—		of excess over—
$46	—$127	15%	—$46
$127	—$210	$12.15 plus 18%	—$127
$210	—$288	$27.09 plus 21%	—$210
$288	—$369	$43.47 plus 24%	—$288
$369	—$454	$62.91 plus 28%	—$369
$454	—$556	$86.71 plus 32%	—$454
$556		$119.35 plus 37%	—$556

Table 6.7. Percentage Method of Withholding— Monthly Payroll Period

(a) SINGLE person—including head of household:

If the amount of wages is: | The amount of income tax to be withheld shall be:

Not over $118 0

Over—	But not over—		of excess over—
$118	—$275	15%	—$118
$275	—$567	$23.55 plus 18%	—$275
$567	—$850	$76.11 plus 21%	—$567
$850	—$1,183	$135.54 plus 26%	—$850
$1,183	—$1,433	$222.12 plus 30%	—$1,183
$1,433	—$1,875	$297.12 plus 34%	—$1,433
$1,875		$447.40 plus 39%	—$1,875

(b) MARRIED person—

If the amount of wages is: | The amount of income tax to be withheld shall be:

Not over $200 0

Over—	But not over—		of excess over—
$200	—$550	15%	—$200
$550	—$908	$52.50 plus 18%	—$550
$908	—$1,250	$116.94 plus 21%	—$908
$1,250	—$1,600	$188.76 plus 24%	—$1,250
$1,600	—$1,967	$272.76 plus 28%	—$1,600
$1,967	—$2,408	$375.52 plus 32%	—$1,967
$2,408		$516.64 plus 37%	—$2,408

Example: A married employee who claims three withholding allowances earned $225 during the past week. What amount should be withheld by the employer for income taxes?

Solution: $19.23   amount of one allowance (Table 6.5, weekly)
× 3   number of allowances claimed by employee
$57.69   nontaxable income

$225 − $57.69 = $167.31   amount subject to withholding tax

$12.15 + 18% of excess over $127 = $19.41 (Table 6.6)

Example: A married employee who claims three allowances receives a monthly salary of $900. What amount should be withheld for income taxes?

Solution: $83.33 × 3 = $249.99   nontaxable income (Table 6.5, monthly)

$900 − $249.99 = $650.01   amount subject to withholding tax

$52.50 + 18% of excess over $550 = $70.50 (Table 6.6)

Federal Insurance Contributions Act (FICA) Tax

FICA tax, commonly called the Social Security tax, was established to provide retirement benefits for eligible citizens. Both employee and employer make matching contributions—up to a specified maximum—into each employee's Social Security account. The law has been changed frequently to provide expanded benefits and coverage at increased cost to the taxpayer.

A Social Security tax withholding table is provided in the *Employers' Tax Guide.* A portion of this table is presented in Table 6.9 on p. 144. The tax to be withheld is to the right of the appropriate wage bracket in these tables. When a copy of the *Tax Guide* is not available or the payroll exceeds the table, *determine the amount of FICA tax to withhold by multiplying the amount of pay by the current tax rate.*

This text uses the 1980 withholding rate for FICA tax, which was 6.13% of the first $25,900 earned by each worker. The maximum FICA tax paid by any employee was $1,587.67 (.0613 × $25,900). Any income in excess of $25,900 is not taxable for FICA tax purposes. Table 6.8 shows the taxable wage base, tax rate, and maximum tax for the years 1980–87.

Table 6.8. FICA (Social Security) Taxes

Year	Taxable Wage	Tax Rate	Maximum Tax
1979	22,900	6.13	1,403.77
1980	25,900	6.13	1,587.67
1981	29,700	6.65	1,975.05
1982	31,800	6.70	2,130.60
1983	33,900*	6.70	2,271.30
1984	36,000*	6.70	2,412.00
1985	38,100*	7.05	2,686.05
1986	40,200*	7.15	2,874.30
1987	42,600*	7.15	3,045.90

*The taxable wage base is established by statute until 1983, when an automatic adjustment mechanism becomes effective. The figures shown for the years 1983–1987 are estimates.

Example: An employee earned $328.40 during the past week. How much should the payroll department withhold for FICA taxes?

Solution: $328.40 × 6.13% = $328.40 × .0613 = $20.13

Example: An employee earned $98.75 last week. How much FICA tax should be withheld?

Solution: $6.05 (Table 6.9)

To calculate the amount of FICA tax withholding on current earnings when new year-to-date accumulated earnings will exceed maximum FICA taxable income:

1. Determine *new* accumulated earnings (accumulated earnings + current earnings).
2. Determine FICA nontaxable income (new accumulated earnings − maximum FICA taxable income).
3. Determine FICA taxable income (current earnings − FICA nontaxable income).
4. Determine FICA withholding amount (FICA taxable income × 6.13%).

Table 6.9. Social Security Employee Tax Table
6.13 percent employee tax deductions

Wages		Tax to be withheld	Wages		Tax to be withheld	Wages		Tax to be withheld	Wages		Tax to be withheld
At least	But less than		At least	But less than		At least	But less than		At least	But less than	
$78.23	$78.39	$4.80	$84.26	$84.43	$5.17	$90.30	$90.46	$5.54	$96.33	$96.50	$5.91
78.39	78.55	4.81	84.43	84.59	5.18	90.46	90.62	5.55	96.50	96.66	5.92
78.55	78.72	4.82	84.59	84.75	5.19	90.62	90.79	5.56	96.66	96.82	5.93
78.72	78.88	4.83	84.75	84.92	5.20	90.79	90.95	5.57	96.82	96.99	5.94
78.88	79.04	4.84	84.92	85.08	5.21	90.95	91.11	5.58	96.99	97.15	5.95
79.04	79.21	4.85	85.08	85.24	5.22	91.11	91.28	5.59	97.15	97.31	5.96
79.21	79.37	4.86	85.24	85.40	5.23	91.28	91.44	5.60	97.31	97.48	5.97
79.37	79.53	4.87	85.40	85.57	5.24	91.44	91.60	5.61	97.48	97.64	5.98
79.53	79.70	4.88	85.57	85.73	5.25	91.60	91.77	5.62	97.64	97.80	5.99
79.70	79.86	4.89	85.73	85.89	5.26	91.77	91.93	5.63	97.80	97.97	6.00
79.86	80.02	4.90	85.89	86.06	5.27	91.93	92.09	5.64	97.97	98.13	6.01
80.02	80.18	4.91	86.06	86.22	5.28	92.09	92.26	5.65	98.13	98.29	6.02
80.18	80.35	4.92	86.22	86.38	5.29	92.26	92.42	5.66	98.29	98.46	6.03
80.35	80.51	4.93	86.38	86.55	5.30	92.42	92.58	5.67	98.46	98.62	6.04
80.51	80.67	4.94	86.55	86.71	5.31	92.58	92.75	5.68	98.62	98.78	6.05
80.67	80.84	4.95	86.71	86.87	5.32	92.75	92.91	5.69	98.78	98.94	6.06
80.84	81.00	4.96	86.87	87.04	5.33	92.91	93.07	5.70	98.94	99.11	6.07
81.00	81.16	4.97	87.04	87.20	5.34	93.07	93.24	5.71	99.11	99.27	6.08
81.16	81.33	4.98	87.20	87.36	5.35	93.24	93.40	5.72	99.27	99.43	6.09
81.33	81.49	4.99	87.36	87.53	5.36	93.40	93.56	5.73	99.43	99.60	6.10
81.49	81.65	5.00	87.53	87.69	5.37	93.56	93.72	5.74	99.60	99.76	6.11
81.65	81.82	5.01	87.69	87.85	5.38	93.72	93.89	5.75	99.76	99.92	6.12
81.82	81.98	5.02	87.85	88.01	5.39	93.89	94.05	5.76	99.92	100.00	6.13
81.98	82.14	5.03	88.01	88.18	5.40	94.05	94.21	5.77			
82.14	82.31	5.04	88.18	88.34	5.41	94.21	94.38	5.78			
82.31	82.47	5.05	88.34	88.50	5.42	94.38	94.54	5.79			
82.47	82.63	5.06	88.50	88.67	5.43	94.54	94.70	5.80			
82.63	82.79	5.07	88.67	88.83	5.44	94.70	94.87	5.81			
82.79	82.96	5.08	88.83	88.99	5.45	94.87	95.03	5.82			
82.96	83.12	5.09	88.99	89.16	5.46	95.03	95.19	5.83			
83.12	83.28	5.10	89.16	89.32	5.47	95.19	95.36	5.84			
83.28	83.45	5.11	89.32	89.48	5.48	95.36	95.52	5.85			
83.45	83.61	5.12	89.48	89.65	5.49	95.52	95.68	5.86			
83.61	83.77	5.13	89.65	89.81	5.50	95.68	95.85	5.87			
83.77	83.94	5.14	89.81	89.97	5.51	95.85	96.01	5.88			
83.94	84.10	5.15	89.97	90.14	5.52	96.01	96.17	5.89			
84.10	84.26	5.16	90.14	90.30	5.53	96.17	96.33	5.90			

The multiples of the withholding for FICA on $100 are

Wage	Tax to be withheld
$100	$6.13
200	12.26
300	18.39
400	24.52
500	30.65
600	36.78
700	42.91
800	49.04
900	55.17
1,000	61.30

Example: Mark Jones has year-to-date earnings of $24,200. His salary this month is $2,700. What will be his deduction for FICA tax?

Solution:

$24,200	accumulated earnings
+ 2,700	current earnings
$26,900	new accumulated earnings
− 25,900	maximum FICA taxable income
$ 1,000	nontaxable income (FICA)

$$\$2,700 - \$1,000 = \$1,700 \text{ taxable} \times .0613 = \$104.21$$

Other Deductions

As mentioned earlier, many other expenses may be deducted from an employee's payroll check. One of the most common deductions is for group insurance premiums—both life and hospitalization insurance. Other common deductions are for credit union payments or savings, saving bonds, contributions to charity, and union dues. Many states require employees to pay a state income tax, which is calculated very much like the federal income tax. Basically, anything can be deducted from an employee's paycheck as long as both employer and employee agree to the transaction.

The Payroll Register

A common tool used by a business when preparing payrolls is the payroll register. A payroll register is used to organize information and calculate gross earnings, withholdings, and net earnings for each employee. An example of a weekly payroll register with entries for an hourly employee and a salaried employee is shown in Table 6.10 on p. 146.

The hourly employee, Wesley Ames, is married and claims three exemptions. He worked 42 hours during the past week and earns $7.50 per hour. His deductions include income tax, FICA tax, $15 for a credit union deposit, and $36.22 for a hospitalization insurance premium.

The salaried employee, Lou Reagan, is single and claims one exemption. She earned a salary of $310 during the past week. Her deductions include income tax, FICA tax, and $27.48 for the hospital insurance premium.

The accuracy of the information in the payroll register should be verified when the register is completed. To verify the entries in the pay columns, add the total of the *Regular Pay* and *Overtime Pay* columns. The sum of

Table 6.10. Payroll Register

Employee	Hours Worked	Rate	Weekly Salary	M/S[1]	Exemp- tions	Regular Pay	Overtime Pay	Gross Pay	Deductions						Net Pay
									FIT[2]	FICA[3]	HI[4]	CU[5]	Total		
Ames	42	$7.50		M	3	300.00	22.50	322.50	41.00	19.77	36.22	15	111.99		210.51
Reagan			$310	S	1	310.00	–0–	310.00	59.40	19.00	27.48		105.88		204.12
						610.00	22.50	632.50	100.40	38.77	63.70	15	217.87		414.63

1. Married/Single
2. Federal Income Tax
3. Social Security Tax
4. Hospitalization Insurance
5. Credit Union

these columns should agree with the *Gross Pay* column total. To verify the accuracy of the entries for deductions, add these column totals and compare with the *Total* deductions column. To verify the entries in the *Net Pay* column, subtract the *Total* deductions from *Gross Pay.*

The information contained in the payroll register is the type of information that is frequently handled by computers in most large businesses. However, there are still hundreds of small businesses that maintain these records by hand.

Information necessary for filing the *Employer's Quarterly Federal Tax Return* (Figure 6.1 on p. 148) can be obtained from the payroll register. This quarterly report must be filed on or before the last day of the month following the end of the calendar quarter.

Exercises

Determine the amount to withhold for federal income tax from the weekly pay of the following taxpayers. Use the appropriate table to find the answer.

	Employee	Weekly Earnings	Marital Status	Exemptions	Federal Income Tax Deduction
1.	Clark, Ed	$304	M	5	
2.	Franks, Jane	$180	S	1	
3.	Harris, Bob	$413	M	4	55.50
4.	Jones, John	$316	M	3	
5.	Martin, C. A.	$168	S	2	
6.	Price, Mary	$312	S	1	58.10

Using a rate of 6.13%, determine the amount to withhold for FICA taxes from the weekly earnings of the following employees. None of the employees have reached the maximum amount of earnings subject to the tax.

	Employee	Weekly Earnings	FICA Tax Deduction
7.	Clark, Ed	$304	
8.	Franks, Jane	$180	
9.	Harris, Bob	$413	
10.	Jones, John	$216	
11.	Martin, C. A.	$168	
12.	Price, Mary	$312	

Figure 6.1. Employer's Quarterly Federal Tax Return

Form **941**
(Rev. April 1980)
Department of the Treasury
Internal Revenue Service

Employer's Quarterly Federal Tax Return

Your name, address, employer identification number, and calendar quarter of return. (If not correct, please change)

Name (as distinguished from trade name)

Trade name, if any

Address and ZIP code

Date quarter ended

Employer identification number

T		
FF		
FD		
FP		
I		
T		

If address is different from prior return, check here ▶

1 Number of employees (except household) employed in the pay period that includes March 12th (complete for first quarter only) . . . .

2 Total wages and tips subject to withholding, plus other compensation . . . . ⟶

3 Total income tax withheld from wages, tips, annuities, gambling, etc. . . . .

4 Adjustment of withheld income tax for preceding quarters of calendar year . . . .

5 Adjusted total of income tax withheld . . . . ⟶

6 Taxable FICA wages paid . . . . $................. multiplied by 12.26% =TAX . .

7 Taxable tips reported . . . . $................. multiplied by 6.13% =TAX . .

8 Total FICA taxes (add lines 6 and 7) . . . . ⟶

9 Adjustment of FICA taxes (see instructions) . . . .

10 Adjusted total of FICA taxes . . . . ⟶

11 Total taxes (add lines 5 and 10) . . . .

12 Advance earned income credit (EIC) payments, if any (see instructions) . . . .

13 Net taxes (subtract line 12 from line 11) . . . .

Record of Federal Tax Deposits (See instructions on page 4)

Deposit period ending:	I. Tax liability for period	II. Date of deposit	III. Amount deposited
Overpayment from previous quarter. . . .			
First month of quarter 1st through 7th day			
8th through 15th day			
16th through 22d day			
23d through last day			
A First month total . . . . [A]			
Second month of quarter 1st through 7th day			
8th through 15th day			
16th through 22d day			
23d through last day			
B Second month total . . . . [B]			
Third month of quarter 1st through 7th day			
8th through 15th day			
16th through 22d day			
23d through last day			
C Third month total . . . . [C]			
D Total for quarter (add items A, B, and C) .			
E Final deposit made for quarter. (Enter zero if the final deposit made for the quarter is included in item D)			

14 Total deposits for quarter (including final deposit made for quarter) and overpayment from previous quarter. (See instructions for deposit requirements on page 4.)

Note: *If undeposited taxes at the end of the quarter are $200 or more, deposit the full amount with an authorized financial institution or a Federal Reserve bank according to the instructions on the back of the Federal Tax Deposit Form 501. Enter this deposit in the Record of Federal Tax Deposits and include it on line 14.*

15 Undeposited taxes due (subtract line 14 from line 13—this should be less than $200). Pay to Internal Revenue Service and enter here . . . . ⟶

16 If line 14 is more than line 13, enter overpayment here ▶ $................ and check if to be: ☐ Applied to next return, or ☐ Refunded.

17 Number of Forms W–4 enclosed. Do not send originals. (See General and Specific Instructions.) . . . .

18 If you are not liable for returns in the future, write "FINAL" (see instructions) ▶   Date final wages paid ▶

Under penalties of perjury, I declare that I have examined this return, including accompanying schedules and statements, and to the best of my knowledge and belief it is true, correct, and complete.

Date ▶   Signature ▶   Title ▶

Please file this form with your Internal Revenue Service Center (see instructions on "Where to File").

Form **941** (Rev. 4–80)

Prepare the payroll register for the Richland Company for the week ending January 18. Time and a half is paid for hours over 40 per week. Use the appropriate wage bracket table to determine the withholding for federal income taxes (FIT). Use a rate of 6.13% to determine the deductions for FICA taxes. Deductions for hospitalization insurance (HI) include: Abbot, $28.43; Harris, $28.43; Jenson, $18.60; Potter, $28.43; and Stewart, $18.60. Deductions for credit union (CU) deposits include: Deen, $10.00; Nelson, $10.00; and Reagan, $20.00. Deductions for retirement plan payments (RP) include: George, $25.00; and Nelson, $15.00. What is the net pay for each employee?

	Employee	Hours Worked	Rate	Weekly Salary	Marital Status	Exemptions
13.	Abbot	44	$7.50		M	4
14.	Deen	40	$8.25		M	2
15.	George			$290	S	1
16.	Harris	46	$6.75		M	0
17.	Jenson	32	$8.00		S	1
18.	Nelson			$360	M	5
19.	Potter	43	$7.25		M	3
20.	Reagan			$265	S	1
21.	Stewart			$287	S	0

Determine the amount to withhold for federal income taxes for the following weekly payroll. Use the percentage method when computing the deductions.

	Employee	Marital Status	Weekly Earnings	Exemptions	Federal Income Tax Withheld
22.	Clark	M	$320	5	__________
23.	Harris	M	$410	4	__________
24.	Franks	S	$210	1	__________
25.	Jones	S	$280	2	__________

Prepare the payroll register for the Richland Company for the week ending March 31. Time and a half is paid for hours over 40 per week. Use the appropriate wage bracket table to determine the withholding for federal income taxes (FIT). Use a rate of 6.13% to figure the deductions for FICA taxes. Deductions for hospitalization insurance (HI) include: Abbot, $28.43; Harris, $28.43; Jenson, $18.60; and Potter $28.43. Deductions for credit union (CU) deposits include: Deen, $10.00; and Reagan, $20.00. Deductions for retirement plan payments (RP) include: George, $25.00; and Nelson, $15.00. What is the net pay for each employee?

	Employee	Hours Worked	Rate	Weekly Salary	Marital Status	Exemptions
26.	Abbot	40	$7.50		M	4
27.	Deen	45	$8.25		M	2
28.	George			$315	M	2
29.	Harris	44	$7.10		M	0
30.	Jackson			$275	S	1
31.	Jenson	37	$8.15		S	1
32.	Nelson			$380	M	5
33.	Potter	40	$7.90		M	4
34.	Reagan			$265	S	1

Determine the amount to withhold for federal income taxes for the following monthly payroll. Use the percentage method in computing the deductions.

	Employee	Marital Status	Monthly Earnings	Exemptions	Federal Income Tax Withheld
35.	Martin	M	$ 740	2	__________
36.	Price	S	$1,352	1	__________
37.	Smith	S	$ 780	2	__________
38.	Wright	M	$ 893	6	__________

Practical Applications

(Use the wage bracket method for finding the federal income tax unless otherwise specified in the problem. All employees participate in Social Security.)

39. An advertising executive receives a monthly salary of $2,350. The company has biweekly payroll periods. How much is deducted from her salary for FICA taxes?

40. An accounting clerk earns $5.80 per hour. He is married and claims two exemptions. How much was deducted from his earnings for income taxes for a week in which he worked 40 hours?

41. Bill is employed as a buyer in a department store. His annual salary is $18,000. He is married and claims three exemptions. His employer has weekly payroll periods. His earnings are subject to deductions for income taxes, FICA taxes, group health and life insurance premiums ($43), and retirement ($38). What is his net pay for the previous week?

42. Betty is treasurer of a real estate investment company and earns a salary of $22,100 annually. She is married and claims only one exemption. Her company has a weekly payroll. Her earnings are subject to deductions for income taxes, FICA taxes, group health and life insurance premiums ($27), and retirement ($33). What is her net pay for the previous week?

43. Jim Wilson is married and claims a total of four exemptions. So far this year, Jim has earned $24,300. This month's gross pay is $2,875. Using the percentage method, calculate Jim's net pay for this month.

44. Arthur is an accountant who made $1,700 this month. Using the wage bracket method, determine how much income tax should be withheld if he is married and claims two exemptions.

45. Pam, a CPA, earns $1,525 a month, is married, and claims only one exemption. Calculate her take-home pay using the wage bracket method for income tax and 6.13% for FICA tax. She also pays $50 each month into a savings account at her credit union and pays $38.50 toward her insurance premium.

46. Richard earns $30,000 a year and is paid monthly. He is single and claims two exemptions. Calculate his net pay for the month of November. Use the wage bracket method for withholding.

47. Theresa Rodriguez is an account executive with a small advertising agency and receives a monthly salary of $2,650. Her earnings to date

(prior to this check) are $24,700. She is married, claims no exemptions, and has a $37.50 insurance premium and FICA tax deducted from her check each month. Use the percentage method to determine her take-home pay.

48. Using the percentage method, calculate Raymond's weekly take-home pay. Raymond has a salary of $18,800, is married, claims four exemptions, and is paid weekly. His weekly deductions include insurance ($15), union dues ($5), credit union ($25), FICA tax, and federal income tax.

Chapter 6
Self-Evaluation

Find the earnings for each of the following. Time and a half is paid for hours worked in excess of 40 hours per week.

1. Salary, $22,620 a year; pay period, monthly; monthly earnings, __________

2. Salary, $1,600 a month; pay period, biweekly; biweekly earnings, __________

3. Wage, $7.80 per hour; hours worked, 40; weekly earnings, __________

4. Wage, $8.25 per hour; hours worked, 42; time and a half is paid for hours over 40 per week; weekly earnings, __________

5. Wage, $2.65 per hour plus $3.00 for each trimmer assembled; hours, 40; trimmers, 50; earnings, __________

6. Commission, 5% on first $10,000 and 8% on remainder; sales, $15,700; earnings, __________

7. Joe is an editor for a publishing company and earns $32,000 a year. He is married and claims five exemptions. His company has a monthly payroll. His earnings are subject to deductions for federal

income tax (use the percentage method), FICA tax (6.13% rate), group health and life insurance ($57), and retirement ($70). What is his net pay for the month?

8. Kim Smith is a buyer for a department store and earns a monthly salary of $1,365. The company has a weekly payroll period. She is single and claims only one exemption.
   (a) Determine the deduction for federal income tax using the wage bracket method.
   (b) Determine the deduction for FICA tax using a 6.13% rate.

9. John's accumulated earnings through November 30 totaled $24,900. How much FICA tax will be deducted from John's December check of $2,417?

Chapter 7
Depreciation

Depreciation is the gradual loss in value of a company's plant assets. Since this loss in value means that, in time, these assets will either be sold at a lower value or will have to be replaced, depreciation is one of the most important items of business expense.

This chapter will provide an opportunity for you to become acquainted with an important phase of accounting—computing depreciation. It will introduce you to the principal methods of computing depreciation, including straight-line, units-of-production, sum-of-the-years-digits, and declining-balance, and thus prepare you for studies in accounting and several other business subjects. A knowledge of the process of depreciation is very important in most career areas in business.

This chapter will enable you to:

1. **explain the meaning of depreciation**

2. **identify and distinguish among the depreciation methods**

3. **perform calculations involving the various depreciation methods**

4. **determine the amount of accumulated depreciation and the book value of a plant asset**

5. **prepare depreciation schedules**

Learning Unit 7.1
Depreciation Based on Years of Service Life (Straight-Line Method)

Assets

Properties owned by a business are called assets. An *asset* is any physical thing (tangible asset) or right (intangible asset) that has a money value. Assets have value because of the benefits that can be received from them.

Two broad categories of assets are (1) current assets and (2) long-term assets. A *current asset* is any asset that may reasonably be expected to be realized in cash, sold, or consumed within a year. Current assets include cash, accounts receivable, merchandise inventory, etc.

Long-term assets provide benefits to a firm that extend beyond one year. One important group of long-term assets are *plant assets,* which are also called *fixed assets.* Plant assets include vehicles, buildings, equipment, land, and other tangible resources that have a life in excess of one year and are used in the normal operations of the business.

All plant assets, with the exception of land, gradually wear out or otherwise lose their usefulness with the passage of time; they are said to depreciate. *Depreciation* is the process of allocating the cost of a plant asset as an expense during the asset's estimated service life.

Understanding the Concept of Depreciation

Why do plant assets depreciate? Plant assets depreciate because of physical wear and tear, technological obsolescence, and/or economic obsolescence.

When is depreciation computed? Depreciation may be computed monthly, quarterly, or at the end of the business year. A business that prepares interim (monthly or quarterly) financial statements will compute depreciation monthly or quarterly. A business that does not prepare interim financial statements will compute depreciation annually. All of the problems in this chapter will involve year-end computations.

What factors are involved in determining the amount of depreciation to recognize during an accounting period? Three factors should be considered:

1. the total cost of the asset
2. the estimated service or useful life of the asset
3. the estimated market value (residual, scrap, salvage, trade-in, or liquidation value) of the asset at the end of its service life

How is the total cost of a plant asset determined? The cost of a plant asset includes the purchase price as well as all expenditures necessary to get the asset in place and ready for use. Typical costs, including sales tax, transportation charges, insurance charges, and installation costs, are added to the purchase price to determine the total cost of a plant asset.

How is depreciation computed? The four principal methods of computing depreciation are straight-line, units-of-production, sum-of-the-years-digits, and declining-balance. Each of these methods will be discussed in this chapter.

Straight-Line Method

The straight-line method of depreciation is the simplest and most frequently used method for financial accounting. Under this method, depreciation is based on years of service life. The loss in value of an asset is divided equally among the years of useful or service life, resulting in equal periodic charges to depreciation expense over the estimated service or useful life of the asset.

To compute depreciation (d) using the straight-line method:

1. Determine the total cost (*c*) of the plant asset.
2. Estimate the years of service or useful life of the asset.
3. Estimate the scrap value (*s*) of the asset.
4. Determine the amount to be depreciated over the life of the asset (total cost − scrap value).
5. Multiply the amount to be depreciated by the annual straight-line depreciation rate (*r*).

This procedure can be summarized in the basic formula for straight-line depreciation:

$$d = (c - s) \times r$$

In this formula, d = the annual depreciation, c = the cost of the asset, s = the scrap value or estimated market value of the asset at the end of its useful life, and r = the annual depreciation rate.

The life of a plant asset can be expressed as a rate. The straight-line depreciation rate for a plant asset is determined by dividing 100% by the number of years of estimated useful life:

$$r = \frac{100\%}{\text{number of years of estimated useful life}}$$

For instance, the annual straight-line depreciation rate for an asset with an estimated life of five years is 20% (100% ÷ 5 = 20%).

Example: The total cost of a machine purchased by the Richland Supply Company was $10,600. The useful life of the asset is estimated to be five years. The scrap value is estimated to be $600. What is the amount of annual depreciation using the straight-line method?[1]

Solution: $d = (c - s) \times r$

$r = 100\% \div$ estimated useful life
$r = 100\% \div 5 = 20\%$, or .2
$d = (\$10,600 - \$600) \times .2$
$d = \$10,000 \times .2 = \$2,000$

The straight-line method of computing depreciation provides a reasonable allocation of costs when usage of the asset is relatively uniform from period to period. Table 7.1 shows the amount of annual depreciation, using the straight-line method, for the machine purchased by the Richland Supply Company. The schedule includes a year zero to show the initial cost of the machine.

Book Value. Plant assets are reported in financial statements at their book value. The *book value* of a plant asset is the cost less total depreciation accumulated up to that time. The book value of the Richland Supply Company machine at the end of the asset's estimated service life of five years is $600 ($10,600 cost − $10,000 accumulated depreciation). An asset can only be depreciated to the estimated *residual* (or *scrap*) *value*. An asset that remains in use beyond the estimated service life should remain on the company's books at the estimated residual value ($600 in our example).

Partial-Year Depreciation Computation. If a plant asset is acquired during the year, less than a full year's depreciation is computed for the first and last years of the service life. Normally, the first day of a month is used in computing depreciation for all plant assets placed in service or retired from service during the first half of the month. The last day of the month is used when the asset was piaced in service or retired during the last half of the month.

[1]Note that these same facts will be used in all the examples throughout the entire chapter.

Table 7.1 Straight-Line Depreciation Schedule

Year	Cost	Depreciation Expense	Accumulated Depreciation	Book Value
0	$10,600	$ –0–	$ –0–	$10,600
1	10,600	2,000	2,000	8,600
2	10,600	2,000	4,000	6,600
3	10,600	2,000	6,000	4,600
4	10,600	2,000	8,000	2,600
5	10,600	2,000	10,000	600

Example: Assume that the Richland Supply Company (see preceding example) purchased the machine on February 14, 1981. How much of the machine's cost should be allocated to depreciation expense for the year 1981? (Notice that depreciation is computed for 11 months.)

Solution: $d = (c - s) \times r$
$d = (\$10,600 - \$600) \times .2$
$d = \$10,000 \times .2$
$d = \$2,000$

$$\text{Depreciation for 1981} = \$2,000 \times \frac{11}{12} = \$1,833.33, \text{ or}$$

$1,833

Exercises

Find the amount to be depreciated and the annual depreciation for each of the following plant assets. Use the straight-line method of computing depreciation.

	Cost	Residual Value	Estimated Service Life
1.	$ 4,300	$ 300	4 years
2.	10,800	800	5 years
3.	19,250	750	8 years
4.	20,175	600	5 years
5.	22,989	1,200	6 years
6.	35,674	3,400	7 years

Determine the number of months to use for depreciation purposes for plant assets purchased on the following dates. The accounting year ends on the date indicated.

	Date Asset Was Purchased	Ending Date of Accounting Year
7.	August 19	December 31
8.	March 11	June 30
9.	January 27	December 31
10.	July 18	August 31
11.	December 3	September 30
12.	February 21	January 31

How much first-year depreciation expense should be reported on the income statement for each of the following plant assets? The income statement is for the year ended December 31. Use the straight-line method of computing depreciation.

	Cost	Residual Value	Service Life	Purchase Date
13.	$10,300	$ 700	8 years	September 25
14.	13,800	1,800	5 years	March 7
15.	21,100	3,500	7 years	July 19
16.	36,509	5,000	6 years	May 12
17.	49,191	3,700	9 years	October 3
18.	56,866	4,300	$4\frac{1}{2}$ years	August 21

Practical Applications

19. Prepare a straight-line depreciation schedule for a delivery truck. The truck cost $8,300 and has an estimated life of five years and an estimated residual value of $800.

20. Jim Gomez, a real estate major at Central College, recently purchased an automobile for $7,752. He is entitled to deduct depreciation on his income tax for use of the car in his business. He estimates the useful life of the car as three years with an estimated trade-in value of $3,300. How much will he be able to deduct each year on his income tax report for depreciation expense if he uses the straight-line method of computing depreciation?

21. A manufacturing representative purchased a photocopying machine for use in his home office. He paid $1,576 for the machine and estimates the useful life to be 10 years with a residual value of $350. Using the straight-line method, how much depreciation expense should the agent record for the first year?

22. A vending machine cost $473. After two years, the accumulated depreciation is $100. What is the book value?

23. A typewriter originally cost $865. The estimated useful life is five years with an estimated trade-in value of $65. The straight-line method is used to compute depreciation. How much depreciation should be recorded at the end of the third year?

24. A desk calculator cost $320 and currently has a book value of $192. How much depreciation has accumulated on the machine?

25. The Hi-Fi Manufacturing Company purchased a machine that had a list price of $8,654. The company incurred the following expenditures to get the machine in place and ready for use: sales tax, 5%; freight charges, $352; and insurance charges, $36. What was the total cost of the machine?

26. A real estate broker purchased a new automobile for $9,895. She estimates the useful life of the car as four years with an estimated trade-in value of $3,500. Using the straight-line method, how much depreciation expense can she deduct each year? What is the annual depreciation rate? What is the book value at the end of the second year?

27. The Cleanrite Cleaners purchased a desk for $919 on October 6. The owner estimates that the desk will have a useful life of 10 years and a trade-in value of $100. The company uses the straight-line method to depreciate all assets. The accounting period for the company ends on December 31. How much depreciation expense should be recorded for the first fiscal year? What is the annual depreciation rate? What is the book value at the end of the second year?

28. Prepare a straight-line depreciation schedule for a machine that cost $16,800. The machine has an estimated service life of 6 years with a residual value of $1,200.

Learning Unit 7.2
Depreciation Based on Productive Capacity (Units-of-Production Method)

Each accounting period in which an asset is used should be charged with a *fair share* of the asset's cost. The straight-line method charges an equal share of the cost of the asset to each accounting period. However, allocating an equal share of an asset's cost to each accounting period may sometimes violate the fair share concept. In some businesses, the use of certain plant assets varies from one accounting period to another. For instance, a highway construction firm may use a road-grading machine for a few weeks and then leave the machine idle for a long period of time.

The *units-of-production* depreciation method attempts to allocate the cost of a plant asset based on *actual* use. Under this method, the estimated life of the asset is computed in terms of the asset's productive capacity rather than in terms of its years of life. The productive capacity of a plant asset may be expressed in terms of hours, miles, number of operations, number of units produced, etc. The depreciation per unit of production is obtained by dividing the amount to be depreciated by the estimated potential number of productive units for the asset.

To compute depreciation (d) using the units-of-production method:

1. Determine the total cost (c) of the plant asset.
2. Estimate the asset's productive capacity.
3. Estimate the scrap value (s) of the asset.
4. Determine the amount to be depreciated over the life of the asset (total cost − residual value).
5. Determine the depreciation per unit of output (amount to be depreciated ÷ units of productive capacity).
6. Multiply the total number of units of production during the accounting period by the depreciation per unit.

This procedure can be summarized in the basic formulas for units-of-production depreciation:

$$d \text{ per unit} = \frac{c - s}{\text{units of productive capacity}}$$

$$d \text{ for year} = d \text{ per unit} \times \text{total units}$$

In these formulas (as in the formula for straight-line depreciation), d = depreciation, c = total cost of the asset, and s = scrap or residual value.

Example: Assume that the estimated productive capacity of the Richland Supply Company machine is 100,000 widgets. How much should the company charge to depreciation expense for a year in which 15,000 widgets were produced?

Solution:

$$d \text{ per unit} = \frac{c - s}{\text{units of productive capacity}}$$

$$d \text{ per unit} = \frac{\$10,600 - \$600}{100,000} = \$.10$$

$$d \text{ for year} = d \text{ per unit} \times \text{total units}$$

$$d \text{ for year} = \$.10 \times 15,000 = \$1,500$$

Exercises

Compute the amount to be depreciated, the depreciation per hour, and the annual depreciation for the following plant assets.

	Cost	Residual Value	Estimated Life (Hours)	Hours Used Last Year
1.	$ 6,450	$ 450	10,000	1,342
2.	42,100	700	7,500	708
3.	67,500	4,500	50,000	5,347
4.	68,050	10,000	135,000	8,901
5.	207,245	25,000	63,500	2,044
6.	57,000	5,000	325,000	46,250

Compute the amount to be depreciated, the depreciation per mile, and the annual depreciation for the following plant assets.

	Cost	Residual Value	Estimated Life (Miles)	Miles Driven Last Year
7.	$ 57,000	$7,000	100,000	2,166
8.	4,175	1,200	85,000	17,203
9.	162,100	4,600	250,000	39,112
10.	3,690	400	90,000	8,674
11.	9,375	750	125,000	26,307
12.	10,960	1,100	170,000	1,865

Practical Applications

13. The Global Cosmetics Company has an airplane that has an expected life of 10,000 flight hours. The company uses the units-of-production method to compute depreciation. The airplane cost $450,000 and has an estimated market value of $150,000 at the end of its service life. How much depreciation should the company record for a year in which the plane was flown 520 hours?

14. A manufacturer purchased a machine at a cost of $395,250. The machine has an estimated productive capacity of 75,000 units and an estimated salvage value of zero. Under the units-of-production method, what is the amount of depreciation for a year in which 10,500 units were produced on the machine?

15. A vending company purchased a delivery truck on September 24, at a cost of $6,795. The life of the truck is estimated at five years or 100,000 miles with a trade-in value of $700. The truck was driven 7,200 miles during the first year, which ended December 31. Using the straight-line method, how much depreciation should be recorded for the first year? Using the units-of-production method, how much depreciation expense should the company record for the first year?

16. A business purchased a truck at a cost of $9,720 on March 4. The truck is estimated to have a service life of four years or 13,500 miles. A trade-in value of zero is anticipated. The accounting year for the firm ends on December 31. During the first year the asset was driven 4,108 miles. Under the straight-line method, how much depreciation

expense should the firm recognize during the first year? Under the units-of-production method, how much depreciation expense should the firm recognize during the first year?

Learning Unit 7.3
Accelerated Depreciation— Sum-of-the-Years-Digits Method

Characteristics of Accelerated Depreciation Methods

In general, a business is not required to use any particular method of depreciation; it may use any method that is systematic and rational. All the methods described in this chapter meet those criteria. The method of depreciation selected by a firm usually is based on whether the pattern of depreciation charges seems reasonable for the asset and the company. It is permissible to use one method for tax purposes and another method for the financial statements.

The units-of-production method (discussed in the preceding unit) may be adopted when the use of the asset varies from period to period. The straight-line method (discussed in Learning Unit 7.1), which depreciates the same amount each year, is satisfactory when the use of the asset is uniform from period to period.

However, some plant assets lose value more quickly in their earlier years than in their later years and therefore do not depreciate the same amount each year. Accelerated methods of computing depreciation are based on the concept that the more valuable portion of the services of some plant assets is received in the early years of the life of the asset. When an accelerated method of depreciation is used, the loss in value of an asset or depreciation is not divided equally among the years. Instead, more depreciation is charged as an expense in the early life of an asset and lesser amounts as the asset gets older. The accelerated methods are often used for tax purposes because more depreciation expense can be charged off during the early years of the asset's life.

In addition, accelerated methods of depreciation can reflect a more realistic apportionment of depreciation. If for some reason an asset must be disposed of earlier than expected, the book value on a straight-line depreciation schedule may be considerably higher than the actual market value.

There are two accelerated methods of computing depreciation: sum-of-the-years-digits method and declining-balance method. The sum-of-the-years-digits method is covered in this learning unit and the declining-balance method in the next learning unit.

Sum-of-the-Years-Digits Method

To compute depreciation (d) using the sum-of-the-years-digits method:

1. Determine the total cost (c) of the asset.
2. Estimate the years of service or useful life of the asset.
3. Estimate the scrap value (s) of the asset.
4. Determine the sum of the years digits.
5. Determine the fraction for the year involved.
6. Multiply the amount to be depreciated by the appropriate fraction.

As it is for the straight-line method, the basic formula to use to obtain annual depreciation under the sum-of-the-years-digits method is:

$$d = (c - s) \times r$$

Unlike the straight-line method, the rate for the sum-of-the-years-digits method is expressed as a different—and smaller—fraction for each year. The numerator of the decreasing fraction changes each year and represents the number of years of estimated useful life remaining at the beginning of the year for which depreciation is being computed. In the first year, the numerator is equal to the number of years over which the plant asset is to be depreciated. In the second year, the numerator is one less; in the third year, two less, and so on. For instance, if the estimated useful life of an asset is five years, the numerator for the fraction in the fourth year would be 2.

The denominator of the fraction remains the same each year and represents the sum of the digits representing the useful life of the asset. There are two methods for obtaining the value for the denominator of the fraction:

1. Add all of the years of the estimated life of the asset, or
2. Use the following formula in which s equals the sum of the years digits and n equals the number of years of estimated useful life:

$$s = \frac{n(n + 1)}{2}$$

Example: Compute the sum of the years digits (denominator of sum-of-the-years-digits fraction) for a machine acquired by the Richland Supply Company if the estimated useful life is five years.

Solution: Method (1): Sum of the years digits $= 1 + 2 + 3 + 4 + 5 = 15$

Method (2): Sum of the years digits $= \dfrac{5(5 + 1)}{2} = \dfrac{5 \times 6}{2} = \dfrac{30}{2} = 15$

Example: The total cost of a machine acquired by the Richland Supply Company was $10,600. The estimated service or useful life of the machine is five years. The estimated scrap value is $600. If the machine was acquired on the first day of the company's fiscal year (business year), how much depreciation expense should be recorded each year of the machine's service life using the sum-of-the-years-digits method? Prepare a depreciation schedule.

Solution: $10,600 − $600 = $10,000 amount to be depreciated.

Year	Amount to be Depreciated	Depreciation Fraction	Annual Depreciation
1	$10,000	$\times \frac{5}{15} =$	$3,333.33 first year
2	$10,000	$\times \frac{4}{15} =$	$2,666.67 second year
3	$10,000	$\times \frac{3}{15} =$	$2,000.00 third year
4	$10,000	$\times \frac{2}{15} =$	$1,333.33 fourth year
5	$10,000	$\times \frac{1}{15} =$	$ 666.67 fifth year
15	sum of the years digits		

Sum-of-the-Years-Digits Depreciation Schedule

Year	Cost	Depreciation Expense	Accumulated Depreciation	Book Value
0	$10,600	$ –0–	$ –0–	$10,600.00
1	10,600	3,333.33	3,333.33	7,266.67
2	10,600	2,666.67	6,000.00	4,600.00
3	10,600	2,000.00	8,000.00	2,600.00
4	10,600	1,333.33	9,333.33	1,266.67
5	10,600	666.67	10,000.00	600.00

Exercises

What is the sum-of-the-years-digits depreciation fraction for the first year for assets with the following estimated lives?

1. 3 years
2. 4 years
3. 6 years
4. 8 years
5. 9 years
6. 12 years
7. 15 years
8. 25 years

Practical Applications

Determine the first year's depreciation and the book value at the end of the first year for the following assets. Use the sum-of-the-years-digits depreciation method. The assets were acquired on January 1 and the accounting year ends on December 31.

9. An office machine purchased by ABC Nursery for $1,752 has an estimated useful life of eight years and an estimated residual value of $100.

10. A delivery truck purchased by Speedy Delivery Service for $7,560 has an estimated service life of four years with an estimated trade-in value of $1,300.

11. Fred's Bookkeeping Service purchased a typewriter for $852. The machine has an estimated service life of five years and an estimated trade-in value of $150.

12. The Universal Construction Company purchased a road grader for $47,250. The machine has an estimated useful life of seven years and an estimated trade-in value of $12,000.

Using the sum-of-the-years-digits method, prepare a depreciation schedule for the following assets.

13. The Hi-Fi Manufacturing Company purchased a machine that cost $9,474.70. The estimated life of the machine is four years and the estimated residual value is $1,000.

14. A real estate broker purchased an automobile for $8,752 on January 1. He is entitled to deduct depreciation on his income tax (for the year ended December 31) for use of the car in his business. He estimates the useful life of the car as three years with an estimated trade-in value of $3,300.

15. The Big State Construction Company acquired a tractor-trailer at a cost of $71,340. The estimated useful life of the equipment is five years with an estimated trade-in value of $23,000.

16. Tri-State Chemical Company purchased a forklift truck for $24,600. The estimated useful life of the equipment is eight years with an estimated trade-in value of $4,000.

Learning Unit 7.4
Accelerated Depreciation— Double-Declining-Balance Method

Another way to compute accelerated depreciation so that the greatest annual depreciation may be deducted in the early years of the life of an asset is to use one of the declining-balance methods. Declining-balance methods use a rate of 125%, 150%, or another percent—up to a maximum of 200%—of the straight-line rate.

The double-declining-balance method uses the maximum rate: 200% of the straight-line rate, or twice the straight-line rate. Since the straight-line depreciation rate = 100% ÷ number of years of estimated useful life, we can say that the double-declining-balance rate = 100% ÷ number of years of estimated useful life × 2.

Unlike the other depreciation methods, the scrap or residual value is not subtracted from the cost of an asset in computing depreciation when using a declining-balance method. To calculate depreciation for the first year, the *original cost* (not cost less residual value) is multiplied by the declining-balance rate. In subsequent years, the decreasing balance (book value of the asset) is multiplied by the declining-balance rate to determine the amount of depreciation to record. As was true with the other depreciation methods, the asset can only be depreciated to the estimated residual value ($600 in our example). The difference between the declining-balance method and the other three methods is that the residual value is not a factor in the computations until the last period of the asset's depreciable life because it is the depreciation limit.

The formula to use in obtaining the annual depreciation for a declining-balance method is:

$$d = bv \times r$$
Annual depreciation = book value × declining-balance rate, or

To compute depreciation using the double-declining-balance depreciation method:

1. Determine the total cost (c) of the asset.
2. Estimate the service life of the asset.
3. Determine the double-declining-balance rate (r) (straight-line rate × 2).

4. Multiply the original cost by the double-declining-balance rate to obtain first-year depreciation.
5. Multiply the book value of the asset by the double-declining-balance rate to obtain depreciation for subsequent years.

Example: The total cost of the machine acquired by the Richland Supply Company was $10,600. The estimated service life of the machine is five years. The estimated residual value is $600. If the machine was acquired on January 1 and the company's accounting year ends on December 31, how much depreciation expense should be recorded each year using the double-declining-balance method? Prepare a depreciation schedule.

Solution: $r = \dfrac{100\%}{\text{number of years of estimated useful life}} \times 2$

$$r = \frac{100\%}{5} \times 2$$

$r = 40\%$ double-declining-balance rate

Year	Book Value	Rate	Depreciation
1	$10,600.00	$\times$ 40% =	$4,240.00
2	$ 6,360.00 ($10,600.00 − $4,240.00) $\times$ 40% =		$2,544.00
3	$ 3,816.00 ($ 6,360.00 − $2,544.00) $\times$ 40% =		$1,526.40
4	$ 2,289.60 ($ 3,816.00 − $1,526.40) $\times$ 40% =		$ 915.84
5	$ 1,373.76 ($ 2,289.60 − $ 915.84) $\times$ 40% =		$ 549.50[1]

Double-Declining-Balance Depreciation Schedule

Year	Cost	Depreciation Expense	Depreciation	Book Value
0	$10,600.00	$ −0−	$ −0−	$10,600.00
1	10,600.00	4,240.00	4,240.00	6,360.00
2	10,600.00	2,544.00	6,784.00	3,816.00
3	10,600.00	1,526.40	8,310.40	2,289.60
4	10,600.00	915.84	9,226.24	1,373.76
5	10,600.00	549.50	9,775.74	824.26*

*Depreciation continues until the asset is disposed of or until the book value declines to the residual value.

[1]The book value at the end of the fifth year is $824.26 ($1,373.76 − $549.50). Depreciation continues until the asset is disposed of or until the book value declines to the residual value.

Comparison of Depreciation Methods

The following is a summary of depreciation methods formulas where

d = depreciation
c = cost
s = scrap value
r = rate
bv = book value
n = number of years of estimated useful life

Straight-Line

$$d \text{ (for year)} = (c - s) \times r$$

$$d \begin{pmatrix} \text{for partial} \\ \text{year} \end{pmatrix} = \frac{\text{months in service}}{12} \times d \text{ (for year)}$$

$$r = \frac{100\%}{\text{number of years of estimated useful life}}$$

$$bv = c - d \text{ (accumulated)}$$

Units-of-Production

$$\text{Per unit: } d = \frac{c - s}{\text{units of productive capacity}}$$

$$\text{For year: } d = d \text{ per unit} \times \text{total units}$$

Sum of the Years Digits

$$d = (c - s) \times r$$

$$r = \frac{\text{number of years of remaining useful life}}{\text{sum of digits of useful life}}$$

$$\text{sum of digits of useful life} = \frac{n(n + 1)}{2}$$

Double-Declining Balance

$$d \text{ (first year)} = c \times r$$

$$d \text{ (subsequent years)} = bv \times r$$

$$r = \text{straight-line rate} \times 2$$

$$bv = c - d \text{ (accumulated)}$$

Table 7.2 Comparison of Depreciation Methods

| Year | Straight-Line (20% Rate) | | Declining-Balance (40% Rate) | | Sum-of-the-Years-Digits | | |
	Depreciation	Book Value 12/31	Annual Depreciation	Book Value 12/31	Rate	Annual Depreciation	Book Value 12/31
0	$....	$10,600	$	$10,600.00	....	$	$10,600.00
1	2,000	8,600	4,240.00	6,360.00	$\frac{5}{15}$	3,333.33	7,266.67
2	2,000	6,600	2,544.00	3,816.00	$\frac{4}{15}$	2,666.67	4,600.00
3	2,000	4,600	1,526.40	2,289.60	$\frac{3}{15}$	2,000.00	2,600.00
4	2,000	2,600	915.84	1,373.76	$\frac{2}{15}$	1,333.33	1,266.67
5	2,000	600	549.50	824.26	$\frac{1}{15}$	666.67	600.00

Table 7.2 provides a comparison of the straight-line, double-declining-balance, and sum-of-the-years digits methods. Figure 7.1 on p. 174 shows the same depreciation patterns graphically. The information used in the comparison in Table 7.2 and Figure 7.1 is the depreciation on the machine acquired by the Richland Supply Company.

Exercises

What is the annual double-declining-balance depreciation rate for assets with the following estimated service lives?

1.	4 years	2.	8 years	3.	6 years	4.	5 years
5.	10 years	6.	15 years	7.	25 years	8.	12 years

Practical Applications

Determine the first year's depreciation and the book value at the end of the first year for the following assets using the double-declining-balance method. The assets were acquired on January 1, and the accounting year ends on December 31.

9. An office machine purchased by ABC Nursery for $1,752 has an estimated useful life of eight years and an estimated residual value of $100.

10. A delivery truck purchased by Speedy Delivery Service for $7,560 has an estimated service life of four years with an estimated trade-in value of $1,300.

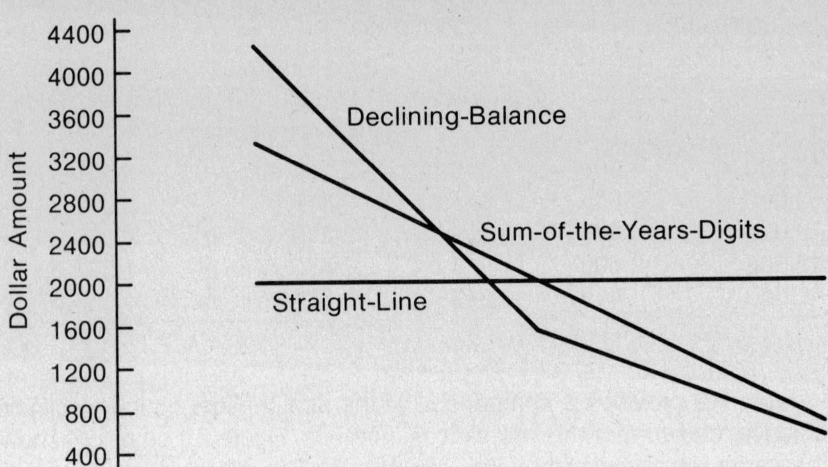

11. Fred's Bookkeeping Service purchased a typewriter for $852. The machine has an estimated service life of five years and an estimated trade-in value of $150.

12. The Universal Construction Company purchased a road grader for $47,250. The machine has an estimated useful life of seven years and an estimated trade-in value of $12,000.

Using the double-declining-balance method, prepare a depreciation schedule for the following assets.

13. The Hi-Fi Manufacturing Company purchased a machine that cost $9,474.70. The estimated life of the machine is four years and the estimated residual value is $1,000.

14. A real estate broker purchased an automobile for $8,752 on January 1. He is entitled to deduct depreciation on his income tax (for the year ended December 31) for use of the car in his business. He estimates the useful life of the car as three years with an estimated trade-in value of $3,300.

15. The Big State Construction Company acquired a tractor-trailer at a cost of $71,340. The estimated useful life of the equipment is five years with an estimated trade-in value of $23,000.

16. Tri-State Chemical Company purchased a forklift truck for $24,600. The estimated useful life of the equipment is eight years with an estimated trade-in value of $4,000.

Chapter 7
Self-Evaluation

1. The XYZ Corporation purchased a postage machine for $5,545. The estimated useful life of the machine is eight years with a residual value of $800. Compute the annual depreciation using the straight-line depreciation method.

2. The Dynamic Novelties Company purchased a stamping machine for $16,800. The estimated life of the machine is 30,000 machine hours with a residual value of $1,800. Compute the depreciation for a period in which the machine was used a total of 2,320 machine hours. Use the units-of-production depreciation method.

3. The XYZ Corporation purchased a postage machine for $5,545. The estimated useful life of the machine is eight years with a residual value of $800. Compute the depreciation for the first year using the sum-of-the-years-digits depreciation method.

4. The XYZ Corporation purchased a postage machine for $5,545. The estimated useful life of the machine is eight years with a residual value of $800. Compute the depreciation for the first year using the double-declining-balance depreciation method.

5. The Cleanrite Cleaners purchased a desk for $319 on October 6. The owner estimates that the desk will have a useful life of ten years and a trade-in value of $50. The accounting period for the cleaners ends on December 31. How much depreciation expense should be recorded for the first year (October 6 through December 31) using the straight-line method?

Chapter 8
Inventory

Businesses inventory (count) various types of resources. In addition to the stock of merchandise maintained by a retailer, most organizations maintain a stock of supplies, tools, equipment, and other types of assets that are subject to a periodic count. In a broad sense, all resources of a business could be considered inventory. However, we will restrict our use of the term *inventory* primarily to the inventories of raw materials, work in progress, and finished goods maintained by a manufacturer and to the merchandise inventory of a retailer. Learning Units 8.1 and 8.2 will provide an opportunity for you to become familiar with the methods used by businesses for determining the cost and valuation of inventory items.

This chapter will enable you to:

1. **identify and distinguish among the four major inventory costing methods: specific identification, FIFO, LIFO, and weighted average cost**

2. **identify and distinguish between the methods used to price inventories: cost and the lower of cost or market**

3. **calculate the amount of inventory (asset) to report on the balance sheet and the amount of cost of merchandise sold (expense) to report on the income statement**

Learning Unit 8.1
Determining the Inventory Balance

Types of Inventory Systems

There are two major inventory systems used in business: the *periodic* inventory system and the *perpetual* inventory system. The periodic system requires a physical count of the items in the inventory to determine the quantities available at any point in time. Under a perpetual inventory system, a record is maintained and an up-to-date inventory figure is available at any time. You may have noticed the salesclerk in a retail store recording the item numbers on sales slips so that the store can maintain accurate records of the quantity remaining in stock. The management of a company must decide whether to use a periodic or a perpetual inventory system. There are many advantages to the perpetual system, but the costs are often high.

Costing the Ending Inventory: Inventory Costing Methods

Most companies take a physical count of the inventory on hand at least once each year. After taking the inventory, the quantity of each item in inventory must be converted into a dollar cost figure for the financial statements. The cost assigned to the inventory (the value of the merchandise) is reported in the asset section of the balance sheet. The cost of merchandise sold (the amount the business paid for the merchandise) is reported as an expense on the income statement.

Since a company usually purchases inventory items throughout the year at different costs, the items in the year-end inventory will have different unit costs. In determining what cost to assign to the ending inventory, the company must, after taking a physical count at the end of its accounting period, either determine the specific cost of each item in the inventory or employ one of the inventory costing methods that are based on certain cash flow assumptions. There are four major methods for determining inventory cost: specific identification; first-in, first-out (FIFO); last-in, first-out (LIFO); and weighted average cost. The information in Table 8.1 will be used to illustrate these four inventory costing methods.

Table 8.1 Inventory Item A-36

Date	Source	Quantity	Unit Cost	Total Cost
January 1	Inventory	10 units	$17	$ 170
March 30	Purchase	10 units	19	190
July 15	Purchase	22 units	20	440
September 30	Purchase	20 units	22	440
December 1	Purchase	15 units	21	315
		77 units		$1,555

Specific Identification. In some situations, it may be possible to use specific invoice prices to cost an inventory because the inventory items can be identified as having been purchased on a particular invoice. Under this method, the value of the inventory is the sum total of each individual item. This method is typically used by a company having a perpetual inventory system with large-unit-cost inventory items. For example, an automobile dealership can use invoices to determine the prices paid for automobiles in stock at the end of an accounting period. Specific identification is impractical for a company having a large volume of small-unit-cost items purchased at different costs throughout the year (such as a sewing notions shop).

When the items in an inventory can be identified with a specific purchase and invoice, specific invoice prices may be used. For example, the company that stocks inventory item A-36 had 21 units in the ending inventory identified as follows:

January 1	Inventory	1 unit	@ $17 = $ 17
March 30	Purchase	2 units	@ $19 = $ 38
September 30	Purchase	6 units	@ $22 = $132
December 1	Purchase	12 units	@ $21 = $252
			Total Cost = $439

When it is impractical to use specific identification, a company may use one of the other inventory costing methods. Each method is based upon a different assumption about the flow of costs through inventory.

First-in, First-out (FIFO). This method is based on the assumption that the items were sold in the order in which they were received, i.e., that the items that were bought first were also sold first. The costs of the last items received are assigned to the ending inventory. Using the FIFO method, the 21 units of A-36 would be included in the inventory at a total cost of $447, as illustrated below:

$$
\begin{array}{lll}
\text{December 1} & \text{15 units} & \text{@ } \$21 = \$315 \\
\text{September 30} & \text{6 units} & \text{@ } \$22 = \$132 \\
& & \text{Total Cost} = \$447
\end{array}
$$

Last-in, First-out (LIFO). This method is based on the assumption that the items bought last were the first to be sold and that, therefore, the items still in stock are the oldest items. The costs of the first items received are assigned to the items in the ending inventory. Using the LIFO method, the 21 units of A-36 would be included in the inventory at a total cost of $380, as illustrated below:

$$
\begin{array}{lll}
\text{January 1} & \text{10 units} & \text{@ } \$17 = \$170 \\
\text{March 30} & \text{10 units} & \text{@ } \$19 = \$190 \\
\text{July 15} & \text{1 unit} & \text{@ } \$20 = \$\ 20 \\
& & \text{Total Cost} = \$380
\end{array}
$$

Weighted Average Cost. Under this method, each item is valued at the weighted average of all costs paid during a time period. To obtain the cost of the items in the ending inventory using this method:

1. Determine the total number of units available during the accounting period.
2. Determine the total cost of those units.
3. Compute the weighted average unit cost; divide the total cost by the total number of units available during the period, i.e.,

$$
\text{Weighted average unit cost} = \frac{\text{Total cost of all units}}{\text{Total number of units available}}
$$

4. Multiply the weighted average unit cost by the number of units in the ending inventory.

Example: If the 21 units of A-36 listed previously are included in the ending inventory, what is the average unit cost? What is the cost of the 21 units?

Solution: Weighted average unit cost $= \dfrac{\$1{,}555}{77} = \$20.19$

Cost of the 21 units $= \$20.19 \times 21 = \$423.99$

Comparison of Inventory Costing Methods. When prices remain unchanged during an accounting period, all of the methods result in the same cost figures. However, when prices change during an accounting period, each method may result in a different cost figure for the ending inventory, as shown below:

Specific identification	$439.00
FIFO	447.00
LIFO	380.00
Weighted average cost	423.99

Pricing the Ending Inventory: Lower of Cost or Market

The value of a company's merchandise inventory can be based on its cost, as we have seen in the preceding discussion of inventory costing methods. Another method of valuing a company's inventory is to compare the cost of the inventory to its current replacement cost in the market. This method is called the *lower of cost or market.* The term *market* refers to the cost of replacing the merchandise on the inventory date. A company using this valuation method will report the cost or market replacement cost, whichever is lower, as the inventory balance.

Example: What is the inventory balance for item A-36 for a company that uses the lower of cost or market valuation method? (Compare FIFO cost method with a $19 per item price.)

Solution: The FIFO cost of 21 units of item A-36 was $447. The current market price of this item is $19 per unit. Therefore, the market price for 21 units is $19 $\times$ 21, or $399. The company should record an inventory balance of $399 for item A-36.

Exercises

A company maintains a stock of item A-37. There were 12 units of this item in the company's ending inventory. Determine the cost that the company should assign to the ending inventory for this item under each of the inventory costing methods.

Inventory Item A-37

Date	Source	Quantity	Unit Cost
January 1	Inventory	8	$25
March 24	Purchase	15	22
June 15	Purchase	20	20
August 19	Purchase	10	24
November 6	Purchase	10	23

1. Specific identification (two of the units were purchased on March 24; two of the units were purchased on August 19; and eight of the units were purchased on November 6).

2. First-in, first-out (FIFO).

3. Last-in, first-out (LIFO).

4. Weighted average cost.

A company maintains a stock of item C-45. There were six units of this item in the ending inventory. Determine the cost that the company should assign to the ending inventory for this item under each of the inventory costing methods.

Inventory Item C-45

Date	Source	Quantity	Unit Cost
January 1	Inventory	2 units	$105
March 22	Purchase	30 units	125
May 30	Purchase	20 units	128
July 12	Purchase	20 units	130
August 27	Purchase	10 units	115

5. Specific identification (four units were purchased March 22; one unit was purchased July 12; and one unit was purchased August 27).

6. First-in, first-out (FIFO).

7. Last-in, first-out (LIFO).

8. Weighted average cost.

A company maintains a stock of item D-43. There were 19 units of this item in the company's ending inventory. Determine the cost that the company should assign to the inventory for this item under each of the inventory costing methods.

Inventory Item D-43

Date	Source	Quantity	Unit Cost
January 1	Inventory	11 units	$ 80
February 15	Purchase	10 units	84
April 30	Purchase	5 units	85
July 1	Purchase	15 units	90
October 17	Purchase	8 units	100
December 8	Purchase	10 units	95

9. Specific identification (one unit was purchased on February 15; three units were purchased on April 30; three units were purchased on July 1; four units were purchased on October 17; and eight units were purchased on December 8).

10. First-in, first-out (FIFO).

11. Last-in, first-out (LIFO).

12. Weighted average cost.

Use cost or market, whichever is lower, to determine the inventory balance for the following items.

	Item	Units	Cost	Market	Inventory Balance
13.	Ladies' 28" pullman	5	$70.00	$72.00	__________
14.	Ladies' 22" pullman	6	$42.95	$41.95	__________
15.	Ladies' handi-tote	10	$35.00	$33.00	__________
16.	Cosmetic case	15	$40.00	$40.95	__________
17.	Garment bag	8	$47.00	$45.50	__________
18.	Mini-tote	12	$18.00	$19.00	__________
19.	27" pullman	4	$59.90	$59.90	__________
20.	30" overseas	2	$74.50	$72.25	__________
21.	Candlesticks (pairs)	3	$15.00	$18.00	__________
22.	Cheese server	10	$13.50	$12.50	__________

Practical Applications

23. Yeager's Sporting Goods had 11 "Super-Beam" flashlights in stock at the start of the year at a cost of $3.83 each. Three purchases were made during the year: ten units at $4.27 each, five units at $4.45 each, and ten units at $4.65 each. There were 13 units in stock at the end of the year.
    (a) How many units were available for sale during the year? 34
    (b) What was the total cost of these units?
    (c) What cost should the company assign to the ending inventory for this item using the weighted average cost method?

24. The ABC Company sells a single product. The company had 17 units in stock at the start of the year at a cost of $181 each. Two purchases were made during the year: 20 units on March 12 at $194 each, and 25 units on September 9 at $203 each. There were 29 units in stock at the end of the year. Which inventory costing method—weighted average cost, FIFO, or LIFO—will result in the lowest inventory cost?

25. The Central Supply Company had the following inventory at the end of the year. Determine the amount to record as the inventory balance in the company's accounting records using the lower of cost or market valuation method.

Item	Inventory Quantity	Unit Cost Price	Unit Market Price	Lower of Cost or Market
A-59	32	$19.90	$18.05	__________
D-66	14	24.42	25.10	__________
E-32	26	9.21	10.75	__________
G-98	22	14.20	13.25	__________
H-12	51	5.35	4.80	__________
J-43	48	17.85	18.65	__________

Learning Unit 8.2
Determining the Cost of Merchandise Sold

As discussed earlier, the cost of merchandise sold (the amount a business pays for the merchandise) is reported as an expense on a company's income statement. Under a perpetual inventory system, a record of this cost is maintained for every item sold. In this way, at the end of the accounting period when the company wants to prepare financial statements, the cost of merchandise sold is already available for entry in the income statement.

A company using a periodic inventory system does not maintain a record of the cost of merchandise sold during the accounting period. At the end of an accounting period when the company wants to prepare financial statements, the cost of merchandise sold must be computed.

To determine the cost of merchandise sold during an accounting period:

1. Determine the amount of merchandise available for sale (beginning merchandise inventory + net purchases).
2. Subtract the ending inventory from the amount of merchandise available for sale.

Example: The Mediterranean Gift Shop uses a periodic inventory system. The merchandise inventory balance at the beginning of the accounting year was $5,000. The shop had net purchases of $70,000 during the year. The ending merchandise inventory was $6,000. What was the amount of merchandise available for sale and the cost of merchandise sold for the year?

Solution: $5,000 + $70,000 = $75,000   merchandise available for sale

$75,000 − $6,000 = $69,000   cost of merchandise sold

The accountant for the Mediterranean Gift Shop may list the $69,000 cost of merchandise sold under expenses on the income statement without providing details about the computation. However, if requested, the accountant will provide a section on the income statement furnishing management and other interested parties a detailed description of the computation of the cost of merchandise sold. A typical income statement presentation of the cost of merchandise sold is illustrated below:

Cost of merchandise sold:

Merchandise inventory, January 1, 19—	$ 5,000
Net purchases	70,000
Merchandise available for sale	$75,000
Less merchandise inventory, December 31, 19—	6,000
Cost of merchandise sold	$69,000

Purchases Account

A company using a periodic inventory system records every acquisition of inventory in its *purchases account*. The costs of all items acquired for sale as well as any other costs (such as transportation charges) associated with the items acquired for sale *increase* the purchases account. This amount is the *delivered cost of the merchandise*. Purchase discounts, i.e., cash discounts offered by suppliers for the early payment of purchase invoices, and purchase returns and allowances *reduce* the purchases account. The delivered cost of the merchandise less purchase discounts and/or returns and allowances results in the *net purchases.*

Example: Purchases by the Mediterranean Gift Shop during 19____ were in the amount of $72,300. There were $1,000 transportation charges on the merchandise purchased for resale. The early payment of invoices enabled the store to deduct $1,300 in purchase discounts. There were $2,000 of purchase returns and allowances. What was the amount of net purchases for the year?

Solution: $72,300 + $1,000 = $73,300$ delivered cost of merchandise

$73,300 - ($1,300 + $2,000) = $70,000$ net purchases

The procedures for determining the cost of merchandise sold are summarized and the relationships diagrammed in Figure 8.1 on p. 187.

Figure 8.1   Determining the Cost of Merchandise Sold

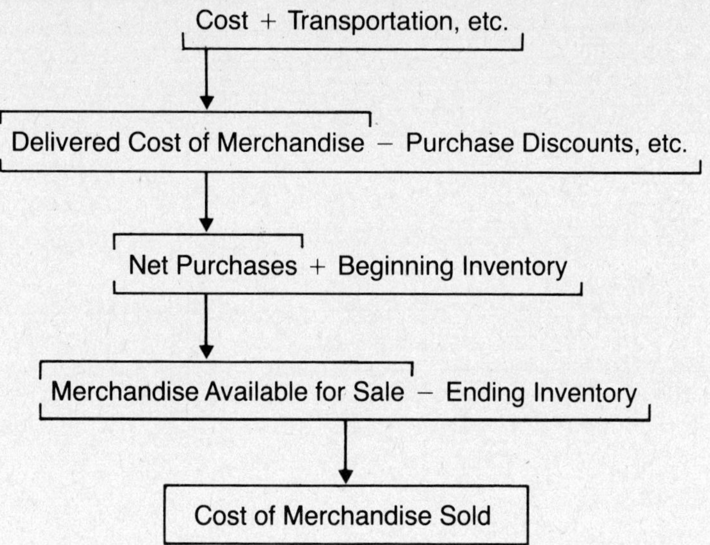

The accountant for the Mediterranean Gift Shop may list the $70,000 net purchases in the cost of merchandise sold section of the income statement without providing details about the computation. However, if requested, the accountant will provide a detailed explanation of the items included in the computation of net purchases. A typical income statement presentation of net purchases is illustrated below:

Purchases		$72,300
Transportation charges		1,000
Delivered cost of merchandise		$73,300
Less:		
Purchase discounts	$1,300	
Purchase returns and allowances	2,000	3,300
Net purchases		$70,000

Exercises

Determine the amount of net purchases for the following retailers:

	Purchases	Trans- portation Charges	Purchase Discounts	Purchase Returns and Allowances	Net Purchases
1.	$313,244	$ 4,000	$6,000	$10,000	__________
2.	$111,500	$ 2,000	$2,200	$ 1,500	__________
3.	$489,753	$15,800	$9,600	$ 3,775	__________
4.	$ 55,245	$ 1,230	$1,054	$ 585	__________
5.	$167,960	$ 3,744	$3,159	$ 1,280	__________
6.	$ 95,335	$ 705	$1,866	$ 299	__________

Determine the cost of merchandise sold for the following retailers:

	Beginning Inventory	Net Purchases	Ending Inventory	Cost of Merchandise Sold
7.	$ 7,000	$ 80,000	$ 9,000	__________
8.	$ 15,500	$125,450	$ 13,740	__________
9.	$ 17,860	$216,741	$ 16,575	__________
10.	$ 26,432	$182,415	$ 28,192	__________
11.	$143,916	$572,442	$106,985	__________
12.	$ 5,476	$ 76,414	$ 10,547	__________

Fill in the missing items in the following tabulation. Each horizontal row is a separate problem.

	Beginning Inventory	Net Purchases	Goods Available for Sale	Ending Inventory	Cost of Merchandise Sold
13.	$ 34,000	_______	$396,544	$36,000	_______
14.	_______	$146,779	$184,658	_______	$162,324
15.	$124,567	$865,938	_______	_______	$896,744
16.	$ 12,656	_______	$ 98,203	$18,057	_______
17.	_______	$347,765	$389,246	$33,545	_______
18.	$103,676	$289,345	_______	_______	$367,823

Fill in the missing items in the following tabulation. Each horizontal row is a separate problem.

	Purchases	Transportation on Purchases	Purchase Discounts	Purchase Returns and Allowances	Net Purchases
19.	$345,722	$ 8,342	$ 6,645	$13,452	_______
20.	$238,017	$ 5,440	$ 4,560	_______	$225,649
21.	$ 55,786	$ 435	1102	$ 276	$ 54,843
22.	_______	$ 1,278	$ 2,015	$ 1,204	$132,765
23.	$883,756	_______	$17,421	$19,592	$871,987
24.	$176,394	$ 1,383	_______	$ 3,482	$170,895

Practical Applications

25. The financial records of the Ornee Company contain the following information. Determine the cost of merchandise sold.

Merchandise inventory, January 1, 19__	$ 45,678.13
Merchandise inventory, December 31, 19__	38,209.86
Purchases	455,778.22
Transportation charges on purchases	4,389.96
Purchase returns and allowances	12,345.89
Purchase discounts	8,868.65

26. The Gourmet Specialty Shop's accounting records contain the following information. Determine the cost of merchandise sold.

Merchandise inventory, January 1, 19—	$ 3,977.34
Merchandise inventory, December 31, 19—	4,802.66
Purchases	52,623.10
Transportation charges on purchases	1,132.42
Purchase returns and allowances	256.47
Purchase discounts	1,047.33

Chapter 8
Self-Evaluation

1. A company maintains a stock of crystal pitchers. There are five units of this item in the ending inventory. Determine the cost that the company should assign to the ending inventory of this item using each of the four inventory costing methods.

Date	Source	Quantity	Unit Cost
January 1	Inventory	4	$15
March 31	Purchase	6	17
June 15	Purchase	12	18
October 13	Purchase	18	21

(a) Specific identification (one unit was in the January 1 inventory; two units were purchased on June 15; and two units were purchased on October 13).

(b) First-in, first-out (FIFO).

(c) Last-in, first-out (LIFO).

(d) Average cost.

2. The Jones Company uses the lower of cost or market valuation method in pricing the ending inventory. The company has 24 silver-plated invitation trays that cost $4.60 each in the ending inventory. The company is selling the trays for $4.75.
   (a) Determine the total cost.
   (b) Determine the total market value.
   (c) Determine the amount that the company should include in the year-end inventory for this item.

3. The Western Wear Shop had purchases of $46,234, purchase discounts of $824.35, and purchase returns and allowances of $234. What was the amount of net purchases?

4. The Westover Specialty Store had a beginning inventory of $33,542 in 19____. Net purchases for the store during the year were $145,675. The cost of the ending inventory was $46,732. What was the cost of merchandise sold?

Chapter 9
Financial Statements and Ratios

Financial statements are a means of presenting information about the financial health and economic activity of a business. Knowledgeable analysis of financial statements permits management and other interested parties to measure business progress and potential. Ratios, which are developed from the information contained in financial statements, are used as a means of effectively analyzing the information in these statements and as a means of comparing current and past statements.

This chapter will enable you to:

1. **analyze the information contained in an income statement and a balance sheet**

2. **compute various financial ratios**

3. **prepare a bank reconciliation statement**

Learning Unit 9.1
Financial Statement Analysis

Financial statements reflect important information about a business's past performance and present financial condition, such as the volume of business, the amount of profit or loss, the worth of the business, and the distribution of assets, liabilities, and capital. It is on the basis of information contained in these statements that management may decide to take corrective action, that a bank may decide to reconsider granting a loan, or that an investor may decide that the purchase of stock in the business is a prudent course of action.

Types of Financial Statements

The two primary accounting statements that are used to present financial information are the income statement and the balance sheet.

Income Statement. The income statement presents the results of financial operations for a period of time, such as a month or a year, in terms of revenues and expenses. The income statement is based on the following formula:

$$\text{Revenues} - \text{Expenses} = \text{Net Income}$$

Figure 9.1 provides an example of an income statement.

Balance Sheet. The balance sheet presents the financial condition of a business at a certain point in time. The balance sheet lists all of a business's *assets* (everything that the business owns or that is owed to it) and all of a business's *liabilities* (everything that the business owes). The balance remaining after the liabilities are subtracted from the assets is the owner's claim on the assets, or the *capital.* The balance sheet is based on the following formula:

$$\text{Assets} = \text{Liabilities} + \text{Capital}$$

Figure 9.2 provides an example of a balance sheet.

Figure 9.1
Central Supply Company
Income Statement
For Year Ended December 31, 19–2

Revenue:		
Net sales		$188,150
Operating expenses:		
Cost of merchandise sold	$82,800	
Salaries expense	33,600	
Wages expense	29,200	
Depreciation expense	5,400	
Advertising expense	4,000	
Utilities expense	3,400	
Supplies used	1,600	
Miscellaneous expense	1,200	
Total expenses		161,200
Net income		$ 26,950

Comparative Financial Statements. Although the information contained in a specific financial statement provides important insights into the financial soundness and future prospects of a business, a more meaningful understanding of the trends and financial condition of a business can be obtained by comparing statements for several periods of time. For this reason, comparative financial statements are often provided management and external users. A comparative statement presents a comparison of the current period with the previous period(s). Figures 9.3 and 9.4 provide examples of comparative statements.

Analysis of Financial Statements

A financial statement, whether comparative or for one period or date, is expressed in dollar amounts. These amounts may be converted to percents to show relationships. Analyses by percents may be expressed either vertically or horizontally.

Vertical Analysis. Vertical analysis compares the items on a financial statement to some base or whole (considered as 100%) within the same

Figure 9.2
Central Supply Company
Balance Sheet
December 31, 19–2

Assets

Current assets:		
Cash		$ 5,000
Accounts receivable		18,000
Supplies		700
Merchandise inventory		40,000
Total current assets		$ 63,700
Plant assets:		
Equipment	$40,000	
Less accumulated depreciation	15,000	$25,000
Building	$50,000	
Less accumulated depreciation	10,000	40,000
Land		15,000
Total plant assets		80,000
Total assets		$143,700

Liabilities

Current liabilities:		
Accounts payable	$20,000	
Notes payable	13,000	
Total current liabilities		$33,000
Long-term liabilities:		
Mortgage payable		29,500
Total liabilities		$ 62,500

Capital

Sam Sims, capital	81,200
Total liabilities and capital	$143,700

statement and time period. Each item is expressed as a percent of the base, which, for an income statement, is usually net sales. To determine the percent relationship of an item to net sales, divide the item by the net sales:

$$\text{Percent of Net Sales} = \frac{\text{Each Item}[1]}{\text{Net Sales}}$$

Example: What is the relationship of the net income of the Central Supply Company for 19–2 to net sales?

Solution: Percent of net sales = Net income ÷ Net sales
= $26,950 ÷ $188,150
= .1432 = 14.32%

A comparative income statement with vertical analysis is illustrated in Figure 9.3.

Figure 9.3
Central Supply Company
Comparative Income Statement with Vertical Analysis
Years Ended December 31, 19–1, and December 31, 19–2

	19–2	Percent	19–1	Percent
Revenue:				
Net sales	$188,150	100.00	$167,340	100.00
Operating expenses:				
Cost of merchandise sold	82,800	44.01	77,210	46.14
Salaries expense	33,600	17.86	31,200	18.64
Wages expense	29,200	15.52	27,800	16.61
Depreciation expense	5,400	2.87	5,100	3.05
Advertising expense	4,000	2.13	4,000	2.39
Utilities expense	3,400	1.81	2,830	1.69
Supplies used	1,600	.85	1,600	.96
Miscellaneous expense	1,200	.64	1,420	.85
Total expenses	$161,200	85.69	$151,160	90.33
Net income	$ 26,950	14.32	$ 16,180	9.67

[1]Note that this formula is an adaptation of the basic percentage formula ($P = B \times R$) that was presented in Chapter 3. In this case, the formula is solved for R, or $R = P/B$, with R = the percent of net sales, P = the amount shown for the item on the income statement, and B = net sales.

In doing a vertical analysis of a balance sheet, each asset is expressed as a percent of total assets (100%), while each liability is expressed as a percent of total liabilities plus capital (which is the same as total assets):

$$\text{Percent of Total Assets} = \frac{\text{Each Item}}{\text{Total Assets}}$$

Example: What is the relationship between cash and total assets for Central Supply Company on December 31, 19–2, expressed as a percent?

Solution: Percent of total assets = Cash ÷ Total assets
$$= \$5,000 \div \$143,700$$
$$= 0.0348 = 3.48\%$$

A comparative balance sheet with vertical analysis is illustrated below, in Figure 9.4.

(Round percents to the nearest hundredth when performing vertical analysis. When rounding, you may find individual numbers that will be off 0.01% or 0.02%. Report the answer you obtain without adjusting it to make the column total an even 100%.)

Horizontal Analysis. Horizontal analysis compares corresponding items for different time periods, showing the percent increase or decrease of each item between time periods. The base for computing percent increase or decrease in a horizontal analysis is the amount of the item in the earliest year. To determine the percent of increase or decrease for an item, (1) determine the dollar amount of increase or decrease from one time period to the next, and (2) divide the amount of increase or decrease by the amount of the item in the base year:

$$\text{Percent of} \begin{cases} \text{Increase} \\ \text{or} \\ \text{Decrease} \end{cases} = \frac{\text{Amount of} \begin{cases} \text{Increase} \\ \text{or} \\ \text{Decrease} \end{cases}}{\text{Amount of Item (Earliest Year)}}$$

Note that the rules and formula outlined above for horizontal analysis are applicable to *both* income statements and balance sheets. A comparative income statement with horizontal analysis is illustrated in Figure 9.5 on page 200; a comparative balance sheet with horizontal analysis, in Figure 9.6 on page 201.

	19–2	Percent	19–1	Percent
Assets				
Current assets:				
Cash	$ 5,000	3.48	$ 3,500	2.52
Accounts receivable	18,000	12.53	17,200	12.37
Supplies	700	.49	850	.61
Merchandise inventory	40,000	27.84	32,100	23.09
Total current assets	$ 63,700	44.33	$ 53,650	38.58
Plant assets:				
Equipment	$ 40,000	27.84	$ 40,000	28.77
Less accumulated depreciation	15,000	10.44	11,600	8.34
	$ 25,000	17.40	$ 28,400	20.42
Building	$ 50,000	34.79	$ 50,000	35.96
Less accumulated depreciation	10,000	6.96	8,000	5.75
	$ 40,000	27.84	$ 42,000	30.20
Land	$ 15,000	10.44	$ 15,000	10.79
Total plant assets	$ 80,000	55.67	$ 85,400	61.42
Total assets	$143,700	100.00	$139,050	100.00
Liabilities				
Current liabilities:				
Accounts payable	$ 20,000	13.92	$ 18,500	13.30
Notes payable	13,000	9.05	14,200	10.21
Total current liabilities	$ 33,000	22.96	$ 32,700	23.52
Long-term liabilities:				
Mortgage payable	$ 29,500	20.53	$ 30,200	21.72
Total liabilities	$ 62,500	43.49	$ 62,900	45.24
Capital				
Sam Sims, capital	$ 81,200	56.51	$ 76,150	54.76
Total liabilities and capital	$143,700	100.00	$139,050	100.00

Figure 9.5
Central Supply Company
Comparative Income Statement with Horizontal Analysis
Years Ended December 31, 19–1, and December 31, 19–2

	Years Ended December 31		Amount of Increase (or Decrease)	Percent of Increase (or Decrease)
	19–2	*19–1*		
Revenue:				
Net sales	$188,150	$167,340	$20,810	12.44
Operating expenses:				
Cost of merchandise sold	82,800	77,210	5,590	7.24
Salaries expense	33,600	31,200	2,400	7.69
Wages expense	29,200	27,800	1,400	5.04
Depreciation expense	5,400	5,100	300	5.88
Advertising expense	4,000	4,000		
Utilities expense	3,400	2,830	570	20.14
Supplies used	1,600	1,600		
Miscellaneous expense	1,200	1,420	(220)	(15.49)
Total expenses	$161,200	$151,160	$10,040	6.64
Net income	$ 26,950	$ 16,180	$10,770	66.56

Example: Using the comparative income statement in Figure 9.5, compute the change that occurred in the cost of merchandise sold for the Central Supply Company during 19–2.

Solution: Amount of increase = $82,800 − $77,210 = $5,590
Percent of increase = $5,590 ÷ $77,210
= 0.0724 = 7.24%

Example: Using the comparative balance sheet in Figure 9.6, compute the percent of increase in the merchandise inventory for Central Supply during 19–2.

Solution: Percent of increase (decrease) = Amount of increase (decrease) ÷ Amount of item (base year)
Amount of increase = $40,000 − $32,100 = $7,900
Percent of increase = $7,900 ÷ $32,100
= 0.2461 = 24.61%

Figure 9.6
Central Supply Company
Comparative Balance Sheet with Horizontal Analysis
December 31, 19–1, and December 31, 19–2

	Year Ended December 31		Amount of Increase (or Decrease)	Percent of Increase (or Decrease)
	19–2	*19–1*		
Assets				
Current assets:				
Cash	$ 5,000	$ 3,500	$ 1,500	42.86
Accounts receivable	18,000	17,200	800	4.65
Supplies	700	850	(150)	(17.65)
Merchandise inventory	40,000	32,100	7,900	24.61
Total current assets	$ 63,700	$ 53,650	$10,050	18.73
Plant assets:				
Equipment	$ 40,000	$ 40,000		
Less accumulated depreciation	15,000	11,600	$ 3,400	29.31
	$ 25,000	$ 28,400	$ (3,400)	(11.97)
Building	$ 50,000	$ 50,000		
Less accumulated depreciation	10,000	8,000	$ 2,000	25.00
	$ 40,000	$ 42,000	$ (2,000)	(4.76)
Land	$ 15,000	$ 15,000		
Total plant assets	$ 80,000	$ 85,400	$ (5,400)	(6.32)
Total assets	$143,700	$139,050	$ 4,650	3.34
Liabilities				
Current liabilities:				
Accounts payable	$ 20,000	$ 18,500	$ 1,500	8.11
Notes payable	13,000	14,200	(1,200)	(8.45)
Total current liabilities	$ 33,000	$ 32,700	$ 300	.92
Long-term liabilities:				
Mortgage payable	$ 29,500	$ 30,200	$ (700)	(2.32)
Total liabilities	$ 62,500	$ 62,900	$ (400)	(.64)
Capital				
Sam Sims, capital	$ 81,200	$ 76,150	$ 5,050	6.63
Total liabilities and capital	$143,700	$139,050	$ 4,650	3.34

Exercises

1. Prepare a vertical analysis of the income statement of the Richland Supply Company for 19–1. Use net sales as the base for comparison of the items.

Richland Supply Company
Income Statement
Year Ended December 31, 19–1

	Amount	Percent
Revenue:		
Net sales	$230,000	100.00
Operating expenses:		
Cost of merchandise sold	124,000	
Salaries expense	35,200	
Wages expense	37,800	
Depreciation expense	4,700	
Advertising expense	5,100	
Utilities expense	4,600	
Supplies used	950	
Miscellaneous expense	870	
Total expenses	$213,220	
Net income	$ 16,780	

2. Prepare a vertical analysis of the balance sheet of the Richland Supply Company. Use total assets as the base for comparison of the items.

Richland Supply Company
Balance Sheet
December 31, 19–1

	Amount	Percent
Assets		
Current assets:		
Cash	$ 8,000	__________
Accounts receivable	21,000	__________
Supplies	1,100	__________
Merchandise inventory	42,000	__________
Total current assets	$ 72,100	__________
Plant assets:		
Equipment	$ 50,000	
Less accumulated depreciation	20,900	__________
	$ 29,100	__________
Building	70,000	
Less accumulated depreciation	27,000	__________
	$ 43,000	__________
Land	29,000	__________
Total plant assets	$101,100	__________
Total assets	$173,200	100.00
Liabilities		
Current liabilities:		
Accounts payable	$ 26,000	__________
Notes payable	17,000	__________
Total current liabilities	$ 43,000	__________
Long-term liabilities:		
Mortgage payable	$ 24,100	__________
Total liabilities	$ 67,100	__________
Capital		
Sam Sims, capital	$106,100	__________
Total liabilities and capital	$173,200	100.00

3. Prepare a horizontal analysis of the following comparative income statement.

Super Sales Company
Comparative Income Statement
Years Ended December 31, 19–1, and December 31, 19–2

	Year ended December 31	
	19–2	19–1
Revenue:		
Net sales	$192,300	$188,000
Operating expenses:		
Cost of merchandise sold	85,000	88,000
Salaries expense	42,000	39,000
Wages expense	16,500	14,200
Depreciation expense	2,200	2,150
Advertising expense	6,200	5,100
Utilities expense	500	600
Supplies used	600	700
Miscellaneous expense	900	1,250
Total expenses	$153,900	$151,000
Net income	$ 38,400	$ 37,000

4. Prepare a horizontal analysis of the comparative balance sheet for Reliance Distributors.

Reliance Distributors
Comparative Balance Sheet
December 31, 19–1, and December 31, 19–2

	December 31	
	19–2	*19–1*
Assets		
Current assets:		
Cash	$ 15,000	$ 13,500
Accounts receivable	18,000	17,200
Supplies	700	850
Merchandise inventory	43,500	42,100
Total current assets	$ 77,200	$ 73,650
Plant assets:		
Equipment	$ 46,000	$ 46,000
Less accumulated depreciation	16,000	14,600
	$ 30,000	$ 31,400
Building	$ 50,000	$ 50,000
Less accumulated depreciation	20,000	18,000
	$ 30,000	$ 32,000
Land	$ 25,000	$ 25,000
Total plant assets	$ 85,000	$ 88,400
Total assets	$162,200	$162,050
Liabilities		
Current liabilities:		
Accounts payable	$ 23,000	$ 17,500
Notes payable	18,000	19,200
Total current liabilities	$ 41,000	$ 36,700
Long-term liabilities:		
Mortgage payable	$ 39,500	$ 40,200
Total liabilities	$ 80,500	$ 76,900
Capital		
Common stock	$ 40,000	$ 40,000
Retained earnings	41,700	45,150
Total liabilities and capital	$162,200	$162,050

Learning Unit 9.2
Financial Ratios

Types of Ratios

A *ratio* is the expression of a relationship between two numbers. A ratio may be computed as a fraction, a decimal, or a percent. Management and other interested individuals and firms use financial ratios developed from financial statements to interpret a business's economic activities and condition. For instance, a bank may determine a company's current ratio of assets to liabilities before granting a loan.

To compute a ratio from the information contained in a financial statement, select two amounts that have a relationship to each other and divide one by the other. Some of the more important ratios that are used in financial analysis are the current ratio, acid test ratio, ratio of plant assets to long-term liabilities, rate of return on total assets, and rate of return on owner's equity. The ratios computed in this learning unit are based on the information contained in the income statement and comparative balance sheet for Yeager's Sporting Goods.

Figure 9.7
Yeager's Sporting Goods
Income Statement
For Year Ended December 31

Revenue:		
Net sales		$114,000
Expenses:		
Cost of merchandise sold	$64,000	
Selling expenses	20,000	
General expenses	10,000	
Total expenses		94,000
Net income		$20,000

Figure 9.8
Yeager's Sporting Goods
Comparative Balance Sheet
December 31, 19–1, and December 31, 19–2

	19–2	19–1
Assets		
Current assets:		
Cash	$ 5,000	$ 13,000
Marketable securities	10,000	2,000
Accounts receivable	30,000	25,000
Notes receivable	5,000	10,000
Merchandise inventory	30,000	34,000
Total current assets	$ 80,000	$ 84,000
Plant assets:		
Equipment	$ 35,000	$ 35,000
Less accumulated depreciation	15,000	14,000
	$ 20,000	$ 21,000
Building	$ 80,000	$ 80,000
Less accumulated depreciation	20,000	18,000
	$ 60,000	$ 62,000
Land	$ 20,000	$ 20,000
Total plant assets	$100,000	$103,000
Total assets	$180,000	$187,000
Liabilities		
Current liabilities		
Accounts payable	$ 26,000	$ 24,000
Notes payable	12,000	19,500
Taxes payable	2,000	1,500
Total current liabilities	$ 40,000	$ 45,000
Long-term liabilities:		
Mortgage payable	$ 40,000	$ 42,000
Total liabilities	$ 80,000	$ 87,000
Capital		
Jim Yeager, capital	$ 60,000	$ 60,000
Bill Yeager, capital	40,000	40,000
Total liabilities and capital	$180,000	$187,000

Current Ratio. The current ratio gives an indication of a company's ability to meet its current liabilities (debts) as they mature (come due). The current ratio is computed by dividing current assets by current liabilities:

$$\text{Current Ratio} = \frac{\text{Current Assets}}{\text{Current Liabilities}}$$

Example: What was the current ratio for Yeager's Sporting Goods on December 31, 19–2?

Solution: Current ratio $= \dfrac{\$80,000}{\$40,000}$

$\qquad\qquad\qquad\quad = 2{:}1 \quad$ (the fraction $\frac{2}{1}$ in ratio form)

A ratio of this type is always read as "something" to 1. The current ratio for Yeager's Sporting Goods is 2:1. This means that for every $1 of current liabilities, the company has $2 of current assets to cover the eventual payments. A 2:1 ratio is generally considered the minimum acceptable ratio by creditors. Whether a company's current ratio is adequate depends on three factors: the nature of the company's business, the composition of its current assets, and the turnover of its current assets.

Acid Test Ratio. The acid test ratio, often called the *quick ratio,* measures the "instant" debt-paying ability of a company. The main difference between this ratio and the current ratio is that only the quick assets (those assets that can easily and quickly be converted to cash) are included in the computation of the acid test ratio. The quick assets include marketable securities, accounts receivable, and notes receivable, as well as cash itself. The acid test ratio is computed by dividing quick assets by current liabilities:

$$\text{Acid Test Ratio} = \frac{\text{Quick Assets}}{\text{Current Liabilities}}$$

Example: What was the acid test ratio for Yeager's Sporting Goods on December 31, 19–2?

Solution: Acid test ratio $= \dfrac{\$50,000}{\$40,000}$

$\qquad\qquad\qquad\qquad = 1.25{:}1$

The acid test ratio for Yeager's Sporting Goods is 1.25:1. An acid test ratio of 1:1 is usually considered satisfactory.

Ratio of Plant Assets to Long-Term Liabilities. The ratio of plant assets to long-term liabilities measures the ability of the company to borrow ad-

ditional funds on a long-term basis. The ratio of plant assets to long-term
liabilities is computed by dividing plant assets by long-term liabilities:

$$\text{Ratio of Plant Assets to Long-Term Liabilities} = \frac{\text{Plant Assets}}{\text{Long-Term Liabilities}}$$

Example: What was the ratio of plant assets to long-term liabilities for
Yeager's Sporting Goods on December 31, 19–2?

$$\text{Solution: Ratio of plant assets to long-term liabilities} = \frac{\$100{,}000}{\$40{,}000}$$
$$= 2.5{:}1$$

The ratio of plant assets to long-term liabilities for Yeager's Sporting
Goods is 2.5:1. This means that for every $1 of long-term liabilities, the
company has $2.50 of plant assets.

Rate of Return on Total Assets. The rate of return on total assets indicates
whether a business is using its assets to best advantage and thus is one
of the measures of the efficiency of the company's management. This ratio
is computed by determining the average total assets and then dividing net
income by the average of total assets:

$$\text{Rate of Return on Total Assets} = \frac{\text{Net Income}}{\text{Total Assets (Average)}}$$

Example: What was the rate of return on total assets for Yeager's Sporting Goods for 19–2?

$$\text{Solution: Average total assets} = \frac{\$180{,}000 + \$187{,}000}{2}$$
$$= \$183{,}500$$

$$\text{Rate of return on total assets} = \frac{\$20{,}000}{\$183{,}500}$$
$$= 0.109 = 10.9\%$$

Rate of Return on Owner's Equity. The rate of return on owner's equity
is a measure of the income yield on the amount invested by the owner(s).
This ratio is computed by dividing net income by average capital:

$$\text{Rate of Return on Owner's Equity} = \frac{\text{Net Income}}{\text{Average Capital}}$$

Example: What was the rate of return on owner's equity for Yeager's
Sporting Goods during 19–2?

Solution: Rate of return on owner's equity $= \dfrac{\$20,000}{\$100,000}$

$$= 0.2 = 20\%$$

Inventory Turnover. The inventory turnover is the number of times the average inventory was sold during the accounting period. It is computed by determining the average inventory and then dividing the cost of merchandise sold by the average inventory:

$$\text{Inventory Turnover} = \frac{\text{Cost of Merchandise Sold}}{\text{Average Inventory}}$$

Example: What was the inventory turnover for Yeager's Sporting Goods during 19–2?

Solution: $\dfrac{\text{Average}}{\text{inventory}} = \dfrac{\$30,000 + \$34,000}{2}$ $\qquad$ $\dfrac{\text{Inventory}}{\text{turnover}} = \dfrac{\$64,000}{\$32,000}$

$$= \$64,000 \div 2 \qquad\qquad\qquad = 2 \text{ times}$$
$$= \$32,000$$

A high inventory turnover is one measure of the efficiency of a company. Although there are no broad generalizations on an acceptable inventory turnover, there is a reasonable turnover rate for each business.

Exercises

Compute the financial ratios using the information contained in the income statement and balance sheet for the Midtown Glass Company.

1. Compute the current ratio for December 31, 19–2.

2. Compute the acid test ratio for December 31, 19–2. The current assets include an inventory of $20,000.

3. Compute the ratio of plant assets to long-term liabilities on December 31, 19–2.

4. Compute the rate of return on total assets for 19–2.

5. Compute the rate of return on owner's equity for 19–2.

6. Compute the inventory turnover for 19–2. The current assets include an inventory of $20,000 for 19–2 and $24,000 for 19–1.

Midtown Glass Company
Income Statement
Year Ended December 31, 19–2

Revenue from sales		$210,000
Expenses:		
Cost of merchandise sold	$80,000	
Selling expenses	42,000	
General expenses	68,000	
Total expenses		190,000
Net income		$ 20,000

Midtown Glass Company
Comparative Balance Sheet
December 31, 19–1, and December 31, 19–2

	19–2	*19–1*
Assets		
Current assets	$ 84,000	$ 62,000
Plant assets	120,000	126,000
Total assets	$204,000	$188,000
Liabilities		
Current liabilities	$ 33,000	$ 35,000
Long-term liabilities	70,000	60,000
Total liabilities	$103,000	$ 95,000
Capital		
Common stock	$ 50,000	$ 50,000
Retained earnings	51,000	43,000
Total capital	$101,000	$ 93,000
Total liabilities and capital	$204,000	$188,000

Practical Applications

7. Western Realty had $75,000 of quick assets in 19–1 and $84,000 in 19–2. The company had $72,000 of current liabilities in 19–1 and $96,000 in 19–2. Was the company in a better position to pay its debts in 19–1 or 19–2? What was the ratio for the better year?

8. Was Midtown Electric in a better position to borrow additional funds on a long-term basis in 19–1 or 19–2? The company had $140,000 of plant assets in 19–1 and $136,000 in 19–2. The long-term liabilities in 19–1 were $89,000 and $82,000 in 19–2. What were the two ratios?

9. The McBee Furniture Company had a beginning inventory of $275,-000 and an ending inventory of $235,000 in 19–2. The cost of merchandise sold for the year was $510,000. What was the inventory turnover?

10. The Lube-All Company had $240,000 of current assets and $125,000 of current liabilities at the end of 19–1. The Global Oil Company had $487,000 of current assets and $236,000 of current liabilities at the end of 19–1. Which company is in a better position to secure a loan from a local bank? Which ratio did you use to obtain your answer? What were the ratios?

11. The Cross-Town Moving and Storage Company had a net income of $72,000 last year on total assets of $600,000. What was the rate of return on total assets?

12. The ABC Company had a net income of $35,000 last year. The owners had an average investment of $218,750 during the year. What was the rate of return on owners' equity?

Learning Unit 9.3
Bank Reconciliation

Bank Statements

Most companies maintain a checking account in which they deposit all cash receipts and from which they pay all invoices. The bank normally mails each depositor a monthly statement, along with copies of deposit slips, cancelled checks, and other documents indicating increases or decreases in the account. An example of a bank statement is illustrated in Figure 9.9.

The information contained on the bank statement should be compared with a depositor's own checking account records. Normally, the balance on the bank statement and the balance in the depositor's records will differ. Errors by the depositor or the bank may account for part of the discrepancy. A discrepancy might also occur because of the period between the time a check or deposit is recorded by the depositor and the time these items are received and recorded by the bank. Also, the bank may have deducted amounts from the depositor's account for service charges, check printing, and deposits that were uncollectible. The monthly statement furnished by most banks provides a form on which to perform the bank reconciliation. Some companies use this form, while other companies prepare a bank reconciliation statement similar to the one shown in Figure 9.10.

Bank Reconciliation Statement

A company should prepare a bank reconciliation statement in which any discrepancies can be discovered and appropriate adjustments made to either or both balances so that they will agree.

Adjustments to Bank Statement Balance. Deposits not recorded on the bank statement are added to the bank statement balance. Outstanding checks (i.e., checks that the bank has not yet received) are subtracted from the bank statement balance. Bank errors may have to be either added to or subtracted from the bank balance, depending on the type of error.

Adjustments to Company Balance. Unrecorded additions to the company's account, such as notes collected by the bank, are added to the company balance. Bank charges, including collection fees, service charges,

STATEMENT OF ACCOUNT

Branch Supply Incorporated
1329 Main Avenue
City

Account
Number
18-4298-7

From:　6/1
To:　6/30

Total Documents Enclosed:　12

AVERAGE BALANCE	BALANCE FROM LAST STATEMENT	DEPOSITS		CHECKS		SERVICE CHARGE	PRESENT BALANCE
		NO.	AMOUNT	NO.	AMOUNT		
1,918.22	2,487.61	3	5,748.00	9	6,882.28	4.50	1,348.83

PLEASE EXAMINE AT ONCE. IF NO ERROR IS REPORTED WITHIN TEN DAYS THE ACCOUNT WILL BE CONSIDERED CORRECT

DETAIL OF TRANSACTIONS (READ ACROSS)

DATE MO. DAY	AMOUNT	DATE MO. DAY	AMOUNT	DATE MO. DAY	AMOUNT
6-2	748.05 −				
6-10	1477.44 −	6-10	218.33 −	6-10	1000.00 +
6-14	82.65 −	6-14	1820.17 −		
6-20	3248.00 +	6-20	900.00 −	6-20	Draft 100.00 −
6-24	719.00 −	6-24	816.64 −		
6-30	*1500.00 +	6-30	Fee* 3.00 −	6-30	SC　1.50 −
	*Note collection and fee				

and check charges, are subtracted from the company balance. Again, company errors may have to be either added to or subtracted from the company balance, depending on the type of error.

Both types of adjustments are summarized below.

Reconciliation

Bank Statement Balance	*Company Balance*
+ Deposits not recorded on statement	+ Unrecorded additions to the account
− Outstanding checks	− Bank charges
± Errors	± Errors

By closely examining the reconciliation statement in Figure 9.10, we will be able to see exactly how a bank reconciliation statement is prepared. The first step is to prepare the heading for the statement, including the name of the company, the name of the statement, and the date or period of time covered by the statement. The next step is to match financial items recorded in the company's records against those on the bank statement.

Figure 9.10
Branch Supply Incorporated
Bank Reconciliation Statement
June 30, 19–1

Balance per bank statement.		$1,348.83	Balance per company records.			$2,056.22
Add:	Deposit of June 30 (deposit in transit)	2,800.00	Add:	Note collected by the bank		1,500.00
		$4,148.83				$3,556.22
Deduct: Outstanding checks			Deduct: Collection fee	$ 3.00		
Check #102	$ 76.40		Service charge	1.50		
Check #104	620.71	697.11	Draft	100.00	104.50	
Adjusted balance per bank statement.		$3,451.72	Adjusted balance per company records.			$3,451.72

The left column of the bank reconciliation statement begins with the final balance on the bank statement ($1,348.83). A deposit mailed on June 30 for $2,800, which does not appear on the bank statement, is added to the bank balance. Outstanding checks #102 for $76.40 and #104 for $620.71, which had been recorded by the company but do not appear on the bank statement, are deducted to obtain an adjusted balance on the bank statement of $3,451.72.

The right column of the bank reconciliation statement begins with the balance in the company's records ($2,056.22). A $1,500 note collected by the bank for Branch Supply is added to the balance. The $3.00 note collection fee, $1.50 service charge, and a $100.00 draft from a supplier, which had been accepted by the bank, are deducted to obtain the adjusted balance ($3,451.72) on the company's records. Since the bank balance and company balance now agree, the bank reconciliation is complete.

Exercises

Reconcile the following bank statements using the format recommended in this learning unit.

1. Western Realty received a bank statement for September. The bank statement shows a balance of $1,025.40, a service charge of $2.90, and a $4 charge for a safe-deposit box rental. A deposit of $730 was en route to the bank on the day the statement was prepared. The following checks had been issued but had not cleared the bank: #55, $180; #57, $600; #58, $26.50. The company's records indicate a cash balance of $955.80. Prepare a bank reconciliation statement to resolve the discrepancies.

2. Midtown Electric received the June bank statement. The bank statement and company records reveal the following information. The bank service charge was $1.75. There was a $3 charge for collecting a note. An error of $.80 was discovered when a check for $198.06 was recorded on the stub as $198.86. A deposit of $460, mailed on June 29, was not shown on the statement. The following checks were written but not included in the bank statement: #84, $72.46; #87, $49.50; #88, $161.47. The bank statement balance was $3,761.62. The stub on the last check written in June showed a balance of $3,942.14. Prepare a bank reconciliation statement.

3. The Lube-All Company received the monthly bank statement for June. The bank statement and company records indicate the following discrepancies. A bank service charge for $3.40; a $2 note collection fee; a deposit for $2,016 for a $2,000 note collected by the bank, including $16 interest earned on the note; and a $360 deposit for rent collected by the bank for Lube-All are included on the bank statement. The company's records indicate that the following checks had been issued but had not been received by the bank when the bank statement had been prepared: #114, $91.66; #118, $266.40; #120, $1,416.00; #121, $33.18. The bank statement balance is $10,023.61. The company's records indicate a cash balance of $5,845.77. Prepare a bank reconciliation statement for Lube-All.

4. The McBee Furniture Company received the monthly bank statement showing a balance of $9,319.35. The balance in the company's cash account reveals a balance of $5,697.77 on the date of the bank statement. The bank statement contained a $9 service charge, a $5 collection fee, an authorized draft for $600, plus a deposit of $2,700 for a $2,500 note plus interest of $200 collected by the bank. An examination of the bank statement reveals that the following checks were outstanding: #204, $130.50; #228, $1,846.20; #230, $496.76; #231, $1,445.61. The company mailed deposits for $1,190 and $1,193.49, but they were en route when the statement had been prepared by the bank. Prepare a bank reconciliation resolving these discrepancies.

Chapter 9
Self-Evaluation

1. Prepare a horizontal analysis for the comparative balance sheet for the Dobson Company.

2. Prepare a vertical analysis of the income statement of the Dobson Company.

3. Determine the following ratios for the Dobson Company for 19–2.
   (a) Current ratio
   (b) Acid test ratio (assume a merchandise inventory of $15,000 for 19–2)
   (c) Plant assets to long-term liabilities
   (d) Rate of return on total assets
   (e) Inventory turnover (beginning inventory, $17,000; ending inventory, $15,000; cost of merchandise sold, $102,000)

4. Determine the correct bank balance for the Dobson Company using the following information for June. A bank service charge for $2.78, a $4 note collection fee, and a $450 deposit for rent collected for the Dobson Company are included on the bank statement. The company records indicate the following checks had been issued but not yet received by the bank when the statement had been prepared: #82, $19.72; #84, $146.20; #85, $37.25. A check for $46.35 had been recorded in the checkbook as $46.55. The bank statement balance is $3,742.60. The company records indicate a cash balance of $3,096.01.

Dobson Company
Income Statement
Year Ended December 31, 19–1

	Amount	Percent
Revenue:		
Net sales	$781,000	__________
Total operating expenses:	508,000	__________
Operating income	$273,000	__________
Less federal income tax	70,900	__________
Net income	$202,100	__________

Dobson Company
Comparative Balance Sheet
December 31, 19–1, and December 31, 19–2

	December 31 19–2	December 31 19–1	Amount of Increase (or Decrease)	Percent of Increase (or Decrease)
Assets				
Current assets	$ 77,000	$ 43,000	__________	__________
Plant assets (net)	214,000	193,000	__________	__________
Total assets	$291,000	$236,000	__________	__________
Liabilities				
Current liabilities	$ 14,000	$ 26,000	__________	__________
Mortgage payable	125,000	117,000	__________	__________
Total liabilities	$139,000	$143,000	__________	__________
Capital				
Walt Dobson, capital	$152,000	$ 93,000	__________	__________
Total liabilities and capital	$291,000	$236,000	__________	__________

Chapter 10
Distribution of Net Income

The main goal of any business is to realize a profit. If the revenues (the amount received from customers for goods and services) exceed the expenses (the costs incurred in selling goods or rendering services to customers), the business realizes a profit. If the expenses exceed the revenues, the business suffers a loss.

After the amount of profit (or loss) is determined and reported on the income statement at the end of each accounting period, this amount must be distributed among the owners of the business. The way profit or loss is distributed is directly related to the way the business is organized.

There are three primary forms of business organization: sole proprietorship (single owner), partnership (two or more owners), and corporation (stockholders).

A sole proprietorship is the most common and least complex form of business ownership. Almost three out of four business firms in the United States are individually owned. A single-owner business is usually small because the capital is limited to the investment of one person. The primary advantage of this type of organization is that the owner receives all of the net profit earned by the business. The primary disadvantage is that the owner must also bear the entire financial burden of any loss incurred by the business. Since the owner receives all the profit (or loss), no special mathematical calculations are required to divide the profit (or loss) at the end of each accounting period.

A variety of methods are used to distribute the net income (or loss) for a partnership or a corporation. The material in the remainder of this chapter explains some of the methods commonly used.

This chapter will enable you to:

1. distinguish among the three primary forms of business ownership: sole proprietorship, partnership, and corporation

2. distribute the net income of a partnership when
    (a) there is equal distribution among the partners
    (b) the distribution is based on a ratio
    (c) the distribution is based on the capital investment of each partner
    (d) one or more of the partners receives a salary and the remainder is distributed based on the capital investment of each partner
    (e) the partners receive a stated rate of interest on their capital investment and a salary, and the remainder is distributed equally

3. distinguish between participating and nonparticipating, cumulative and noncumulative stock

4. distribute the net income of a corporation when
    (a) the corporation has only common stock outstanding
    (b) the corporation has both common and preferred stock outstanding
    (c) the preferred stock is participating and/or cumulative

Learning Unit 10.1
Distribution of Net Income for a Partnership

Characteristics of a Partnership

A *partnership* is a form of business organization in which two or more persons mutually agree to pool their investments, skills, and/or energies to carry on a business for profit. A partnership can be formed on the basis of an oral contract, although a written contract, known as *articles of partnership,* is recommended.

The articles of partnership is a legal agreement setting forth, among other things, the responsibilities and restrictions, as well as the method of distribution of profits and losses, of the partnership. In the absence of a written agreement (or if the written agreement does not specify the manner in which net income will be distributed), the profits are divided among the partners on an equal basis.

Under a partnership arrangement, responsibilities and net income may be divided in any way that is mutually agreeable. However, profits are usually distributed on the basis of the amount of time, skill, and/or capital contributed by each partner.

Some of the typical methods of dividing business profits and losses are illustrated in the examples below. For purposes of these examples, assume that Ames, Bell, and Crews organized a partnership known as ABC Enterprises. The net profit earned by the partnership the first year was $48,600. Let's examine some of the ways this profit could be divided in accordance with the terms of different partnership agreements.

Example: *Net Income Is Distributed Equally Among the Partners.* If the partnership agreement specifies that net income will be shared equally, or if there is no formal agreement, how is the net income distributed?

Solution: The net income is divided by the number of partners.

$$\frac{\$48,600}{3} = \$16,200 \quad \text{per partner}$$

Example: *The Distribution of Net Income Is Based on a Ratio.* The partnership agreement specifies that net income will be shared at a ratio of 3:2:1 (3 shares for Ames, 2 shares for Bell, and 1 share for Crews). Describe the distribution.

Solution: The net income is multiplied by a ratio fraction computed for each partner. The denominator of the ratio fraction is the sum of the shares of all the partners. The numerator is the number of shares that the individual partner is entitled to.

$$3 + 2 + 1 = 6$$

$$\frac{3}{6} \times \$48{,}600 = \$24{,}300 \quad \text{Ames's share of the net income}$$

$$\frac{2}{6} \times \$48{,}600 = \$16{,}200 \quad \text{Bell's share of the net income}$$

$$\frac{1}{6} \times \$48{,}600 = \$\ 8{,}100 \quad \text{Crews's share of the net income}$$

Example: *The Distribution of Net Income Is Based on the Amount of Capital Invested by Each Partner.* Compute the distribution of net income if the partners have invested the following amounts: Ames, \$16,000; Bell, \$22,000; Crews, \$12,000.

Solution: The total net income is multiplied by an investment ratio fraction computed for each partner. The denominator of the ratio fraction is the total capital investment of all the partners. The numerator is the capital investment of the individual partner.

$$\$16{,}000 + \$22{,}000 + \$12{,}000 = \$50{,}000 \quad \text{Total capital}$$

$$\frac{\$16{,}000}{\$50{,}000} = .32 = 32\% \quad \text{Ames's investment}$$

$$\frac{\$22{,}000}{\$50{,}000} = .44 = 44\% \quad \text{Bell's investment}$$

$$\frac{\$12{,}000}{\$50{,}000} = .24 = 24\% \quad \text{Crews's investment}$$

$$\$48{,}600 \times .32 = \$15{,}552 \quad \text{Ames's share of net income}$$

$$\$48{,}600 \times .44 = \$21{,}384 \quad \text{Bell's share of net income}$$

$$\$48{,}600 \times .24 = \$11{,}664 \quad \text{Crews's share of net income}$$

Example: *One or More of the Partners Receives a Salary, and the Remainder of the Net Income Is Distributed Based on the Amount of Capital Invested.* If the partnership agreement specifies that Crews, who is manager, will be paid an annual salary of $15,000, how is the net income distributed? (Assume the same investment amounts as in the previous example.

Solution: (1) The salary (or salaries) are subtracted from the net income to find the amount to be distributed.

(2) The amount to be distributed is multiplied by an investment ratio fraction computed for each partner to find income distribution (see preceding example).

(3) Salaried partners receive income distribution *plus* salary.

$48,600	Net income
− 15,000	Salaries
$33,600	Remainder to be distributed

$33,600 × .32 = $10,752   Ames's share of net income

$33,600 × .44 = $14,784   Bell's share of net income

$33,600 × .24 = $8,064 + $15,000 = $23,064
Crews's share of net income

Example: *The Partners Receive a Stated Rate of Interest on Their Capital and Salaries, and the Remainder of the Net Income Is Distributed Equally.* The partnership agreement stipulates that 10% interest will be paid on each partner's invested capital. In addition, Ames will receive a salary of $18,000; Bell, $20,000; and Crews, $15,200. The remainder will be distributed equally. Describe the distribution.

Solution: (1) The capital investment of each partner is multiplied by the rate of interest to find each partner's interest amount.

(2) Total salaries and total interest are subtracted from net income to find the amount to be distributed.

(3) The amount to be distributed is divided by the number of partners.

$16,000 × .10 = $1,600   Interest on Ames's investment
$22,000 × .10 = $2,200   Interest on Bell's investment
$12,000 × .10 = $1,200   Interest on Crews's investment
$5,000   Total interest

$18,000   Ames's salary
20,000   Bell's salary
15,200   Crews's salary
$53,200   Total salary

$48,600   Net income
− 5,000   Interest allowance
− 53,200   Salary allowance
−$ 9,600   Deficiency to be divided equally

$1,600 + $18,000 − $3,200 = $16,400   Ames's share

$2,200 + $20,000 − $3,200 = $19,000   Bell's share

$1,200 + $15,200 − $3,200 = $13,200   Crews's share

A summary of the procedures involved in the mathematical distribution of net income is provided in Table 10.1 on page 227.

Exercises

Distribute the net profit or net loss for the following partnerships.

1. Ames, Bell, and Crews made a profit of $47,100. The partners plan to share equally.
   Ames __________
   Bell __________
   Crews __________

2. Moore, Nolen, and Rogers made a $64,800 profit. There is no formal division ratio agreed upon.
   Moore __________
   Nolen __________
   Rogers __________

3. Spears, Tison, and Young made a profit of $86,100. Using a 2:3:2 ratio, divide the profit.
   Spears __________
   Tison __________
   Young __________

Table 10.1
Distribution of Income for a Partnership

Distribution method	Mathematical procedures
Equal Distribution	$\text{Distribution} = \dfrac{\text{Net Income}}{\text{Number of Partners}}$
Preagreed Ratio	$\text{Distribution} = \dfrac{\text{Number of Shares of Each Partner}}{\text{Sum of Shares of All Partners}} \times \text{Net Income}$
Initial Investment Ratio	$\text{Distribution} = \dfrac{\text{Capital Investment of Each Partner}}{\text{Total Capital Investment}} \times \text{Net Income}$
Salary and Capital Investment	$\text{Amount to Be Distributed} = \text{Net Income} - \text{Salaries}$ $\text{Distribution} = \dfrac{\text{Capital of Each}}{\text{Total Capital}} \times \text{Amount to Be Distributed}$
Interest on Capital, Salary, and Equal Distribution	$\text{Interest for Each} = \text{Capital of Each} \times \text{Rate of Interest}$ $\text{Amount to Be Distributed} = \text{Net Income} - (\text{Total Interest} + \text{Total Salaries})$ $\text{Distribution} = \dfrac{\text{Amount to Be Distributed}}{\text{Number of Partners}}$

4. Cook, Collins, and Case had a loss of $98,120. Using a ratio of 5:3:3, divide the loss.

   Cook _________
   Collins _________
   Case _________

5. Jones invested $28,000, Miles invested $14,000, and Moody invested $42,000. The partners agreed upon a return based on their capital investment. Distribute the $67,140 profit.

   Jones _________
   Miles _________
   Moody _________

6. Kane invested $36,000, Lott invested $24,000, and Lowe invested $20,000. Distribute a profit of $76,900, based on each partner's capital investment.

   Kane ___________

   Lott ___________

   Lowe ___________

7. The profit for Pool, Wagner, and Weems is distributed on the basis of their investment after all salaries are paid. Each of them receives a salary of $9,000. Pool invested $10,000; Wagner, $30,000; and Weems, $40,000. The net profit was $11,160.

   Pool ___________

   Wagner ___________

   Weems ___________

8. In the partnership of Phipps, McMeens, and Harris, Phipps receives a salary of $20,000, and McMeens a salary of $22,000. Phipps invested $36,000; McMeens, $24,000; and Harris, $20,000. If the profit is distributed based on the capital investment, distribute the net profit of $63,500 after paying the salaries.

   Phipps ___________

   McMeens ___________

   Harris ___________

Practical Applications

9. In forming a new partnership, Guy invested $20,000, Nail invested $28,000, and Ross invested $32,000. They agreed to receive an 8% return on their investment, each having a salary of $10,000, with the remainder to be divided equally. Distribute the net income of $62,800 to the three partners.

   Guy ___________

   Nail ___________

   Ross ___________

10. Reel and Roy reorganize their partnership and bring in Rood as a new partner. There is a net profit of $31,640. Reel receives a salary of $18,000, 8% on his investment of $40,000, and an equal share of the remainder; Roy receives a salary of $15,000, 8% on her investment of $60,000, and an equal share of the remainder; and Rood

receives a salary of $14,000, 8% on his new investment of $50,000, and an equal share of the remainder. Determine each partner's share of the net profit.

Reel _____________

Roy _____________

Rood _____________

11. Townley and Thomas have decided to form a partnership. They have agreed that Townley will invest $40,000 cash, and Thomas will invest land and a building valued at $60,000. The following plans for division of net profit are being considered. Determine the division of the net income if the projected income for the first year is $23,000.

(a) The net income is to be divided equally.
Townley _____________ Thomas _____________

(b) Townley and Thomas are to divide on a 2:3 ratio.
Townley _____________ Thomas _____________

(c) Net income is to be divided according to the amount invested.
Townley _____________ Thomas _____________

(d) Townley will receive a salary of $15,000; Thomas, a salary of $12,000; with the remainder divided equally.
Townley _____________ Thomas _____________

Learning Unit 10.2
Distribution of Net Income for a Corporation

Characteristics of a Corporation

A *corporation* is the most complex form of business organization. It is a legal entity: an artificial being created by law and established through a state or federal charter. The charter grants the corporation many of the rights, duties, and powers of a person.

Ownership in a corporation is represented by shares of stock and is measured by the number of shares a person owns. Persons who invest in a corporation by purchasing stock are *stockholders* or *shareholders.* Division of the ownership into shares represented by stock certificates provides a basis for distributing profits to the owners. A portion of the profit is distributed to the owners of the corporation (the stockholders) on each share they own and is called a *dividend.* Dividends may be distributed in cash, other assets, or the corporation's own stock.

Computation of Stock Dividends

A corporation may issue two classes of stock: common stock and preferred stock (see Figure 10.1). *Common stock* represents a share of corporation ownership but carries no guarantee about the size of dividends. *Preferred stock* also represents a share of corporation ownership, but this class of stock has a preset dividend that in most cases is limited.

Common Stock. When only common stock is issued by the corporation, the dividend paid per share is determined by dividing the total dividends declared by the number of shares outstanding (the number of shares that have been issued).

Example: The Mull Corporation has 25,000 shares of common stock outstanding. What is the dividend per share in a year in which the board of directors declared dividends totaling $60,000?

Solution: $\dfrac{\$60,000}{25,000} = \$2.40$ dividend per share

Preferred Stock. Most stock is issued with a par value (amount) printed on the stock certificate. The par value of a stock is an arbitrary value established in the charter of the issuing corporation and does not necessarily reflect the market value of the stock. Preferred stock is granted priority over common stock in the payment of dividends; in other words, dividends on preferred stock are always paid first (and therefore computed first).

Dividend payments on preferred stock are usually limited to a fixed dollar amount per share or to a specified percent of par value. When the dividend is fixed as a dollar amount per share, the preferred dividend paid per share is determined by multiplying the dollar amount by the number of preferred shares. When the dividend is fixed as a percent of par value, the preferred dividend paid per share is determined by multiplying the par value by the specified percent.

Specimens of Common and Preferred Stock Certificates

Source: Courtesy of the NCR Corporation, Dayton, Ohio.

Example: Carl Stout owns 100 shares of preferred stock. What is the total dividend that he can expect to receive from the corporation each year (a) if it is $4 preferred stock; (b) if it is 5%, $100 par value stock?

Solution: (a) 100 × $4 = $400   annual dividend on 100 shares
(b) $100 × .05 = $5   dividend per share
$5 × 100 = $500   annual dividend on 100 shares

Preferred stock may be participating or nonparticipating. *Participating* preferred stock can earn dividends in excess of the specified percentage or dollar amount. (*Nonparticipating* stock cannot earn dividends above this rate.) After the common stockholders have received a specified dividend per share (usually equal to the preferred dividend), the participating preferred stockholders have a right to participate with the common stockholders in any additional dividends declared.

Example: The Wilson Corporation has 6,000 shares of $5 nonparticipating preferred stock and 50,000 shares of common stock. The board of directors declared dividends totaling $180,000. What dividends will be paid on the preferred and common stock?

Solution: 6,000 × $5 = $30,000   preferred dividends
$180,000 − $30,000 = $150,000   common dividends

Example: Assume that the preferred stock in the preceding example is fully participating. If the board of directors declared dividends totaling $180,000, what dividends will be paid on the preferred and common stock after each common share has received a specified dividend of $1.88?

Solution: 6,000 × $5 = $30,000   preferred dividends
$1.88 × 50,000 = $94,000   specified common dividends
$180,000 − ($30,000 + $94,000)
= $56,000   excess dividends

$$\frac{\$56,000 \text{ excess dividends}}{6,000 + 50,000 \text{ total shares}} = \$1 \quad \text{per share extra dividend}$$

Preferred stockholders' dividend:

Regular dividend	$ 30,000
Extra dividend (6,000 × $1) =	6,000
Total dividend	$ 36,000

Common stockholders' dividend:

Specified dividend	$ 94,000
Extra dividend (50,000 × $1) =	50,000
Total dividend	$144,000

Preferred stock, in addition to being participating or nonparticipating, may be cumulative or noncumulative. If the stock is *noncumulative,* the right to receive dividends is forfeited in any year in which the dividends are not paid. If the stock is *cumulative,* unpaid dividends accumulate, and the preferred stockholder has a legal claim to any past unpaid dividends. Dividends due from years in which no dividend was declared must be paid to the owners of cumulative preferred stock before any dividends are paid to other stockholders.

Example: The Walker Corporation has 3,000 shares of $4, noncumulative preferred stock outstanding. Because of a net loss last year, the board of directors limited the payment of dividends on preferred stock to $3 per share. If $18,000 dividends are declared this year, the preferred stockholders have a right to what amount of dividends?

Solution: 3,000 × $4 = $12,000   preferred dividends (stated annual amount only)

Example: Assume that the stock in the previous example is cumulative preferred stock. What amount of dividends do the preferred stockholders have a right to?

Solution: 3,000 × $1 = $3,000   unpaid dividends from last year
3,000 × $4 = $12,000   stated annual dividend

Unpaid dividends	$ 3,000
Present annual dividends	12,000
Total dividends	$15,000

(This dividend must be paid before any dividends can be paid to common stockholders.)

Exercises

Determine the dividends per share for the following stock issues.

	Shares outstanding	Class of stock	Dividend declared	Special instructions
1.	30,000	Common	$ 64,000	
2.	10,000	Common	$ 50,000	
	2,000	$5, preferred		
3.	100,000	Common	$150,000	
	10,000	5%, $100		
4.	180,000	Common	$685,000	
	25,000	5%, $80 par		
5.	10,000	Common	$119,000	specified dividend on common stock— $5 per share
	7,000	$5 participating		
6.	180,000	Common	$685,000	preferred dividend previous year— $3 per share
	25,000	8%, $50 par cumulative		
7.	20,000	Common	$180,000	preferred dividend previous year— none paid
	15,000	$4 cumulative		
8.	50,000	Common	$205,000	specified dividend on common stock— $1.85 per share
	5,000	$6 participating		

Determine the amount of the declared dividend that will be used for each class of stock.

	Dividend last year	Declared dividend	Class of stock
9.	$1	$307,000	90,000 common
	$3		20,000 5%, $80 par cumulative
10.	$2	$138,000	30,000 common
	$4		3,000 8%, $100 par cumulative
11.	$1	$152,600	20,000 common $4 specified
	$4		8,000 $4 participating

12.	$.50 $2	$950,000	200,000 common 50,000 $6 preferred cumulative
13.	$.30	$73,250	29,500 common 0 $5 preferred participating
14.	$2.10 $8	$1,625,000	250,000 common $4 specified 50,000 8%, $100 par participating
15.	$.80 $2	$2,772,000	1,200,000 common 210,000 8%, $50 par cumulative
16.	$1.10 $2	$74,800	40,000 common 8,000 preferred 7%, $100 par

Practical Applications

17. P & P Co., Inc. had a net income of $45,000 for the previous year. The board of directors voted to retain $24,000 of the net income and pay the remainder as dividends. Determine the dividend per share for the following situations: (a) Assume that there are 18,500 shares of common stock outstanding. (b) Assume that the outstanding shares of stock include 3,000 shares of 6%, $80 par, preferred stock and 15,000 shares of common stock.

18. Gresham, Inc. has had the following outstanding stock for each of its first three years of operation: 4,000 shares of 7%, $100 par, cumulative preferred stock and 50,000 shares of common stock. Determine the dividends per share for each class of stock for each of the years of operation. (a) $14,000 dividends were declared in the first year. (b) $50,000 dividends were declared in the second year. (c) $228,000 dividends were declared in the third year.

19. CCC, Inc. had a net income of $1,360,000 for the past year. The board of directors voted to retain 60% of the net income and pay the remainder as dividends. Determine the total amount of dividends for each class of stock under the following assumptions. (a) There are 400,000 shares of common stock outstanding. (b) There are 50,000

shares of 5%, $100 par participating preferred stock outstanding and 100,000 shares of common stock outstanding with a specified dividend of $1.89. (c) No dividends were paid for the previous year. There are 10,000 shares of $3 cumulative, preferred stock; 40,000 shares of 5%, $80 par, preferred stock; and 100,000 shares of common stock outstanding.

Chapter 10
Self-Evaluation

Distribute the net profit for the following partnerships.

1. Shield and Ames agreed to share profits equally for their partnership. The net profit for the current year is $39,780.
   Shield _________
   Ames _________

2. Justin, Mallory, and Timmons have an agreement whereby Mallory receives a salary of $8,000 and Timmons a salary of $14,000. They share any remaining profit on a 5:3:2 ratio. If the net profit for this year is $56,000, what is the share for each partner?
   Justin _________
   Mallory _________
   Timmons _________

3. Travis invested $50,000 cash and Duke invested a building and land valued at $30,000 into their partnership. They agreed to share net profits on the basis of their capital investment. How much did each receive from a profit of $48,864?
   Travis _________
   Duke _________

4. Elam, Goodner, and Drake invested $30,000, $50,000, and $20,000, respectively, in their partnership. They agreed to receive a stated rate

of interest of 10% on their investment and share the remainder equally. How much did each receive from a net profit of $51,010?

Elam _________

Goodner _________

Drake _________

5. JMT has stock outstanding as follows: 6,000 shares of 6%, $100 par and 80,000 shares of common stock. The board of directors voted to declare $236,000 for dividends. How much did each class of stock receive for dividends?

(a) preferred _________

(b) common _________

6. Molkraft, Inc., had a net profit of $85,000 this year. The board of directors voted to pay 60% of the profit as dividends to 3,000 6%, $100 par, participating preferred and 20,000 common shareholders. How much dividend did each class of stock receive?

(a) 6%, $100 par, participating _________

(b) common _________

7. S & A, Inc., had a net income of $1,238,000 this year. The board of directors voted to set aside the $38,000 toward an interest payment on a bond issue and to retain 30% of the remainder. Distribute the dividends for the following classes of outstanding stock: 4,000 shares of 5%, $80 par cumulative, preferred, on which a $3 dividend was paid last year; 10,000 shares of $7 preferred stock on which a dividend of $4 was paid last year; 1,000,000 shares of common stock on which a dividend of $1 was paid last year. What was the dividend per share for each class of stock?

(a) 5%, $80 par, cumulative preferred _________

(b) $7 preferred _________

(c) common _________

PART FOUR
THE MATHEMATICS OF FINANCE

Business finance is primarily concerned with the source, cost, and applications of funds. Financial considerations of where to obtain and how to make the most effective use of funds are constantly affecting decisions made by the management of a business. For a business, the three basic sources of funds are (1) funds invested by owners, (2) funds borrowed from creditors, and (3) earnings retained by the business (not paid out in dividends). These sources provide funds for short-term, intermediate-term, and long-term financing.

Most of the funds obtained for short-term financing (less than one year) are obtained indirectly from vendors, through the purchase of materials and merchandise on credit; from commercial banks that extend loans; and from sales finance companies that finance inventories. Funds for long-term financing are obtained from owners through their investment or from earnings retained by business for debt retirement and expansion. Another important source of long-term funds, especially for corporations, are bonds and mortgages on land, buildings, and equipment.

The chapters in this part of your text provide an opportunity for you to become better acquainted with the cost and sources of funds obtained by business.

Chapter 11
Short-Term Credit

Businesses usually acquire goods and services on credit; that is, the business is permitted a period of time following a purchase before payment must be made. Credit for supplies, merchandise, and services is usually extended on *open account.* The buyer makes an oral or implied promise to pay for the goods or services, usually within 30 to 60 days. Normally, there are no interest charges for credit extended on open account.

Credit extended for periods in excess of 60 days is usually granted on the basis of a formal instrument of credit such as a *promissory note.* Promissory notes are used in settlement of an open account and in borrowing and lending money. Two kinds of notes are used in business: noninterest-bearing and interest-bearing notes.

A promissory note is an unconditional promise in writing made by one person to another, signed by the maker, to pay on demand or at a definite time a specific sum of money to order or to bearer. The elements of an interest-bearing promissory note are illustrated in Figure 11.1.

Interest is the price paid for the use of money and is the amount paid in excess of the amount originally borrowed. The computation of simple interest and bank discount is discussed in this chapter.

This chapter will enable you to:

1. **calculate simple interest for a short-term credit transaction**

2. **determine the principal, rate, and time of the loan when one of these factors is missing**

3. **determine the maturity date for a short-term credit transaction**

4. **describe the elements of a promissory note**

5. **distinguish between simple interest and bank discount**

6. **calculate the discount on a promissory note**

Figure 11.1 Promissory Note (Interest Bearing)

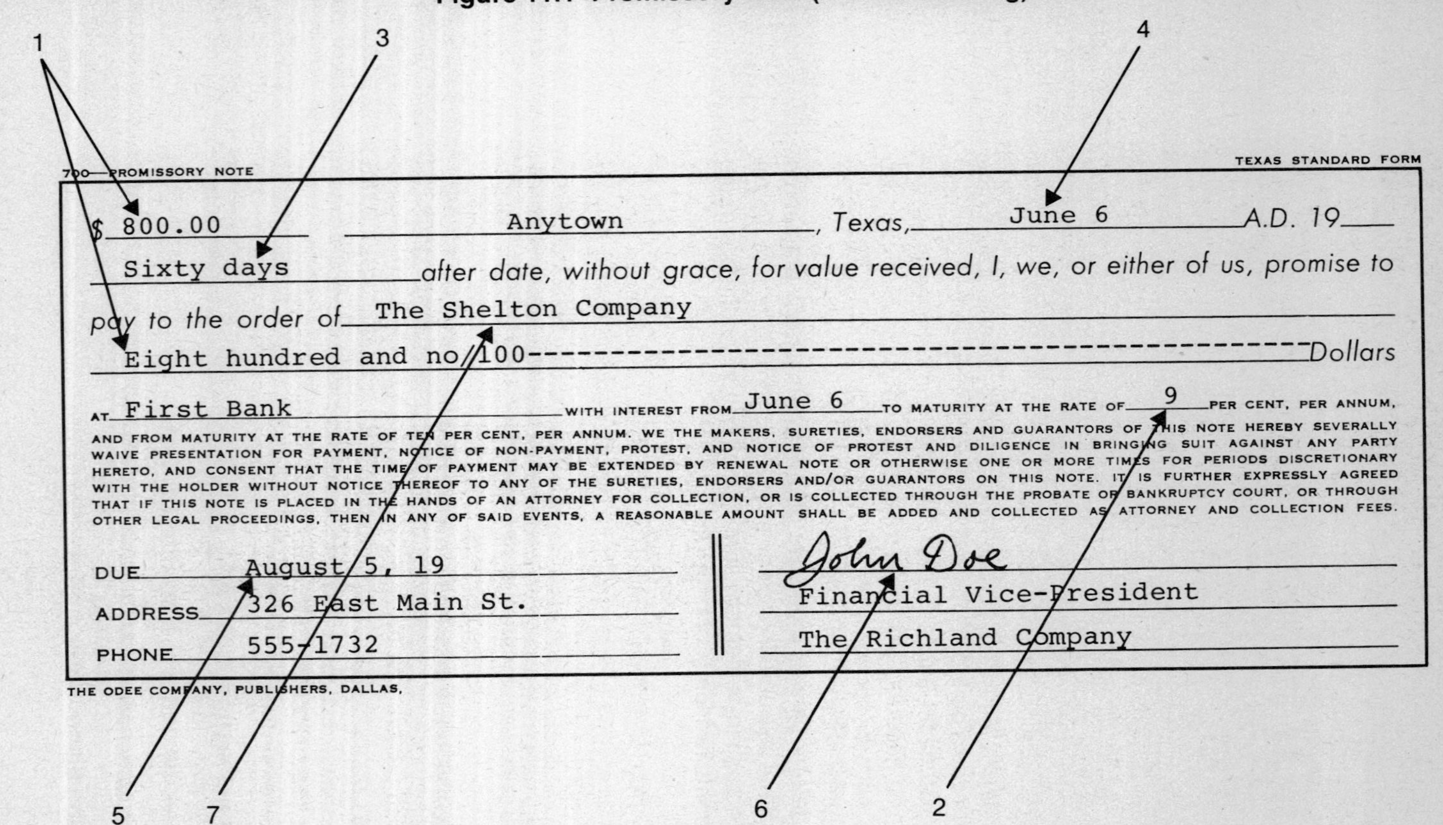

1. The *principal* ($800.00) is the amount of the debt. It is the amount of money borrowed in the credit transaction.

2. The *rate* (9 percent) expresses the value paid for use of the borrowed money. It is usually stated in annual, or yearly, terms.

3. The *time* (60 days) is the period for which the money is borrowed.

4. The *date* (June 6) is the date the note was issued.

5. The *maturity date* (August 5) is the day the principal and interest are due. It is often called the due date.

6. The *maker* (The Richland Company) is the individual or company issuing the note and borrowing the money.

7. The *payee* (The Shelton Company) is the individual or company extending the credit.

Learning Unit 11.1
Simple Interest

Simple Interest Formula

Interest is the price that is paid for the privilege of using someone else's money for a specified period of time. It is a kind of "rental" fee that must be paid to the lender along with the original sum borrowed.

The amount of interest charged on a loan or debt depends on three things:

1. *Principal* (*P*)—the amount of money borrowed
2. *Rate* (*R*)—the percent of interest that is charged annually
3. *Time* (*T*)—the number of days, months, or years in the term of the loan

The basic formula for computing simple interest is:

$$I = P \times R \times T$$

The percent, or rate, of interest is usually expressed on a *yearly* basis. Although time may be given in days and months, as well as years, time is always converted to years to make rate and time correspond.

Time is most easily expressed as a fraction of a year. When time is expressed in years, the denominator of the time fraction is 1. When time is expressed in months, the denominator is 12. And, as we shall see later, when time is expressed in days, the denominator will be either 365 for the "exact" year or 360 for the "ordinary" year.

Example: The Bilco Company borrowed $1,000 for three months at a rate of 10%. What is the amount of simple interest on the loan? (The fractional forms of principal, rate, and time are used to simplify computation.)

Solution: $I = P \times R \times T$

$$I = \frac{\overset{10}{\cancel{\$1{,}000}}}{1} \times \frac{10}{\underset{1}{\cancel{100}}} \times \frac{\overset{1}{\cancel{3}}}{\underset{4}{\cancel{12}}}$$

$$I = \frac{\overset{5}{\cancel{\$10}}}{1} \times \frac{\overset{5}{\cancel{10}}}{1} \times \frac{1}{\underset{\underset{1}{2}}{\cancel{4}}} \qquad\qquad I = \frac{\$5}{1} \times \frac{5}{1} \times \frac{1}{1}$$

$$I = \$25$$

Example: $4,000 was borrowed for two years at an interest rate of 12%. How much simple interest will be charged?

Solution: $I = P \times R \times T$

$$I = \frac{\overset{40}{\cancel{\$4,000}}}{1} \times \frac{12}{\underset{1}{\cancel{100}}} \times \frac{2}{1}$$

$$I = \frac{\$40}{1} \times \frac{12}{1} \times \frac{2}{1}$$

$$I = \$960$$

Exact Time and Ordinary Time

When the term of a loan is expressed in days, either exact time or ordinary time may be used in computing interest. *Exact time* is based on a 365-day year and is always used by the federal government and federal reserve banks in their dealings with branch banks.

Ordinary time is based on a 360-day year (each month is assumed to have 30 days). Ordinary time was formerly used by many commercial institutions. However, because of recent emphasis on maximum interest rate ceilings, many banks and lending institutions no longer use ordinary interest but exact interest instead.

Exact (365-Day Year) Interest Method

In calculating exact interest, the denominator of the time fraction is 365 (the exact number of days in a year), and the numerator is the exact number of days in the term of the loan:

$$T = \frac{\text{exact number of days in the term of the loan}}{365}$$

The numerator of the time fraction (exact number of days in the term of the loan) may be calculated by (1) counting the days on a pocket calendar; (2) mathematically computing the exact number of days, based on the exact number of days in each month; or (3) using a special table (The Number of Each Day of the Year, Appendix D) that denotes the number of each day in the year.

To calculate days by using a calendar, simply begin counting with the day after the origination date of the loan (the day the loan was made) and continue until the due date. Notice that the *last day* of the term of the loan (the due date) *is* counted, but the *first day* of the loan *is not*.

The process required in the mathematical computation of the exact number of days is illustrated in the example below.

Example: Determine the number of days between May 12 and September 18.

Solution: May has 31 days.

$$31 - 12 =$$

19	days remaining in May
30	days in June
31	days in July
31	days in August
18	days in September
129	total days

Use of the special table, The Number of the Day of the Year, found in Appendix D, is probably the most convenient method of determining the exact number of days within a time period. In this table, each day of the year is listed in consecutive order and is assigned a "day number" from 1 to 365. To determine the exact number of days in the term of a loan, subtract the day number of the origination date from that of the due date.

Example: The term of a loan extends from March 7 to June 15. Determine the number of days in the term.

Solution:

	Day Number	
June 15 =	166	
March 7 =	− 66	
	100	days from March 7 to June 15

To determine the exact number of days in the term of a loan when the term extends beyond the end of a calendar year, the table can be used in two steps:

1. Calculate the number of days from the origination date to December 31.
2. To this amount add the number of days remaining in the term from January 1 until the due date.

Example: Using exact time, find the number of days from November 12 to February 15.

Solution:

	Day Number
December 31 =	365
November 12 =	−316
	49
January 1–February 15 =	+ 46
	95 days from November 12 to February 15

After the proper time fraction has been determined, exact interest can then be calculated by using the basic interest formula.

Example: The Shelton Company borrowed $800 on January 15 at a rate of 9%. The loan was due on March 16. What was the amount of exact interest on the loan?

Solution:

$$\left.\begin{array}{l} \text{March 16} = \quad 75 \\ \text{January 15} = -15 \\ \hline \qquad\quad 60 \quad \text{days} \end{array}\right\} \text{(Calculate exact time.)}$$

$$I = P \times R \times T$$

$$I = \frac{\$800}{1} \times \frac{9}{100} \times \frac{\overset{12}{\cancel{60}}}{\underset{73}{\cancel{365}}}$$

$$I = \frac{\$8}{1} \times \frac{9}{1} \times \frac{12}{73}$$

$$I = \$11.84$$

Ordinary (360-Day Year) Interest Method

In calculating ordinary interest, each month is assumed to have 30 days. Thus, for instance, any three-month period would be considered 90 days (3 × 30). The denominator of the time fraction for ordinary interest is 360 (12 × 30). After the proper time fraction has been determined, ordinary interest can then be calculated by using the basic interest formula, as shown on page 244.

Example: Field Plumbing Company borrowed $800 for two months at a rate of 9%. What was the amount of ordinary interest on the loan?

Solution: 2 months = 60 days (2 × 30)

$$I = P \times R \times T$$

$$I = \frac{\$\cancel{800}}{1} \times \frac{9}{100} \times \frac{\cancel{60}^{\;1}}{\cancel{360}_{\;6}}$$

$$I = \frac{\$8}{1} \times \frac{9}{1} \times \frac{1}{6}$$

$$I = \$12$$

Maturity Value

The total amount of money that must be repaid by the borrower on a loan that has matured (become due) is the *maturity value*. Maturity value (*MV*) is the sum of the principal (*P*)—the amount originally borrowed—and any interest (*I*) on the loan. The formula for finding maturity value is:

$$MV = P + I$$

Thus, to determine maturity value:

1. Calculate the interest on the loan.
2. Add the interest and the principal.

Example: John's barber shop secured a 90-day, $1,000 note at 10% due on April 4. How much money must be repaid to the bank on April 4?

Solution: (1) $I = P \times R \times T$

$$I = \frac{\$1,000}{1} \times \frac{10}{100} \times \frac{90}{365}$$

$$I = \$24.66$$

(2) $MV = P + I$

$$MV = \$1,000 + \$24.66$$

$$MV = \$1,024.66$$

Exercises

Find the amount of ordinary interest on the following promissory notes.

	Principal	Rate	Time	Interest
1.	$ 3,000.00	6%	36 days	————
2.	$ 5,000.00	7%	90 days	————
3.	$ 4,000.00	8%	145 days	————
4.	$ 1,400.00	9%	60 days	————
5.	$11,000.00	8%	300 days	————
6.	$ 6,200.00	6.5%	45 days	————
7.	$ 9,300.00	10%	42 days	————
8.	$ 4,060.00	9%	90 days	————
9.	$ 4,000.00	7.25%	60 days	————
10.	$ 1,900.00	11%	48 days	————
11.	$ 800.00	8.5%	137 days	————
12.	$ 2,640.00	12%	150 days	————
13.	$ 1,296.57	5.5%	80 days	————
14.	$ 570.50	6.75%	36 days	————
15.	$ 1,200.00	12%	95 days	————

Find the amount of simple interest on the following promissory notes using the exact interest method.

	Principal	Rate	Time	Interest
16.	$ 800.00	8%	90 days	————
17.	$ 1,200.00	9%	150 days	————
18.	$ 976.00	7%	146 days	————
19.	$14,000.00	8.5%	225 days	————
20.	$ 7,328.00	11%	310 days	————
21.	$ 5,722.00	10%	125 days	————
22.	$ 1,000.00	6%	146 days	————
23.	$ 3,000.00	8%	100 days	————
24.	$ 350.00	15%	30 days	————
25.	$ 820.00	11%	150 days	————

Determine the difference between the ordinary interest and the exact interest on the following promissory notes.

	Terms of the Note	Ordinary Interest	Exact Interest	Difference
26.	$600 at 7% for 60 days	______	______	______
27.	$1,300 at 8% for 90 days	______	______	______
28.	$3,600 at 11% for 320 days	______	______	______
29.	$8,500 at 8.5% for 120 days	______	______	______
30.	$730 at 5% for 80 days	______	______	______

Practical Applications

(When time is given in days, use exact time unless otherwise instructed.)

31. AAA Appliances issued a promissory note for the $12,542 balance on open account with a supplier. The note is for 90 days at a rate of 8%. What is the maturity value of the note?

32. Edsel Realtors loaned $500 to one of its salespersons on a four-month, 6% promissory note. How much must the salesperson pay the firm when the note matures in four months?

33. Ben Phillips borrowed $300 from an uncle to pay the tuition and purchase books for courses he enrolled in at Central Community College. He agreed to repay the loan in four months with interest of 7%. How much interest will he pay for the loan?

34. Fun House Novelties obtained a 90-day, 11% loan from a supplier. What is the interest charge on the loan if the principal was $5,000?

35. Bob's Transfer and Storage borrowed $9,000 on a 12%, 120-day note. How much interest will be charged on the note?

36. An open account with a balance of $22,500 was paid with a promissory note. The note was issued for six months at a rate of 9%. What is the maturity value of the note?

37. A small business owner borrowed $3,500 at 9% for 18 months. How much principal and interest will be repaid upon maturity of the loan?

38. Mrs. Wilson, a high school English teacher, borrowed $6,000 to buy a new car. She was able to get an 11% loan for four years. How much will she have paid for the car after it is completely paid for?

Learning Unit 11.2
Finding the Principal, Rate, and Time

There are occasions when the amount of interest on a loan is known, but one of the other factors in the interest formula is missing. If all but one of the interest factors are known, the missing factor can be calculated by using a variation of the interest formula.

Beginning with the basic interest formula, $I = P \times R \times T$, solutions can be obtained for the principal, the rate, and the time by isolating the unknown on one side of the equation as discussed in Chapter 3. (When solving for principal, rate, or time, the denominator in the time fraction could be either 360 or 365. For convenience only, the examples and problems used in this unit will use a 360-day year.)

Calculating the Principal

Use the interest formula and isolate P:

$$I = P \times R \times T$$

$$\frac{I}{R \times T} = \frac{P \times (R \times T)}{(R \times T)}$$

$$\frac{I}{R \times T} = P \quad \text{after cancellation}$$

Example: The interest on a 6%, 60-day loan was $8. What was the amount borrowed?

$$\text{Solution: } P = \frac{I}{R \times T} = \frac{\$8}{(6 \div 100) \times (60 \div 360)} = \frac{\$8}{(6 \div 100) \times (1 \div 6)}$$

$$= \frac{8}{(1 \div 100)} = \frac{8}{1} \times \frac{100}{1} = \$800$$

Calculating the Rate of Interest

Using the interest formula, isolate R:

$$I = P \times R \times T$$

$$\frac{I}{P \times T} = \frac{P \times R \times T^{1}}{P \times T}$$

$$\frac{I}{P \times T} = R$$

Example: What is the rate of interest on a 60-day loan for $400 if the interest on the loan is $6?

$$\text{Solution: } R = \frac{I}{P \times T} = \frac{\$6}{(\$400 \div 1) \times (60 \div 360)}$$

$$= \frac{\$6}{(\$400 \div 1) \times (1 \div 6)} = \frac{\$6}{(\$400 \div 6)}$$

$$= \frac{\$6}{1} \times \frac{6}{400} = \frac{36}{400} = \frac{9}{100} = 9\%$$

Calculating the Time

Using the interest formula, isolate T:

$$I = P \times R \times T$$

$$\frac{I}{P \times R} = \frac{(P \times R) \times T}{(P \times R)}$$

$$\frac{I}{P \times R} = T \quad \text{after cancellation}$$

Example: The interest on a 12%, $700 loan is $14. What is the time on the loan?

[1] $P \times R \times T = R \times P \times T$; therefore, divide by $(P \times T)$ to isolate R.

Solution: $T = \dfrac{I}{P \times R} = \dfrac{\$14}{(\$700 \div 1) \times (12 \div 100)}$

$$= \dfrac{\$14}{(7 \div 1) \times (12 \div 1)} = \dfrac{\$14}{\$84} = \dfrac{7}{42} = \dfrac{1}{6} \text{ of a year}^2$$

$$T = \dfrac{1}{6} \times \dfrac{360 \text{ days}}{1} = 60 \text{ days}$$

Figure 11.2 will help you remember the correct formula to calculate the principal, rate, or time when the algebraic solution is not used. To determine the formula needed to solve for the principal, rate, or time, cover the unknown factor in Figure 11.2. The remaining arrangement of factors will be the necessary formula to solve for the unknown factor. (Of course, I will always be the numerator.)

Figure 11.2 Calculating Principal, Rate, and Time

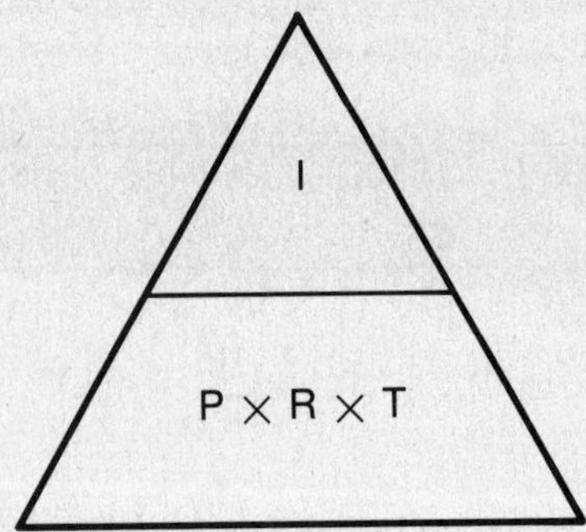

Exercises

Find the principal for the following loans (one year = 360 days).

	Time	Rate	Interest	Principal
1.	90 days	8%	$ 80.00	_______
2.	120 days	9%	$ 24.00	_______
3.	60 days	7%	$ 11.20	_______

[2]The time formula provides an answer showing the fractional or decimal portion of a year. The portion of a year must be multiplied by 360 (ordinary) or 365 (exact) to obtain the number of days on the loan. Multiply by 12 to obtain the number of months.

	Time	Rate	Interest	
4.	60 days	5%	$ 10.25	___
5.	30 days	10%	$ 69.50	___
6.	60 days	11%	$169.95	___

Find the rate of interest for the following loans (one year = 360 days).

	Principal	Time	Interest	Rate
7.	$5,000.00	60 days	$100.00	___
8.	$ 700.00	120 days	$ 28.00	___
9.	$1,710.00	300 days	$ 44.00	___
10.	$4,800.00	72 days	$ 62.40	___
11.	$3,160.00	180 days	$146.65	___
12.	$ 855.00	280 days	$ 33.25	___

Find the time for the following loans (one year = 360 days).

	Principal	Rate	Interest	Time
13.	$2,000.00	7%	$ 14.00	___
14.	$ 372.00	14%	$ 8.68	___
15.	$4,000.00	8.5%	$ 42.50	___
16.	$1,440.00	4%	$ 51.20	___
17.	$6,152.00	9%	$ 23.07	___
18.	$5,700.00	7%	$133.00	___

Practical Applications

(In the following problems, one year = one year, 12 months, or 360 days.)

19. If V. W. Jones invested $2,500 at 6%, how many days would it be before his investment earned $75?

20. If V. W. Jones wishes to earn $100 interest on his investment during a six-month investment period, what rate of interest must he obtain in order to do so? (See problem number 19.)

21. Mary Greene would like to supplement her annual income by $100 per month through investments. If she obtained a 6% rate, how much would she need to invest to earn this supplement?

22. T. D. Street borrowed $7,500 for 90 days. The cost of the loan was $150. What rate of interest did he pay?

23. What amount of money will Somerset Realty have to deposit in a savings account to have an additional $600 in 120 days? The rate of interest for money deposited in the account is 5%.

24. At what rate of interest will Bill's Barber Supply have to invest $13,000 for 120 days to earn approximately $500?

25. In how many days will a $15,000 savings deposit by Wester's Office Supply earn $187.50? The rate of interest paid on the savings account is 5%.

26. Bill Postwait paid $27 interest on a 9%, 90-day promissory note. What amount of money did he borrow?

Learning Unit 11.3
Bank Discount

Bank Discount vs. Simple Interest

As we saw in the last unit, interest on a loan or note can be paid on the due date (simple interest transaction). However, interest on a loan or note can also be paid on the origination date by deducting the interest amount *in advance* from the original amount of the note (bank discount transaction). The original amount of the note is the *maturity value*; the interest deducted in advance from the maturity value is the *bank discount.*

Bank discount (*BD*) is calculated on the basis of the maturity value (*MV*) of the loan or note, the rate of discount (*R*), and the time period (*T*), or term of the note:

$$BD = MV \times R \times T$$

The bank discount is then deducted from the maturity value of the loan to calculate the *net proceeds* (*NP*), the amount that the borrower actually receives:

$$NP = MV - BD$$

On the due date of the loan or note, the borrower must repay only the original amount of the note—the maturity value—because the interest has already been paid.

In order to see how bank discount is computed and how the elements, formulas, and procedures in a bank discount transaction compare with those in a simple interest transaction, let's examine the following example.

Example: The Alpha Printing Company obtained a *bank discount note* for $1,000 for one year at a 6% discount rate. The Beta Printing Company obtained a *simple interest note* for $1,000 for one year at a 6% interest rate. Find (a) the net proceeds of the discount note and (b) the maturity value of the interest note.

Solution: (a) *Bank Discount Note*

$$BD = MV \times R \times T$$

$$BD = \frac{\$1,000}{1} \times \frac{6}{100} \times \frac{1}{1}$$

$$BD = \$60$$

$$NP = MV - BD$$

$$NP = \$1,000 - \$60$$

$$NP = \$940$$

$$\$1,000 = \text{maturity value} \begin{cases} \text{amount "borrowed"} \\ \text{and} \\ \text{amount to repay} \end{cases}$$

$$\$60 = \text{bank discount} \begin{cases} \text{calculated on basis of} \\ \text{maturity value and} \\ \text{paid on origination date} \end{cases}$$

$$\$940 = \text{net proceeds} \begin{cases} \text{amount received} \\ \text{by borrower} \end{cases}$$

(b) *Simple Interest Note*

$$I = P \times R \times T$$

$$I = \frac{\$1,000}{1} \times \frac{6}{100} \times \frac{1}{1}$$

$$I = \$60$$

$$MV = P + I$$

$$MV = \$1,000 + \$60$$

$$MV = \$1,060$$

$$\$1,000 = \text{principal} \begin{cases} \text{amount borrowed} \\ \text{and} \\ \text{amount received by borrower} \end{cases}$$

$$\$60 = \text{interest} \begin{cases} \text{calculated on basis} \\ \text{of principal and} \\ \text{paid on due date} \end{cases}$$

$$\$1,060 = \text{maturity value} \begin{cases} \text{amount} \\ \text{to repay} \end{cases}$$

To reemphasize: In the bank discount transaction, Alpha Printing Company receives $940—it has paid nothing out of its own pocket. At the end of one year (upon maturity), Alpha will have to pay the bank $1,000 ($940 actually received plus $60 in interest). Thus, the amount "borrowed" ($1,000) is also the amount that has to be repaid (the maturity value).

Example: Medical Lab Services borrowed $8,000 from the Downtown Bank on a 12%, 90-day note. What were the bank discount and net proceeds on the loan? (Use exact time for the rate.)

Solution: $BD = MV \times R \times T$

$$BD = \frac{\$8,000}{1} \times \frac{12}{100} \times \frac{90}{365} = \$236.71$$

$$NP = MV - BD$$

$$NP = \$8,000 - \$236.71 = \$7,763.29$$

Discounting Notes—General

As we discussed in the beginning of this chapter, a promissory note is a promise in writing to pay the maturity value of a loan at a specified time.

We have seen that promissory notes can be written at simple interest or simple discount.

Promissory notes are classified as notes payable (liability) and notes receivable (asset). As we have seen in the preceding examples, a note (note payable) may be signed by the borrower to obtain a loan from a bank. However, a promissory note is also a *negotiable* instrument, which means that it may be sold (note receivable) to a third party for cash, in payment for goods or services, or to discharge a debt. Banks are the usual purchasers of promissory notes and do so at a discount. For instance, if a business needs cash to meet unexpected or unusual expenses, notes owned by the business may be taken to a bank and discounted. The bank determines the maturity value of the note, deducts the bank discount (interest charged for holding the note to the maturity date), and gives the net proceeds to the business.

The bank discount and net proceeds of notes sold to a bank and then discounted may be found by applying the discount formulas that we learned earlier: $BD = MV \times R \times T$ and $NP = MV - BD$. However, before being able to apply these formulas, we must take a closer look at the concept and value of Time (T) as it applies to notes discounted after the origination date.

As we saw earlier in this unit, for notes discounted *on* their origination date, the discount is applicable to the total duration of the note. Therefore, we saw that *Time* (T), for purposes of the formula, *is equal to the number of years, months, or days in the term of the note.*

However, a note that is held and then sold to a bank at discount is discounted *after* the origination date. The discount on this note is applicable only to the period of time in which the bank holds the note. Therefore, Time (T), for purposes of the formula, is the number of years, months, or days *remaining* in the term of the note after the bank takes possession. This period of time is generally referred to as the *discount period.*

To summarize:

Notes discounted on origination date	}	T = original term of the note
Notes discounted after origination date	}	T = discount period (days remaining in the term of the note)

The procedures required in calculating the discount period are described in detail in the following discussion on noninterest-bearing notes.

Discounting Noninterest-Bearing Notes

Promissory notes may be interest bearing or noninterest bearing. A noninterest-bearing note makes no provision for interest, i.e., the maker promises to pay only the principal when the note matures.

As we just explained, we will be able to determine net proceeds (how much the business will receive) on a discounted noninterest-bearing note by applying the discount formulas learned earlier ($BD = MV \times R \times T$ and $NP = MV - BD$), but we must first determine the discount period.

Calculating Maturity Date and Discount Period

The first step in determining the discount period is to calculate the *maturity date* of the note, i.e., the day the note is due and payable.

To calculate the maturity date, the exact number of days in the term of the loan must be determined. Any of the methods described for determining exact time in computing interest (calendar count, mathematical computation based on exact days in the month, or use of the special table in Appendix D) may be applied. However, here again, the exact number of days can be determined most conveniently by using The Number of Each Day of the Year Table:

1. Find the day number of the origination date.
2. Add the number of days in the term of the note to the day number of the origination date to find the day number of the maturity date.
3. Find the date in the table that corresponds to the day number of the maturity date.

Example: What is the maturity date on a 90-day note issued by the Shelton Company on March 24?

Solution:

Origination Date		Day Number		Maturity Date
March 24	=	83		
Length of note	=	+90 days		
		173	=	June 22

After determining the maturity date of the note, the number of days remaining on the note—the discount period—can be calculated. Using the table in Appendix D:

1. Find the day number of the discount date.

2. Subtract the day number of the discount date from the day number of the maturity date.

Example: If the Shelton Company discounts a 90-day, $3,000 note at the bank on April 5, how long will the bank hold the note (what is the discount period)? (The maturity date was obtained in the preceding example.)

Solution:

		Day Number
Maturity date	= June 22	173
Day discounted	= April 5	− 95
Discount period	=	78 days

After determining the discount period (the value of T in the discount formula), bank discount and net proceeds can then be computed.

Example: What are the bank discount and net proceeds for a 90-day, $3,000 note discounted by the Shelton Company on April 5? The current bank discount rate is 9%.

Solution: The discount period is 78 days (from preceding example).

$$BD = MV \times R \times T$$

$$BD = \frac{\$3,000}{1} \times \frac{9}{100} \times \frac{78}{365}$$

$$BD = \$57.70$$

$$NP = MV - BD$$

$$NP = \$3,000 - \$57.70$$

$$NP = \$2,942.30 \quad \text{amount Shelton Company will receive}$$

To summarize: To find net proceeds on a noninterest-bearing note:

1. Determine the maturity date.
2. Determine the discount period.
3. Determine the bank discount.
4. Determine the net proceeds.

Discounting Interest-Bearing Notes

The procedures for discounting an interest-bearing note are similar to those for a noninterest-bearing note, with one exception: the maturity value of the note must be *calculated*, i.e., interest must be computed and added to the principal. In the case of noninterest-bearing notes, the maturity value is simply equal to the principal.

An important thing to keep in mind when calculating bank discount and net proceeds on an interest-bearing note is that two separate transactions have taken place. In the first transaction, a note is issued, an interest rate established, and a maturity value determined. In the second transaction, the note is sold to the bank and discounted.

To find the net proceeds on a discounted interest-bearing note:

1. Determine the amount of *interest* on the note.
2. Determine the *maturity value* of the note.
3. Determine the *maturity date* of the note.
4. Determine the *discount period*.
5. Determine the *bank discount*.
6. Determine the *net proceeds*.

Example: The Brigham Company received a 60-day, 9% note from a customer for $5,200 on June 7. What were the net proceeds if the note was discounted at the bank on June 21 at a rate of 12%? (Use ordinary time to compute interest and the counting method to determine number of days.)

Solution: (1) $I = P \times R \times T$

$$= \$5,200 \times \frac{9}{100} \times \frac{60}{360}$$

$$= \$78 \quad \text{interest}$$

(2) $\$5,200 + \$78 = \$5,278$ maturity value of the note

(3)

Term of the note		60
June (days)	30	
Date of the note	7	
Days remaining in June	23	
July (days)	31	
Total		54
Due date in August		6

(4)

June (days)	30	
Date of discount	21	
Days remaining in June		9
July (days)		31
Due date of the note in August		6
Discount period		46 days

$$(5) \quad BD = MV \times R \times T$$

$$= \$5{,}278 \times \frac{12}{100} \times \frac{46}{360} = \$80.93 \quad \text{bank discount}$$

$$(6) \quad NP = MV - BD$$

$$= \$5{,}278 - \$80.93 = \$5{,}197.07 \quad \text{net proceeds}$$

Bank Discount Terms, Symbols, and Formulas

BD = bank discount (interest deducted by the bank on the day of the loan)
NP = net proceeds (amount of the loan less the bank discount)
T = discount period (length of time the bank holds a discounted note)
R = discount rate (rate of interest charged by the bank)
MV = maturity value (amount due on a note on the maturity date)
$BD = MV \times R \times T$ (*bank discount = maturity value × discount rate × discount period*)
$NP = MV - BD$ (*net proceeds = maturity value − bank discount*)

Exercises

Determine the maturity date for the following notes.

	Origination Date	Time	Maturity Date
1.	May 10, 1979	90 days	__________
2.	February 22, 1979	30 days	__________
3.	February 8, 1980	150 days	__________
4.	August 6, 1979	60 days	__________
5.	November 6, 1980	120 days	__________
6.	March 6, 1979	75 days	__________
7.	January 3, 1981	135 days	__________
8.	July 8, 1980	80 days	__________
9.	April 18, 1979	300 days	__________
10.	October 4, 1980	230 days	__________

Determine the bank discount and net proceeds for the following noninterest-bearing notes. (Use the exact year.)

	Principal, Time, Discount Rate	Bank Discount	Net Proceeds
11.	$3,000, 80 days, 9%	_______	_______
12.	$920, 150 days, 8%	_______	_______
13.	$1,380, 70 days, 6.5%	_______	_______
14.	$1,900, 210 days, 7.29%	_______	_______
15.	$1,300, 240 days, 11%	_______	_______
16.	$3,800, 330 days, 7%	_______	_______
17.	$12,000, 360 days, 6.75%	_______	_______
18.	$11,000, 200 days, 8.25%	_______	_______
19.	$763, 90 days, 7%	_______	_______
20.	$479, 60 days, 5%	_______	_______

Determine the maturity date and maturity value of the following notes. (Use exact interest.)

	Principal	Rate	Time	Origination Date	Maturity Date	Maturity Value
21.	$2,000	8%	60 days	March 6, 1979	_______	_______
22.	$4,000	10%	90 days	April 14, 1979	_______	_______
23.	$ 960	7.75%	30 days	February 6, 1980	_______	_______
24.	$6,070	6.5%	45 days	June 10, 1980	_______	_______
25.	$2,140	11%	120 days	August 16, 1981	_______	_______
26.	$7,520	10%	160 days	November 5, 1980	_______	_______
27.	$4,200	6.25%	210 days	December 3, 1979	_______	_______
28.	$3,100	9%	90 days	May 10, 1980	_______	_______
29.	$1,240	8.5%	70 days	April 18, 1981	_______	_______
30.	$2,110	6.75%	100 days	June 7, 1980	_______	_______

Practical Applications

The Richland Company received the following notes. They were discounted at the Commercial Bank of North Texas at 8.5%. Determine the bank discount and the net proceeds for each note received. (Use exact interest.)

	Origination Date	Principal	Time	Rate	Bank Discount Date	Bank Discount	Net Proceeds
31.	July 22	$ 5,000	60 days	7%	August 1	_______	_______
32.	February 18	$ 1,600	120 days	8%	March 9	_______	_______
33.	March 25	$ 3,200	90 days	8%	April 24	_______	_______
34.	July 3	$ 4,700	180 days	9%	September 1	_______	_______
35.	December 15	$ 8,000	30 days	7.5%	December 20	_______	_______
36.	September 6	$ 900	45 days	6.5%	September 16	_______	_______
37.	June 7	$ 2,800	90 days	7.75%	June 17	_______	_______
38.	May 10	$ 2,150	60 days	7%	May 20	_______	_______
39.	August 8	$12,000	30 days	9%	August 8	_______	_______
40.	January 6	$ 4,300	180 days	6%	February 5	_______	_______

Chapter 11
Self-Evaluation

1. Determine the interest for the following note using the simple interest formula and the ordinary year.
   $2,200 for 60 days at 9%

2. Determine the interest for this note using the exact year.
   $3,000 for 73 days at 10%

3. Solve for the missing factor (I, P, R, or T).
   (a) $800 for 60 days, $12 interest
   (b) 90 days at 8%, $50 interest
   (c) $1,440 for 90 days at 9%
   (d) $1,300 for 30 days, $13 interest

4. Determine the maturity date of the following short-term notes.
   (a) A 60-day note dated May 17
   (b) A 100-day note dated November 1

5. Determine the net proceeds of the following noninterest-bearing note.
    $3,700 for 80 days at 8%

6. Determine (a) the maturity date and (b) the maturity value of the
    following note.
    $7,000, 8%, 90-day note dated June 7

7. Determine the net proceeds for the following note.
    $2,700 for 150 days at 8%, dated July 22; discounted August 21 at
    10%

Chapter 12
The Time Value of Money

Financial institutions are in a highly competitive market. Their income is derived from interest on the money they loan. The amount available for loans comes from individuals' investments and deposits. To be competitive, compound interest is paid to encourage more investors to deposit their savings with a particular institution. The material in this chapter contains computations pertaining to compound interest, present value, ordinary annuities, sinking funds, and amortizations.

This chapter will enable you to:

1. **calculate compound interest using the compound interest formula**

2. **calculate rate and time using the compound interest formula**

3. **calculate compound amounts and compound interest using a compound interest table**

4. **calculate present value amounts using a present value table**

5. **calculate the amount of an ordinary annuity using an annuity table**

6. **calculate the present value of an ordinary annuity using a present value of annuity table**

7. **calculate the periodic payment for a sinking fund**

8. **calculate the periodic payment to amortize a debt**

Learning Unit 12.1
Compound Interest

Compound Interest vs. Simple Interest

How is compound interest different from simple interest? *Simple interest* is computed only once and only on the principal. On the other hand, *compound interest* (which, technically, means "interest earned on interest") is computed periodically, and interest is earned not only on the principal but also on all interest accumulated since the original deposit.

The difference between simple interest and compound interest is illustrated in the example below.

Example: Investor X makes an investment of $1,000 for one year at 8% simple interest. Investor Y makes the same investment at the same terms, but interest is compounded quarterly. What is the difference in earnings between the simple interest and compound interest investments?

Solution: *Simple Interest*

$$I = P \times R \times T$$

$$= \frac{\$1,000}{1} \times \frac{8}{100} \times \frac{1}{1}$$

$$= \$80$$

Compound Interest

First Quarter $\quad I = \dfrac{\$1,000}{1} \times \dfrac{8}{100} \times \dfrac{1}{4} = \quad \$20.00$

Second Quarter $\quad I = \dfrac{\$1,020}{1} \times \dfrac{8}{100} \times \dfrac{1}{4} = \quad 20.40$

Third Quarter $\quad I = \dfrac{\$1,040.40}{1} \times \dfrac{8}{100} \times \dfrac{1}{4} = \quad 20.81$

Fourth Quarter $\quad I = \dfrac{\$1,061.21}{1} \times \dfrac{8}{100} \times \dfrac{1}{4} = \quad 21.22$

$$\text{Total Interest} = \$82.43$$

When interest is compounded quarterly, $2.43 more ($82.43 − $80.00) is earned.

In the example, we can see exactly what takes place when interest is compounded. Each time that interest is computed, the interest is added to the previous principal. That total then becomes the principal for the next interest period. After the first computation, interest is being paid on a new, higher principal balance, and thus more interest is generated.

Compound Interest Tables

In the preceding example, when $1,000 was invested for one year at 8% interest compounded quarterly, four different calculations of simple interest were needed to determine the final compound interest amount. A simpler, far less tedious method of calculating compound interest is the use of the compound interest table (see Table 12.1 and Appendix E).

However, in order to be able to use this table, we must be able to determine:

1. the compound interest rate, and
2. the number of compound interest periods in the term of the investment

Compound Rate. The compound interest rate is expressed as a rate per compound period. Therefore, the annual interest rate must be converted to its corresponding rate per period (i).

To determine this rate, divide the annual interest rate by the number of compound interest periods in one year.

Example: What is the interest rate per compound period when 12% interest is compounded quarterly?

Solution: $i = \dfrac{.12}{4 \text{ (four quarters in one year)}} = .03 = 3\%$ per quarter

Compound Interest Period. The compound interest period is the interval at which interest is computed and added to the previous principal. Compound interest is traditionally calculated on a semiannual, quarterly, or monthly basis, although some institutions compound daily or even hourly. In order to compute compound interest, the term of the investment must be converted to its total number of compound interest periods (n).

Example: How many times will interest be compounded if interest is compounded quarterly for ten years?

Solution: There are four quarters, or compound periods, in one year. Therefore, $4 \times 10 = 40$ (periods in ten years), or $n = 40$.

Use of Tables. Given the same facts as in the first example at the beginning of this chapter ($1,000 for one year at 8% compounded quarterly), the compound amount and compound interest can be computed using the compound interest table, according to the following steps:

1. Determine the number of interest periods (n).
    (1 year $\times$ 4 quarters per year $= 4$ interest periods)
2. Determine the interest rate per period.
    (8% annual rate $\div$ 4 quarters per year $= 2$% per period)
3. Using the compound interest table, find the compound interest factor for the two items determined in steps 1 and 2. [Note that the compound interest table found in Appendix E is presented in combination with other tables that we will be using later in this chapter. These tables are organized on the basis of the percent rate found in the top left corner of each page. To find the compound factor, (1) locate the page with the appropriate rate (in our example, 2%), (2) find the appropriate number of interest periods in the "Periods" column (in our example, 4), and (3) read across to the compound factor (in our example, 1.08243216) in the compound amount column. For illustration purposes, the portion of the 2% table that is required to solve the example is reproduced in Table 12.1.]
4. Determine the compound amount.
    (principal $\times$ compound factor, or $1,000 \times 1.08243216 = $1,082.43)
5. Find the amount of compound interest.
    (compound amount $-$ principal)

$$
\begin{array}{rl}
\$1,082.43 & \text{compound amount} \\
-\ 1,000.00 & \text{principal} \\
\hline
\$\ \ \ 82.43 & \text{compound interest}
\end{array}
$$

Example: Determine the interest on $2,000 invested for two years at 12% compounded monthly. Use the compound interest table contained in Appendix E for your solution.

Solution: (1) 2 years $\times$ 12 interest periods per year $= 24$ periods
(2) 12% annual rate $\div$ 12 interest periods per year $= 1$%
(3) Compound factor from the table $= 1.26973465$
(4) $2,000 investment $\times$ 1.26973465 $= $2,539.47
(5)

$$
\begin{array}{rl}
\$2,539.47 & \text{compounded amount} \\
-\ 2,000.00 & \text{principal} \\
\hline
\$\ \ 539.47 & \text{compound interest}
\end{array}
$$

Table 12.1 Compound Interest Table

Periods	1%	1 1/4%	1 1/2%	1 3/4%	2%	2 1/4%	2 1/2%
0	1.	1.	1.	1.	1.	1.	1.
1	1.01	1.0125	1.015	1.0175	1.02	1.0225	1.025
2	1.0201	1.02515625	1.030225	1.03530625	1.0404	1.04550625	1.050625
3	1.030301	1.03797070	1.04567838	1.05342411	1.061208	1.06903014	1.07689063
4	1.04060401	1.05094534	1.06136355	1.07185903	1.08243216	1.09308332	1.10381289
5	1.05101005	1.06408215	1.07728400	1.09061656	1.10408080	1.11767769	1.13140821
6	1.06152015	1.07738318	1.09344326	1.10970235	1.12616242	1.14282544	1.15969342
7	1.07213535	1.09085047	1.10984491	1.12912215	1.14868567	1.16853901	1.18868575
8	1.08285671	1.10448610	1.12649259	1.14888178	1.17165938	1.19483114	1.21840290
9	1.09368527	1.11829218	1.14338998	1.16898721	1.19509257	1.22171484	1.24886297
10	1.10462213	1.13227083	1.16054083	1.18944449	1.21899442	1.24920343	1.28008454

Compound Interest Formula

Another way of computing compound interest and the compound amount (ending balance) of an investment is by using the compound interest formula:

$$MV = P(1 + i)^n$$

where:

MV = maturity value (compound amount)

P = principal

i = interest rate per compound interest period

n = number of compound interest periods over the life of the investment

Using the same problem ($1,000 invested for one year at 8% compounded quarterly), we would have:

MV = ?

P = $1,000

i = 2%, or .02 (8% ÷ 4 quarters)

n = 4 (1 year × 4 quarters per year)

Thus:

$$MV = \$1,000 (1 + .02)^4$$

In the algebra of exponents, the expression $(1.02)^4 = 1.02 \times 1.02 \times 1.02 \times 1.02$.

Performing this multiplication process is no small task. Conveniently, the compound interest table lists the values for combinations of $(1 + i)^n$. These values show how much an investment of $1 per period would amount to compounded over various numbers of interest periods and at various rates.

Therefore, just as before, after locating the 2% page in Appendix E, we find 4 in the "Periods" column and read across to the compound amount column to find the compound factor (1.08243216), which is the value of $(1 + i)^n$, or $(1.02)^4$ for our problem.

Thus:

$$MV = \$1,000 \times 1.08243216 = \$1,082.43$$

Since $MV = P + I$ (see Chapter 11),

$$\$1,082.43 = \$1,000 + I$$
$$\$1,082.43 - \$1,000 = I$$
$$I = \$82.43 \quad \text{compound interest}$$

This formula will also be required later in this chapter to compute the compound rate and/or the term of a compound investment as well as annuity values.

Exercises

Using the simple interest formula, determine the compound interest for the following short-term investments.

	Principal	Rate	Time	Interest
1.	$1,800	8% semiannually	1 year	__________
2.	$2,000	6% quarterly	2 years	__________
3.	$5,000	7% quarterly	2 years	__________
4.	$6,000	9% semiannually	3 years	__________
5.	$3,700	10% annually	5 years	__________

Using the compound interest table, determine the maturity value and compound interest for the following notes.

	Principal	Rate	Time	Maturity Value	Compound Interest
6.	$ 1,000	6% quarterly	1 year	__________	__________
7.	$ 1,200	5% quarterly	2 years	__________	__________
8.	$ 5,000	5% semiannually	5 years	__________	__________

	Principal	Rate	Time	Maturity Value	Compound Interest
9.	$ 6,200	10% semiannually	3 years	_______	_______
10.	$14,000	6% annually	7 years	_______	_______
11.	$17,300	12% monthly	4 years	_______	_______
12.	$ 1,900	8% quarterly	6 years	_______	_______
13.	$ 3,300	15% monthly	3 years	_______	_______
14.	$ 4,700	11% quarterly	2 years	_______	_______
15.	$62,000	8% semiannually	10 years	_______	_______

Practical Applications

16. The Smiths invested $3,000 in an account for each of their three children. The accounts paid 7% compounded quarterly. Determine the balance of each account for the following:
    (a) The oldest child withdrew the balance after six years to help with college expenses.
    (b) The second child withdrew the balance after eight years to invest in a business.
    (c) The third child withdrew the balance after nine and one-half years to make a down payment on a house.

17. TCD, Inc., invested $25,000 of unappropriated funds in an account that paid 12% compounded monthly. How much interest had the deposit earned after two years?

18. If Jack Tyler invested $5,000 compounded semiannually at 5% seven years ago, what is the present balance in the account?

19. The Ace Company invested $6,000 for four years at 5% compounded quarterly.
    (a) Determine the maturity value.
    (b) Determine the compound interest.

Learning Unit 12.2
Finding the Principal, Rate, and Time

The compound interest formula, $MV = P(1 + i)^n$, may be used as a financial planning tool. Not only can it be used to determine the amount of interest and the end balance of a compound investment, but its variations can also be used to find the principal, rate, or time.

Finding the Principal

A variation of the compound interest formula can be used to determine how much money is presently required to accumulate into a predetermined future maturity value at a stated rate of interest for a specified amount of time.

Example: John would like to buy a car three years from now using the proceeds of a 12% investment that is compounded quarterly. If the projected car price is $6,000, how much money must be invested today to earn the price of the car?

Solution: Use the compound interest formula and isolate P; then solve using the compound interest table.

$$MV = P(1 + i)^n$$

$$P = \frac{MV}{(1 + i)^n} \quad \text{[Divide both sides of the equation by } (1 + i)^n \text{ to isolate } P.]$$

$$MV = \$6,000$$

$$i = .03 \ (12\% \div 4)$$

$$n = 12 \ (4 \text{ quarters in one year} \times 3 \text{ years})$$

$$P = ?$$

$$P = \frac{\$6,000}{(1 + .03)^{12}}$$

$$P = \frac{\$6,000}{1.42576089} \quad \text{(from the Compound Interest Table)}$$

$$P = \$4,208.28$$

The principal, or current amount, of a compound investment is referred to as the *present value* and will be discussed and illustrated in detail in the next learning unit.

Finding the Rate

A variation of the compound interest formula can be used to determine the compound rate when the amount of the investment, the term of the investment, the compound interest period, and the accumulated amount are known.

Example: What annual interest rate compounded quarterly would be needed for a $3,500 investment to mature to $5,000 after three years?

Solution: $MV = P(1 + i)^n$

$$\frac{MV}{P} = (1 + i)^n \qquad \text{[Divide both sides of the equation by } P \text{ to isolate } (1 + i)^n.]$$

$MV = \$5,000$

$P = \$3,500$

$n = 12$ (4 quarters in one year $\times$ 3 years)

$i = ?$

$$\frac{\$5,000}{\$3,500} = (1 + i)^{12}$$

$$1.42857142 = (1 + i)^{12}$$

Using the compound interest table:

(a) Find 12 in the "Periods" column.
(b) Skim the numbers in the compound amount column on each page until the number on the left side of the equation is found.[1]
(c) Find the quarterly rate in the top left corner of the page (in our example, 3.5%).
(d) Multiply the quarterly rate by 4 (quarters) to find the annual rate (14%).

The annual rate of interest required is 14%.

[1] The table value corresponding to compound periods (n) of 12 and an interest rate (i) of 3.5% is larger than the left side of the equation, but 3.5% is the smallest i value that will guarantee the desired maturity value.

Finding the Time (Number of Interest Periods)

A variation of the compound interest formula can be used to determine the term of the investment (i.e., the number of compound interest periods) when the amount of the investment, the compound interest period, the compound amount, and the interest rate are known.

Example: How long would it take for \$1,500 to mature into \$4,000 if 10% interest is compounded quarterly?

Solution: $MV = P(1 + i)^n$

$\dfrac{MV}{P} = (1 + i)^n$ [Divide both sides of the equation by P to isolate $(1 + i)^n$.]

$MV = \$4,000$

$P = \$1,500$

$i = 2.5\%$, or .025 ($10\% \div 4$)

$n = ?$

$\dfrac{\$4,000}{\$1,500} = (1 + .025)^n$

$2.66666667 = (1 + .025)^n$

Using the compound interest table:
(a)   Find the 2.5% interest rate page.
(b)   Read down the compound amount column until the number on the left side of the equation is found.[2]
(c)   Read left horizontally to the "Periods" column to find time (number of periods).

The number of periods (n) is 40. Therefore, the money will have to be invested for 40 quarters, or 10 years.

[2]The table value corresponding to an interest rate (i) of 2.5% and periods (n) of 40 is larger than the left side of the equation, but 40 is the smallest n value that will guarantee the desired maturity value.

Exercises

In the following problems, determine the annual interest rate.

	Principal	Maturity Value	Time	Compound Period	Annual Rate
1.	$1,000	$3,000	7 years	Quarterly	_______
2.	$1,700	$2,700	$3\frac{1}{2}$ years	Semiannually	_______
3.	$2,500	$4,700	8 years	Semiannually	_______
4.	$ 500	$ 800	6 years	Quarterly	_______
5.	$ 450	$ 600	5 years	Annually	_______
6.	$1,050	$2,000	9 years	Annually	_______

In the following problems, determine the amount of time.

	Principal	Maturity Value	Time	Compound Period	Annual Rate
7.	$1,200	$2,800	_______	Quarterly	12%
8.	$ 500	$ 750	_______	Semiannually	10%
9.	$2,800	$3,500	_______	Annually	8%
10.	$1,400	$1,900	_______	Quarterly	6%
11.	$2,350	$4,200	_______	Monthly	18%
12.	$1,000	$1,950	_______	Annually	7%

Practical Applications

13. How long would it take for $2,000 to mature into $4,250 if 10% interest is compounded quarterly?

14. Ralph Jones would like to have $8,500. If money is currently earning 8% compounded quarterly, how long will it take Ralph's $3,300 to mature to his desired amount?

15. Three years ago Bill Wilson placed $17,500 in a savings account that compounded interest semiannually. If Bill has $21,000 today, what rate of interest did he earn?

16. Karen Jeter would like to buy a car valued at $6,500 four years from now. If she currently has $3,950, what interest rate must she obtain to satisfy her goal if interest is compounded monthly?

Learning Unit 12.3
Present Value

Definition of Present Value

Present value is a measure of the current value of a predetermined future sum of money. It is the amount that an individual or business would have to invest *right now* at the current interest rate in order to end up with some predetermined future sum of money (for instance, $10,000 three years from now). The ability to determine present value is necessary for the success of any individual's or business's long-range financial plans.

In problems involving present value, the ending, or future, value is known, and the beginning, or present, value must be determined. In the preceding chapter on short-term credit, some of the problems that we had to consider involved present value. For instance, in determining the principal, or P, using a variation of the simple interest formula,

$$P = \frac{I}{R \times T}$$

we were actually determining present value—the current amount of investment necessary to earn a stated amount of interest. In determining the net proceeds of a discounted note, we were again actually determining the present value—the present worth of a future maturity value.

Present Value Formula

In the preceding unit we saw how a variation of the compound interest formula, along with the compound interest table, could be used to find present value (principal) at compound interest. However, use of this method for determining present value results in having to divide by a very long decimal number (for instance, in the last unit we had to divide $6,000 by 1.42576089).

Therefore, calculating present value is more easily done by using a formula and table that require multiplication rather than division of the compound factor.

The formula for present value (*PV*) is:

$$PV = MV \times (1 + i)^{-n}$$

where:

PV = present value
MV = maturity value
i = interest rate per compound interest period
n = number of compound interest periods over the life of the investment

This formula requires the use of the Present Value Table found in Appendix F. This table is set up and used in much the same way as the Compound Interest Table. Whereas the Compound Interest Table lists the values of $(1 + i)^n$ (the amount of compound interest per \$1 invested for various periods and rates), the Present Value Table lists the values of $(1 + i)^{-n}$ (the present value of \$1 in the future for various periods and rates).

The present value formula and table can be used to solve the same problem that was presented in the preceding unit, solving for the principal (*P*) by using the compound interest factor.

Example: John would like to buy a car three years from now using the maturity value of a 12% investment that is compounded quarterly. If the projected car price is \$6,000, how much money must be invested today?

Solution: $PV = MV \times (1 + i)^{-n}$

MV = \$6,000

i = .03 (12% ÷ 4)

n = 12 (4 quarters in one year × 3 years)

PV = \$6,000 × $(1 + .03)^{-12}$

Using the Present Value Table in Appendix F, find the present value factor for the number of interest periods (12) and the interest rate per period (3%). [Locate the 3% page, find 12 in the *n* column, and read across to the present value factor (.70137988) in the "Present Value" column.]

PV = \$6,000 × .70137988   (from the Present Value Table)

PV = \$4,208.28

Exercises

Using the Present Value Table, determine the present value of these notes.

	Maturity Value	Rate	Time	Present Value
1.	$ 2,000	4% annually	2 years	————
2.	$ 4,000	6% annually	3 years	————
3.	$ 4,000	7% quarterly	3 years	————
4.	$ 5,000	5% semiannually	4 years	————
5.	$ 7,000	8% semiannually	5 years	————
6.	$ 4,800	5% quarterly	4 years	————
7.	$ 1,600	9% semiannually	3 years	————
8.	$ 5,300	12% quarterly	2 years	————
9.	$ 18,000	8% quarterly	7 years	————
10.	$ 62,000	7% semiannually	10 years	————
11.	$ 36,000	5% annually	12 years	————
12.	$145,000	8% semiannually	15 years	————
13.	$ 19,000	12% monthly	1 year	————
14.	$ 23,000	9% quarterly	6 years	————

Practical Applications

15. Julia Ray is an investment officer for the First Bank. Last week she purchased three notes. What is the present value of each of the notes?
    (a) A $4,300 note due in four years with 8% interest compounded quarterly
    (b) A $2,380 note due in two years with 6% interest compounded semiannually
    (c) A $10,127 note due in five years with 7% interest compounded quarterly

16. What is the present value of a ten-year bond issue of $100,000 if 7% interest is compounded semiannually?

17. John Dumas is planning to sell a house he inherited and to invest the money in a savings account that pays 8% compounded semiannually.

He would like to have a savings account balance of $50,000 after ten years. How much must he invest from the sale of the house in order to have that amount?

18. In order to pay for his college education, Phil's parents want to establish a savings account at age 6 that would provide $16,000 for Phil at age 18. If 6% interest is compounded quarterly, how much money must his parents place into the savings account?

19. Sara Jones would like to retire in ten years and have $50,000 at that time. What single deposit must be made today to mature to $50,000 if 10% interest is compounded quarterly?

Learning Unit 12.4
Annuities

Types of Annuities

In the beginning of this chapter, we saw that compound interest basically involves a *single* amount of payment that is invested all at *one time*. An *annuity*, however, is a *series* of payments (usually but not necessarily equal in amount) that are made at regular *intervals of time*. Although the term *annuity* may indicate it, the payment interval does not have to be a year.

The regular payment received from an insurance policy when it is cashed in after retirement is one obvious example of an annuity. However, examples of annuities also include mortgage payments, installment payments, social security payments—and any other payments made at regular intervals.

There are two basic types of annuities: an annuity certain and a contingent annuity. An annuity is *contingent* if the beginning or ending date is uncertain. Payments on an ordinary life insurance policy are an example of a contingent annuity, since the beginning payment is contingent on the death of the insured. When an annuity has a specified beginning and ending date, it is called an *annuity certain.* Payments made under an installment plan would be an example of an annuity certain.

The type of annuity to be studied in this chapter is the annuity certain. There are two types of annuities certain: *ordinary annuity* and *annuity due*. If the regular payment is made at the end of a period, the annuity is referred to as an *ordinary annuity*. If the payment is made at the beginning of a period, the annuity is referred to as an *annuity due*. Only the ordinary annuity will be discussed.

Ordinary Annuities

In order to demonstrate an ordinary annuity and its formulas, let's suppose that Will Wilson decided to begin saving for his retirement by depositing $1,200 at the end of every year in a savings account that pays 6% interest compounded annually. How much will Mr. Wilson have accumulated in his savings account after seven years?

By using the compound interest formula and table to find the maturity value of $1 deposited each year for seven years, we would have:

		MV	
Year One	$1(1.06)^6 =$	$1.41851911	(6 years' interest)
Year Two	$1(1.06)^5 =$	1.33822558	(5 years' interest)
Year Three	$1(1.06)^4 =$	1.26247696	(4 years' interest)
Year Four	$1(1.06)^3 =$	1.19101600	(3 years' interest)
Year Five	$1(1.06)^2 =$	1.12360000	(2 years' interest)
Year Six	$1(1.06)^1 =$	1.06000000	(1 year's interest)
Year Seven	1 $=$	1.00000000	(no interest)
		$8.39383765	

One dollar deposited at the end of each year for seven years would mature to $8.39. Therefore, $1,200 deposited at the end of each year for seven years would amount to $10,072.61 ($1,200 × 8.39383765).

Annuity Formula

Using the compound interest method to calculate annuities (as demonstrated in the preceding example) would require, for a problem involving, say, monthly payments for ten years, 120 interest calculations (12 × 10).

Fortunately, there are a special annuity formula and annuity tables that can be used to speed up and simplify annuity calculations. The formula for finding the maturity value of an annuity is:

$$MV = P \times \frac{(1 + i)^n - 1}{i}$$

where:

MV = maturity value
P = amount of each payment
i = compound interest rate per payment period
n = number of periods (or payments) over the life of the annuity

or, in its shortened form:

$$MV = P \times S_{\overline{n}|i}$$

where:

$$S_{\overline{n}|i} = \frac{(1 \times i)^n - 1}{i}$$

The annuity table in Appendix G lists values for combinations of $S_{\overline{n}|i}$ and is set up and used in the same way [by locating the appropriate rate page and number of periods (n)] as the compound interest and present value tables studied in the preceding units. In this case, of course, the annuity factor will be found in the "Amount of Annuity" column. The values in the annuity table reflect how much an investment of $1 per period would amount to over various numbers of interest periods at various interest rates.

Let's go back to the same annuity problem that we solved in the beginning of this unit by using the compound interest formula and table, but this time we will use the annuity formula and table. The facts of the problem are repeated in the following example.

Example: Will Wilson decided to begin saving for his retirement by depositing $1,200 at the end of every year in a savings account that pays 6% interest compounded annually. How much will Mr. Wilson have accumulated in his savings account after only seven years?

Solution: $MV = P \times S_{\overline{n}|i}$

P = $1,200

i = 6%

n = 7

$S_{\overline{n}|i}$ = 8.39383765   (from annuity table in Appendix G)

MV = $1,200 × 8.39383765

MV = $10,072.61

Present Value of Ordinary Annuities

The present value of an ordinary annuity is the *single deposit* (principal) necessary to yield, through compounding and periodic payments (withdrawals), the maturity value of an annuity.

The present value of an annuity can be calculated by using the present value of an annuity formula and table. The formula for finding present value of an annuity is:

$$PV = P \times \frac{1 - (1 + i)^{-n}}{i}$$

where:

PV = present value
P = amount of each payment (withdrawal)
i = compound interest rate per payment period
n = number of periods (or payments) over the life of the annuity

or, in its shortened form:

$$PV = P \times A_{\overline{n}|i}$$

where:

$$A_{\overline{n}|i} = \frac{1 - (1 + i)^{-n}}{i}$$

The Present Value of an Annuity Table in Appendix H lists values for combinations of

$$A_{\overline{n}|i} \left[\text{or } \frac{1 - (1 + i)^{-n}}{i} \right]$$

and is set up and used in the same way as the other tables, except that the present value annuity factor is found in the "Present Value of Annuity" column. This table shows how much $1 payable periodically is worth today, according to various interest rates and payment periods.

Example: How much money must be deposited today in order to withdraw $1,000 a year for the next five years if 8% interest is compounded annually?

Solution: $PV = P \times A_{\overline{n}|i}$

$P = \$1,000$

$i = 8\%$

$n = 5$

$A_{\overline{n}|i} = 3.99271004$ (from Present Value of an Annuity Table)

$PV = \$1,000 \times 3.992710$

$PV = \$3,992.71$

Maximum Number of Withdrawals

A variation of the formula for calculating the present value of an ordinary annuity can be used to determine the maximum number of withdrawals a specific annuity will pay.

Example: If $10,000 is used to buy an annuity that will pay $300 a month, how many full payments will be received if interest of 9% is compounded monthly?

Solution: $PV = P \times A_{\overline{n}|i}$

$\dfrac{PV}{P} = A_{\overline{n}|i}$ (Divide both sides of the equation by P to isolate $A_{\overline{n}|i}$.)

$PV = \$10,000$

$P = \$300$

$i = .75\%$

$n = ?$

$\dfrac{\$10,000}{\$300} = A_{\overline{n}|} .75\%$

$33.33333333 = A_{\overline{n}|} .75\%$

Using the Present Value of an Annuity Table, look up the $\frac{3}{4}\%$ (.75%) rate page and find the largest n (period) where the table value ($A_{\overline{n}|}$ .75%) is less than 33.33333333. The table shows that, when $n = 38$, $A_{\overline{n}|}$ .75% = 32.95808016; therefore, 38 full withdrawals, or payments, are possible.

Exercises

Find the accumulated amount of an annuity using the appropriate table in the appendix and the formula $MV = P \times S_{\overline{n}|i}$.

	Payment per Time Period	Length of Time	Annual Interest and Compound Period	Maturity Value
1.	$ 200 per month	$3\frac{1}{2}$ years	12%, monthly	________
2.	$ 500 per quarter	6 years	8%, quarterly	________
3.	$1,000 per year	9 years	7%, annually	________
4.	$ 250 per month	$1\frac{3}{4}$ years	15%, monthly	________
5.	$ 300 per quarter	10 years	10%, quarterly	________

Find the present value of an ordinary annuity using the appropriate table in the appendix and the formula $PV = P \times A_{\overline{n}|i}$.

	Withdrawal per Time Period	Length of Time	Annual Interest and Compound Period	Present Value
6.	$2,500 per year	8 years	6%, annually	________
7.	$ 100 per month	4 years	9%, monthly	________
8.	$ 600 per quarter	$2\frac{1}{4}$ years	6%, quarterly	________
9.	$ 300 per quarter	$5\frac{1}{2}$ years	10%, quarterly	________
10.	$1,200 per year	7 years	8%, yearly	________

Practical Applications

11. Jan Jeffers is saving $300 every three months in a savings account that pays 8% compounded quarterly. How much money will Jan have in her account after four and one-half years?

12. Bill Jones is saving $100 each month for his children's future college expenses. How much will Bill's account have in it after four years if interest of 6% is compounded monthly?

13. Sam Strothers is saving $2,000 each year in an account that pays 7% compounded annually in order to buy a house. How much money will Sam have after 13 years?

14. Cindy Holiday wants to go into business for herself someday. Toward that goal, she is depositing $1,800 a year into a savings account paying 8% interest compounded annually. How much money will Cindy have accumulated after seven years?

15. How many full payments will be received from an annuity that costs $5,000 if the payments are $300 a quarter and interest of 8% is compounded quarterly?

16. If $12,000 is used to purchase an annuity that will pay $400 a month and interest of 15% is compounded monthly, how many full payments will be received from the annuity?

17. Sally Snead sold her restaurant for $10,000 down and quarterly payments of $950 for eleven years. If money is worth 8% and is com-

pounded quarterly, what is the equivalent cash price for the restaurant?

18. Jerry Smith wants to set up an annuity that will pay monthly checks of $250 to his daughter to cover living expenses while in college. How much will Mr. Smith pay for the annuity if interest of 6% is compounded monthly for four years?

19. Jim Kelley plans to retire in 12 years. If he saves $500 every three months and interest is 8% compounded quarterly, how much money will Jim have when he retires?

20. Roland McKenzie wants to take a world cruise in five years. If he saves $1,000 every six months and interest is 8% compounded semiannually, how much money will he accumulate by the time for his trip?

Learning Unit 12.5
Sinking Funds and Amortization

Sinking Funds

Often a business will know that it will need a certain amount of money on some future date to finance an anticipated obligation (e.g., expand facilities, replace equipment, repay a debt). In such situations, it is necessary to determine the amount that must be set aside or invested each period (annuity) to obtain this amount. An annuity that is established to reach a certain and specific maturity value (equal periodic deposits plus compound interest) is a *sinking fund*.

As explained in the preceding learning unit, to find the maturity value of an ordinary annuity, we use the formula:

$$MV = P \times S_{\overline{n}|i}.$$

In a sinking fund, the amount of the obligation (MV), the term, and the current interest rate are known (remember that $S_{\overline{n}|i}$ represents the relationship of the term and rate). The object of a sinking fund problem is to determine the amount of the periodic payment (P). This is done by solving for P in the annuity formula. The result is:

$$P = \frac{MV}{S_{\overline{n}|i}}, \text{ or } P = MV \times \frac{1}{S_{\overline{n}|i}}$$

To save time, a table of values for $1/S_{\overline{n}|i}$ has been derived and can be found in Appendix I (see the "Sinking Fund" column). This table is read in the same manner as previous annuity tables. The values in this table reflect the periodic amounts that must be deposited to grow to $1 over various numbers of interest periods at various rates.

Example: Gary Wilson plans to replace his current office copier in four years at an estimated cost of $15,000. How much should he put into a sinking fund account each quarter if interest is currently 8% compounded quarterly?

Solution: $P = MV \times \dfrac{1}{S_{\overline{n}|i}}$

$MV = \$15,000$

$i = 2\% \ (8\% \div 4)$

$n = 16$

$\dfrac{1}{S_{\overline{n}|i}} = .05365013$ (from the Sinking Fund Table)

$P = \$15,000 \times .05365013$

$P = \$804.75$

In the above example the amount of interest earned can be determined by multiplying the number of payments by the amount of a payment and then subtracting that result from the maturity value.

$$P \times n = \$804.75 \times 16 = \$12,876$$

$$
\begin{array}{rl}
\$15,000 & \text{maturity value} \\
-\ 12,876 & \text{payments} \\
\hline
\$\ 2,124 & \text{interest}
\end{array}
$$

Amortization

In general, when sinking funds are established to retire a future debt or obligation, the equal periodic payments retire only the principal of that debt. When both the principal and interest are retired by a series of equal periodic payments, the process is known as *amortization*. The most familiar example of amortization is the monthly payments that homeowners make to pay off real estate mortgages. Note that the equal periodic payments in a sinking fund *earn interest*, while the equal periodic payments in an amortization *pay off interest* as well as part of the principal.

To calculate the amount of the equal periodic payment needed to retire both principal and interest on a long-term debt, refer back to the present value of an annuity formula (Learning Unit 12.4):

$$PV = P \times A_{\overline{n}|i}$$

and solve for *P*:

$$P = \frac{PV}{A_{\overline{n}|i}}, \text{ or } P = PV \times \frac{1}{A_{\overline{n}|i}}$$

Amortization calculations can be simplified by using the Amortization Table in Appendix J. This table lists the values for combinations of $1/A_{\overline{n}|i}$ and shows the periodic payment necessary to pay off a loan of $1, according to various interest rates and payment periods and based on an annuity worth $1 today. [Note that the debt itself is the present (or beginning) value of the annuity.]

Example: Sam and Mary Jones bought a $20,000 tractor. They agreed to pay 20% down and the balance in monthly payments for four years. What was the amount of each payment if the interest was 12%?

Solution: $P = PV \times \dfrac{1}{A_{\overline{n}|i}}$

$PV = \$16,000\ (\$20,000 - \$4,000\ \text{down payment})$

$i = 1\%\ (12\% \div 12)$

$n = 48$

$\dfrac{1}{A_{\overline{n}|i}} = .02633384$ (from the Amortization Table)

$P = \$16,000 \times .02633384$

$P = \$421.34$ per month

In the above example the amount of interest paid can be found by subtracting the present value from the amount determined by multiplying the monthly payment by the number of payments.

$$P \times n = \$421.34 \times 48 = \$20,224.32$$

$$
\begin{array}{rl}
\$20,224.32 & \text{total payments} \\
-\ 16,000.00 & \text{principal} \\
\hline
\$\ 4,224.32 & \text{interest paid}
\end{array}
$$

Exercises

Using the Sinking Fund Table, determine the amount of the periodic payment (P) for each sinking fund.

	Maturity Value	Rate	Compound Period	Time
1.	$ 80,000	8%	Quarterly	7 years
2.	$ 30,000	6%	Semiannually	12 years
3.	$ 75,000	5%	Annually	20 years
4.	$ 14,000	10%	Quarterly	6 years
5.	$ 25,000	9%	Semiannually	15 years
6.	$110,000	12%	Quarterly	3 years
7.	$ 42,000	7%	Semiannually	10 years
8.	$ 8,000	6%	Annually	8 years

Using the Sinking Fund Table, determine the amount of the periodic payment (P), the total amount of payments, and the total amount of interest in the maturity value for each sinking fund.

	Maturity Value	Rate	Compound Period	Time
9.	$ 21,000	8%	Quarterly	4 years
10.	$ 6,000	12%	Monthly	2 years
11.	$ 18,000	5%	Semiannually	17 years
12.	$ 11,000	9%	Monthly	4 years
13.	$ 36,000	7%	Quarterly	5 years
14.	$150,000	6%	Quarterly	8 years
15.	$ 28,000	9%	Monthly	3 years
16.	$ 17,500	6%	Quarterly	4 years

Using the Amortization Table, determine the periodic payment required to amortize each of the following debts.

	Present Value	Rate	Compound Period	Time
17.	$ 30,000	6%	Semiannually	20 years
18.	$ 8,000	8%	Quarterly	3 years

	Present Value	Rate	Compound Period	Time
19.	$ 60,000	8%	Annually	15 years
20.	$100,000	5%	Semiannually	8 years
21.	$ 24,000	7%	Quarterly	10 years
22.	$ 5,200	8%	Quarterly	4 years
23.	$ 32,000	9%	Semiannually	13 years
24.	$ 50,000	12%	Monthly	4 years

Using the Amortization Table, determine the amount of the periodic payment (P), the total amount to be repaid, and the amount of interest included.

	Present Value	Rate	Compound Period	Time
25.	$ 4,000	8%	Quarterly	10 years
26.	$ 15,000	10%	Semiannually	18 years
27.	$ 14,500	6%	Monthly	$2\frac{1}{2}$ years
28.	$ 25,000	9%	Semiannually	20 years
29.	$ 9,400	14%	Semiannually	3 years
30.	$ 87,000	9%	Monthly	$3\frac{1}{2}$ years
31.	$ 50,000	5%	Annually	5 years
32.	$ 32,000	10%	Quarterly	10 years

Practical Applications

33. The citizens of Hurst Hills voted to issue bonds totaling $500,000 to build an addition to the municipal complex. The bonds will mature in 20 years. If a sinking fund earning 8% compounded semiannually is set up, how much must be deposited every six months to retire the bonds at maturity?

34. Robin Hartley would like to buy a new car in four years and pay cash. Determine the following if the projected cost of the car is $8,000. She is able to set up a sinking fund that pays 9% compounded monthly.
    (a) How much will she need to deposit in the fund each month to have the money she needs?
    (b) How much of the maturity value is interest?
    (c) How much of the maturity value is deposits?

35. DFW International is planning an expansion of their plant in ten years at an estimated cost of $1,000,000. The business will establish a sinking fund at 8% compounded quarterly to finance the project.
   (a)   How much will need to be deposited each quarter?
   (b)   How much of the maturity value is interest?
   (c)   How much of the maturity value is deposits?

36. Betty Crampton purchased a new $7,500 automobile by paying $1,-500 down and signing a 12% note for four years. How much is the monthly payment?

37. Charles and Lindy Finney borrowed $5,000 to add a room to their house. The three-year, 9% loan will be repaid with monthly payments.
   (a)   What is the Finneys' monthly payment?
   (b)   How much interest will be paid on the loan?

38. John Nix borrowed $40,000 to finance the construction of the building for Nix-Nax Antiques. His loan was at 12% semiannually for 20 years.
   (a)   How much was the semiannual payment?
   (b)   How much interest will be paid on the loan?
   (c)   How much is the total cost of the building?

Chapter 12
Self-Evaluation

Using the simple interest formula, determine the compound interest for the following note.

1. $1,600 at 6% compounded quarterly for one year

Using the compound interest table, determine the maturity value for the following notes.

2. $2,700 at 8% quarterly for two years

3. $3,100 at 12% monthly for four years

Using the compound interest formula and table, find the following:

	Principal	Maturity Value	Time	Compound Period	Annual Rate
4.	$1,000	$2,000	$6\frac{1}{2}$ years	Quarterly	_______
5.	$1,500	$4,500	_______	Semiannually	10%

Using the Present Value Table, determine the present value for the following.

6. $1,800 at 9% semiannually for three years

7. $12,000 at 10% quarterly for four years

8. $17,000 at 12% monthly for two years

9. Beth Jennings is saving $200 a month. How much money will she have in four years if interest is compounded monthly at 9%?

10. How much money must be deposited today in order to withdraw $500 a quarter for three years if interest is compounded quarterly at 8%?

11. If $7,000 is used to purchase an annuity that will pay $300 a month and interest of 12% is compounded monthly, how many full payments will the annuity make?

12. The residents of Mayfair passed a $250,000 bond program to finance the construction of two neighborhood parks. A 12-year sinking fund was established at 8% compounded quarterly to redeem the bonds.
(a) What quarterly payment is needed to finance the sinking fund?
(b) How much of the maturity value is deposits?
(c) How much of the maturity value is interest?

13. To purchase a $14,000 recreational vehicle, the Bakers made monthly payments for four years on a 9% loan.
(a) How much was each payment?
(b) How much interest was paid on the loan?
(c) What was the total cost of the van?

Chapter 13
Consumer Credit

Credit has become an accepted part of the American way of life. Credit permits persons to purchase items, albeit at an additional charge, that they might not otherwise be able to afford and eliminates the need to carry money. Although consumers must pay for the convenience of buying on credit, credit purchases by both consumers and businesses have been steadily increasing.

As in the case of most other services, businesses usually pass the cost of credit transactions on to the consumers. In order to make the public aware of the true cost of credit and to allow consumers to compare credit terms, a common basis for stating consumer costs for credit services was stipulated in the Federal Consumer Protection Act (better known as the Federal Truth in Lending Act), which became effective in 1969.

Regulation Z of the Federal Reserve System implements the provisions of this act. Under the provisions of the regulation, a seller is required to disclose the total finance charges (direct and indirect) as well as the annual percentage rate (the interest rate equivalent to the finance charges).

This chapter examines two types of consumer credit: installment plans and open-end credit. When you have successfully completed this chapter, you will be able to:

(1) **identify the elements of installment loans**

(2) **calculate the finance charges and the annual percentage rate for installment loans**

(3) **identify the elements of open-end credit transactions**

(4) **calculate the finance charges and the annual percentage rate for open-end loans**

Learning Unit 13.1
Installment Loans

Elements of Installment Loans

An installment loan is a type of "buy-now, pay-later" consumer credit that is given in return for a series of fixed (usually equal) payments made at equal intervals over a fixed period of time. This is the type of credit that is most often used by consumers to buy more expensive items, such as automobiles, furniture, and appliances. The basic elements of an installment loan are: the down payment, the installment loan principal, the installment price, and the finance charge.

Down Payment. The down payment for an installment loan is usually a small cash payment made at the time of purchase but sometimes includes a trade-in. The down payment may be an agreed-on fixed amount, a percent of the total purchase price, or a percent of the cash price. The amount of the down payment varies according to the item purchased (usually 10% of the cash price for furniture and appliances) and sometimes according to the credit rating of the customer.

Installment Loan Principal. The installment loan principal is the unpaid balance of the cash price (cash price minus down payment) and is the amount that is financed.

Installment Price. The installment price is the total price a customer must pay for an item. It is the sum of the down payment and the installment payments (which include the finance charge). The installment price is sometimes referred to as the deferred payment price.

Finance Charge. The finance charge is the total amount of extra money paid for the privilege of buying on credit and is computed by subtracting the cash price from the installment price.

Example: Cora Shook bought a couch, agreeing to pay $20 as a down payment and monthly payments of $10 each for 24 months. The cash price was $220. Determine (a) the installment loan principal, (b) the installment price, and (c) the finance charge.

Solution: (a)

	$220	cash price
−	20	down payment
	$200	installment loan principal

(b)

	$240	24 payments at $10 each
+	20	down payment
	$260	installment price

Figure 13.1 Annual Percentage Rate Table for Monthly Payment Plans

NUMBER OF PAYMENTS	ANNUAL PERCENTAGE RATE															
	18.00%	18.25%	18.50%	18.75%	19.00%	19.25%	19.50%	19.75%	20.00%	20.25%	20.50%	20.75%	21.00%	21.25%	21.50%	21.75%
	(FINANCE CHARGE PER $100 OF AMOUNT FINANCED)															
1	1.50	1.52	1.54	1.56	1.58	1.60	1.62	1.65	1.67	1.69	1.71	1.73	1.75	1.77	1.79	1.81
2	2.26	2.29	2.32	2.35	2.38	2.41	2.44	2.48	2.51	2.54	2.57	2.60	2.63	2.66	2.70	2.73
3	3.01	3.06	3.10	3.14	3.18	3.23	3.27	3.31	3.35	3.39	3.44	3.48	3.52	3.56	3.60	3.65
4	3.78	3.83	3.88	3.94	3.99	4.04	4.10	4.15	4.20	4.25	4.31	4.36	4.41	4.47	4.52	4.57
5	4.54	4.61	4.67	4.74	4.80	4.86	4.93	4.99	5.06	5.12	5.18	5.25	5.31	5.37	5.44	5.50
6	5.32	5.39	5.46	5.54	5.61	5.69	5.76	5.84	5.91	5.99	6.06	6.14	6.21	6.29	6.36	6.44
7	6.09	6.18	6.26	6.35	6.43	6.52	6.60	6.69	6.78	6.86	6.95	7.04	7.12	7.21	7.29	7.38
8	6.87	6.96	7.06	7.16	7.26	7.35	7.45	7.55	7.64	7.74	7.84	7.94	8.03	8.13	8.23	8.33
9	7.65	7.76	7.87	7.97	8.08	8.19	8.30	8.41	8.52	8.63	8.73	8.84	8.95	9.06	9.17	9.28
10	8.43	8.55	8.67	8.79	8.91	9.03	9.15	9.27	9.39	9.51	9.63	9.75	9.88	10.00	10.12	10.24
11	9.22	9.35	9.49	9.62	9.75	9.88	10.01	10.14	10.28	10.41	10.54	10.67	10.80	10.94	11.07	11.20
12	10.02	10.16	10.30	10.44	10.59	10.73	10.87	11.02	11.16	11.31	11.45	11.59	11.74	11.88	12.02	12.17
13	10.81	10.97	11.12	11.28	11.43	11.59	11.74	11.90	12.05	12.21	12.36	12.52	12.67	12.83	12.99	13.14
14	11.61	11.78	11.95	12.11	12.28	12.45	12.61	12.78	12.95	13.11	13.28	13.45	13.62	13.79	13.95	14.12
15	12.42	12.59	12.77	12.95	13.13	13.31	13.49	13.67	13.85	14.03	14.21	14.39	14.57	14.75	14.93	15.11
16	13.22	13.41	13.60	13.80	13.99	14.18	14.37	14.56	14.75	14.94	15.13	15.33	15.52	15.71	15.90	16.10
17	14.04	14.24	14.44	14.64	14.85	15.05	15.25	15.46	15.66	15.86	16.07	16.27	16.48	16.68	16.89	17.09
18	14.85	15.07	15.28	15.49	15.71	15.93	16.14	16.36	16.57	16.79	17.01	17.22	17.44	17.66	17.88	18.09
19	15.67	15.90	16.12	16.35	16.58	16.81	17.03	17.26	17.49	17.72	17.95	18.18	18.41	18.64	18.87	19.10
20	16.49	16.73	16.97	17.21	17.45	17.69	17.93	18.17	18.41	18.66	18.90	19.14	19.38	19.63	19.87	20.11
21	17.32	17.57	17.82	18.07	18.33	18.58	18.83	19.09	19.34	19.60	19.85	20.11	20.36	20.62	20.87	21.13
22	18.15	18.41	18.68	18.94	19.21	19.47	19.74	20.01	20.27	20.54	20.81	21.08	21.34	21.61	21.88	22.15
23	18.98	19.26	19.54	19.81	20.09	20.37	20.65	20.93	21.21	21.49	21.77	22.05	22.33	22.61	22.90	23.18
24	19.82	20.11	20.40	20.69	20.98	21.27	21.56	21.86	22.15	22.44	22.74	23.03	23.33	23.62	23.92	24.21
25	20.66	20.96	21.27	21.57	21.87	22.18	22.48	22.79	23.10	23.40	23.71	24.02	24.32	24.63	24.94	25.25

(c) $260   installment price
    − 220   cash price
    $ 40   finance charge (This amount must be reported
             on a disclosure statement for the installment
             loan.)

Annual Percentage Rate (APR)

As discussed earlier, truth-in-lending requires the seller to disclose not only the amount of the finance charge but also the *annual percentage* (or interest) *rate* to which the finance charge is equivalent. Regulation Z provides the guidelines for reporting this rate and tables for determining the rate. The interest rates from the tables recognize the reduction of the installment principal with each payment. A portion of the Annual Percentage Rate (APR) Table is reproduced in Figure 13.1 on page 295, and another portion of the table in Appendix K.

Use the following steps to determine the APR from the tables provided in Regulation Z:

1. Divide the finance charge by the installment loan principal and multiply by $100. (This will give the finance charge for each $100 financed.)
2. Find the number of payments in the first column, follow horizontally across the page until you find the amount nearest the amount obtained in step 1. Read the percent rate at the top of the column. This is the APR that is reported on the disclosure statement.

Example: Assuming the same facts as in the preceding example, determine the APR equivalent of the finance charge.

Solution: (1) $40.00 ÷ $200 = .20 × $100 = $20.00

(2)   Find 24 in the first column and read across to the number nearest $20.00. ($20.11 is nearest to $20.00.)

The APR at the top of this column is 18.25%.

In fulfilling the requirements of the Federal Truth in Lending Act, the lender must provide the borrower a form known as a disclosure statement that gives the charges for the particular loan and the APR as determined using Regulation Z guidelines. The disclosure statement that would be used for the preceding loan would appear as shown in Figure 13.2.

Figure 13.2 Disclosure Statement of Loan (facing page)

DATE

AMOUNT OF LOAN:

DEBTOR
NUMBER
& STREET
CITY AND
STATE   ZIP CODE

DESCRIPTION
OF COLLATERAL

CREDITOR:

Forest Hill State Bank

6401 Wichita

Fort Worth, Texas 76119

DISCLOSURE STATEMENT OF LOAN

STATEMENT OF TRANSACTION

Date of Cash Advance:________________

1. Proceeds .... $ *200*

2. Less:

    a. Prepaid finance charge ...... $__________

    b. Required deposit balance ..... $__________

    Total Prepaid Finance Charge and
    Required Deposit Balance .... $__________

3. Net (1 less 2) .... $ *200*

4. Other Charges:

    a. Filing fees & record search .... $__________

    b. Taxes .... $__________

    c. Certificate of title fee .... $__________

    d. License registration fees ...... $__________

    e. Other official fees .... $__________

    f. Insurance:

        Property damage .... $__________

        Credit life .... $__________

        Credit accident and health ... $__________

        Total other charges............. $__________

        Less: charges paid...............................

    Balance Other Charges...................... $__________

5. Amount Financed (Sum 3 + 4)............ $ *200*

6. **FINANCE CHARGE** .... $ *40*

7. Total of Payments (sum 1, 4 and 6) ...... $ *240*

8. **ANNUAL PERCENTAGE RATE** .... *18.25* %

PAYMENTS

This loan is payable:

☐ In one payment, due on demand if no demand on________________.

☐ In__________ successive monthly installments of $__________
   each beginning__________________with a final installment of
   $__________due and payable on or before__________

☐ In__________successive monthly installments of $__________
   each beginning__________________with a final Balloon Payment
   of $__________due on or before__________, which Bank
   is under no obligation to refinance.

The **Finance Charge** accrues from the "Date of Cash Advance" shown in the Statement of Transaction, but if no date is there given it accrues from the date of this Statement.

INSURANCE

Property Damage Insurance, if written in connection with this loan, may be obtained by Debtor through any person of his choice. If Debtor desires property insurance to be obtained through Bank, the cost will be $__________ for __________ months (including policy fee).

Credit Life and Accident and Health Insurance is not required in connection with this loan. No charge is included for credit insurance unless Debtor signs the appropriate statement below:

The cost of insurance for the term of the credit will be $__________ for credit life and $__________for credit accident and health.

I desire credit life, health and accident   I desire credit life insurance only.
insurance.

_______________ _______________   _______________ _______________
Date   Signature   Date   Signature

I DO NOT desire credit life or
health or accident insurance

_______________ _______________
Date   Signature

PREPAYMENT IN FULL

A credit for prepayment is obtainable as follows:

☐ Debtor may prepay this loan in full at any time without penalty, and the finance charge will abate from date of payment.

☐ Debtor may prepay the unpaid balance of this loan in full at any time and obtain a credit of any unearned finance charge based on the "Rule of 78's".

DEFAULT CHARGE

☐ All past due interest and principal shall bear interest after maturity at the rate of 10% per annum. If the obligations are referred to an attorney for collection, Debtor shall pay an additional 10% of the principal and interest then due as attorneys' fees.

☐ If any installment is not received within ten days after its due date, the Debtor shall pay a late charge equal to 5% of the amount of the installment or, if deferred at holder's option, a charge for deferrment equal to the difference between the refund for prepayment in full at the date of deferrment and the refund for prepayment in full as of one month prior to the date of deferrment multiplied by number of months of deferrment. All past due principal and interest shall bear interest at the rate of 10% per annum. If the obligations are referred to an attorney for collection, Debtor shall pay an additional 10% of the principal and interest then due as attorneys' fees.

SECURITY

This loan is secured by a security interest in all deposits now or hereafter made or maintained by Debtor with Bank. If checked below, this loan is also secured as follows:

☐ By a security interest in the above described collateral created in a Security Agreement of even date between Debtor and Bank. After-acquired property of Debtor now or hereafter in Bank's possession will be subject to the security interest and future and other indebtedness is and will be secured.

☐ By the following security interest(s) covering the collateral identified below which also will cover after-acquired property and any property of Debtor now or hereafter in Bank's possession and which secures and will secure future and other indebtedness:

I ACKNOWLEDGE RECEIPT OF A COPY OF THIS STATEMENT.

____
Debtor

FORM 41   ORIGINAL

Example: Mr. Franco bought a refrigerator agreeing to pay 10% of the cash price as a down payment and monthly payments of $50 each for 16 months. The cash price was $750. Determine (a) the down payment, (b) the installment loan principal, (c) the installment price, (d) the finance charge, and (e) the APR.

Solution: (a) $750 × .10 = $75   down payment

(b)
$$\begin{array}{ll} \$750 & \text{cash price} \\ -\ 75 & \text{down payment} \\ \hline \$675 & \text{installment loan principal} \end{array}$$

(c)
$$\begin{array}{ll} \$\ 75 & \text{down payment} \\ 800 & \text{16 payments of }\$50 \\ \hline \$875 & \text{installment price} \end{array}$$

(d)
$$\begin{array}{ll} \$875 & \text{installment price} \\ -\ 750 & \text{cash price} \\ \hline \$125 & \text{finance charge} \end{array}$$

(e) $125 ÷ $675 = .18519 × $100 = $18.519

On the table, follow 16 payments across to $18.42 (the nearest number); the APR = 24.75%.

Exercises

Determine the APR for the following credit transactions. Use the tables in Appendix K for your solutions.

	Finance Charge	Amount Financed	Number of Payments	APR
1.	$38.00	$528.00	12	_______
2.	$60.00	$750.00	15	_______
3.	$ 2.50	$ 55.00	6	_______
4.	$ 5.00	$136.00	8	_______
5.	$24.00	$320.00	10	_______
6.	$80.00	$500.00	20	_______
7.	$10.00	$200.00	10	_______
8.	$48.00	$528.00	24	_______
9.	$ 3.00	$ 70.00	5	_______
10.	$ 8.00	$140.00	10	_______

Determine the finance charges and APR for each of the following purchases.

	Item	Cash Price	Down Payment	Monthly Payments Number	Monthly Payments Amount
11.	Mower	$500.00	$ 50.00	12	$42.00
12.	Ring	$790.00	$100.00	15	$50.00
13.	Watch	$ 55.00	20%	6	$ 8.00
14.	Lamp	$150.00	10%	8	$18.00
15.	Clock	$370.00	1/5	10	$32.00
16.	Stereo	$467.00	1/10	20	$25.00
17.	Radio	$200.00	$ 50.00	10	$17.00
18.	Television	$530.00	$100.00	24	$22.00
19.	Server	$ 54.95	10%	5	$10.50
20.	Tent	$140.00	1/4	10	$11.50

21. If $460 is financed for 15 months and there was a $92 charge for the financing, what is the APR?

22. Determine the APR for this loan: finance charge, $42; amount financed, $300; number of payments, 12.

23. Determine the finance charges and APR for the following purchase: Marie Pack bought a new freezer that had a cash price of $870. She agreed to pay 10% down and 24 monthly payments of $40.

24. Dave Reddig bought a riding mower for $50 down and ten payments of $50 each. Determine the finance charge and the APR if the cash price is $500.

25. As an officer of the loan department of the First Bank, one of your responsibilities is to prepare disclosure statements for all loans up to two years in length. Determine the APR for each of the following loans:

    Loan #14-26 for $450 to be paid in nine months with a finance charge of $30.

    Loan #14-27 for $800 to be paid in 20 months with a finance charge of $128.

    Loan #14-28 for $625 to be paid in 24 months with a finance charge of $65.

Loan #14-29 for $1,500 to be paid in 18 months with a finance charge
of $175.

Loan #14-30 for $300 to be paid in 12 months with a finance charge
of $24.

Learning Unit 13.2
Open-End Charge Accounts

Characteristics of Open-End Credit

Like installment loans, open-end credit enables the consumer to buy now
and pay later. However, unlike installment loans, open-end credit enables
the consumer to receive additional credit before the first credit is paid off.
In addition, there is no definite time period within which payment must be
made and no down payment required. Credit card accounts and revolving
charge accounts are examples of this type of credit.

Under open-end credit, a finance charge is imposed each month on the
unpaid balance. (The finance charge is usually $1\%-1\frac{1}{2}\%$ per month or
$12\%-18\%$ per year.) Buyers may elect to pay either the *entire* bill each
month, in which case the finance charge can be avoided, or only a *portion*
of the bill, in which case the finance charge must be paid. A prescribed
minimum payment may be required, according to the amount owed, and
a limit may be imposed on the amount a buyer may charge, according to
the buyer's income and credit history.

Calculating the Unpaid Balance
and Finance Charges

To determine the unpaid balance on a charge account:

1. Determine the finance charge for the month (unpaid balance $\times$
   finance rate).
2. Determine the amount to be credited to the balance (payment $-$
   finance charge).
3. Subtract the amount to be credited from the account balance.

To determine the finance charges for a given period, total the finance charges from each month within the period.

Example: Ray Garza had a balance of $117.20 on his credit card account. The finance charge is $1\frac{1}{2}\%$ of the unpaid balance. Determine the unpaid balance and the total finance charges after the third month if he has made monthly payments of $30, $30, and $40.

Solution: First Month:

Account balance		$117.20
Payment on 31st day	$30.00	
Finance charge ($117.20 × .015)	− 1.76	
Credited to balance		28.24
New balance		$ 88.96

Second Month:

Account balance		$88.96
Payment on 30th day	$30.00	
Finance charge ($88.96 × .015)	− 1.33	
Credited to balance		28.67
New balance		$60.29

Third Month:

Account balance		$60.29
Payment on 31st day	$40.00	
Finance charge ($60.29 × .015)	− .90	
Credited to balance		39.10
New balance		$21.19

Total finance charge $1.76
                     1.33
                      .90
               $3.99

When making computations for months in which additional purchases have been made, remember that finance charges are computed *only on the previous month's balance*, and not on the current month's purchases.

Example: Ray Garza had a balance of $21.19 on his credit card account. The finance charge is $1\frac{1}{2}\%$. He made a $175 purchase during the first month and an $86 purchase during the third month. He made payments of $20, $30, and $40 during the three months. Determine the unpaid balance and total finance charges for the three-month period.

Solution: First month:

Account balance		$ 21.19
Purchase on 16th day		175.00
Payment on 31st day	$20.00	
Finance charge ($21.19 × .015)	− .32	
Credited to account		19.68
New balance		$176.51

Second month:

Account balance		$176.51
Payment on 30th day	$30.00	
Finance charge ($176.51 × .015)	− 2.65	
Credited to account		27.35
New balance		$149.16

Third month:

Account balance		$149.16
Purchase on 22d day		86.00
Payment on 31st day	$40.00	
Finance charge ($149.16 × .015)	− 2.24	
Credited to account		37.76
New balance		$197.40

Total finance charge $ .32
2.65
2.24
$5.21

Annual Percentage Rate

Like installment loans, the annual percentage equivalent of the finance charge must be determined and disclosed.

To determine the APR for an open-end account, multiply the interest rate per period by the number of interest periods per year.

Example: Ray Garza is charged $1\frac{1}{2}\%$ per month on the unpaid balance. Determine the APR.

Solution:

$$\begin{array}{ll} 1\frac{1}{2}\% \ (.015) & \text{interest charge per interest period} \\ \underline{\times\ 12} & \text{number of interest periods per year} \\ 18\% & \text{APR} \end{array}$$

Exercises

Determine the ending balance and the APR for each of the following open-end accounts.

	Beginning Balance	Payment	Periodic Rate
1.	$214.00	$50.00	1%
2.	$190.00	$40.00	1%
3.	$173.40	$40.00	$1\frac{1}{2}\%$
4.	$315.60	$70.00	$1\frac{1}{2}\%$
5.	$ 97.00	$20.00	$1\frac{3}{4}\%$
6.	$125.00	$25.00	1%
7.	$ 74.00	$10.00	$1\frac{3}{4}\%$
8.	$ 47.20	$20.00	$\frac{3}{4}\%$
9.	$163.10	$80.00	$1\frac{1}{2}\%$
10.	$ 46.00	$35.00	$1\frac{1}{2}\%$

Determine the ending balance for each of the following open-end accounts.

	Beginning Balance	Purchases	Payment	Periodic Rate
11.	$146.00	$ 32.00	$ 20.00	$1\frac{1}{2}\%$
12.	$ 86.32	$ 44.00	$ 25.00	1%
13.	$ 26.00	$149.50	$ 15.00	$1\frac{1}{2}\%$
14.	$ 46.95	$ 82.00	$ 40.00	$\frac{1}{2}\%$
15.	$117.80	—	$ 30.00	1%

	Beginning Balance	Purchases	Payment	Periodic Rate
16.	$246.82	$ 46.50	$ 50.00	$1\frac{1}{4}\%$
17.	$500.00	—	$125.00	$\frac{3}{4}\%$
18.	$427.00	$113.00	$100.00	$1\frac{1}{4}\%$
19.	—	$557.95	—	$1\frac{1}{2}\%$
20.	$557.95	$120.00	$200.00	$1\frac{1}{2}\%$

21. The Buyalot Charge Company billed one of its credit card customers for a $180.65 purchase. The financing rate for the company is 1.33%. Compute the finance charge for next month if the customer paid $40.

22. The balance at the beginning of the month on Charles Jones's credit card account was $93. What was the balance at the end of the month if he had a purchase of $119.95 and a payment of $50. The financing rate is $1\frac{1}{2}\%$.

Chapter 13
Self-Evaluation

Use the tables in Appendix K to solve the following problems.

1. Calculate the APR for the following loan: finance charge, $28; amount financed, $360; number of payments, 10.

2. If the finance charge is $50, the amount financed is $600, and the number of payments is 12, what is the APR?

3. Calculate the finance charge and APR for this chair: cash price, $180; down payment, $50; number of monthly payments, 10; amount of monthly payments, $15.

4. Jan Price bought a new leather coat with a cash price of $235. She agreed to pay $25 down and to make 12 monthly payments of $20 each. Compute the finance charge and the APR for the loan.

5. Calculate the ending balance and the APR for the following open-end account: beginning balance, $187; payment, $40; finance rate, $1\frac{1}{3}\%$.

6. Calculate the ending balance for the following open-end account: beginning balance, $519.67; purchase, $65.30; payment, $120; finance rate, $1\frac{1}{2}\%$.

Chapter 14
Investments

Individuals and businesses may wish to put their savings, profits, or other accumulated cash to work for them. There are a variety of investment opportunities available to individuals and businesses with money to invest. One option is to deposit money in a savings account. Although, under this option, the rate of return is low and protection against inflation limited, the money is secure because deposits are insured up to $100,000 by the Federal Deposit Insurance Corporation or the Federal Savings and Loan Insurance Corporation.

Real estate is another investment opportunity. The acquisition of the right piece of property at the right time and at the right price protects against inflation and may provide the owner with income tax advantages while he or she owns the real estate and with a handsome profit when he or she decides to sell. More information about real estate is provided in the next chapter.

Another investment vehicle available to individuals and businesses is the purchase of corporate stocks and bonds. Although this type of investment carries some degree of risk, the amount of money realized often exceeds the returns from other forms of investments. This chapter explains some of the investment aspects of stocks and bonds.

This chapter will enable you to:

1. **understand the terminology associated with stocks and bonds**

2. **compute the earnings per share, price-earnings ratio, and dividend yield on common stock**

3. **understand the meaning of discounts and premiums on bonds**

4. **determine the price of a bond**

5. **compute the total cost of a bond**

6. **determine the current yield on a bond**

Learning Unit 14.1
Investment in Stocks

Corporations often raise money by selling stock to the public, who, in turn, purchase the stock as an investment vehicle. Investors buy stock with two goals in mind: (1) to receive a current income by sharing current company earnings (dividends) and (2) to realize a future profit on stock that has grown in value to more than its purchase price (capital gain). The investor receives a certificate from the corporation that states the name of the owner, the number of shares, the par value, and the class of stock.

Since the price of stock is determined solely by the law of supply and demand, the price of a stock can vary in the short term—even on a daily basis. Therefore, investors regularly check on the performance of stocks by examining the stock quotations in the financial pages of newspapers. Stock quotations give an account of the previous day's stock activities, including the highest and lowest selling price of the day as well as the difference between the day's closing price and the closing price of the last session in which the stock was traded. Table 14.1 illustrates the type of information found on the financial pages and explains what this information means.

Table 14.1 The Financial Page: Stock Quotations

Yearly				Sales[5]				
High[1]	Low[2]	Stock[3]	Dividend[4]	100s	High[6]	Low[7]	Last[8]	Net Change[9]
$65\frac{3}{8}$	$56\frac{7}{8}$	ATT	4.20	908	$59\frac{5}{8}$	$59\frac{1}{8}$	$59\frac{1}{8}$	$-\frac{1}{8}$
$62\frac{1}{4}$	45	CBS	2.40	500	$45\frac{3}{4}$	$45\frac{1}{8}$	$45\frac{3}{8}$	$-\frac{5}{8}$
$286\frac{1}{8}$	$244\frac{1}{2}$	IBM	4.50	568	$258\frac{3}{4}$	$257\frac{1}{8}$	$258\frac{1}{4}$	$-\frac{3}{8}$
$32\frac{1}{2}$	$22\frac{5}{8}$	RCA	1.20	290	25	$24\frac{7}{8}$	$24\frac{7}{8}$	$-\frac{1}{8}$
$11\frac{7}{8}$	$7\frac{3}{4}$	TWA	—	207	$11\frac{3}{8}$	$11\frac{1}{8}$	$11\frac{1}{4}$	$-\frac{1}{8}$

1. Highest price during the past year
2. Lowest price during the past year
3. Abbreviated name of the company
4. Annual dividends paid by the company
5. Number of shares traded during the day
6. Highest price for the day
7. Lowest price for the day
8. Last transaction for the day
9. Amount of increase or decrease from the previous day

Stocks are listed alphabetically. Preferred stock is distinguished from common stock by the use of "pf." Prices per share are quoted in eighths, quarters, or halves. For example, $65\frac{3}{8}$ means $65.375 per share.

The stock of major corporations is sold principally through a stock exchange. The New York Stock Exchange is the largest exchange in the United States and handles more than 80% of the stock transactions negotiated through a stock exchange. The American Stock Exchange is the next largest exchange.

The stock of smaller, lesser known corporations is sold in the over-the-counter securities market. The over-the-counter market is a countrywide network of thousands of dealers, linked together by telephone and other communication devices.

Most of the transactions on the stock exchanges are negotiated through members of the exchange called *stockbrokers*. Stockbrokers are responsible for bargaining for the best possible price—whether a stock is being bought or sold. Stockbrokers charge a commission, or fee, that is based on the value and number of shares involved in the transaction. Shares are sold in "round lots" (100 or more shares) and "odd lots" (less than 100 shares).

Evaluation of Stocks

While there is no sure way to predict market behavior or "to beat the market," there are several indicators that can be used to evaluate the performance and potential of stocks. Among these are: (1) the earnings per share, (2) the price-earnings ratio, and (3) the dividend yield. These figures are commonly quoted in the financial pages of daily newspapers.

Earnings per Share. Earnings per share show the *theoretical* portion of total earnings that a stockholder owns on one share of stock. (Do not confuse earnings per share with dividends. Dividends are the earnings that are *actually* distributed to investors and represent only a portion of earnings.)

The earnings per share for common stock are computed by dividing the corporate net income after taxes and after payment of preferred dividends by the outstanding shares of common stock.

Example: The ABC Corporation has 10,000 shares of common stock outstanding. The company does not have any preferred stock outstanding. What are the earnings per share of common stock for a year in which the company had after tax earnings of $37,500?

Solution:

$$\frac{\text{after tax net income}}{\text{shares of common stock outstanding}} = \frac{\$37,500}{10,000}$$

$$= \$3.75 \quad \text{earnings per share}$$

Price-Earnings Ratio. The price-earnings ratio indicates how much investors are currently paying for $1 of a company's earnings. A higher-than-normal P/E ratio usually is interpreted as indicating a good growth stock, while a lower-than-normal P/E ratio usually is interpreted as indicating a good income stock. However, determining what is "normal" for a given stock is the responsibility of the investor and requires careful assessment over a period of time.

The price-earnings ratio for common stock is computed by dividing the market price per share by the earnings per share.

Example: The earnings per share for the ABC Corporation were $3.75. If the market price per share is $45, what is the price-earnings ratio?

Solution: $\dfrac{\text{market price per share}}{\text{earnings per share}} = \dfrac{\$45}{\$3.75} = 12$

The price-earnings ratio for the common stock of ABC Corporation is 12 to 1. This means that a share of the stock was selling for 12 times the earnings per share.

Dividend Yield. The dividend yield expresses the rate of return on common stock in terms of cash dividends and is used to indicate whether a stock price is reasonable. Dividend yield is expressed as a percent and is computed by dividing the annual dividend per share by the current market price.

Example: The annual dividend paid on Texas Utilities stock is $1.52. If the stock is currently selling for $20 per share, what is the dividend yield?

Solution: $\dfrac{\text{annual dividend}}{\text{current market price}} = \dfrac{\$1.52}{\$20} = .076, \text{ or } 7.6\%$

Exercises

What is the price per share of the following stocks?

	Stock	Quote	Price
1.	ACF	$30\frac{5}{8}$	_______
2.	AtlRich	$46\frac{3}{4}$	_______
3.	Beech	$32\frac{1}{8}$	_______
4.	Cousins	$1\frac{1}{2}$	_______
5.	duPont	$104\frac{1}{8}$	_______
6.	EastUtl	$16\frac{1}{4}$	_______
7.	ForMK	$17\frac{7}{8}$	_______
8.	IntTT	$29\frac{3}{8}$	_______
9.	Jantzen	$14\frac{7}{8}$	_______
10.	Litton	$16\frac{3}{4}$	_______
11.	McDnld	$45\frac{3}{4}$	_______
12.	NCR	$44\frac{5}{8}$	_______

The net income after taxes and payments of preferred dividends for several corporations are shown below. Compute the earnings per share for the common stock of each of the following examples.

	Net Income	Shares of Common Stock Outstanding	Earnings per Share
13.	$ 126,000	90,000	_______
14.	$ 13,160	47,000	_______
15.	$ 279,300	142,500	_______
16.	$ 208,800	87,000	_______
17.	$ 200,576	313,400	_______
18.	$ 350,568	162,300	_______
19.	$ 24,684	56,100	_______
20.	$10,342,195	897,760	_______
21.	$ 139,968	145,800	_______
22.	$ 674,179	306,445	_______

Compute the price-earnings ratio and dividend yield for the common stock for the following examples. Assume that each corporation retains 20% of the earnings and pays the remainder as a dividend.

	Market Price per Share	Earnings per Share	Price-Earnings Ratio	Dividend Yield
23.	$ 17.00	$ 1.35	————	————
24.	$ 57.63	$ 2.60	————	————
25.	$ 26.63	$ 1.60	————	————
26.	$ 6.63	$ .30	————	————
27.	$ 9.50	$ .53	————	————
28.	$ 24.75	$ .76	————	————
29.	$113.00	$10.70	————	————
30.	$ 28.00	$ 2.00	————	————

Practical Applications

31. A share of Avon is quoted at $45\frac{7}{8}$ in today's newspaper. What is the price per share?

32. The last transaction for GAF common stock on the New York Stock Exchange today was for $11\frac{1}{8}$ per share. What was the price per share?

33. The XYZ Corporation had net income after taxes of $150,000. Dividends on preferred stock were $30,000. The corporation has 140,000 shares of common stock outstanding. What were the earnings per share of common?

34. PPG common stock is currently selling for $26 per share. The earnings per share are $1.60. What is the price-earnings ratio for the stock?

35. The common stock of K Mart is currently selling for $24 per share. The annual dividend per share is $.56. What is the dividend yield on the stock?

Learning Unit 14.2
Investment in Bonds

The bond market is divided into four categories: U. S. government bonds, municipal bonds, corporate bonds, and corporate convertible bonds. Our discussion will be limited to corporate bonds.

Corporate bonds (see Figure 14.1) are issued by a company to raise capital. When a company issues bonds, it is actually borrowing money from investors. A bond is somewhat like a promissory note: it is a written promise (1) to repay a specified amount on a certain date and (2) to pay a fixed rate of interest from the day the bond is issued to the day the bond is redeemed. The amount that must be repaid is the *principal*, which is the face value, or par value, of the bonds. Each bond issue has terms that the corporation

Figure 14.1 Sample Corporate Bond

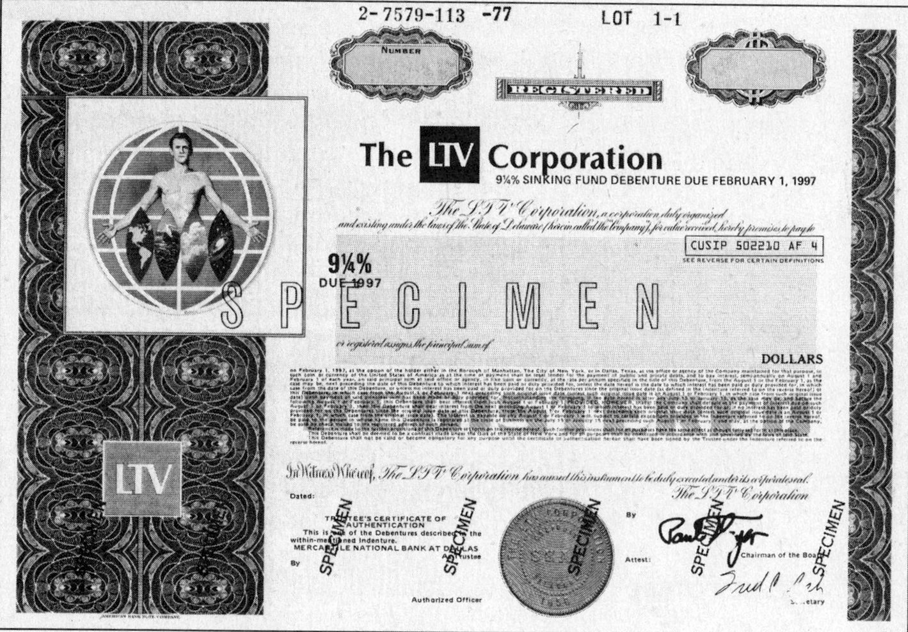

Source: Used by permission of the LTV Corporation.

must meet. The terms are stated in a legal document called the *indenture*. A *trustee* is appointed for each bond issue to protect the interests of the bond owners by making certain that the corporation complies with the terms of the indenture.

The bond indenture may require that the corporation put up *collateral* to secure the loan. The collateral for a bond issue may be the physical assets of the company, such as land, buildings, and equipment. Bonds that are secured by the pledge of assets are called *mortgage bonds*. Bonds that are not secured by collateral are called *debenture bonds*. Debentures are backed only by the general credit of the corporation.

Bond owners receive interest payments, usually semiannually, which are an expense for the corporation. The corporation may maintain a register of the names and addresses of the bond owners and mail the interest payments. This type of bond is called a *registered bond*. Some bonds have negotiable coupons attached, which must be redeemed at a bank. This type of bond is called a *coupon bond*.

There is an element of risk involved in the purchase of bonds: risk that the interest will not be paid, that the principal will not be repaid, or that the price of the bonds will decline. The degree of risk for a particular bond is estimated—primarily on the basis of its security features—by credit rating services, such as Moody's, Dun and Bradstreet, and Standard and Poor's. Bond ratings range from an AAA (best possible security risk) down to C (highly speculative). The degree of risk influences the price that buyers are willing to pay for bonds.

Corporate bonds are bought and sold on the securities exchanges or on the over-the-counter market. Bond transactions are reported daily in the financial pages of many newspapers. Separate listings are provided for different types of bonds. Table 14.2 illustrates the type of information found in the financial pages and explains what this information means.

Current Price of Bonds

Bond prices fluctuate daily. Since the interest rates of bonds are fixed, the only way to market bonds competitively against current interest rates is to adjust the selling price. When interest rates go up, the price of bonds tends to go down so that the interest payment on the bond will be competitive. When interest rates go down, the price of bonds tends to go up because the fixed interest payments make the bonds more attractive.

Although bonds are usually issued in denominations (par value, or face value) of $1,000, bonds are usually sold at a *premium* (more than $1,000) or at a *discount* (less than $1,000) in order to reflect the fluctuations in

Table 14.2 The Financial Page: Bond Quotations

Bonds[1]	Volume[2]	High[3]	Low[4]	Close[5]	Net Change[6]
CIT 8.85s82	5	$101\frac{3}{8}$	$101\frac{3}{8}$	$101\frac{3}{8}$	—
CNA $8\frac{1}{2}$ 95	10	$88\frac{5}{8}$	$88\frac{5}{8}$	$88\frac{5}{8}$	—
PPG 9s95	100	$101\frac{3}{4}$	$101\frac{3}{4}$	$101\frac{3}{4}$	$-\frac{1}{4}$
RCA $9\frac{1}{4}$s90	7	$104\frac{7}{8}$	104	104	$+1$
Sears $4\frac{3}{4}$ 83	13	$87\frac{5}{8}$	$87\frac{1}{8}$	$87\frac{1}{8}$	$+\frac{1}{8}$

1. Abbreviated name of the company; interest rate; and, year of maturity
2. Number of bonds traded during the day (in 100s)
3. Highest price for the day
4. Lowest price for the day
5. Last transaction for the day
6. Amount of increase or decrease from the previous day

current interest rates. Bond prices are quoted as a percent of the face value and in relationship to 100% (i.e., $1,000), regardless of the denomination.

To determine the *current price* of a bond, multiply the quoted price by $1,000.

Example: CIT bonds are currently being quoted at $101\frac{3}{8}$. CNA bonds are currently being quoted at $88\frac{5}{8}$. What is the current price of each bond?

Solution: $101\frac{3}{8} = 1.01375 \times \$1,000$
$= \$1,013.75$ price of each CIT bond

$88\frac{5}{8} = .88625 \times \$1,000$
$= \$\ \ 886.25$ price of each CNA bond

Bond Costs

Because interest is paid only to the owner of a bond, a bond purchaser must pay the seller not only the current bond price, but also all accrued interest since the last interest payment.

To determine the *total cost* of a bond (disregarding broker's commission):

1. Compute the current bond price.
2. Compute the interest ($I = P \times R \times T$).
3. Add the current price and the accumulated interest.

Example: A $1,000, 8.85% CIT bond was purchased for $101\frac{3}{8}$. Interest on the bond is paid semiannually on December 31 and June 30. What was the total cost of the bond, disregarding brokerage fees, if purchased on March 31?

Solution: (1) Price of the bond = 1.01375 × $1,000 = $1,013.75

(2) Interest for three months = $1,000 × .0885 × $\dfrac{3}{12}$ = $22.13

(3) Total cost of the bond = $1,013.75 + $22.13 = $1,035.88

Some bonds are *convertible*. A convertible bond may be converted into a specified number of shares of common stock at a stated price per share. The market price of a convertible bond depends on both the value of the stock and the interest that the bond pays.

Some bonds are *callable*. A callable bond may be redeemed by the corporation *prior* to the maturity date. For instance, if interest rates fall after the bond has been issued, the corporation may call the old bonds for redemption and issue new bonds.

Sometimes interest is called *yield*. Investors who buy bonds on a short-term basis are interested in the *current yield*.

To determine the current yield on a bond:

1. Compute the annual interest.
2. Compute the current price of the bond.
3. Divide the annual interest by the current price.

Example: What is the current yield on a $1,000, 8.85% CIT bond that is currently selling for $101\frac{3}{8}$?

Solution: (1) Annual interest = $1,000 × .0885 × $\dfrac{1}{1}$ = $88.50

(2) Price of the bond = 1.01375 × $1,000 = $1,013.75

(3) Current yield = $88.50 ÷ $1,013.75 = 8.7%

Exercises

The denomination of the following bonds is $1,000. Determine the price of each bond based on the quoted price at the close of the bond market today. What is the annual interest on each bond?

	Bond	Quote	Current Price	Annual Interest
1.	APL $10\frac{3}{4}$97	98	__________	__________
2.	ATT $3\frac{1}{4}$s84	$77\frac{1}{4}$	__________	__________
3.	ConEd 3s81	87	__________	__________
4.	Deere $5\frac{1}{2}$01	$89\frac{1}{2}$	__________	__________
5.	DukeP $7\frac{3}{8}$02	$83\frac{3}{4}$	__________	__________
6.	Exxon 6s97	$78\frac{7}{8}$	__________	__________
7.	GMA 5s80	$93\frac{1}{2}$	__________	__________
8.	Greyh $6\frac{1}{2}$90	$85\frac{1}{4}$	__________	__________
9.	Honey 6.1s92	$79\frac{1}{2}$	__________	__________
10.	LTV 5s88	$53\frac{3}{4}$	__________	__________
11.	PAA $4\frac{1}{2}$s84	73	__________	__________
12.	Xerox 6s95	$87\frac{1}{2}$	__________	__________

13. Are the bonds in problems 1–12 selling for a premium or a discount?

14. Does your answer to problem 13 suggest that interest rates are high or low at this point in time?

What is the current yield on the following $1,000 bonds?

	Bond	Quote	Current Yield
15.	Arco 8.70s81	$101\frac{3}{8}$	__________
16.	Arms $8\frac{1}{2}$01	97	__________
17.	Bendx $9\frac{1}{4}$81	$102\frac{1}{2}$	__________
18.	Ford $8\frac{1}{8}$90	$99\frac{1}{4}$	__________
19.	MKT 4s90	$6\frac{1}{2}$	__________
20.	Woolw 9s99	$98\frac{1}{2}$	__________

The following $1,000 bonds pay interest semiannually. Determine the total cost of each bond, disregarding brokerage fees.

	Bond	Quote	Last Interest Payment	Date Purchased	Total Cost
21.	AMAX 8s86	96	June 30	September 30	_______
22.	AAirl $4\frac{1}{4}$s92	$55\frac{1}{8}$	December 31	March 31	_______
23.	BellPa $8\frac{5}{8}$06	$99\frac{3}{4}$	June 30	November 30	_______
24.	Mobil $8\frac{1}{2}$01	98	December 31	April 30	_______

Practical Applications

25. Pfizer $1,000, 4% convertible bonds are currently quoted at 75.
    What is the current price of one of these bonds?
    What is the current yield on one of these bonds?
    What is the semiannual interest on these bonds?

26. What is the total cost of a $1,000 MGM, 10% bond currently quoted at $99\frac{3}{8}$?

27. What is the current price of a Sears $1,000, $7\frac{3}{4}$% bond that is quoted at $97\frac{1}{2}$?

28. What is the current yield on a TWA $1,000, 5% bond that is selling for $580?

Chapter 14
Self-Evaluation

1. What is the price of Schlitz common stock that is quoted in today's paper at $11\frac{5}{8}$?

2. What are the earnings per share for the common stock of a corporation that has 47,000 shares outstanding when the net income after taxes and payment of preferred dividends is $58,750?

3. Determine the price-earnings ratio for a share of RCA common stock. The earnings per share are $1.40 and the selling price is $25\frac{3}{8}$.

4. What is the dividend yield on a share of RCA common stock if the stock is purchased for $25\frac{3}{8}$ and pays annual dividends of $1.40?

5. What is the current price of a UAL $1,000, 8% bond that is quoted at $114\frac{1}{2}$?

6. What is the semiannual interest on a $1,000, $6\frac{1}{4}$% GMA bond that is selling for a quoted price of 85?

7. What is the total cost, disregarding brokerage fees, for a $1,000, $7\frac{1}{2}$% General Electric bond that is currently selling for $92\frac{7}{8}$?

PART FIVE
THE MATHEMATICS OF OTHER BUSINESS AREAS

This part of the text provides an opportunity for you to become familiar with the mathematics of real estate, insurance, transportation, and business statistics. Your success in business will be enhanced by an understanding of these math concepts.

Chapter 15
The Mathematics of Real Estate

The term *real estate* refers to the type of property that is classified as realty; that is, land and all improvements on or to the land. According to the U.S. Department of Commerce, almost three-fourths of the total national wealth in the United States is represented by land, land resources, and real estate improvements. Obviously, real estate is an important area of business activity in this country.

Land is a scarce and limited resource. Inherent in the structure of every society is a system designed to deal with the multitude of relationships concerning land. In this country, the magnitude of the real estate business is such that it dwarfs most other fields of endeavor. Real-estate-related activities touch the lives of millions of people: those who acquire real estate for residential or business purposes as well as those who deal in real estate as an occupation, including brokers, investors, appraisers, and builders. As a resource, real estate is continually being bought, sold, improved, financed, leased, managed, and appraised.

This chapter will provide an opportunity for you to become better acquainted with some specific aspects of real estate activity: the compensation paid brokers for handling real estate sales transactions; the points involved in financing real estate; the taxes levied on real property by various units of local government; and percentage leases involved in the rental of shopping centers, stores, and offices used by businesses.

This chapter will enable you to:

1. **explain the meaning of various terms used in the real estate industry: commission, points, ad valorem taxes, assessment, percentage leases, etc.**

2. calculate the amount of commission on real estate transactions

3. compute the rate of commission or price of the property in real estate transactions

4. determine the cost of title insurance

5. calculate loan origination costs on real estate transactions

6. demonstrate an understanding of how real estate taxes are levied

7. calculate real estate taxes

8. determine the total rent paid or percentage rate on a percentage lease

Learning Unit 15.1
Real Estate Commissions

Calculating a Broker's Commission

A real estate *broker* negotiates the sale, purchase, lease, or exchange of realty and helps arrange financing for these transactions. For these services, the broker receives a fee, or *commission*, usually a specified percent of the amount of a sale.

To determine the amount of commission, multiply the amount of the sale by the rate of commission.[1]

Example: A house sold for $43,000. The selling broker received a 6% commission on the sale. What amount of commission did the broker receive?

Solution: $43,000 × .06 = $2,580 commission

Calculating Split Commissions

Most active brokers have associates who perform various functions in the broker's office. They may receive 40 to 60% of the commission for the transactions that they handle for their broker.

To calculate a commission that is divided by the broker and the associate:

1. Determine the total commission (amount of sale × rate of commission).
2. Determine the associate's share (total commission × associate's rate).
3. Subtract the associate's share from the total commission.

Example: A house sold for $56,000. The commission on the sale was 7%. If the broker's associate receives 40% of the commission, what amount of commission will the associate receive? What amount of commission will the broker receive?

---

[1] This is yet another use of the basic percentage formula ($P = B \times R$) studied earlier, where B = the amount of the sale, R = commission percent, and P = commission.

Solution: $56,000 × .07 = $3,920   commission

$3,920 × .4 = $1,568   associate's commission

$3,920 − $1,568 = $2,352   broker's commission

Calculating the Rate of Commission

To determine the rate of commission when the sales price of the property and the commission are known, divide the amount of commission by the sales price of the property.[2]

Example: A house sold for $38,000. The broker received a commission of $1,900. What was the rate of commission?

Solution: $1,900 ÷ $38,000 = .05, or 5%   rate of commission

Calculating the Sales Price of the Property

To determine the sales price of a piece of property when the rate of commission and amount of commission are known, divide the amount of commission by the rate of commission.[3]

Example: A broker who charges 6% commission received a commission of $3,900 for handling the sale of a house. What was the sales price of the house?

Solution: $3,900 ÷ .06 = $65,000   sales price

Valuation of Real Estate

One of the primary functions of a real estate broker is to appraise the market value of a given parcel of real estate so that a selling price or purchase price can be suggested. Three of the primary methods for estimating real estate value are: (1) net amount (owner's value) method, (2) market survey method, and (3) income method.

---

[2]These are variations of the basic percentage formula: $R = P ÷ B$ or $B = P ÷ R$, where R = rate of commission, P = commission amount, and B = amount of sale.

[3]See footnote 2.

Net Amount (Owner's Value). The *selling price* of a piece of property is often based on (1) the minimum amount that the owner specifies he or she must *actually receive* (owner's estimate of value) and (2) the rate of commission that the broker charges.

This specified amount (called the *net amount*) is the amount that must remain *after* the broker's commission has been paid. (The *list price* of a piece of property is the price that is *asked* and is usually set higher than the required selling price to allow some leeway in the bargaining negotiations.)

To determine the selling price based on net amount, divide the net amount by the complement of the rate of commission.

Example: The owner wants $45,000 net after payment of the broker's fee. What must the selling price be to provide the broker a 6% commission?

Solution: 100% − 6% = 94%   percent of selling price to be received by the owner

94% = $45,000   net amount to be received by the owner

$45,000 ÷ .94 = $47,872   selling price for the property

Market Survey Method. Real estate value may also be estimated on the basis of a market survey conducted by the broker. A market survey is a comparative investigation of the recent selling prices of similar properties in the area—often on a per-square-foot basis.

To estimate the value of property based on the per-square-foot prices of similar properties:

1. Determine the number of square feet in the property to be sold.
2. Multiply the square feet by the comparative price per square foot.

Example: Bill Fowler contacted Cohn Realty to obtain information about listing his home (having the following dimensions) for sale. Cohn Realty did a market survey and found that several com-

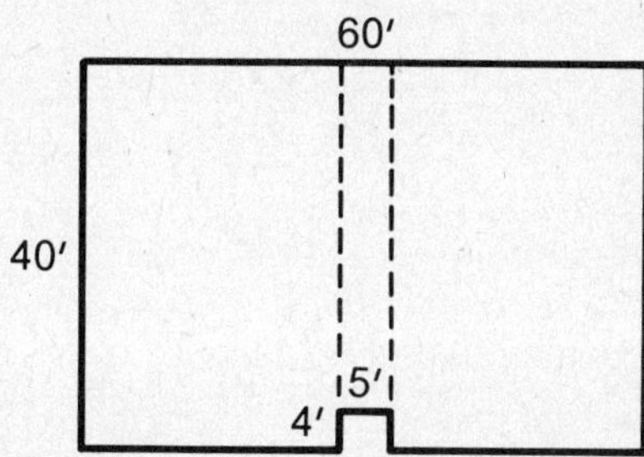

parable houses in the area sold recently for $25 to $28 per square foot. Bill and the realtor mutually agreed to ask $28 per square foot for Bill's home. What selling price should the realtor suggest for the house?

Solution: Employing the formula length $\times$ width $=$ area,

$$(40 \times 27.5) + (40 \times 27.5) + (5 \times 36) = 2{,}380 \text{ square feet}$$

or

$$(60 \times 40) - (5 \times 4) = 2{,}380 \text{ square feet}$$

$2{,}380 \times \$28 = \$66{,}640$ suggested selling price for the house

Income Method. A third method of estimating real estate value is on the basis of the anticipated income the property will earn. This method is especially applicable in the valuation of investment, or income-producing, property for a potential buyer.

In order to be able to screen and evaluate investment properties, the broker may consider the following factors:

1. client's capitalization rate (return "on" capital)
2. rate of return "of" capital
3. net operating income of the property

1.   *Capitalization rate.* The capitalization rate is the client's *desired* rate of return "on" his or her investment capital. This rate is a percent established by the client based on a number of factors including alternative investment opportunities.

Example: Cohn Realty has a client who wants to purchase commercial property. The client could invest in a savings account that would yield $6\frac{1}{2}\%$ interest. The client believes that a real estate investment should yield an additional 1% annually because of the relative nonliquidity of the investment, $1\frac{1}{2}\%$ for the risk of loss, and 1% for the entrepreneurial requirement. What is the client's desired rate of return on capital?

Solution: $6\frac{1}{2}\% + 1\% + 1\frac{1}{2}\% + 1\% = 10\%$ capitalization rate (return "on" capital)

2.   *Rate of return of capital.* This factor represents the annual rate of return that a property must yield to return an investment over its economic life. This rate is a percent obtained by dividing 100% by the years of estimated economic life.

Example: A building has an estimated economic life of 50 years. What rate of return of capital must the property yield to return the investment in 50 years?

Solution: 100% ÷ 50 = 2%   rate of return "of" capital

3. *Net operating income.* The net operating income of a property is based on the projected total revenue earned by the property less operating expenses.

The client's capitalization rate plus the rate of return of capital for a specific property is the total required rate of return. To determine the value of the property, divide the projected net operating income for the property by the *total* required rate of return.

Example: Cohn Realty has located a piece of commercial property that has an annual projected net operating income of $10,000. The economic life of the property is 50 years. What is the value of the property?

Solution:

10%	rate of return on capital
+ 2%	rate of return of capital
12%	total required rate of return on the property

$10,000 ÷ .12 = $83,333.33, or $83,000   value of the property

Exercises

Find the amount of commission earned by the broker in the following real estate transactions.

	Sales Price of the Property	Rate of Commission	Amount of Commission
1.	$106,000	6%	________
2.	$ 54,000	7%	________
3.	$ 67,000	5%	________
4.	$ 32,000	$5\frac{1}{2}$%	________
5.	$ 46,000	$6\frac{1}{2}$%	________
6.	$ 70,000	7%	________

Calculate the amount of commission received by the associate in the following real estate transactions.

	Sales Price of the Property	Broker's Rate of Commission	Total Commission	Associate's Percent of Commission	Associate's Commission
7.	$74,000	5%	————	50%	————
8.	$53,000	7%	————	40%	————
9.	$36,000	6%	————	60%	————
10.	$61,000	$5\frac{1}{2}$%	————	45%	————
11.	$48,000	7%	————	55%	————
12.	$69,000	6%	————	50%	————

Find the rate of commission that was charged in the following real estate transactions.

	Sales Price of the Property	Amount of Commission	Rate of Commission
13.	$ 27,000	$1,620	————
14.	$ 66,000	$3,300	————
15.	$ 54,000	$2,970	————
16.	$ 79,000	$3,160	————
17.	$120,000	$6,000	————
18.	$ 84,000	$5,880	————

Find the sales price in the following transactions.

	Amount of Commission	Rate of Commission	Sales Price of the Property
19.	$ 4,600	5%	————
20.	$11,480	7%	————
21.	$ 6,480	6%	————
22.	$ 3,440	4%	————
23.	$11,760	6%	————
24.	$ 7,840	7%	————

Practical Applications

25. Jim Bates's house sold for $82,000. The associate involved in the transaction received 55% of the broker's 7% commission. How much commission did the associate receive?

26. A house sold for $50,000. The 6% commission charged by the broker for selling the house was divided as follows: 20% to the associate who obtained the listing and one half of the balance to the associate who made the sale. How much commission was received by each associate?

27. The 6% commission received by a broker was $2,700. What was the sales price of the property?

28. The broker received a commission of $6,160 for selling a house for $88,000. What rate of commission did he charge?

29. Joe Ennis listed his home with a broker and specified that he wants $49,000 net after payment of the broker's fee. What must the selling price of the home be to provide the broker a 6% fee?

30. Allan Beal listed his house with a realtor. The house has 2,350 square feet. After conducting a market survey the realtor recommended an asking price of $25.50 per square foot. At what price should the realtor list the house?

31. James Riley wants to purchase some commercial property as an investment. He wants to realize a return on capital of 10%. He is considering an investment in property that has an annual projected net operating income of $4,000. The estimated economic life of the property is 25 years. What is the value of the property?

32. How many square feet are in the houses diagrammed below?

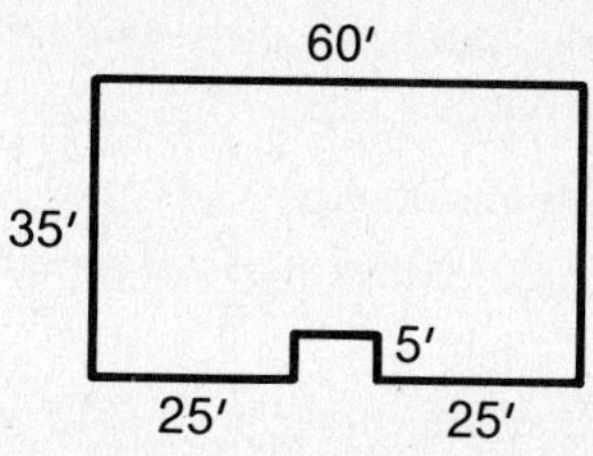

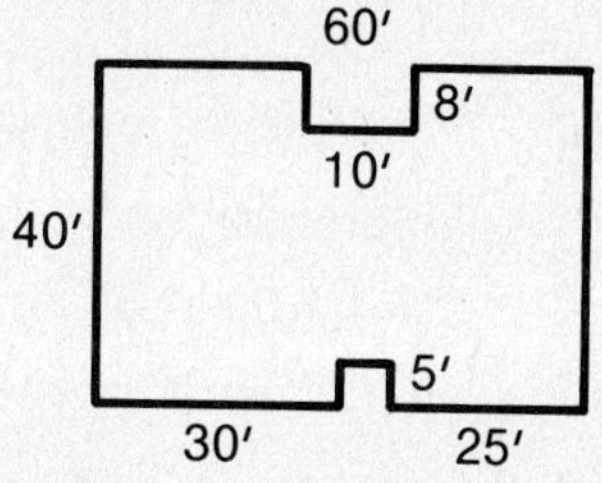

Learning Unit 15.2
Elements of Cost in a Closing

The elements of cost in a real estate closing are: (1) commissions; (2) title assurance charges and legal fees; (3) loan-related charges and fees; and (4) property taxes and related charges.

Commissions

Commissions are typically 5% to 6% of the sales price when a broker is used. Commissions on sales of lots and land may run up to 10%. The process of calculating commissions was discussed in the previous unit.

Title Assurance Charges and Legal Fees

Title assurance charges include the costs of title search and title insurance. A buyer may also incur fees for legal counsel in handling the closing. Both the buyer and lender want assurances that the title to the property has no claims or liens filed against it. Title insurance typically costs from $3.50 to $6.50 per thousand dollars of value. To find the cost of title insurance, determine the number of thousands in the sales price of the property and then multiply that figure by the rate per thousand.

Example: Mortgage financing is being arranged for a house that is being bought for $50,000. The fee for the attorney providing legal counsel to the buyer and checking the title and deed is $150. The cost of title insurance is $5.50 per $1,000 of the sales price of the property. How much title assurance charges and legal fees will the buyer pay?

Solution: $50,000 ÷ 1,000 = 50   number of 1,000's in $50,000

50 × $5.50 = $275   cost of title insurance

$275 + $150 = $425   title assurance charges and legal fees

Loan-Related Charges and Fees

The major cost items that must be considered in obtaining mortgage financing are loan origination (service fee points), mortgage discount points, property survey, appraisal, prepaid interest, hazard insurance, and the attorney fees of the lender.

Loan Origination Fees (Service Fee Points). Service fee points are a charge to cover the expenses incurred in initiating a mortgage loan with a lending firm and typically amount to 1% of the amount borrowed.

To determine the amount of a lender's service charge, multiply the number of points by the amount of the loan.

Example: Mortgage financing is being arranged for a $45,000 loan on a house. The lender charges a one-point loan origination fee. What is the amount of the fee?

Solution: $45,000 \times .01 = \$450$ loan origination fee

Government Loan Origination Fees (Mortgage Discount Points). Government-regulated mortgage loans, such as FHA (Federal Housing Administration) and VA (Veterans' Administration) loans, are usually offered at lower interest rates than mortgage loans on the general market. When the current market interest rates are higher than the interest ceilings on government loans, lenders charge mortgage discount points (prepaid interest) in order to avoid losing the interest they could obtain on the open market.

Since federal regulations prohibit lending institutions from charging more than a specified amount of interest on government loans, mortgage discount points must be paid by the *seller*.

One percent (one mortgage discount point) is required to make up for each $\frac{1}{8}$% interest rate loss. The mortgage discount (prepaid interest) is determined by multiplying the percent value of the discount points (remember that 1 point = 1%) by the amount of the loan.

Example: The Southern Savings and Loan Association is negotiating a 9% FHA loan for $45,000. The current interest rate on mortgage loans is $9\frac{1}{4}$%. How many mortgage discount points and what amount of prepaid interest must the association charge in order to avoid the interest rate loss?

Solution: If the association approves the FHA loan, it will suffer a $\frac{1}{4}$% interest rate loss. Two mortgage discount points are therefore required since $\frac{1}{4}$% equals $\frac{2}{8}$%. Since each point is equal to 1% of the loan, the mortgage discount is $900 (.02 \times \$45,000)$.

Property Taxes and Related Charges

The lender or mortgage company will generally make arrangements to pay the taxes on the property. Normally, the estimated property tax for the year is prorated on a monthly basis and added to the payments due each month for the mortgage interest, principal, and insurance on the property. The next unit will discuss real estate taxes in more detail.

Exercises

Determine the title assurance charges and legal fees that the buyer will pay in the following transactions.

	Sales Price of the Property	Attorney Fee	Title Insurance Rate per $1,000	Cost of Title Insurance	Assurance Charges and Legal Fee
1.	$63,000	$125	$5.30	_______	_______
2.	$84,000	$175	$4.80	_______	_______
3.	$42,000	$150	$6.20	_______	_______
4.	$29,000	$300	$6.50	_______	_______
5.	$56,000	$225	$5.70	_______	_______
6.	$48,000	$200	$5.90	_______	_______

Determine the loan-related charges for the following mortgage loans.

	Amount of Loan	Loan Origination Fee	Mortgage Discount Points	Loan-Related Charges
7.	$65,000	1%	0	_______
8.	$42,000	2%	3	_______
9.	$59,000	1%	0	_______
10.	$71,000	1%	0	_______
11.	$33,000	2%	4	_______
12.	$37,000	2%	2	_______

Practical Applications

13. Jerry Williams wants to obtain a $32,000, 9% VA loan from the Metroplex Savings and Loan Association. The current market rate of

interest is $9\frac{1}{2}\%$. How many mortgage discount points will be required to obtain the loan? What amount of mortgage discount or prepaid interest will Jerry have to pay the savings and loan?

14. Mike Terry is buying a house for $52,000. The rate for title insurance is $6 per thousand. How much will Terry pay for title insurance?

15. Bill Morgan is negotiating a $44,000 conventional loan with a savings and loan association. The association charges a $75 application fee plus a one-point loan origination fee. What are the total charges for the application fee and loan origination fee?

Learning Unit 15.3
Real Estate Taxes

The real estate, or property, tax is the primary source of revenue for local governments. Property taxes are used by local communities to provide a variety of services, such as schools, fire and police protection, city streets and lights, emergency medical facilities, auditoriums, and recreational facilities. Real estate taxes are levied so that each taxpayer will share the cost of these various government services.

Assessment and Taxation Procedures

Property taxes vary from state to state and from one community to another within a state, but the method of computing real estate taxes is the same. Real estate taxes are levied in proportion to the value of each taxpayer's property and are known as *ad valorem* taxes. An ad valorem tax is based on the value of the property subject to taxation. The responsibility for valuing real estate for tax purposes is usually assigned to an assessor who is elected or appointed to office.

Assessment practices vary among communities. While property in some communities may be assessed, or valued, for tax purposes at 15% or 20% of its market value, legal requirements in other communities may demand an assessment of 100% of market value. Regardless of the local policy, all property in the same community is usually assessed at the same percent of its market value.

The tax rate is also established by the local government and is usually expressed as dollars or cents per hundred or per thousand dollars of assessed value.

Computing Real Estate Taxes

To compute the amount of tax that will be levied on a particular parcel of real estate:

1. Determine the assessed value of the property (market value × assessment rate).
2. Determine the number of 100's (or 1,000's) in the assessed value (assessed value ÷ 100 [or 1,000]).
3. Multiply the number of 100's (or 1,000's) by the tax rate.

Example: Jack Jason's home has a market value of $60,000. The assessed value of property in the city is 65% of market value, and the tax rate is $.85 per $100 of assessed valuation. What are the annual city taxes on the house?

Solution: (1) $60,000 × .65 = $39,000   assessed value

(2) $39,000 ÷ 100 = 390   number of 100's in $39,000

(3) 390 × $.85 = $331.50   annual city taxes

Real estate is often subject to taxation by several local units of government. The total tax rate may include the rates of various units of governments such as city, county, and school.

To compute taxes on property subject to taxation by several local units:

1. Determine the total tax rate (add rates of various governmental units).
2. Determine the number of 100's (or 1,000's) in the assessed value.
3. Multiply the number of 100's (or 1,000's) by the total tax rate.

Example: Jim Bagwell's home has an assessed valuation of $45,000. Tax rates per $100 of assessed valuation are: school, $1.76;

city, $.85; county, $.22; and water district, $.04. What are the total tax rate and total taxes on Jim's home?

Solution:
(1) $1.76 + $.85 + $.22 + $.04 = $2.87   total tax rate
(2) $45,000 ÷ 100 = 450   number of 100's in $45,000
(3) 450 × $2.87 = $1,291.50   total taxes

Exercises

Calculate the amount of tax for the following parcels of real estate subject to a tax rate per $100 assessed value.

	Market Value	Assessment Rate	Assessed Value	Tax Rate per $100	Amount of Tax
1.	$50,000	65%	_______	$1.45	_______
2.	$76,000	100%	_______	$ .85	_______
3.	$32,000	15%	_______	$4.75	_______
4.	$46,000	35%	_______	$3.20	_______
5.	$95,000	75%	_______	$1.40	_______
6.	$62,000	60%	_______	$ .95	_______
7.	$78,000	80%	_______	$1.10	_______
8.	$49,000	25%	_______	$2.85	_______

Calculate the amount of tax for the following parcels of real estate subject to a tax rate per $1,000 assessed value.

	Market Value	Assessment Rate	Assessed Value	Tax Rate per $1,000	Amount of Tax
9.	$80,000	60%	_______	$ 9.72	_______
10.	$49,000	87%	_______	$ 7.41	_______
11.	$92,000	30%	_______	$13.35	_______
12.	$75,000	20%	_______	$15.48	_______
13.	$54,000	100%	_______	$ 6.39	_______
14.	$32,000	65%	_______	$17.10	_______
15.	$76,000	75%	_______	$ 8.74	_______
16.	$98,000	90%	_______	$11.25	_______

Practical Applications

17. An office building has a market value of $450,000. The assessed value for commercial property in the city is 75%, and the tax rate per $1,000 is $6.42. What are the annual taxes?

18. Jean Oberman is interested in buying a home that has a market value of $55,000. She phoned the local tax assessor and learned that all local taxes will be levied on 45% of the market value of the house and that the tax rates per $100 of assessed value are: school, $1.92; city, $.65; and county, $.14. What are the total annual taxes on the house?

19. Jake Jacobs purchased a home for $68,000 in a city with an assessment rate of 40%. The tax rate is $4.22 per $100 of assessed value. How much of his total tax was spent on education if 56% of the local taxes was spent by the local school system?

20. Fred Fontain owns a house that he rents for $375 per month. The assessed value of the property is $40,000, and the total tax rate is $3.15 per hundred. Total depreciation and repairs on the house were $2,240 last year. How much were the taxes on the house last year? How much net income did he realize on the property?

Learning Unit 15.4
Percentage Leases

A lease is a contract under which a tenant rents property from a landlord. The tenant acquires possession and use of the property for a specified period of time, called the *term*, in return for rent or other compensation. The company or person renting the property is the tenant, or *lessee*. The landlord, or owner, of the property is the *lessor*.

Calculating Percentage Rent

It is a common practice for businesses to rent office or store space in commercial buildings or shopping centers on a *percentage lease*. Under this type of lease, the lessee agrees to pay a percentage of the volume of sales and services sold on the premises, often in addition to a base rent. Percentage rentals range from as low as 2% for department stores to as high as 75% for parking lot space.

To calculate the annual rent obligation under a percentage lease:

1. Determine the percentage rent (annual gross sales × percentage rental rate).
2. Determine the base rent (monthly rent × 12).
3. Add the percentage rent and base rent.

Example: Victor's Hobby Shop has a lease that requires a base rent of $175 per month plus 7% of gross sales. If the gross sales last year were $125,000, what was the total rent for the year?

Solution: (1) $125,000 × .07 = $8,750 percentage rent

(2) $175 × 12 = $2,100 base rent

(3) $8,750 + $2,100 = $10,850 total rent for the year

Calculating Percentage Rate

To calculate the percentage rate of a lease when the amount of base rent, gross sales, and rent paid are known:

1. Determine the percentage rent (total rent − base rent).
2. Divide the percentage rent by gross sales.

Example: Miller's Carpets has a lease that requires a base rent of $300 per month plus a percentage of gross sales. The total rent for the year was $8,600, and gross sales totaled $100,000. What percentage rate was contained in the lease?

Solution: (1) $8,600   total rent
             − 3,600   base rent
               $5,000   percentage rent

(2) $5,000 ÷ $100,000 = .05, or 5%   percentage rate

Exercises

Find the total rent for the year under the following leases.

1. Spencer's Fabric Center pays a monthly rental of $225 plus 6% of gross sales. Last year the gross sales were $250,000. What was the total rent for the year?

2. The Barber and Beauty Supply Company has a lease requiring $350 per month base rental plus 4% of gross sales. If total sales for the year were $300,000, what was the average monthly rent?

3. West Side Office Supply pays a monthly base rent of $275 plus 5% of gross sales in excess of $100,000. What was the total rent paid for the previous year if gross sales were $400,000?

4. Abe's Sporting Goods has a percentage lease that requires a $200 monthly base rent plus 8% of gross sales over $80,000. What was the total rent paid for a year in which gross sales amounted to $330,000?

Find the percentage rate contained in the following leases.

5. Lammon's Paint and Wallpaper pays a base rent of $250 per month plus a percentage of gross sales. If total sales for the year were $400,000 and total rent paid was $19,000, what percentage rate was contained in the lease?

6. Ben's Antique Shop paid a total rent of $18,000 last year on gross sales of $150,000. The lease does not include a base rental. What percentage rate is required by the lease?

7. Louella's Fashions pays a monthly base rent of $175 plus a percentage of gross sales. Gross sales last year were $250,000, and the total rent paid was $10,850. What percentage rate is required by the lease?

8. Jane's Florist has a percentage lease that requires a monthly base rent of $150. Last year a total rent of $10,200 was paid on gross sales of $120,000. What percentage rate is required by the lease?

Chapter 15
Self-Evaluation

1. Joe Barnes sold his home through a real estate broker for $56,400. What was the amount of commission earned by the realtor if the rate of commission is 6%?

2. The Brooks Real Estate Agency charges a 10% commission for the sale of lots for residential construction. Associates receive 60% of the commission for sales transactions that they handle. How much commission will an associate receive on the sale of a lot for $15,500?

3. A broker assisted in the sale of a house for $48,700 and received a commission of $2,678. What was the rate of commission charged by the broker?

4. A broker sold some commercial property and earned a commission of $8,120. If the broker charges 5% commission, what was the selling price of the property?

5. Sam Samson's home has 2,050 square feet. Comparable houses in the area have recently sold for $27.50 per square foot. What is the market value of Sam's home?

6. A realtor has obtained a listing from a homeowner who wants $56,900 net for his house. What must the selling price of the house be for the broker to receive a commission of 6%?

7. A homeowner is selling his house for $39,000. The attorney fee is $125, and the cost of title insurance is $6.25 per thousand. What are the total legal fee and title insurance charges?

8. Ed Beal is buying a new house for $73,000. The savings and loan association charges a $75 application fee and a one-point loan origination fee. What is the total cost of these two items?

9. Bill Walters is obtaining a 9% FHA loan from a savings and loan association. If the current market rate of interest is $9\frac{5}{8}\%$, how many mortgage discount points will be required to obtain the loan?

10. The assessment rate in Centerville is 65% of the market value. The tax rate per hundred is $2.95. What is the amount of taxes that will be levied on a house that has a market value of $72,700?

11. The market value of a building is $235,000. The tax rate in the community is $3.45 per hundred. The rate of assessment is 40%. What are the annual taxes on the property?

12. Martha's Novelties has a lease that requires a base rent of $125 per month plus 4% of gross sales. What is the total rental charge for a month in which gross sales were $7,500?

Chapter 16
The Mathematics of Insurance

Insurance is a means of providing persons or businesses with protection against financial loss resulting from some perilous event, such as fire, theft, accident, or death. Insurance is based on the principles of shared risk and shared loss. Under these principles, payments are made by persons subject to a common risk and are pooled in order to provide funds with which to reimburse, or *indemnify*, those who experience a loss.

Insurance involves a financial agreement, or indemnity contract, in the form of a *policy* between the *insurer* (insurance company) and the *insured* person or business. The insurer, in return for a fee called a *premium*, agrees to provide the insured protection against the risk of financial loss covered by the insurance policy.

This chapter examines three basic types of insurance: automobile, fire, and life. Automobile and fire insurance provide protection against the loss of property, while life insurance protects against the loss of earning power.

This chapter will enable you to:

1. **recognize and apply insurance terms such as policy, premium, indemnity, risk, coinsurance, beneficiary, and liability**

2. **distinguish between the various types of automobile insurance**

3. **compute the cost of various automobile coverages**

4. **determine the maximum liability of the insurance company under an automobile policy for various types of losses**

5. compute the premium on a fire insurance policy if the rate and amount of insurance are known

6. compute the short-rate premium on a fire insurance policy if the policy is cancelled at the request of the insured

7. compute the amount of indemnity for a fire loss when a coinsurance clause is involved

8. distinguish among the three basic types of life insurance policies: term, endowment, and whole life (ordinary life and limited payment life)

9. compute the premium on life insurance policies on an annual, semiannual, quarterly, and monthly basis

Learning Unit 16.1
Automobile Insurance

There are two basic types of automobile insurance: (1) liability insurance and (2) comprehensive and collision insurance. *Liability insurance* provides financial protection for bodily injury or property damage inflicted on *others* by the insured. *Comprehensive* and *collision insurance* protects against damage or loss of the insured's *own* automobile.

Liability Insurance—Coverage

Bodily-Injury Liability. Liability coverage for bodily injury is often quoted as "10/20 coverage." This means that the insurer will pay a maximum of $10,000 for the bodily injury inflicted to one person involved in an accident and a maximum of $20,000 for the bodily injuries inflicted to all victims of the same accident. The distribution of these amounts is illustrated in the following example.

Example: Pam Vargo was in an automobile accident in which two persons won claims for bodily injury. The first claim was for $3,000, and the second claim for $16,000. Pam has a policy with 10/20 bodily injury liability limits. How much will her insurance company pay?

Solution: Her insurance company will pay $13,000 ($3,000 + $10,-000). The total injury claims are less than $20,000, but the second claim was over the $10,000 maximum that the insurance company will pay for any one person's injury. Therefore, the insurance company will pay only $10,000 toward the second claim, and Pam will have to pay $6,000.

Property-Damage Liability. In many states, the maximum amount that an insurance company will pay for damage to the property of others for any single accident is $5,000.

Example: Abe Marko was in an automobile accident in which two persons won claims for property damage. The first claim was for $2,000, and the second claim for $4,000. Abe has a policy that provides $5,000 property-damage liability coverage. How much will his insurance company pay?

Solution: The total property-damage claims were $6,000. The maximum that the insurance company will pay is $5,000. Therefore, Abe will have to pay $1,000 to settle the claims.

Liability Insurance—Premium Costs

The premium for automobile liability insurance is based on a number of factors:

1. Driver class (age, marital status, and sex of the driver)
2. Use of the car (business or pleasure)
3. Territory in which the car is located (city, suburban, or rural, with least populous areas having lowest premiums)

Table 16.1 provides an example of selected annual rates for bodily-injury liability for maximum limits of $10,000 and $20,000 and property-damage liability for a maximum limit of $5,000. While most states use a large number of driver rate classes, only three are used in this illustration.

Higher maximum limits for bodily-injury and property-damage liability insurance are available for an additional premium. Table 16.2 provides an example of the additional cost of higher limits.

The total premium for increased coverage is determined by multiplying the basic coverage premiums from Table 16.1 by the appropriate percent in Table 16.2.

Example: Mark Ambrose is 23 years old and lives in territory 3. What is the premium for 10/20/5 automobile liability protection? What is the premium for 25/50/10 limits?

Table 16.1 Automobile Liability Insurance Rate Table

	Territory 1		Territory 2		Territory 3	
Class*	B.I.	P.D.	B.I.	P.D.	B.I.	P.D.
1	$39	$52	$47	$ 60	$ 71	$ 69
2	72	96	86	111	131	127
3	57	76	68	87	103	100

*Class 1: Nonbusiness use, no male driver under 25 or female driver under 21.
Class 2: Business or nonbusiness use, male driver under 25 or female driver under 21.
Class 3: Business use, no male driver under 25.

Bodily-Injury Liability			Property-Damage Liability	
Maximum Limits		Percent of Basic 10/20 Rates	Maximum Limits	Percent of $5,000 Rate
$ 20,000 and $ 40,000		129	$ 10,000	105
25,000 and 50,000		138	25,000	108
50,000 and 100,000		160	50,000	113
100,000 and 300,000		184	100,000	118

Solution: $131   B.I. basic rate for class 2, territory 3

    127   P.D. basic rate for class 2, territory 3

$258   total annual premium for 10/20/5 limits

$131 $\times$ 1.38 = $180.78   B.I. rate for 25/50 maximum limits

$127 $\times$ 1.05 = $133.35   P.D. rate for a $10,000 maximum limit

$314.13   total annual premium for 25/50/10 limits

Comprehensive and Collision Insurance—Coverage

Comprehensive Coverage. Comprehensive insurance protects the insured's automobile against fire, theft, and any other cause of physical damage that is not specifically excluded. (The principal risk that is excluded is collision.) Comprehensive insurance containing a deductible clause can be purchased for a lower premium. A deductible clause reduces the amount that the insurance company will pay for each claim.

Example: Joe Amon's automobile was completely destroyed by fire. His automobile policy contained a $50 deductible comprehensive clause. The value of the car was determined to be $4,000 at the time of the loss. How much will he be reimbursed by his insurance company for the loss?

Solution: $4,000 − $50 = $3,950   amount of reimbursement

Collision Coverage. Collision insurance protects against damage to the insured's own automobile, including damage caused in one-car accidents. The insurance policy always contains a deductible clause of $50 or more. As in the case of comprehensive insurance, the deductible clause reduces the amount that the insurance company will pay for each claim.

Example: Jim Jones was involved in a single-car accident that caused $700 damage to his automobile. His automobile policy provided $100 deductible collision coverage. How much will he be reimbursed by his insurance company for the loss?

Solution: $700 − $100 = $600   reimbursement

Comprehensive and Collision Insurance—Premium Costs

The premium for automobile comprehensive insurance is based on a number of factors:

1. symbol group (value of the car when new)
2. car age group
3. territory in which the car is driven
4. policy limits

An additional factor, the class of the driver, is used in determining the premium for collision insurance. The following tables provide information about the symbol groups and age groups used in computing the premiums for comprehensive and collision coverage.

Table 16.3 Symbol Groups for Comprehensive and Collision Insurance

Original Price of Automobile	Symbol* Group
$2,751 to $3,700	4
$3,701 to $5,000	5
$5,001 to $6,500	6

*Symbol for medium-priced cars only.

Table 16.4 Age Groups for Comprehensive and Collision Insurance

Age Group	Definition*
1	All automobiles of the current model year
2	All automobiles of the first preceding model year
3	All automobiles of the second preceding model year
4	All other automobiles

*For the purpose of this definition, the current model year changes effective October 1 of each calendar year.

The following comprehensive and collision rate tables provide some typical rates for the three automobile symbol groups and the four age groups described in Tables 16.3 and 16.4.

As we discussed earlier, a deductible clause reduces the amount that the insurer would have to pay in case of accident. As Tables 16.5 and 16.6 show, the higher the deductible, the lower the premium.

Table 16.5 Automobile Comprehensive Insurance Rate Table

Symbol Group	Age Group	Territory 1			Territory 2		
		Full Coverage	$50 Ded.	$100 Ded.	Full Coverage	$50 Ded.	$100 Ded.
4	1	$ 71	$50	$29	$53	$37	$21
	2	64	45	26	47	33	19
	3	54	38	22	40	28	16
	4	43	30	17	31	22	13
5	1	$ 91	$64	$37	$67	$47	$27
	2	81	57	33	60	42	24
	3	68	48	28	50	35	20
	4	54	38	22	77	28	16
6	1	$115	$81	$47	$85	$60	$34
	2	102	72	42	77	54	30
	3	85	60	35	64	45	25
	4	68	48	38	51	36	20

Example: Bill Bagwell bought a new automobile for $6,200. He obtained an automobile insurance policy that provides full-coverage comprehensive insurance. If he lives in territory 1, what is the annual premium for the coverage? How much less would $50 deductible comprehensive cost?

Solution: The premium for symbol group 6, age group 1, territory 1, full-coverage comprehensive is $115. The cost of $50 deductible comprehensive is $81. Therefore, he could obtain $50 deductible comprehensive for $34 less ($115 − $81 = $34).

Table 16.6   Automobile $200 Deductible Collision Insurance Rate Table*

Symbol Group	Age Group	Territory 1 Class			Territory 2 Class		
		1	2	3	1	2	3
4	1	$123	$360	$161	$ 93	$272	$121
	2	117	342	153	89	258	115
	3	105	306	137	79	231	103
	4	93	270	121	70	204	91
5	1	$148	$432	$193	$112	$326	$146
	2	141	410	183	106	310	138
	3	126	367	164	95	277	124
	4	111	324	145	84	244	109
6	1	$173	$504	$225	$131	$380	$170
	2	164	478	214	124	361	161
	3	147	428	191	111	323	144
	4	130	378	169	98	285	127

*The methods for determining collision premiums for other deductible amounts are:
$ 50 deductible—charge 157% of $200 deductible collision premium.
$100 deductible—charge 133% of $200 deductible collision premium.
$500 deductible—charge 47% of $200 deductible collision premium.

Example: Bill Bagwell wants to insure his new $6,200 automobile for $200 deductible collision insurance. Bill is 23 years old and lives in territory 1. How much will this coverage cost? How much more would he have to pay for $50 deductible collision coverage?

Solution: The annual premium for symbol group 6, age group 1, territory 1, class 2 (see Table 16.6), $200 deductible collision coverage is $504. The premium for $50 deductible collision is $791.28 ($504 × 1.57 = $791.28). He would pay $287.28 more for $50 deductible collision than $200 deductible collision ($791.28 − $504 = $287.28).

Exercises

Determine the amount of insurance settlement in the following cases.

	Amount of Liability Insurance	Bodily-Injury Claims			Property-Damage Claims	Total B.I. Settlement	Total P.D. Settlement
		1	2	3			
1.	10/20/5	$ 6,000	$ 8,000	$ 9,000	$ 4,000	_______	_______
2.	10/20/5	$ 7,000	$ 9,000		$ 6,000	_______	_______
3.	10/20/10	$12,000	$16,000		$ 8,000	_______	_______
4.	20/40/10	$ 8,000	$11,000	$12,000	$13,000	_______	_______
5.	25/50/25	$ 2,000	$ 5,000		$31,400	_______	_______
6.	50/100/25	$49,000			$17,000	_______	_______

Determine the annual premium for the following automobile liability insurance coverage.

	Insurance	Class Driver	Insurance Territory	Amount of Insurance	Annual Premium
7.	Bodily Injury	1	3	10/20	_______
8.	Property Damage	1	3	$5,000	_______
9.	Bodily Injury	3	2	10/20	_______
10.	Property Damage	3	2	$5,000	_______
11.	Property Damage	2	1	$25,000	_______
12.	Bodily Injury	1	1	25/50	_______
13.	Property Damage	3	3	$10,000	_______
14.	Bodily Injury	2	2	20/40	_______

Determine the annual premium for comprehensive insurance for the following automobiles.

	Automobile Symbol Group	Automobile Age Group	Insurance Territory	Coverage	Annual Premium
15.	5	2	2	$50 Ded.	_______
16.	4	3	2	Full Coverage	_______
17.	6	1	1	$100 Ded.	_______
18.	4	4	1	Full Coverage	_______
19.	6	3	2	$100 Ded.	_______
20.	4	2	1	$50 Ded.	_______
21.	5	4	1	Full Coverage	_______
22.	6	1	2	$100 Ded.	_______

Determine the annual premium for collision insurance for each of the following automobiles.

	Automobile Symbol Group	Automobile Age Group	Territory	Class Driver	Coverage	Annual Premium
23.	6	4	1	3	$200 Ded.	_______
24.	4	2	1	1	$200 Ded.	_______
25.	5	1	2	2	$ 50 Ded.	_______
26.	5	3	1	3	$500 Ded.	_______
27.	4	2	2	1	$100 Ded.	_______
28.	6	4	2	3	$ 50 Ded.	_______
29.	6	3	1	2	$200 Ded.	_______
30.	4	1	2	2	$100 Ded.	_______

Practical Applications

31. Due to a blowout, Judy Bell's automobile swerved and struck a tree. The damage to her car amounted to $937. Her automobile policy includes $100 deductible collision. How much reimbursement will she receive from the insurance company?

32. Bob Carswell, age 27, who lives in territory 2, wants to obtain insurance that will protect him against liability arising from death or injury

caused by his automobile. He wants to be protected up to $10,000 for one person and $20,000 for two or more people injured in the same accident. He also wants protection up to $5,000 for property damage caused by his car. The car is not used in business. What is the annual premium for 10/20/5 liability coverage?

33. The Richland Company wants to obtain bodily-injury and property-damage liability insurance on an automobile. There are no drivers under 25 years of age. The automobile will be used in business and will be driven in territory 1. What is the premium for maximum limits of 100/300/25?

34. How much more does a 22-year-old male driver have to pay for $50 deductible collision insurance than a 29-year-old male driver? Both drivers live in territory 2 and purchased the same model automobile during the past month for a price of $4,500. Neither car is used in business.

Learning Unit 16.2
Fire Insurance

Fire insurance provides financial protection against property damage resulting from fire. Extended coverage is usually included to provide financial protection from damage due to smoke or to measures taken to prevent the spread of fire. Insured property may include homes, commercial buildings, inventories, equipment, etc.

Premium Costs

The cost of fire insurance depends on a number of factors, including:

1. type of structure (flammability of construction material, such as brick or wood)
2. location of structure (congestion of area or nearby fire hazards)
3. contents of structure (degree of flammability)

4. proximity to fire protection facilities
5. term of the policy
6. amount of the policy

The annual premium rate for fire insurance is usually expressed in terms of cents per $100 of insurance.

To calculate the annual premium for fire insurance coverage:

1. Determine the number of times $100 is contained in the amount of insurance.
2. Multiply that number by the premium rate.

Example: What is the annual premium on $47,000 of fire insurance at a premium rate of $.54$\frac{1}{2}$ per $100?

Solution: $47,000 \div $100 = 470$ number of $100's in $47,000

$470 \times $.545 = 256.15 annual premium

Long-Term Policies

To encourage property owners to purchase fire insurance for periods longer than one year, some insurance companies offer reduced rates. Sample fire insurance rates for periods longer than one year are presented in Table 16.7. Multiple-year rates generally reduce the cost of the insurance.

Table 16.7   Sample Long-Term Rates

Period	Long-Term Rate
2 years	1.85 times the annual rate
3 years	2.7 times the annual rate
4 years	3.55 times the annual rate
5 years	4.4 times the annual rate

To determine the premium for a long-term policy, multiply the annual premium by the long-term rate.

Example: What is the premium on a $73,000 three-year policy at an annual premium rate of $.46 per hundred?

Solution: $73,000 ÷ $100 = 730   number of $100's in $73,000

730 × $.46 = $335.80   annual premium

$335.80 × 2.7 = $906.66   three-year premium

Short Rates

Sometimes a fire insurance policy is in effect for less than a year due to the insured's need for only temporary protection or to cancellation of the policy by the insured. The premium for such policies is computed according to special short-term rates. These rates vary. Whereas multiple-year rates for long-term policies generally reduce the costs of fire protection, short rates for policies in effect less than one year generally increase these costs. In case of cancellation, the insurance company returns the difference between the regular annual premium and the short-rate premium.

To determine a short-rate premium, multiply the annual premium by the short rate.

Example: The Richland Company obtained a $35,000 fire policy on a building for one year at a premium rate of $.87 per $100. The building was sold and the policy cancelled three months later. The short-rate premium was 40% of the annual premium. How much was the short-rate premium?

Solution: $35,000 ÷ $100 = 350   number of $100's in $35,000

350 × $.87 = $304.50   annual premium

$304.50 × .4 = $121.80   short-rate premium.

Coinsurance

In order to encourage property owners to purchase full insurance coverage, many policies contain a coinsurance clause. A coinsurance clause requires, as a condition for full payment in the event of loss, that the insured carry coverage that is at least a specified percent (often 80%) of the total value of the property.

If the amount of insurance coverage at the time of loss is less than the specified percent, the insurance company will indemnify the insured on a pro rata basis, according to this formula:

$$\text{Indemnity} = \frac{\text{insurance carried}}{\text{insurance required}} \times \text{amount of loss}$$

Example: A house valued at $67,000 is insured for $40,000 under a fire policy having an 80% coinsurance clause. Fire damaged the property to the extent of $16,000. How much indemnity will the insured receive?

Solution: Insurance carried = $40,000

Insurance required = $53,600 ($67,000 × .8)

Amount of loss = $16,000

$$\text{Indemnity} = \frac{\$40,000}{\$53,600} \times \$16,000$$

Indemnity = $11,940.30

Exercises

Calculate the premium for each of the following fire insurance policies.

	Amount of Insurance	Annual Premium Rate per $100	Term	Premium
1.	$50,000	$.162	1 year	_______
2.	$43,000	$.226	3 years	_______
3.	$76,000	$.185	2 years	_______
4.	$30,000	$.146	5 years	_______
5.	$45,000	$.242	4 years	_______
6.	$28,000	$.138	1 year	_______
7.	$66,000	$.225	5 years	_______

Find the short-rate premium for each of the following one-year policies that were cancelled at the request of the insured before the term expired.

	Amount of Insurance	Annual Premium Rate per $100	Annual Premium	Short Rate	Short-Rate Premium
8.	$19,000	$.334	_______	72%	_______
9.	$75,000	$.260	_______	19%	_______
10.	$46,000	$.432	_______	52%	_______
11.	$87,000	$.278	_______	64%	_______
12.	$90,000	$.180	_______	31%	_______
13.	$42,000	$.345	_______	22%	_______

Determine the amount of reimbursement by the insurance company for the following fire losses.

	Amount of Insurance	Property Loss	Property Value	Coinsurance Clause	Amount of Indemnity
14.	$ 40,000	$15,000	$ 49,000	80%	________
15.	$ 62,000	$23,000	$ 74,000	80%	________
16.	$ 28,000	$ 7,000	$ 33,000	90%	________
17.	$ 36,000	$18,000	$ 43,000	80%	________
18.	$ 55,000	$ 6,000	$ 75,000	80%	________
19.	$100,000	$ 5,000	$142,000	80%	________
20.	$ 24,000	$ 9,000	$ 32,000	80%	________
21.	$ 80,000	$41,000	$ 93,000	90%	________

Practical Applications

22. Joe Washington sold his home and returned his fire policy to the insurance company for cancellation. The policy had been in force 27 days and the short-rate premium was 20% of the annual premium of $168. How much premium refund did he receive?

23. Jack Smith insured his house for $40,000 with a three-year fire policy. The annual rate per $100 of insurance is $.165. What is the cost of the three-year policy?

24. Mort Mikel currently insures his real estate office building for $120,000 under a one-year fire policy. The annual rate is $.224 per $100 coverage. How much annual savings would he realize if he changed to a five-year policy?

25. A house was valued at $78,000 when a $22,000 fire loss occurred. The owner carried a $60,000 fire policy that contained an 80% coinsurance clause. How much indemnity was paid by the insurance company?

26. A building worth $120,000 is insured for $90,000 by a fire policy that contains an 80% coinsurance clause. What is the insurer's liability for fire damage of $22,000?

Learning Unit 16.3
Life Insurance

Life insurance protects the dependents and survivors of the insured from financial loss resulting from the death of the insured. There are three basic types of life insurance: (1) term, (2) whole-life (ordinary life and limited-payment life), and (3) endowment.

The cost of life insurance depends, among other things, on the age of the insured (cost increases with age), the sex of the insured (increased life expectancy for females decreases cost), the type of policy, and the amount of coverage. Premium rates differ among companies. Table 16.8 provides some typical rates.

Table 16.8   Annual Premiums per $1,000 Insurance*

Age Nearest Birthday		5-Year Renewable Term	Ordinary Life	20-Pay Life	20-Year Endowment
Male	Female				
20	25	2.37	10.13	16.44	35.18
25	30	2.58	12.07	18.87	35.85
30	35	2.88	14.30	21.42	36.41
35	40	3.73	17.18	24.50	37.24
40	45	5.30	20.94	28.27	38.73
45	50	7.74	25.91	33.07	40.68
50	55	12.16	33.10	39.84	45.42
55	60	19.55	42.95	48.83	—
60	65	27.03	52.50	56.97	—

*The semiannual rate is 51 percent of the annual rate; the quarterly rate is 26 percent of the annual rate; and the monthly rate is 9 percent of the annual rate.

Term Insurance

Term insurance is the least expensive type of life insurance: it provides only temporary protection and develops no equity or cash value for the policyholder. Under a term policy, protection is provided for only a specific period of time, usually one to 20 years. The insured pays the premium and the insurance company agrees to pay the insured's beneficiaries the amount of insurance carried (face value of the policy) if the death of the insured occurs during the term of the policy. If the insured is living when the term expires, the insurance is terminated. Term policies usually permit the insured to renew the coverage or convert to another form of life insurance before the policy expires.

Term policies can be used to provide maximum insurance protection at a minimum cost to young families with children to support and educate. Term policies are also used to purchase life insurance for plane or boat trips—the term in such cases is the duration of the trip.

To calculate the monthly permium for term insurance:

1. Determine the annual rate per $1,000 from Table 16.8.
2. Determine the number of 1,000's in the face value of the policy.
3. Determine the annual premium (number of 1,000's × rate of premium).
4. Multiply the annual premium by the monthly rate factor (see * at the end of Table 16.8).

Example: What is the monthly premium for a $100,000 five-year renewable term policy for a female, age 25?

Solution: (1) $2.37 = rate per $1,000

(2) $100,000 ÷ $1,000 = 100   number of 1,000's in $100,000

(3) $2.37 × 100 = $237   annual premium

(4) $237 × .09 = $21.33   monthly premium

Ordinary Life Insurance

Ordinary life insurance policies are the most widely purchased and offer "permanent" life insurance protection during the insured's life. (The protection under this type of policy is "permanent" insofar as there is no termination date and the policy never has to be renewed.) In order to keep the policy in effect, premiums must be paid as long as the insured lives. Upon the death of the insured, the face value of the policy is paid to the beneficiary.

In addition to providing insurance protection, ordinary life insurance policies build up an equity, or cash value, which is the amount the insured would receive if he or she cancelled the policy. Under this type of coverage, the insured has the options of converting the cash value to other types of insurance policies, borrowing on the policy for normal lifetime needs, or using the cash value for retirement needs. Premiums remain the same and, over the long term, the net cost may turn out to be even less than the cost of term insurance.

The monthly premium for ordinary life insurance can be calculated by using the same four-step procedure that was described for calculating the monthly premium of term insurance, except that the rate for ordinary life from Table 16.8 is used.

Example: What is the monthly premium for a $25,000 ordinary life policy for a female, age 25?

Solution: $10.13 = rate per $1,000

$25,000 ÷ 1,000 = 25   number of 1,000's in $25,000

$10.13 × 25 = $253.25   annual premium

$253.25 × .09 = $22.79   monthly premium

Limited-Payment Life Insurance

Limited-payment life insurance policies provide permanent protection just as ordinary life insurance policies, but require premium payments for only a limited number of years (often to age 65). However, these payments are sufficiently larger so that an amount approximately equivalent to the total that would be paid during a lifetime for ordinary life insurance will be paid during the limited-payment period. Although the premiums are higher under this type of policy, lifetime coverage can be paid for during the peak income-earning years.

A limited-payment life insurance policy with payments for 20 years is called a 20-pay life policy. If the insured is living at the end of 20 years, no more payments are required, and protection is provided for the remainder of the insured's life. Upon the insured's death, the insurance company pays the insured's beneficiary the face value of the policy.

The monthly premium for limited-payment life insurance can be calculated by using the four-step procedure illustrated for calculating term insurance premiums except that the rate for limited-payment life from Table 16.8 is used.

Example: What is the monthly premium for a $25,000, 20-pay life policy for a female, age 25?

Solution: $16.44 = rate per $1,000

       $25,000 ÷ 1,000 = 25   number of 1,000's in $25,000

       $16.44 × 25 = $411   annual premium

       $411 × .09 = $36.99   monthly premium

Endowment Insurance

Endowment policies are similar to term and limited-payment life policies in two respects: (1) premiums are paid for a fixed period of time (typically 10, 15, or 20 years for endowment policies), and (2) if the insured dies during the policy period, the beneficiary receives the face value of the policy. However, endowment policies are different in that if the insured is alive when the policy period ends, the insured receives the face value. (The insurance protection ceases upon payment to the insured.)

Since endowment premiums not only purchase insurance protection in the event an insured dies, but also "save" an equivalent cash amount in the event the insured lives, the cost of these policies is high.

The monthly premium for endowment policies can be calculated by following the four-step procedure used for calculating term insurance premiums except that, in this case, the endowment rate is applied.

Example: What is the monthly premium for a $25,000, 20-year endowment policy for a female, age 25?

Solution: $35.18 = rate per $1,000

       $25,000 ÷ 1,000 = 25   number of 1,000's in $25,000

       $35.18 × 25 = $879.50   annual premium

       $879.50 × .09 = $79.16   monthly premium

Exercises

What is the annual premium per $1,000 life insurance in the following situations? (Use Table 16.8.)

	Age	Sex	Type of Insurance	Annual Premium
1.	30	Male	Ordinary life	__________
2.	45	Male	20-pay life	__________

3.	40	Female	20-year endowment	_________
4.	30	Female	Ordinary life	_________
5.	20	Male	5-year renewable term	_________
6.	30	Female	5-year renewable term	_________

What is the annual premium for the following life insurance policies?

	Age	Sex	Type of Insurance	Face Value	Annual Rate per $1,000	Annual Premium
7.	35	Female	5-year term	$100,000	_________	_________
8.	35	Female	Ordinary life	$25,000	_________	_________
9.	35	Female	20-pay life	$25,000	_________	_________
10.	35	Female	20-year endowment	$25,000	_________	_________
11.	45	Male	Ordinary life	$10,000	_________	_________
12.	25	Male	5-year term	$50,000	_________	_________
13.	50	Female	20-pay life	$15,000	_________	_________
14.	40	Male	20-year endowment	$10,000	_________	_________

A male, age 30, plans to purchase $10,000 life insurance. Complete the amount of periodic premium payment for each of the following types of policies and methods of payment.

	Type of Insurance	Annually	Semiannually	Quarterly	Monthly
15.	5-year term	_________	_________	_________	_________
16.	Ordinary life	_________	_________	_________	_________
17.	20-pay life	_________	_________	_________	_________
18.	20-year endowment	_________	_________	_________	_________

Practical Applications

19. Jane Smith plans to purchase a $20,000 ordinary life insurance policy on her 25th birthday. How much annual saving will she realize if she elects an annual payment rather than quarterly premium payments?

20. Jack Brown is 25 years of age and has several dependents. He plans to purchase term insurance and make annual premium payments. How much insurance protection can he obtain for an annual premium of approximately $180?

21. A partnership insured the life of one of the partners, Jim Moors, age 55, with a $100,000, 5-year renewable term policy. How much is the annual premium?

22. The MBO Corporation provides each of its chief executives a $50,000 term insurance policy. Barbara Ingle, age 45, has been promoted to vice-president, marketing. How much is the annual premium?

Chapter 16
Self-Evaluation

1. What is the annual premium on $56,000 of fire insurance at a premium rate of $.63\frac{1}{2}$ per $100?

2. The ABC Company obtained a $235,000 fire policy on a building for one year at a premium rate of $.93 per $100. The building was sold and the policy cancelled three months later. The short-rate premium was 40% of the annual premium. What was the amount of the short-rate premium?

3. A house valued at $84,000 is insured for $52,000 under a fire policy having an 80% coinsurance clause. The house had $21,000 fire damage. How much indemnity will the insured receive?

4. Joan has decided to purchase a $25,000 limited-payment life policy. The annual premium per $1,000 for a 20-pay life policy for a female, age 25, is $16.44. The monthly rate is 9% of the annual rate. What is the monthly premium for the policy?

5. Evelyn is planning to purchase a 20-year endowment policy in the amount of $25,000. The annual premium rate per $1,000 for a female, age 25, is $35.18. The quarterly rate is 26% of the annual rate. What is the quarterly premium for the policy?

6. Joe Thomas was in an auto accident from which two persons won claims for bodily injury. The first claim was for $8,532, and the second claim for $17,650. Joe has an auto policy with 10/20 bodily-injury liability limits. How much will his insurance company pay?

Chapter 17
The Mathematics of Transportation

Commercial transportation is a major factor in the economy of every nation. It is an important service industry that facilitates the movement of goods and services along channels of distribution.

Transportation costs are an important consideration in the cost of goods sold. Therefore, the ability to compute transportation costs, as well as the ability to choose the most economical shipment method, are desirable business skills.

This chapter will enable you to:

1. **identify various weight classifications**

2. **calculate costs of transportation using various freight rates**

3. **calculate the break point between two rate classifications**

4. **calculate costs of transportation when there are ancillary costs**

Learning Unit 17.1
Weights and Rates

Transportation costs are usually assigned by the weight of the shipment. Three of the most common weight classifications used by transportation companies are: (1) the *hundredweight* (100 pounds), (2) the *ton* (2,000 pounds), and (3) the *long ton* (2,240 pounds). These weight classifications and their symbols are summarized in Table 17.1.

Table 17.1   Weight Classifications

Term	Symbol	Weight
hundredweight	cwt.	100 pounds
ton	T	2,000 pounds
long ton	L Tn	2,240 pounds

Transportation charges can be divided into two main categories: (1) the *line-haul rate*, which includes the cost of moving a shipment of goods from the point of origination to the point of destination, and (2) the *ancillary rate*, which includes the costs for additional or special services. For instance, a rail company that makes a special stop en route to drop off a partial carload of lumber would charge the lumber company an ancillary charge for this service. (Ancillary charges are discussed in detail in the next unit.)

Line-Haul Rates

Line-haul rates are usually set by weight classification and stated in minimum weight groups. Transportation companies use prepared rate schedules for quoting rates to customers. A typical rate schedule is shown in Table 17.2.

Before the rate can be applied to find the cost of moving goods, the total weight of the shipment must be converted into the weight classification to which the rate is applicable. For instance, if the transportation rate is expressed per hundredweight, the weight of the shipment is divided by 100.

Table 17.2   Rate Schedule: Dallas to Houston

Minimum Weight	cwt. Rate
1,000 pounds	$2.39
10,000 pounds	1.97
20,000 pounds	1.85
34,000 pounds	1.50
50,000 pounds	1.34

If the transportation rate is expressed per ton, the shipment weight is divided by 2,000. And if the rate is expressed per long ton, the shipment weight is divided by 2,240. Therefore, to determine transportation costs:

1. Divide the shipment weight (in pounds) by the appropriate rate weight classification (100; 2,000; or 2,240).
2. Multiply that number by the transportation rate.

Example: Using Table 17.2, determine the costs of transporting a 19,200-pound shipment of goods.

Solution: (1)   19,200 pounds ÷ 100 = 192 cwt.

(2)   192 × $1.97 = $378.24   shipping costs

By examining Table 17.2, we can see that there is a minimum charge for small shipments. In this case, the minimum charge for hauling between Dallas and Houston is $23.90 [(1,000 ÷ 100) × $2.39]. Thus, any shipment of less than 1,000 pounds would cost $23.90.

From Table 17.2, we can also see that the rate per weight classification goes down as the minimum weight group goes up. Notice that the weight groups are *minimum* weight groups. In the preceding example, the stated rate for a shipment of 19,200 pounds was $1.97—the rate of the 10,000-pound weight group—because it fell short of the 20,000-pound minimum of the next (and lower) rate group.

By setting a minimum charge for small shipments and by decreasing the rate as the total shipment weight increases, transportation companies encourage their customers to ship in maximum quantities—a policy that makes for more efficient utilization of transportation facilities and equipment. Thus, if the customer in the example were to increase the shipment by 800 pounds to meet the 20,000-pound minimum requirement, the cost would be based on the lower rate of $1.85.

Example: The customer in the preceding example increased his shipment by 800 pounds. Using Table 17.2, determine the costs of transporting a 20,000-pound shipment of goods

Solution: (1)   20,000 pounds ÷ 100 = 200 cwt.

              (2)   200 × $1.85 = $370.00   shipping costs

Exercises

Find the charges for shipping the following. Round to the nearest cent.

1. 2,700 pounds at $1.24 cwt.

2. 3,900 pounds at $2.21 cwt.

3. 27,900 pounds at $17.50 per ton

4. 43,232 pounds at $16.25 per long ton

5. 6,845 pounds at $1.71 cwt.

6. 28,790 pounds at $14.50 per ton

7. 13,750 pounds at $.66 cwt.

8. 22,400 pounds at $30.75 per long ton

9. 36,750 pounds at $19.25 per ton

10. 38,000 pounds at $38 per long ton

Using the following rate schedule, find the charge for each of the following shipments.

Rate Schedule: Wichita to Topeka

Minimum Weight	cwt. Rate
2,000 pounds	$1.68
10,000 pounds	1.53
25,000 pounds	1.33
40,000 pounds	1.13

11. 8,600 pounds

12. 14,300 pounds

13. 1,800 pounds

14. 27,800 pounds

15. 7,920 pounds

16. 41,370 pounds

17. 17,510 pounds

18. 33,600 pounds

19. 40,900 pounds

20. 23,100 pounds

21. A carload of cattle weighing 23,200 pounds was shipped from Oklahoma City to Kansas City. The rate was $1.27 per cwt. What was the transportation charge?

22. A rancher bought three loads of winter hay weighing 27,840 pounds, 17,650 pounds, and 4,520 pounds. The transportation cost was $18 per ton. How much were the total transportation costs?

23. Find the transportation costs of a carload of coal weighing 70,000 pounds at $16 a long ton.

Learning Unit 17.2
Break Point and Ancillary Costs

Break Point

To begin this unit, let's take another look at the last example in the preceding unit in which the customer increased his shipment of 19,200 pounds by 800 pounds to meet the 20,000-pound minimum of the next—and lower—rate group. Notice that even if the customer had no other goods to ship, it still would have been cheaper for the customer to pay the extra freight on the 800 pounds. (The total transportation costs for 19,200 pounds at the $1.97 rate were $378.24. The total transportation costs for 20,000 pounds at the $1.85 rate were $370.00.)

Thus, we can see that at some point between the minimum weight of one classification and the minimum weight of the next classification, it becomes cheaper to pay the extra freight of the higher weight classification in order to take advantage of the correspondingly lower rate. This point is called the *break* or *break-even point*.

Example: Using the rate schedule from the preceding unit, calculate the cost of shipping 8,500 pounds at the 1,000-pound rate and the 10,000-pound rate. Which is cheaper to use? (For easy reference, the rate schedule is repeated in Table 17.3.)

Table 17.3   Rate Schedule: Dallas to Houston

Minimum Weight	cwt. Rate
1,000 pounds	$2.39
10,000 pounds	1.97
20,000 pounds	1.85
34,000 pounds	1.50
50,000 pounds	1.34

Solution: *1,000-Pound Classification*

8,500 ÷ 100 = 85 cwt.

85 × $2.39 = $203.15   shipping costs

10,000-Pound Classification

10,000 ÷ 100 = 100 cwt.

100 × $1.97 = $197.00   shipping costs

$203.15   cost at 1,000-pound classification
197.00   cost at 10,000-pound classification
$ 6.15   difference

Even though the shipment is not 10,000 pounds, it is cheaper to use the 10,000-pound rate.

The following formula is used to determine the break point between weight classifications for this and other problems. Assume the rate is quoted per hundredweight.

$$\text{Break point} = \frac{\text{higher weight} \times (\text{lower rate} \div 100)}{(\text{higher rate} \div 100)}$$

In the preceding example, the break point between 1,000 pounds at $2.39 and 10,000 pounds at $1.97 can be calculated in this way:

$$\frac{10,000 \times (\$1.97 \div 100)}{(\$2.39 \div 100)} = \frac{197}{.0239}$$
$$= 8,242 \text{ pounds}$$

Therefore, for any shipment of less than 8,242 pounds, it would be cheaper for the customer to pay for the exact number of pounds in the shipment at $2.39 per hundredweight. For any shipment of more than 8,242 pounds, it would be cheaper for the customer to pay for 10,000 pounds at $1.97 per hundredweight.

Example: Determine the break point between the 10,000-pound weight classification and the 20,000-pound weight classification with rates stated per cwt.

Solution:
$$\frac{\text{higher weight} \times (\text{lower rate} \div 100)}{(\text{higher rate} \div 100)}$$
$$= \frac{20,000 \times (\$1.85 \div 100)}{(\$1.97 \div 100)}$$
$$= \frac{370}{.0197}$$
$$= 18,781 \text{ pounds} \quad \text{break point}$$

Rate schedules sometimes indicate the break point for each weight classification. Table 17.4 shows a schedule with that information.

Table 17.4
Rate Schedule with Break Points: Dallas to Houston

Minimum Weight	cwt. Rate	Break Point
1,000 pounds	$2.39	8,242 pounds
10,000 pounds	1.97	18,781 pounds
20,000 pounds	1.85	27,567 pounds
34,000 pounds	1.50	44,666 pounds
50,000 pounds	1.34	

Ancillary Costs

Line-haul rates apply from point of origination to point of destination. There are occasions when a customer may want goods delivered to several different destinations. The goods may be combined into one shipment with partial deliveries made along the route.

For instance, if a company in Denver, Colorado, needs one shipment of 8,000 pounds delivered to Colorado Springs and another shipment of 8,000 pounds delivered to Pueblo, they may find it beneficial to combine the shipments into one, pay the total rate to Pueblo, and pay an ancillary—or extra—charge for stopping in transit and unloading a partial shipment. (Stopping in transit means that the stop must occur at a point between origin and final destination.) Other ancillary costs might include storage, refrigeration, or distribution.

Table 17.5
Rate Schedule with Ancillary Charge:
From Denver

| | To Pueblo | | | | To Colorado Springs | | |
Minimum Weight (pounds)	cwt. Rate	Minimum Charge	Break Point (pounds)	Minimum Weight (pounds)	cwt. Rate	Minimum Charge	Break Point (pounds)
5,000	$1.19	$ 59.50	12,226	5,000	$.99	$ 49.50	13,484
15,000	.97	145.50	21,907	15,000	.89	133.50	22,471
25,000	.85	212.50	28,235	25,000	.80	200.00	28,125
30,000	.80	240.00		30,000	.75	225.00	

Stop-off charge for Colorado Springs: $30.00

Example: Garza Corporation, located in Denver, wants a 15,000-pound shipment delivered in Pueblo and another 15,000-pound shipment delivered in Colorado Springs. Would it be less expensive to ship them separately or as a combined shipment to Pueblo with a stop-off charge for unloading at Colorado Springs?

Solution: *Separate Shipments*

Pueblo
15,000 ÷ 100 = 150 cwt.
150 × $.97 = $145.50

Colorado Springs
15,000 ÷ 100 = 150 cwt.
150 × $.89 = $133.50

$145.50   cost to Pueblo
 133.50   cost to Colorado Springs
$279.00   total cost of separate shipments

Combined Shipment
(15,000 + 15,000) ÷ 100 = 300 cwt.

300 × $.80 = $240   transportation costs
           30   stop-off charge (ancillary cost)
      $270   total cost of combined shipment

$279.00   separate costs
 270.00   combined costs
$ 9.00   saving using combined shipment

Combining the shipments and paying a stop-off charge would be the less expensive way for the company in the preceding example to ship the goods. The company doing the shipping—not the transportation company— is responsible for examining the shipping alternatives and selecting the less expensive method.

Example: Calculate the transportation costs for two shipments of 8,000 pounds each. One shipment is from Denver to Pueblo, the other from Denver to Colorado Springs. Assume the two are (a) shipped separately, (b) combined, with a stop-off charge for Colorado Springs. (Use Table 17.5.)

Solution: (a)   *Separate Shipments*
8,000 ÷ 100 = 80 cwt.   8,000 ÷ 100 = 80 cwt.
80 × $1.19 = $95.20   80 × $.99 = $79.20

$ 95.20   cost to Pueblo
  79.20   cost to Colorado Springs
$174.40   total cost of separate shipments

(b) *Combined Shipment*

$(8,000 + 8,000) \div 100 = 160$ cwt.

$160 \times \$.97 = \$155.20$	transportation costs
30.00	stop-off charge (ancillary cost)
$\$185.20$	total cost of combined shipment

$185.20	combined costs
174.40	separate costs
$ 10.80	saving using separate shipments

Exercises

Determine the break point for the following rate schedule.

Rate Schedule: Cheyenne to Casper

	Minimum Weight	cwt. Rate	Break Point
1.	1,000 pounds	$2.10	__________
2.	5,000 pounds	$1.97	__________
3.	15,000 pounds	$1.82	__________
4.	25,000 pounds	$1.69	__________
	40,000 pounds	$1.49	

Complete the following rate schedule by calculating the minimum charge and break point for each weight classification.

Rate Schedule: Pittsburgh to Washington

	Minimum Weight	cwt. Rate	Minimum Charge	Break Point
5.	4,000 pounds	$1.67	__________	__________
6.	15,000 pounds	$1.58	__________	__________
7.	30,000 pounds	$1.43	__________	__________
8.	50,000 pounds	$1.23	__________	__________
9.	80,000 pounds	$ .92	__________	

Using the following rate schedules, determine the transportation cost for each of the following shipments.

Rate Schedule: Memphis to Nashville

Minimum Weight	T Rate	Minimum Charge	Break Point
10,000 pounds	$23.00	$115	34,782 pounds
40,000	20.00	400	56,000
70,000	16.00	560	87,500
100,000	14.00	700	117,857
150,000	11.00	825	

Stop-off charge: $50.00

Rate Schedule: Memphis to Knoxville

Minimum Weight	T Rate	Minimum Charge	Break Point
10,000 pounds	$26.00	$130	42,307 pounds
50,000	22.00	550	69,090
80,000	19.00	760	101,052
120,000	16.00	960	121,875
150,000	13.00	975	

Stop-off charge: $50.00

10. Determine the separate costs of two shipments of grain weighing 28,000 pounds each. One shipment is to be delivered to Nashville and one to Knoxville.

11. Determine the combined cost of the two 28,000-pound shipments in the preceding problem paying the rate to Knoxville. There will be a stop-off charge at Nashville.

12. A shipment of 60,000 pounds was delivered to Nashville; another shipment of 70,000 pounds was delivered to Knoxville. What were the separate costs of the two shipments?

13. Determine the combined cost of the two shipments in the preceding problem paying the rate to Knoxville. There will be a stop-off for partial delivery at Nashville.

14. Would it be less expensive for the customer to pay separate shipping charges or combined shipping charges on the following two shipments: 80,000 pounds to Nashville, 100,000 pounds to Knoxville? What is the difference in the cost between the two alternatives?

Chapter 17
Self-Evaluation

1. Find the charge for shipping 41,780 pounds at a T rate of $18.40.

2. What is the charge for shipping 1,916 pounds at $.93 per cwt.

3. Find the cost of transporting a carload of coal weighing 76,000 pounds at $15 per L Tn.

4. Find the break point for the following two weight classifications:
   Minimum weight, 10,000 pounds; cwt. rate, $1.83
   Minimum weight, 18,000 pounds; cwt. rate, $1.68

5. Use the following information to determine whether two shipments should be sent separately or combined with a stop-off charge. The Garza Company needs to make two 16,000-pound shipments. The first shipment is to Pueblo, the second to Colorado Springs. The minimum weight classification to Pueblo is 15,000 pounds; the rate is $1.97. The minimum weight classification to Colorado Springs is 15,000 pounds; the rate is $.89. The minimum weight classification to Pueblo is 30,000 pounds at $.80 with a stop-off charge for Colorado Springs set at $30.

Chapter 18
Business Statistics

Success in business depends to a considerable extent on the ability to read and accurately interpret statistical information. The word *statistics* refers to the process of collecting, organizing, presenting, analyzing, and interpreting numerical data or information. Analysis of statistical information enables managers to identify relationships, make forecasts, and formulate business decisions.

Statistics involves the process of arranging the information so that the facts can be analyzed and interpreted and conclusions reached. The analysis of data may be aided by computing one or more measures of central tendency. The information is often presented to management in the form of tables and charts. Tables and charts facilitate analysis and interpretation of the data.

This chapter explains some of the ways statistics are interpreted, as well as the forms in which data are presented to management for analysis.

This chapter will enable you to:

1. **describe the use of statistics in business decision making**

2. **calculate measures of central tendency for both grouped and nongrouped data**

3. **prepare a summary table for use by management**

4. **distinguish between some of the more commonly used graphs**

5. **prepare various types of graphs**

6. **distinguish between reference tables and summary tables**

Learning Unit 18.1
Measures of Central Tendency

In order to obtain any useful or meaningful information from a group of statistical data, it is customary to derive a single fact from the data that can be used to describe or represent the entire group. One of the most common ways of describing a group of numbers is in terms of the average. The *average* is a central value around which all the numbers in a group tend to cluster. In this way, the average is a measure of the *central tendency* of the data.

The three most common averages are: (1) the *arithmetic mean*, (2) the *median*, and (3) the *mode*. The selection of one of these measures of central tendency must be based on which one will most accurately represent the given collection of values.

Arithmetic Mean

The arithmetic mean is the arithmetic average. It is the "average" that most people are familiar with and refer to when discussing average weight, average height, average temperature, etc.

To find the arithmetic mean of a series of values:

1. Add the various values in the series.
2. Divide the sum by the number of values in the series.

As an equation, this is expressed:

$$\text{Arithmetic mean} = \frac{\text{sum of values}}{\text{number of values}}$$

Example: The hourly wages of the employees in the maintenance department of the Hemphill Manufacturing Company are: Cox, $8.45; Doyle, $7.60; Hall, $5.45; and Miller, $4.85. What is the average (mean) hourly wage?

Solution: Mean = $\dfrac{\text{sum of values}}{\text{number of values}}$

Mean = $\dfrac{\$8.45 + \$7.60 + \$5.45 + \$4.85}{4}$

Mean = $\dfrac{\$26.35}{4}$

Mean = $\$6.59$ hourly wage

Weighted Mean

When the numbers in a group are not of equal importance, the numbers must be adjusted to reflect their relative importance before an accurate average can be determined. Each number is multiplied by a "weight" to show its relative importance within the group.

To find the weighted mean:

1. Determine the weighted value of all the numbers in the group (number × appropriate weight).
2. Add the weighted values of all the numbers.
3. Divide the sum by the total number of weights.

Example: Ralph Wilson earned two A's and three B's in the courses he completed at Central Community College last semester. The college uses a three-point grading system and assigns three points for each A, two points for each B, and one point for each C. What was his grade-point average for the following schedule of courses?

Course	Semester Credit Hours		Grade	Grade Points
Accounting	3	×	2 (B)	6
Economics	3	×	2 (B)	6
Golf	1	×	3 (A)	3
Science	4	×	2 (B)	8
Speech	3	×	3 (A)	9
	14			32

Solution: Mean = $\dfrac{6 + 6 + 3 + 8 + 9}{14} = \dfrac{32}{14}$

Mean = 2.29   grade-point average

Median

The arithmetic mean may not always accurately measure the central tendency of a given group of numbers. For instance, the mean is not a representative average for a group of numbers in which there are a few very high or very low numbers. In situations in which the group contains a few values that greatly differ from the others, a more representative average may be the *median*, or middle number in the group. The median separates the group into two equal subgroups: half the numbers fall above the median, and half fall below.

In order to find the median, the numbers must first be arranged in order of size, from lowest to highest or highest to lowest. (Such an ordered arrangement is called an *array* of numbers.)

To find the position held by the median number:

1. Arrange the numbers in an array.
2. Add the total number of items (n) plus one.
3. Divide the sum by two.

These steps can be summarized and most easily remembered in the formula:

$$\text{Median position} = \frac{n + 1}{2}$$

When an array contains an *odd* number of items, the median will be the exact middle number. When an array contains an *even* number of items, the *median position* will be between the two middle values. The *median number* is the arithmetic mean of these two middle values.

Example: The five students who took a business math make-up exam had the following scores: 84, 77, 74, 73, and 32. What was the average (mean and median) grade on the make-up exam?

Solution:

$$
\begin{array}{l}
84 \\
77 \\
74 \quad \text{median grade} \\
73 \\
\underline{32} \\
340 \div 5 = 68 \quad \text{mean grade}
\end{array}
$$

$$\text{Median position} = \frac{n + 1}{2}$$

$$\text{Median position} = \frac{5 + 1}{2} = \frac{6}{2} = 3$$

3d position number = 74; therefore, 74 = median grade

Example: Eight members of a local men's club purchased new cars during the month of June. The prices paid were (rounded to the nearest \$100) \$4,500; \$6,300; \$5,800; \$7,200; \$6,900; \$3,900; \$8,100; and \$6,700. What was the median price?

Solution:

Position	1	2	3	4	5	6	7	8
Array	\$3,900	4,500	5,800	6,300	6,700	6,900	7,200	8,100

$$\text{Median position} = \frac{n + 1}{2}$$

$$= \frac{8 + 1}{2}$$

$$= 4.5\text{th position, or halfway between the 4th and 5th positions}$$

$$\text{Median price} = \frac{\$6,300 + \$6,700}{2}$$

$$= \$6,500 \quad \text{mean of middle values}$$

Mode

The mode of a group of numbers is the value that occurs the greatest number of times. If two different numbers appear more than any others and both appear the same number of times, the array is *bimodal*. Similarly, three such numbers would make the array *trimodal*. If all of the numbers are different, the group has no mode.

To find the mode:

1. Arrange the numbers in an array.
2. Identify the most frequently occurring value or values.

Example: The number of lawnmowers sold each day during the past week by the lawn and garden department of a department store was: 6, 3, 2, 4, 7, and 7. What was the average (mode) number of lawnmowers sold each day by the department?

Solution: $\left.\begin{array}{c} 7 \\ 7 \end{array}\right\}$ mode

6
4
3
2

Exercises

1. The weights of the linemen on the varsity football team are: 219, 234, 227, 254, 238, 246, 242, and 246. Find the average weight: (a) the mean, (b) the median, and (c) the mode.

2. The grades on a business math exam were 71, 90, 78, 62, 71, 68, 93, 87, 59, 91, 74, and 83. Find the average grade: (a) the mean, (b) the median, and (c) the mode.

3. The salaries of the employees in the accounting department of Northeast Tool and Equipment are: $24,000, $14,000, $11,000, $9,000, and $7,000. Determine: (a) the mean, (b) the median, and (c) which is the more representative average.

4. Glen Wilson had daily sales of $214, $143, $297, $287, and $264 last week. What were his average (mean and median) daily sales?

5. A student received the following scores on four exams: 96, 84, 90 and 86. What is the student's average (mean) grade in the course?

6. Bill Autrey had games of 197, 174, and 187 at Central Bowl during a recent bowling contest. What was his average (mean) for the competition?

7. Wanda scored the following points in the first seven basketball games of the season: 16, 23, 18, 29, 14, 21, and 23. What was the average number of points she scored per game according to (a) the mean, (b) the median, and (c) the mode?

8. Joe drove 528 miles in 11 hours. How many miles per hour did he average?

Learning Unit 18.2
Grouped Data

We have seen that before raw data can be summarized or described, the data must be arranged in a usable form. We have used one such arrangement—the array—in determining the median and mode for a small number of values.

However, when dealing with large numbers of values, it is far less tedious to arrange the values by classes and to analyze the data on the basis of the *number of values* within the class, rather than on the basis of the *values themselves*. The process of (1) distributing data into classes and (2) keeping track of the number, or frequency, of values in each class is a *frequency distribution*.

To best illustrate this process, let's now examine the frequency distribution table set up for the following problem. An explanation of the steps required for (1) setting up the frequency distribution table, (2) determining the mean, (3) determining the median, and (4) determining the modal class for grouped data will follow.

Example: Using a frequency distribution, determine the mean, the median, and the modal class for the following group of values:

250	649	267	372
291	482	329	325
273	511	335	255
392	522	480	274

Solution:

Class Intervals	Tally	Frequency(f)	Midpoint	f × Midpoint
250–349	||||| ||||	9	300	2,700
350–449	||	2	400	800
450–549	||||	4	500	2,000
550–649			+ 1	600	+ 600
		16		6,100

1. *Setting up a frequency distribution.*

   a. *Determine the class interval.*

Data is organized into classes according to class intervals. A *class interval* is the difference between the lower number of one class and the lower number of the next class. The number of class intervals, as well as the size of the interval, is usually established according to the range of the data involved and the needs of the researcher. However, for convenience, the intervals are usually round numbers and are the same size. [In our example, the smallest number is 250 and the largest is 649; thus a table from 250 to 649 includes all values. The difference between the upper (649) and lower (250) limits gives a range of 400. This range can conveniently be divided into four classes, with 100 as the class interval.]

    b.   *Classify each given value in the appropriate class, making a tally as each value is classified.*

Note that in making this tally, we are keeping track of the *number of values* that fall within the class—*not the values themselves*. (For instance, in our example, the first value in the group of data—250—falls within the 250–349 interval, so one tally mark is put in the *Tally* column next to that interval. This procedure is followed for each and every value in our group of data.)

    c.   *Determine and record the frequency of the classes.*

The total tally in each class is the frequency (f) of the class or, in other words, the number of values falling within a class. [In our example, the frequency of the 450–549 class is four (four tally marks).]

  2.   *Determine the arithmetic mean.*[1]

    a.   *Determine the midpoint of each interval.*

The midpoint of an interval is the arithmetic mean of the lower number of that interval and the lower number of the next interval. (For instance, in our problem, the midpoint of the 350–449 interval is

$$\frac{\text{sum of values}}{\text{number of values}} = \frac{350 + 450}{2} = 400.)$$

    b.   *Multiply the midpoint of each interval by the frequency (f) of that interval ($f \times$ midpoint).*
    c.   *Add the products.*

(In our problem, the sum of the products is 6,100.)

    d.   *Divide by the frequency total.*

---

[1]Note that with grouped data, the arithmetic mean and the median are only estimates.

The frequency total is the total number of values in all class intervals or, in other words, the total number of items in the raw data. (In our problem, this is 6,100 ÷ 16 = 381.25. Thus, the arithmetic mean of our group of data is 381.25.)

3. *Determining the median.*

    a. *Divide the total frequency by 2 to determine the position that the median value holds in the tally.*

[In our problem, the position of the median is (16 ÷ 2), or 8.]

    b. *Using the tally column, count upward until the class in which the median position is located is found.*

(In our problem, the bottom classes contain only 1 + 4 + 2, or 7, items, so the 8th item is in the 250–349 class. The median class is 250–349.)

    c. *Determine how many values fall in class intervals that are smaller than the median class interval.*

(In our problem, since the median class interval is the smallest class interval, there are *no* values below, or smaller than, the median class interval.)

    d. *Subtract the value found in step c from the median position found in step a.*

[In our problem, we have eight (8–0).]

    e. *Using the number values found in step d as a numerator and a frequency of the median class interval (total frequency within the class interval) as a denominator, form a fraction to be multiplied by the class interval.*

[In our problem, step d yields eight values. There are nine values in the median class, and the class interval is 100. Therefore, (8 ÷ 9) × 100 equals $88\frac{8}{9}$, or 88.89.]

    f. *Add the result of step e to the lower limit of the median class interval to arrive at the median.*

(In our problem, 250 + 88.89, or 338.89 = median.)

4. *Determine the modal class.*

Although the mode cannot be determined for grouped data, the *modal class* is that class in a frequency distribution that has the highest frequency.
[In our problem, the 250–349 class is the modal class since it has the highest frequency (nine).]

Exercises

Use a frequency distribution to calculate the (a) mean, (b) median, and (c) modal class for the following problems.

1. Use four class intervals.

29	39	117	0	17	25
131	48	162	120	182	111
65	122	150	82	79	31
191	75	198	59	99	40

2. Use four class intervals.

7	2	5	6	3	1	6	7	2	1
8	2	5	6	4	7	5	8	2	11
9	1	1	7	3	9	3	3	1	7
5	6	8	4	2	4	9	6	9	1

3. The distribution of grades on a business math exam was as follows:

Grades	Number of Grades
40–49	1
50–59	3
60–69	7
70–79	9
80–89	9
90–99	4

Find the (a) mean, (b) median, and (c) modal class.

4. An income survey taken at a local shopping center revealed the following statistical information. Use the data to find the (a) mean income, (b) median income, and (c) modal income class.

Income Range	Shoppers
$ 8,000–11,999	27
12,000–15,999	32
16,000–19,999	21
20,000–23,999	12
24,000–27,999	9
28,000–31,999	6

5. A mileage survey was taken in a used-car dealership. The mileage figures (rounded to the nearest 1,000 miles) were taken from every car on the lot. Find the (a) mean, (b) median, and (c) modal class.

Miles Driven (1,000's)	Number of Cars
10–69	79
70–129	121
130–189	32

Learning Unit 18.3
Presentation of Statistical Data

After statistical data has been collected, organized, tabulated, and interpreted, the significance of the data frequently must be presented and communicated to others. Two of the most common methods of communicating statistical information are: (1) tables (communication of data in condensed, word form) and (2) graphs (communication of data in condensed, visual form).

Tables

Some tables function merely as repositories for a collection of data. Examples of repository tables are those found in the appendices of reports and publications. Other tables summarize a body of collected information. All tables should have a title (so the reader will know what facts are being presented) and should give the source of the information. An example of a summary table is Table 18.1 on page 388.

Graphs

Graphs provide a visual description of a collection of information and are usually more effective than tables in displaying the meaning of that information. Graphs are easier to read and interpret and can show the relationships that exist between and among the data.

Four of the most common graphs are bar graphs, line graphs, circle

Table 18.1   How U.S. Has Changed in Four Decades

People	1940 *(Given in 1,000s)*	Today *(Given in 1,000s)*	Change
Northeast	35,977	49,081	Up 36%
Midwest	40,143	58,251	Up 45%
South	41,666	70,627	Up 70%
West	13,883	40,100	Up 189%
Urban	74,424	163,560	Up 120%
Rural	57,246	54,500	Down 5%
Under age 20	45,306	71,819	Up 59%
Age 20–60	77,344	122,186	Up 58%
Age 65 and over	9,019	24,054	Up 167%
Blacks	12,866	25,467	Up 98%
Total Population	131,669	218,059	Up 66%

Source: *U.S. News & World Report,* September 10, 1979, pp. 66–67.

graphs, and pictographs. All types of graphs should have a title to show what facts are being pictured and a scale to show increasing or decreasing values. The scale should be clearly labeled, starting at 0 or the point of origin for dollar amounts, etc.

Bar Graphs

A bar graph shows the relationships between similar or related values through the placement of horizontal or vertical bars. The bars in the following graph of average tuition charges (Figure 18.1) are placed vertically.

A component bar graph is used to supplement the information presented in a bar graph by focusing on a particular relationship within a category. Figure 18.2 is a component bar graph that distinguishes between enrollment in privately and publicly controlled institutions of higher education.

Line Graphs

A line graph uses points connected by a line to present information. A line graph is particularly useful in displaying data in which there is a time relationship. The time element is usually plotted horizontally and the other variable vertically. The changing of the 18–24–year-old segment of the U.S.

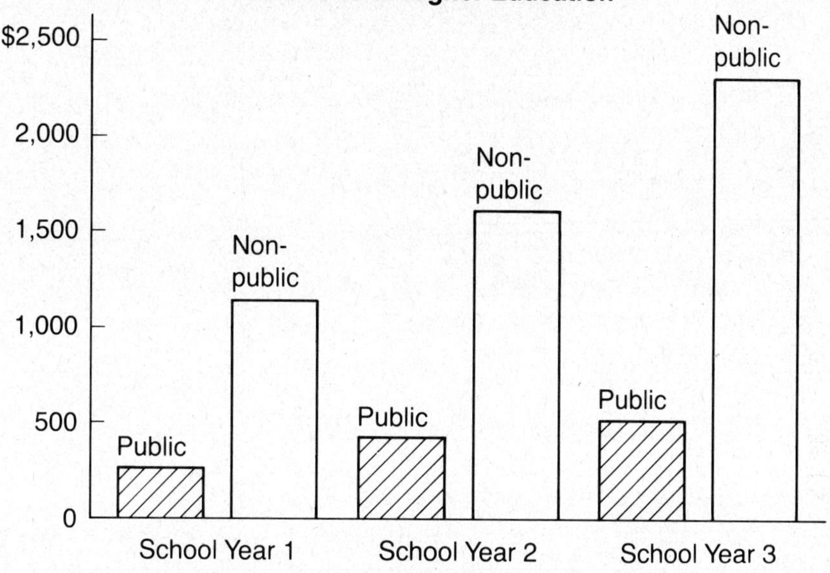

Figure 18.1
Average Tuition Charges
Institutions of Higher Education

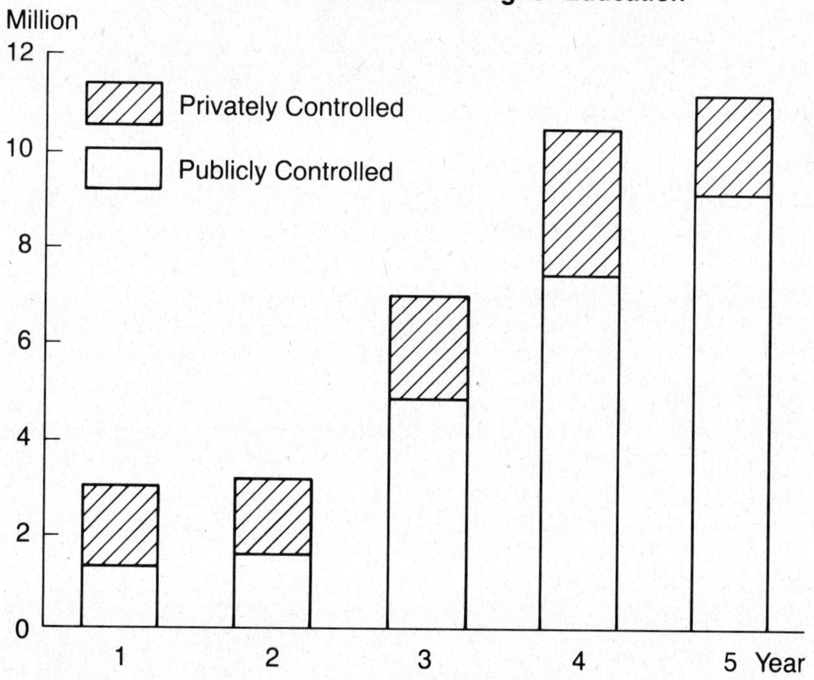

Figure 18.2
Enrollment in Institutions of Higher Education

population enrolled in institutions of higher education might be reported as follows (Figure 18.3):

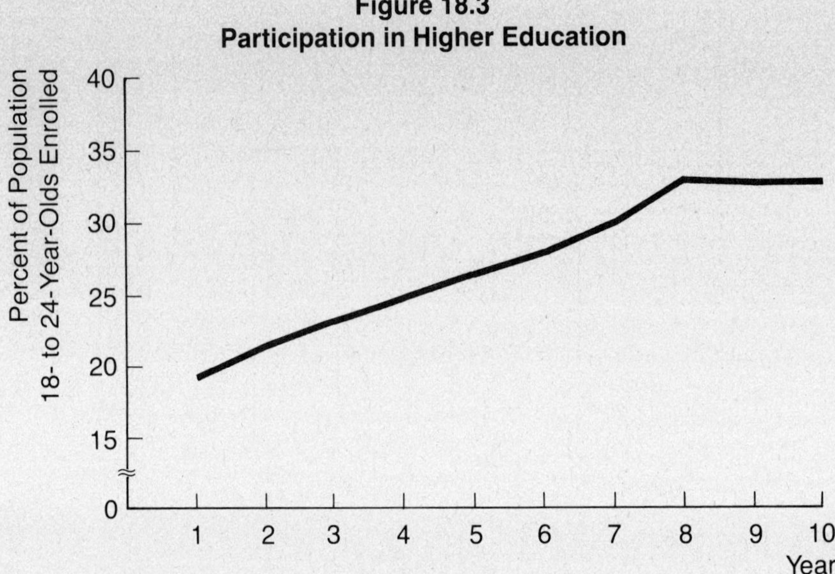

Circle Graphs

Circle graphs (sometimes called pie charts) use a circle as the basis for presenting data. Circle graphs are useful in showing the distribution or breakdown of the various parts of some whole. The whole—the entire circle—represents 100% (360°), and each item of data is converted to a percent and depicted in a corresponding area of the circle. The number of degrees required for a percent item can be determined by multiplying the percent of an item by 360°. For instance, 5% of a circle equals .05 × 360°, or 18°, of the circle.

Consider, for instance, the relationship between the sales accounted for by a company's top salesman and the sales of the rest of the sales force. The top salesman sold $100,000 worth of goods, while total sales amounted to $400,000. A circle graph of this record might be drawn as follows (Figure 18.4):

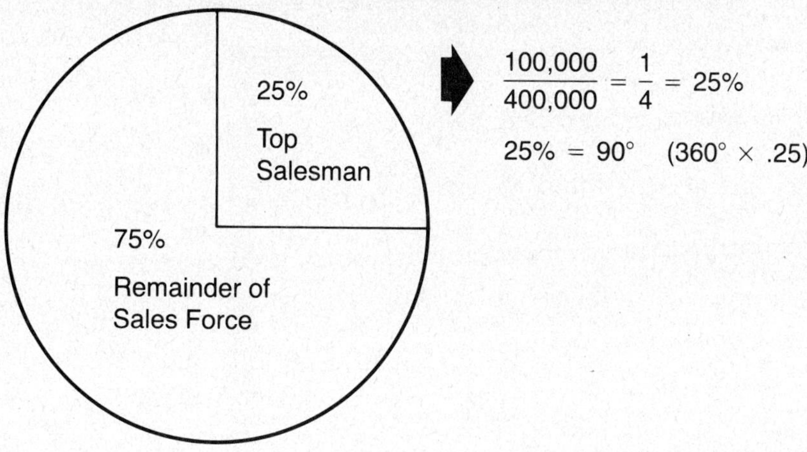

$$\frac{100,000}{400,000} = \frac{1}{4} = 25\%$$

$$25\% = 90° \quad (360° \times .25)$$

Pictographs

A modified form of the horizontal bar graph, a pictograph uses pictures (instead of bars) to represent quantity. Although it presents data in a simple, easy-to-read format, the pictograph is not exact in depicting a portion of a value and is therefore less accurate. The changing size of the average U.S. household between 1790 and 1975 was depicted as shown in Figure 18.5 on page 392.

Exercises

1. The sales and cost of goods sold for the Richland Company during the past four years are shown below. Prepare a bar graph similar to that in Figure 18.1.

Year	Sales	Cost of Goods Sold
1975	$ 75,000	$ 40,000
1976	125,000	65,000
1977	150,000	85,000
1978	170,000	120,000

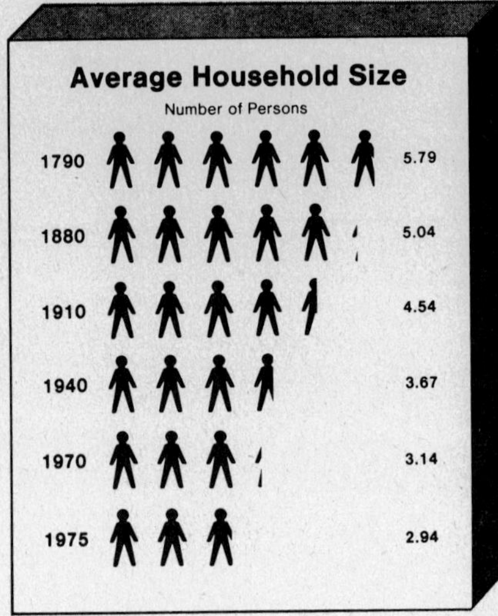

Source: *U.S. Population: 200 Years of Growth and Change,* Road Maps of Industry No. 1887, The Conference Board, July, 1976.

2. The selling price and cost per unit for widgets sold by the Richland Company during the past four years is shown below. Using this information, prepare a component bar graph similar to that in Figure 18.2.

Year	Selling Price	Cost per Unit
1975	$3.75	$2.75
1976	4.25	3.00
1977	4.50	3.25
1978	4.50	3.50

3. Employee turnover for the Richland Company during the past six years is shown on the next page. Using this information, prepare a line graph similar to that in Figure 18.3.

Year	*Turnover*
1973	76
1974	63
1975	47
1976	58
1977	36
1978	42

4. Trading activity on the New York Stock Exchange has increased dramatically in recent years. In 1966, there were 3.2 billion shares traded on registered stock exchanges: 69% on the New York Stock Exchange, 23% on the American Stock Exchange, and 8% on the other stock exchanges. In 1976, there were 7 billion shares traded on registered stock exchanges: 80% on the New York Stock Exchange, 9% on the American Stock Exchange, and 11% on the other stock exchanges. Complete the following pie charts.

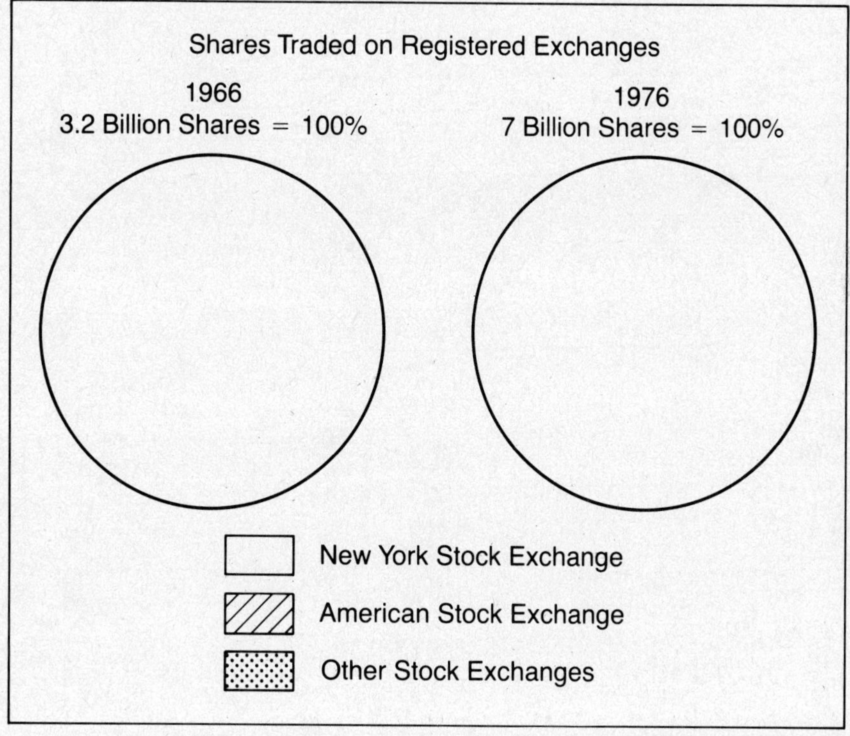

5. Prepare two pie charts based on the following figures comparing federal spending and federal income for fiscal 1979. The figures provide the source of each dollar received by the federal government and how each dollar is spent by the federal government.

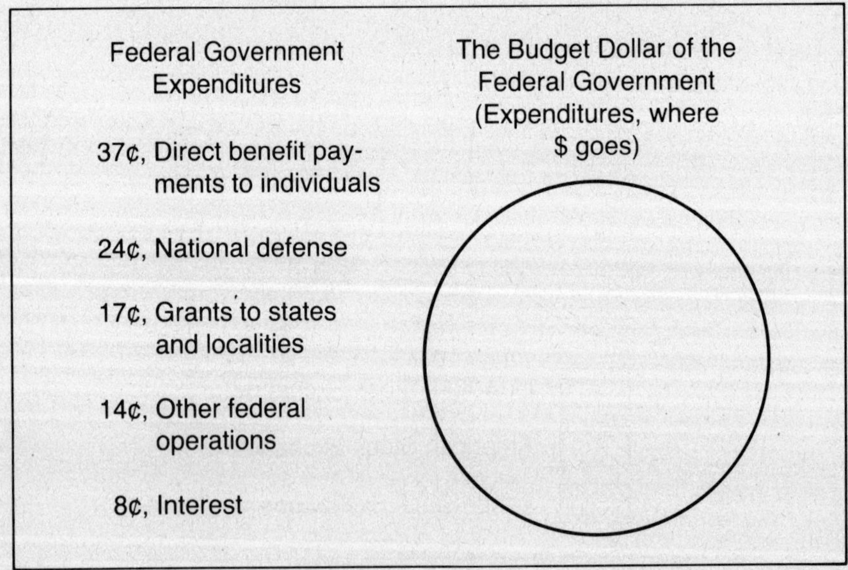

6. The interest on corporate bonds is subject to the federal income tax, whereas the interest on state and municipal bonds is exempt from federal income taxation. For this reason, investors are willing to accept a lower return on state and municipal bonds because the after tax return is equivalent to higher yields on corporate bonds.

Prepare a summary table, similar to Table 18.1, to show the equivalent yields on taxable and nontaxable bonds for selected taxable incomes. If a joint return taxpayer has a taxable income of $20,000 to $24,000, the marginal tax rate is 32%, and the taxable yield equivalent to a 7% tax exempt yield is 10.29%. This information has already been recorded in the table below. Complete the summary table using the following facts:

taxable income $32,000–$36,000, tax bracket 42%, yield 12.07%
taxable income $44,000–$52,000, tax bracket 50%, yield 14.00%
taxable income $76,000–$88,000, tax bracket 58%, yield 16.67%
taxable income $120,000–$140,000, tax bracket 64%, yield 19.44%

Equivalent Yields for Taxable and Nontaxable Bonds at Selected Levels of Taxable Income

Selected Taxable Incomes (joint return)	Tax Bracket (marginal tax rate)	Equivalent Taxable Yields if Tax Exempt Yield Is 7%
$20,000 to $24,000	32%	10.29%

Chapter 18
Self-Evaluation

1. Determine the (a) mean, (b) median, and (c) mode for the following series of test scores: 82, 91, 77, 71, 86, 64, 95, 57, 82, 68, 90, 71.

2. Female shoppers in a grocery store were asked how many times a month they went into a supermarket to shop for food or nonfood items. Find the (a) mean, (b) median, and (c) modal class for the results listed below.

Shopping Trips	Shopper
1–5	7
6–10	12
11–15	38
16–20	20
21–25	11

3. Prepare two circle graphs showing the level of educational attainment for men and women who are employed by the XYZ Corporation.

Men		Women	
Level	Percent	Level	Percent
Elementary	31	Elementary	10
Secondary	54	Secondary	28
College	15	College	62

4. Prepare a component bar graph showing the percent of unemployed men and women from the following information:

Year	Unemployed Men	Unemployed Women
1950	70%	30%
1960	65%	35%
1970	55%	45%
1975	58%	42%

Appendices

Appendix A
The Metric System

The United States is in the process of converting from the English to the metric system. The conversion is scheduled to be completed during the 1980's; by that time, 90% of the world will be using the same basic metric measurements.

Business students need to become familiar with the metric system and the advantages that this system offers over our present system. This appendix offers you an opportunity to become better acquainted with the metric system. The material in this appendix will help you be able to:

1.   **identify basic measurements in the metric system**

2.   **indicate multiples of the basic measurements**

3.   **write numbers with many digits using the decimal as the only mark of punctuation**

4.   **convert metric measurements by decimal adjustment**

5.   **solve business problems that contain metric measurements**

Metric Conversion

How far? Do you mean in inches, feet, yards, or miles? *How heavy?* Do you mean in ounces, pounds, or tons? *How much?* Do you mean fluid ounces, pints, quarts, or gallons? One of the advantages of the metric system is that there is only one basic unit for weight, another for length, and one for capacity. The *gram* is the basic unit of weight and is equal to about 1/28 of an ounce; the *meter* is the basic unit of length and is equal to 39.37 inches; and the *liter* is the basic unit of capacity and is equal to 1.0567 liquid quarts or .906 dry quarts.

A change to the metric system will not require a change in our numbering system. The same digits (0, 1, 2, 3, etc.) are used in the metric system. The decimal is also the basic punctuation for value determination in the metric system. As you move to the right of the decimal, the quantity of the number will decrease. As you move to the left of the decimal, the quantity of the number will increase.

There are two minor style differences between the metric system and our present numbering system. First, under the metric system, a number that contains only a decimal portion is always preceded by a zero. For example, the values 0.352 and 0.006 may not be written as .352 and .006. Second, the metric system uses a space, instead of a comma, to separate values within a number. The following examples illustrate this difference:

English Style	*Metric Style*
3,000,000	3 000 000
14,326.92635	14 326.926 35

Metric unit measurements are identified by lower case letters unless the unit name is taken from a proper name. When the symbol is taken from a proper name, a capital letter is used for the first letter. Since the letters are symbols and not abbreviations, they are not followed by a period or a space if more than one symbol is involved. A partial list of the symbols used for the base units in the metric system is presented in the following table.

Metric Base Units

Measure	*Name*	*Symbol*
length	meter	m
weight (mass)	gram	g
volume (capacity)	liter	L*

*The American National Metric Council has adopted the use of *L* as the symbol for liter. Other sources may use *l*.

Under this system, 7 meters, for instance, is stated as 7 m; 6 grams as 6 g; and 3 liters as 3 L.

The prefix symbol is combined with the basic unit to express magnitude. For example, 8 meters is expressed as 8 m, while 800 meters is expressed as 8 hm.

The metric system is based on a decimal system that uses multiples of 10 (1, 10, 100, etc.; 0.1, 0.01, 0.001, etc.). Fractions used in a metric system are 1/10, 1/100, 1/1000, etc.

The metric system is based on exponents of 10. The basic metric units (gram, meter, liter, etc.) are the focal point of the system and are considered to be 10^0. Prefixes representing different powers of ten are attached to these basic units to indicate multiple or decimal values. Prefixes used to express a value greater than one are deka, hecto, kilo, etc. Prefixes used to express a value less than one are deci, centi, milli, etc. The following is a list of prefixes and the powers of ten that each prefix represents:

$$
\begin{array}{rcrcl}
\text{kilo} & = & 1{,}000\ X & = & 10^3 \\
\text{hecto} & = & 100\ X & = & 10^2 \\
\text{deka} & = & 10\ X & = & 10^1 \\
\text{—} & & & & 10^0 \\
\text{deci} & = & 0.1\ X & = & 10^{-1} \\
\text{centi} & = & 0.01\ X & = & 10^{-2} \\
\text{milli} & = & 0.001\ X & = & 10^{-3}
\end{array}
$$

The symbols for the most common metric prefixes are shown in the following table.

Symbols for Metric Prefixes

Value	Name	Symbol
10	deka-	da*
100	hecto-	h
1 000	kilo-	k
0.1	deci-	d
0.01	centi-	c
0.001	milli-	m

*The American National Metric Council has adopted the use of *da* as the symbol for deka-. Other sources may use *dk*. You may also encounter the spelling *deca-*.

The following two rules apply when the prefix indicates a value greater than one (deka, hecto, kilo, etc.):

1. *Multiply to convert a large metric value into a smaller metric value.*

Example: Change 5 kilometers (km) to meters (m).

Solution: Kilo is the prefix for 1000, which is 10^3 or $10 \times 10 \times 10$. To multiply 1000, move the decimal 3 digits to the right. Therefore, 5 km would be 5×1000m or 5000m.

2. *Divide to convert a small metric value into a larger metric value.*

Example: Change 400 liters (L) to hectoliters (hL).

Solution: Hecto is the prefix for 100, which is 10^2 or 10×10. To divide by 100, move the decimal 2 digits to the left. Therefore, 400 L would be $400 \div 100$ or 4 hL.

The following two rules apply when the prefix indicates a value less than one (deci, centi, milli, etc.):

1.   *Multiply to convert a small metric value to a larger metric value.*

Example: Change 8000 milligrams to grams.

Solution: Milli is the prefix for 0.001, which is 0.1^3 or $0.1 \times 0.1 \times 0.1$. To multiply by 0.001, move the decimal 3 digits to the left. Therefore, 8000 mg would be 8000 mg $\times$ 0.001 or 8 g.

2.   *Divide to convert a large metric value to a smaller metric value.*

Example: Convert 5 meters (m) to centimeters (cm).

Solution: Centi is the prefix for 0.01, which is 0.1^2 or 0.1×0.1. To divide by 0.01, move the decimal 2 digits to the right. Therefore, 5 m would be 5 m $\div$ 0.01 or 500 cm.

Exercises

Write the symbols for the following measurements.

1. meter	2. gram	3. dekameter
4. decigram	5. liter	6. hectoliter
7. centimeter	8. kilometer	9. milligram
10. kiloliter	11. millimeter	12. dekaliter
13. milliliter	14. hectogram	15. decimeter
16. deciliter	17. centiliter	18. kilogram

Write the prefix and base unit for the following.

19. mg	20. daL	21. g	22. dL	23. cm
24. hg	25. km	26. dag	27. cL	28. hL
29. mm	30. kL	31. kg	32. dam	

Express each of the following numbers in the metric system.

33. 17,468.32657   34. 11,578.55   35. 14.893257

36. 97,486.3241   37. 897,463.77   38. 86.55329

39. 1,736,439,621   40. .7945213   41. 17,436,321.66217

42. .963408

Express the following numbers as metric numbers and add.

43. 10,469.62
       77.54612
      694.00264
    47,364.1
    ____

44.   76,149
         77.17623
      4,836.111
    1,436,621
    ____

45.   14,431.6
          5.368214
    101,436
        931.47721
    ____

46. 1,736,531
         0.4592014
       461.3098
       924.9985
    ____

47.   0.96143
             0.064
       764,123.5
     1,495,641
    ____

Change the following metric values into the unit of measurement indicated.

48. 3 km ___________ m   49. 6 000 mg ___________ g

50. 200 L ___________ hL   51. 2 m ___________ cm

52. 3 000 mm ___________ m   53. 24 g ___________ cg

54. 4 dam _____________ m 55. 3 600 m _____________ km

56. 160 g _____________ dag 57. 8 hm _____________ m

58. 3 kL _____________ hL 59. 2 m _____________ mm

60. 30 000 mm _____________ dam 61. 4 g _____________ cg

62. 3 hL _____________ dL 63. 5 000 cm _____________ dam

64. 50 kg _____________ g 65. 8 km _____________ m

66. 3 000 mg _____________ g 67. 500 L _____________ daL

68. 6 000 mm _____________ m 69. 10 200 m _____________ mm

70. 460 g _____________ mg 71. 70 000 mm _____________ dam

72. 18 hL _____________ daL

Convert 2 m to the following.

73. _____________ dam 74. _____________ dm

75. _____________ km 76. _____________ cm

77. _____________ mm

Convert 4 000 000 mg to the following.

78. _____________ cg   79. _____________ dag

80. _____________ hg   81. _____________ kg

82. _____________ dg

Practical Applications

83. The distance between two cities is 352 km. If a truck driver averages 88 km an hour, how long will it take to make the trip?

84. Pam Rase, a secretary, drove 3.6 km each direction to work. If she worked 220 days last year, how many km did she drive?

85. If a field measures 402 m on each side, how many m of wire would be needed to put a four-strand wire fence around the field?

86. Rubin Lewis, a service station operator, started the week with 8.2 kL of gasoline. During the week he bought an additional 5.3 kL.
    (a) If he sold 11.2 kL of gasoline during the week, how many kL did he have left?
    (b) How many L would this be?

87. Nancy Evans has driven her new car 5 296 km and used 32 daL of gasoline. What is the average km per L for this distance?

88. Fran Stewart froze 32 cartons of berries. If each carton contained 3.5 hg of berries, what was the total kg of berries frozen?

Answers
Appendix A Exercises

1. m   2. g   3. dam

4. dg   5. L   6. hL

7.	cm	8.	km	9.	mg

7. cm   8. km   9. mg

10. kL   11. mm   12. daL

13. mL   14. hg   15. dm

16. dL   17. cL   18. kg

19. milligram   20. dekaliter   21. gram

22. deciliter   23. centimeter   24. hectogram

25. kilometer   26. dekagram   27. centiliter

28. hectoliter   29. millimeter   30. kiloliter

31. kilogram   32. dekameter   33. 17 468.326 57

34. 11 578.55   35. 14.893 257   36. 97 486.324 1

37. 897 463.77   38. 86.553 29   39. 1 736 439 621

40. 0.794 521 3   41. 17 436 321.662 17   42. 0.963 408

43. 58 605.268 76   44. 1 517 683.287 23   45. 116 804.445 424

46. 1 737 917.767 501 4   47. 2 259 765.525 43   48. 3 000

49. 6   50. 2   51. 200

52. 3   53. 2 400   54. 40

55. 3.6   56. 16   57. 800

58. 30   59. 2 000   60. 3

61. 400   62. 3 000   63. 5

64. 50 000   65. 8 000   66. 3

67. 50   68. 6   69. 10 200 000

70. 460 000   71. 7   72. 180

73. 0.2   74. 20   75. .002

76. 200   77. 2000   78. 400 000

79. 400   80. 40   81. 4

82. 40 000   83. 4 hours   84. 1 584 km

85. 6 432 m   86. 2.3 kL; 2 300 L   87. 16.55 km

88. 11.2 kg

Appendix B
Computer Number Systems

Computers are here to stay! The electronic computer has become a vital part of the information (data processing) system of most business organizations. The decreasing cost of computers will cause even the small firm of the future to rely more heavily on the computer for its data processing operations. Because of the increasing importance of the computer, business students should become better acquainted with computer number systems.

The computer, which can process data in millionths of a second, is capable of performing a variety of functions including addition, subtraction, multiplication, division, and the comparison of two quantities. Despite its speed, it is still only a machine—it can do nothing without being given a detailed set of instructions called a program. Data and instructions are transmitted to the computer in the form of coded electrical impulses.

There are three number systems used in computer operations: binary (base 2), octal (base 8), and hexadecimal (base 16). This appendix will help you become familiar with the binary system. An understanding of the binary system is essential to understanding and using the octal and hexadecimal systems in computer operations.

This appendix will enable you to:

1.   **explain how and why the binary system is used in computers**

2.   **explain digit and place value in the binary system**

3.   **change binary numbers to decimal numbers**

4.   **change decimal numbers to binary numbers**

5.   **perform calculations with binary numbers**

The Binary System

A computer is a machine—a complicated arrangement of simple electronic switches. Because a switch has only two positions, on and off, a computer is forced to work in a number system with only two symbols. One of the symbols represents the on position (usually denoted as 1) and the other symbol represents the off position (usually denoted as 0). This is a base 2 system, commonly called a binary system, because the word binary means something made up of two parts.

The value of a number in the decimal system depends on two things: the digits (0, 1, 2, 3, 4, 5, 6, 7, 8, 9) and the positional notation (each place has ten times the value of the place to its right because there are ten digits). The value of a number in the binary system depends on the same two things, digit value and place value. The binary system differs in the number of digits (0 and 1) and in place value (each place has only twice the value of the place to its right because there are only two digits).

128	64	32	16	8	4	2	1	Base-two place values
10,000,000	1,000,000	100,000	10,000	1,000	100	10	1	Base-ten place values

The beginning numbers in the decimal and binary systems appear as follows:

Decimal Number	Binary Number	Binary Positional Interpretation
0	0	0 ones
1	1	1 one
2	10	1 two + 0 ones
3	11	1 two + 1 one
4	100	1 four + 0 twos + 0 ones
5	101	1 four + 0 twos + 1 one
6	110	1 four + 1 two + 0 ones
7	111	1 four + 1 two + 1 one
8	1000	1 eight + 0 fours + 0 twos + 0 ones
9	1001	1 eight + 0 fours + 0 twos + 1 one
10	1010	1 eight + 0 fours + 1 two + 0 ones

Computers are forced to work in the binary system; fortunately, humans are not. In a system with only two numbers, those numbers must be repeated many times when numbers get large. For example, 212 in binary notation is 11010100. Although we normally do arithmetic calculations using decimal numbers, there are occasions in business when it is helpful to be acquainted with the binary system.

Changing binary numbers to decimal numbers. To change a binary number to a decimal number, multiply each digit by its place value and add the results.

Example: Change the binary number 101001 to a decimal number.

Solution:

Binary number	1	0	1	0	0	1
Multiply	×	×	×	×	×	×
Place values	32	16	8	4	2	1
Add the results	32 +	0 +	8 +	0 +	0 +	1 = 41

Changing decimal numbers to binary numbers. To change a decimal number to a binary number, divide repeatedly by 2. The remainders are the required binary digits. Check your answer by changing the binary number back to a decimal number.

Example: Change 22 to a binary number.

Solution: $22 \div 2 = 11$, remainder 0

$11 \div 2 = 5$, remainder 1

$5 \div 2 = 2$, remainder 1

$2 \div 2 = 1$, remainder 0

$1 \div 2 = 0$, remainder 1

10110   binary number

Check:

Binary number	1	0	1	1	0
Multiply	×	×	×	×	×
Place values	16	8	4	2	1
Add the results	16 +	0 +	4 +	2 +	0 = 22 decimal number

Adding in the binary system. Three combinations of digits are possible in binary addition. The addition table for the binary system is shown below. Notice that addition in the binary system is the same as in the decimal system except for the third combination of digits ($1 + 1 = 10$). Be sure to exercise caution when using the "carrying process" in addition.

Combinations of Digits in Binary Addition

```
   0        0        1
 + 0      + 1      + 1
 ———      ———      ———
   0        1       10
```

+	0	1
0	0	1
1	1	10

Example: Add 1001 and 1101 in the binary system. Check your answer by changing the binary numbers to decimal numbers and adding.

Solution:
$$\begin{array}{r} 1001 \\ +1101 \\ \hline 10110 \end{array}$$

Check:
$$\begin{array}{rcr} 1001 &=& 9 \\ +1101 &=& +13 \\ \hline 10110 &=& 22 \end{array}$$

Subtracting in the binary system. Four combinations of digits are possible in binary subtraction. Notice that subtracting in the binary system is the same as in the decimal system except for the fourth combination of digits $(10 - 1 = 1)$. Be sure to exercise caution when using the "borrowing process" in subtraction.

Combinations of Digits in Binary Subtraction

$$\begin{array}{cccc} 0 & 1 & 1 & 10 \\ -0 & -1 & -0 & -1 \\ \hline 0 & 0 & 1 & 1 \end{array}$$

Example: Subtract 101 from 1110 in the binary system. Check your answer by changing the binary numbers to decimal numbers and subtracting.

Solution:
$$\begin{array}{r} 1110 \\ -\ 101 \\ \hline 1001 \end{array}$$

Check:
$$\begin{array}{rcr} 1110 &=& 14 \\ -\ 101 &=& -\ 5 \\ \hline 1001 &=& 9 \end{array}$$

Multiplying in the binary system. Multiplication is performed the same way in all number systems.

Example: Multiply 10011 by 101, in the binary system. Check your answer by changing the binary numbers to decimal numbers and multiplying.

Solution:

$$
\begin{array}{r}
10011 \\
\times\quad 101 \\
\hline
10011 \\
10011 \\
\hline
1011111
\end{array}
$$

Check:

$$
\begin{array}{rcr}
10011 & = & 19 \\
\times\quad 101 & = & \times\ 5 \\
\hline
1011111 & = & 95
\end{array}
$$

Dividing in the binary system. Division is performed the same way in the binary system as in the decimal system.

Example: Divide 1111 by 101 in the binary system. Check your answers by changing the binary numbers to decimal numbers and dividing.

Solution:

$$
\begin{array}{r}
11 \\
101\overline{)1111} \\
101 \\
\hline
101 \\
101 \\
\hline
0
\end{array}
$$

Check: $101\overline{)1111} = 5\overline{)15}$ with quotient $11 = 3$

Exercises

Change the following binary numbers to decimal numbers.

1. 101

2. 100

3. 111

4. 1000

5. 1010

6. 1101

7. 1111

8. 1011

9. 10101

10. 11000

11. 10011

12. 10001

13. 11011   14. 10111   15. 100000

16. 100110   17. 111001   18. 110100

19. 1001000   20. 1101011   21. 1011000

22. 1110000   23. 10100001   24. 10010010

Change the following decimal numbers to binary numbers.

25. 6   26. 13   27. 27   28. 33   29. 41

30. 43   31. 55   32. 58   33. 64   34. 65

35. 72   36. 84   37. 96   38. 98   39. 101

40. 125   41. 160   42. 166   43. 189   44. 200

45. 224   46. 288   47. 384   48. 424

Add the following binary numbers. Check your answers.

49.   101   50.   100   51.   101
     +110   +101   +111

52.   111   53.   1011   54.   1001
     +111   +1111   +1011

55.   1001   56.   1101   57.   1011
     +1111   +1110   +1100

58.   1010   59.   1111   60.   10101
     +1101   +1111   +11011

61.   10011   62.   11111   63.   10101
     +10111   +11111   +10111

64.   100101   65.   10111   66.   110101
     +110001   +11000   +111110

| 67. | 111011
+111111 | 68. | 111111
+111111 | | |

Subtract the following binary numbers. Check your answers.

69.	111 − 11	70.	111 −110	71.	111 −111
72.	111 −101	73.	1011 − 111	74.	1101 − 111
75.	1011 − 101	76.	1111 − 100	77.	1001 −1001
78.	10011 − 1001	79.	10011 − 1101	80.	11011 − 1010
81.	11101 − 1000	82.	10111 − 1111	83.	11111 − 1001
84.	11111 −10000	85.	10111 −10010	86.	10111 −10000
87.	11111 −10101	88.	11111 −11011		

Perform the following binary multiplications. Check your answers.

| 89. | 111
× 101 | 90. | 1001
× 111 | 91. | 1110
×1101 |
| 92. | 1111
×1001 | 93. | 1111
×1011 | | |

Perform the following binary divisions. Check your answers.

94. $111\overline{)1110}$ 95. $110\overline{)100100}$ 96. $1000\overline{)11000}$

97. $1001\overline{)110110}$ 98. $100\overline{)1000000}$

Practical Applications

99. A computer operator experiences difficulty with the computer. The following binary numbers appear in the register. Find their equivalent decimal number to help determine the problem.
    (a) 1011   (b) 11001
    (c) 110001   (d) 111110

100. A programmer wants to check to see if the program of instructions has been correctly coded for the computer. In order to make the check, she needs to convert the following decimal numbers to binary numbers. Make the conversion for her.
    (a) 17   (b) 23
    (c) 49   (d) 105

Answers
Appendix B Exercises

1. 5	2. 4	3. 7
4. 8	5. 10	6. 13
7. 15	8. 11	9. 21
10. 24	11. 19	12. 17
13. 27	14. 23	15. 32
16. 38	17. 57	18. 52
19. 72	20. 107	21. 88
22. 112	23. 161	24. 146
25. 110	26. 1101	27. 11011
28. 100001	29. 101001	30. 101011
31. 110111	32. 111010	33. 1000000
34. 1000001	35. 1001000	36. 1010100

37. 1100000   38. 1100010   39. 1100101

40. 1111101   41. 10100000   42. 10100110

43. 10111101   44. 11001000   45. 11100000

46. 100100000   47. 110000000   48. 110101000

49. 1011   50. 1001   51. 1100

52. 1110   53. 11010   54. 10100

55. 11000   56. 11011   57. 10111

58. 10111   59. 11110   60. 110000

61. 101010   62. 111110   63. 101100

64. 1010110   65. 101111   66. 1110011

67. 1111010   68. 1111110   69. 100

70. 1   71. 0   72. 10

73. 100   74. 110   75. 110

76. 1011   77. 0   78. 1010

79. 110   80. 10001   81. 10101

82. 1000   83. 10110   84. 1111

85. 101   86. 111   87. 1010

88. 100   89. 100011   90. 111111

91. 10110110   92. 10000111   93. 10100101

94. 10   95. 110   96. 11

97. 110   98. 10000   99. 11; 25; 49; 62

100. 10001; 10111; 110001; 1101001

Appendix C
Using the Electronic Calculator

The small electronic hand-held calculator has become a valuable tool to the business person at work, the student at school, or the money manager at home. Calculators come in a multitude of sizes with innumerable variations in their capabilities.

This material is designed to introduce you to the basic functions of a calculator and to show how it can be used in solving business-related problems.

Calculator Features. Most hand-held electronic calculators have the following features to simplify the solving of mathematical problems.

Floating Decimal—The answer provided is complete to the digit capacity of the machine. Most hand-held calculators have eight digit capacities.

Automatic Constant—A multiplier or divisor may be held for repeated use. A constant factor for addition or subtraction may also be retained.

Control Keys. Following is a description of the control keys contained on most hand-held calculators. If the keys on your calculator vary, check with the manufacturer's instruction booklet to help you determine which key offers the same features.

(ON) Off-On Switch—Move the switch to the ON position for calculator operation.

⑦⑧⑨ Numeral Keys—Numbers are entered using the standard ten-
④⑤⑥ key keyboard.
①②③
⓪

⊕ Plus Key—Enters addends into the machine and indicates the addition function.

⊖ Minus Key—Enters subtrahends into the machine and indicates the subtraction function.

⊗ Multiplication Key—Enters multipliers into the machine and indicates the multiplication function.

⊘ Division Key—Enters dividends into the machine and indicates the division function.

⊜   Equal Key—Enters the multiplicands and the divisors into the machine and completes the multiplication and division cycle. On some calculators, this key also completes addition and subtraction cycles.

⊙   Decimal Key—Enters the decimal in each factor at its appropriate place.

⊘   Percent Key—Enters the factor as a percent and adjusts the decimal appropriately in the answer.

ⓒ   Clear Key—Clears the machine of all entries and prepares the machine for new calculations.

ⓒⓔ   Clear Entry Key—Clears only the number showing on the display. This key does not destroy numbers already entered into the machine.

Some calculators have a memory bank to store numbers that can be recalled for later use. The controls for this feature are usually $M+$ and $M-$.

Machine Logic. One of the first things you will need to learn about your calculator is whether it is programmed using algebraic logic or arithmetic logic. You will be able to determine which logic your machine uses by working a simple addition or subtraction problem.

Work the following problem to determine whether your machine uses arithmetic or algebraic logic.

Example:
$$\begin{array}{r} 56 \\ -23 \\ \hline 33 \end{array}$$

1.   Turn machine to ON
2.   Clear machine by depressing C
3.   Enter 56 on the keyboard and depress +
4.   Enter 23 on the keyboard and depress −

If your calculator gives the answer as 33, it is programmed with *arithmetic logic*. If the answer on your machine is 79, it is programmed with *algebraic logic*.

The difference between arithmetic logic and algebraic logic must be compensated for only when adding or subtracting:

Arithmetic—the + or − key is depressed *after* the number is entered on the keyboard.

Algebraic—the + or − key is depressed *before* the number is entered on the keyboard.

Addition:

41.14
6.23
9.47

Arithmetic Logic

Turn machine to (ON)
Clear machine by depressing (C)
Enter (4)(1)(·)(1)(4) depress (+)
Enter (6)(·)(2)(3) depress (+)
Enter (9)(·)(4)(7) depress (+)
Read the answer 56.84

Algebraic Logic

Turn machine to (ON)
Clear machine by depressing (C)
Enter (4)(1)(·)(1)(4) depress (+)
Enter (6)(·)(2)(3) depress (+)
Enter (9)(·)(4)(7) depress (=)
Read the answer 56.84

Subtraction:

72.18
−49.15
‾‾‾‾‾
23.03

Arithmetic Logic

Turn machine to (ON)
Clear machine by depressing (C)
Enter (7)(2)(·)(1)(8) depress (+)
Enter (4)(9)(·)(1)(5) depress (−)
Read the answer 23.03

Algebraic Logic

Turn machine to (ON)
Clear machine by depressing (C)
Enter (7)(2)(·)(1)(8) depress (−)
Enter (4)(9)(·)(1)(5) depress (=)
Read the answer 23.03

Multiplication: 8.724
                       ×   9.6
                       83.7504

Turn machine to (ON)
Clear machine by depressing (C)
Enter (8)(·)(7)(2)(4) depress (×)
Enter (9)(·)(6) depress (=)
Read the answer of 83.7504

Division: $78.465 \div 27.35 = 2.8689213$

Turn machine to (ON)
Clear machine by depressing (C)
Enter (7)(8)(·)(4)(6)(5) depress (÷)
Enter (9)(·)(6) depress (=)
Read the answer of 2.8689213

Constant Operations

Most electronic calculators retain constant multipliers and divisors for repeated use in problem solving. Use the following steps if your calculator retains constants for multiplication and division.

Multiplication: Set the constant (number to be used repeatedly) with the × key to solve the following problem:

$$9 \times 5 = 45$$
$$14 \times 5 = 70$$
$$17 \times 5 = 85$$

Enter (5) depress (×)
Enter (9) depress (=)
Read the answer 45

Enter (1)(4) depress (=)
Read the answer 70
Enter (1)(7) depress (=)
Read the answer 85

Division: Set the constant (number to be used repeatedly) with
the $=$ key to solve the following problem:

$56 \div 8 = 7$
$72 \div 8 = 9$
$96 \div 8 = 12$

Enter ⑤ ⑥ depress ÷
Enter ⑧ depress =
Read the answer 7

Enter ⑦ ② depress =
Read the answer 9
Enter ⑨ ⑥ depress =
Read the answer 12

Multiple Operations

The electronic calculator is capable of handling several calculations at
once without having to obtain an intermediate answer. This will greatly
simplify and speed up calculations for many business problems. For example, to calculate the interest for $1,496 \times .08 \times 130 \div 360$, use the
following steps:

Example: Turn machine to ⓞₙ
Enter ① ④ ⑨ ⑥ depress ⊗
Enter · ⓪ ⑧ depress ⊗
Enter ① ③ ⓪ depress ÷
Enter ③ ⑥ ⓪ depress =
Read the answer 43.217777
(Round to $43.22)

Appendix D
The Number of the Day of the Year

Day of Month	Jan.	Feb.	Mar.	April	May	June	July	Aug.	Sept.	Oct.	Nov.	Dec.	Day of Month
1	1	32	60	91	121	152	182	213	244	274	305	335	1
2	2	33	61	92	122	153	183	214	245	275	306	336	2
3	3	34	62	93	123	154	184	215	246	276	307	337	3
4	4	35	63	94	124	155	185	216	247	277	308	338	4
5	5	36	64	95	125	156	186	217	248	278	309	339	5
6	6	37	65	96	126	157	187	218	249	279	310	340	6
7	7	38	66	97	127	158	188	219	250	280	311	341	7
8	8	39	67	98	128	159	189	220	251	281	312	342	8
9	9	40	68	99	129	160	190	221	252	282	313	343	9
10	10	41	69	100	130	161	191	222	253	283	314	344	10
11	11	42	70	101	131	162	192	223	254	284	315	345	11
12	12	43	71	102	132	163	193	224	255	285	316	346	12
13	13	44	72	103	133	164	194	225	256	286	317	347	13
14	14	45	73	104	134	165	195	226	257	287	318	348	14
15	15	46	74	105	135	166	196	227	258	288	319	349	15
16	16	47	75	106	136	167	197	228	259	289	320	350	16
17	17	48	76	107	137	168	198	229	260	290	321	351	17
18	18	49	77	108	138	169	199	230	261	291	322	352	18
19	19	50	78	109	139	170	200	231	262	292	323	353	19
20	20	51	79	110	140	171	201	232	263	293	324	354	20
21	21	52	80	111	141	172	202	233	264	294	325	355	21
22	22	53	81	112	142	173	203	234	265	295	326	356	22
23	23	54	82	113	143	174	204	235	266	296	327	357	23
24	24	55	83	114	144	175	205	236	267	297	328	358	24
25	25	56	84	115	145	176	206	237	268	298	329	359	25
26	26	57	85	116	146	177	207	238	269	299	330	360	26
27	27	58	86	117	147	178	208	239	270	300	331	361	27
28	28	59	87	118	148	179	209	240	271	301	332	362	28
29	29		88	119	149	180	210	241	272	302	333	363	29
30	30		89	120	150	181	211	242	273	303	334	364	30
31	31		90		151		212	243		304		365	31

Note. In leap years, after February 28, add 1 to the tabulated number.

Appendices E-J

<table>
<thead>
<tr><th>Rate
¼%</th><th>E
Compound
Amount</th><th>F
Present
Value</th><th>G
Amount of
Annuity</th><th>H
Present Value
of Annuity</th><th>I
Sinking
Fund</th><th>J
Amortization</th><th></th></tr>
<tr><td>n</td><td>$(1 + i)^n$</td><td>$(1 + i)^{-n}$</td><td>$S_{\overline{n}|i}$</td><td>$A_{\overline{n}|i}$</td><td>$1/S_{\overline{n}|i}$</td><td>$1/A_{\overline{n}|i}$</td><td>n</td></tr>
</thead>
<tbody>
<tr><td>1</td><td>1.0025 0000</td><td>0.9975 0623</td><td>1.0000 0000</td><td>0.9975 0623</td><td>1.0000 0000</td><td>1.0025 0000</td><td>1</td></tr>
<tr><td>2</td><td>1.0050 0625</td><td>0.9950 1869</td><td>2.0025 0000</td><td>1.9925 2492</td><td>0.4993 7578</td><td>0.5018 7578</td><td>2</td></tr>
<tr><td>3</td><td>1.0075 1877</td><td>0.9925 3734</td><td>3.0075 0625</td><td>2.9850 6227</td><td>0.3325 0139</td><td>0.3350 0139</td><td>3</td></tr>
<tr><td>4</td><td>1.0100 3756</td><td>0.9900 6219</td><td>4.0150 2502</td><td>3.9751 2446</td><td>0.2490 6445</td><td>0.2515 6445</td><td>4</td></tr>
<tr><td>5</td><td>1.0125 6266</td><td>0.9875 9321</td><td>5.0250 6258</td><td>4.9627 1766</td><td>0.1990 0250</td><td>0.2015 0250</td><td>5</td></tr>
<tr><td>6</td><td>1.0150 9406</td><td>0.9851 3038</td><td>6.0376 2523</td><td>5.9478 4804</td><td>0.1656 2803</td><td>0.1681 2803</td><td>6</td></tr>
<tr><td>7</td><td>1.0176 3180</td><td>0.9826 7370</td><td>7.0527 1930</td><td>6.9305 2174</td><td>0.1427 8928</td><td>0.1442 8928</td><td>7</td></tr>
<tr><td>8</td><td>1.0201 7588</td><td>0.9802 2314</td><td>8.0703 5110</td><td>7.9107 4487</td><td>0.1239 1035</td><td>0.1264 1035</td><td>8</td></tr>
<tr><td>9</td><td>1.0227 2632</td><td>0.9777 7869</td><td>9.0905 2697</td><td>8.8885 2357</td><td>0.1100 0462</td><td>0.1125 0462</td><td>9</td></tr>
<tr><td>10</td><td>1.0252 8313</td><td>0.9753 4034</td><td>10.1132 5329</td><td>9.8638 6391</td><td>0.0988 8015</td><td>0.1013 8015</td><td>10</td></tr>
<tr><td>11</td><td>1.0278 4634</td><td>0.9729 0807</td><td>11.1385 3642</td><td>10.8367 7198</td><td>0.0897 7840</td><td>0.0922 7840</td><td>11</td></tr>
<tr><td>12</td><td>1.0304 1596</td><td>0.9704 8187</td><td>12.1663 8277</td><td>11.8072 5384</td><td>0.0821 9370</td><td>0.0846 9370</td><td>12</td></tr>
<tr><td>13</td><td>1.0329 9200</td><td>0.9680 6171</td><td>13.1967 9872</td><td>12.7753 1555</td><td>0.0767 7595</td><td>0.0782 7595</td><td>13</td></tr>
<tr><td>14</td><td>1.0355 7448</td><td>0.9656 4759</td><td>14.2297 9072</td><td>13.7409 6314</td><td>0.0702 7510</td><td>0.0727 7510</td><td>14</td></tr>
<tr><td>15</td><td>1.0381 6341</td><td>0.9632 3949</td><td>15.2653 6520</td><td>14.7042 0264</td><td>0.0655 0777</td><td>0.0680 0777</td><td>15</td></tr>
<tr><td>16</td><td>1.0407 5882</td><td>0.9608 3740</td><td>16.3035 2861</td><td>15.6650 4004</td><td>0.0613 3642</td><td>0.0638 3642</td><td>16</td></tr>
<tr><td>17</td><td>1.0433 6072</td><td>0.9584 4130</td><td>17.3442 8743</td><td>16.6234 8133</td><td>0.0576 5587</td><td>0.0601 5587</td><td>17</td></tr>
<tr><td>18</td><td>1.0459 6912</td><td>0.9560 5117</td><td>18.3876 4815</td><td>17.5795 3250</td><td>0.0543 8433</td><td>0.0568 8433</td><td>18</td></tr>
<tr><td>19</td><td>1.0485 8404</td><td>0.9536 6700</td><td>19.4336 1727</td><td>18.5331 9950</td><td>0.0514 5722</td><td>0.0539 5722</td><td>19</td></tr>
<tr><td>20</td><td>1.0512 0550</td><td>0.9512 8878</td><td>20.4822 0131</td><td>19.4844 8828</td><td>0.0488 2288</td><td>0.0513 2288</td><td>20</td></tr>
<tr><td>21</td><td>1.0538 3352</td><td>0.9489 1649</td><td>21.5334 0682</td><td>20.4334 0477</td><td>0.0464 3947</td><td>0.0489 3947</td><td>21</td></tr>
<tr><td>22</td><td>1.0564 6810</td><td>0.9465 5011</td><td>22.5872 4033</td><td>21.3799 5488</td><td>0.0442 7278</td><td>0.0467 7278</td><td>22</td></tr>
<tr><td>23</td><td>1.0591 0927</td><td>0.9441 8964</td><td>23.6437 0843</td><td>22.3241 4452</td><td>0.0422 9455</td><td>0.0447 9455</td><td>23</td></tr>
<tr><td>24</td><td>1.0617 5704</td><td>0.9418 3505</td><td>24.7028 1770</td><td>23.2659 7957</td><td>0.0404 8121</td><td>0.0429 8121</td><td>24</td></tr>
<tr><td>25</td><td>1.0644 1144</td><td>0.9394 8634</td><td>25.7645 7475</td><td>24.2054 6591</td><td>0.0388 1298</td><td>0.0413 1298</td><td>25</td></tr>
<tr><td>26</td><td>1.0670 7247</td><td>0.9371 4348</td><td>26.8289 8619</td><td>25.1426 0939</td><td>0.0372 7312</td><td>0.0397 7312</td><td>26</td></tr>
<tr><td>27</td><td>1.0697 4015</td><td>0.9348 0646</td><td>27.8960 5865</td><td>26.0774 1585</td><td>0.0358 4736</td><td>0.0383 4736</td><td>27</td></tr>
<tr><td>28</td><td>1.0724 1450</td><td>0.9324 7527</td><td>28.9657 9880</td><td>27.0098 9112</td><td>0.0345 2347</td><td>0.0370 2347</td><td>28</td></tr>
<tr><td>29</td><td>1.0750 9553</td><td>0.9301 4990</td><td>30.0382 1330</td><td>27.9400 4102</td><td>0.0332 9093</td><td>0.0357 9093</td><td>29</td></tr>
<tr><td>30</td><td>1.0777 8327</td><td>0.9278 3032</td><td>31.1133 0883</td><td>28.8678 7134</td><td>0.0321 4059</td><td>0.0346 4059</td><td>30</td></tr>
<tr><td>31</td><td>1.0804 7773</td><td>0.9255 1653</td><td>32.1910 9210</td><td>29.7933 8787</td><td>0.0310 6449</td><td>0.0335 6449</td><td>31</td></tr>
<tr><td>32</td><td>1.0831 7892</td><td>0.9232 0851</td><td>33.2715 6983</td><td>30.7165 9638</td><td>0.0300 5569</td><td>0.0325 5569</td><td>32</td></tr>
<tr><td>33</td><td>1.0858 8687</td><td>0.9209 0624</td><td>34.3547 4876</td><td>31.6375 0262</td><td>0.0291 0806</td><td>0.0316 0806</td><td>33</td></tr>
<tr><td>34</td><td>1.0886 0159</td><td>0.9186 0972</td><td>35.4406 3563</td><td>32.5561 1234</td><td>0.0282 1620</td><td>0.0307 1620</td><td>34</td></tr>
<tr><td>35</td><td>1.0913 2309</td><td>0.9163 1892</td><td>36.5292 3722</td><td>33.4724 3126</td><td>0.0273 7533</td><td>0.0298 7533</td><td>35</td></tr>
<tr><td>36</td><td>1.0940 5140</td><td>0.9140 3384</td><td>37.6205 6031</td><td>34.3864 6510</td><td>0.0265 8121</td><td>0.0290 8121</td><td>36</td></tr>
<tr><td>37</td><td>1.0967 8653</td><td>0.9117 5445</td><td>38.7146 1171</td><td>35.2982 1955</td><td>0.0258 3004</td><td>0.0283 3004</td><td>37</td></tr>
<tr><td>38</td><td>1.0995 2850</td><td>0.9094 8075</td><td>39.8113 9824</td><td>36.2077 0030</td><td>0.0251 1843</td><td>0.0276 1843</td><td>38</td></tr>
<tr><td>39</td><td>1.1022 7732</td><td>0.9072 1272</td><td>40.9109 2673</td><td>37.1149 1302</td><td>0.0244 4335</td><td>0.0269 4335</td><td>39</td></tr>
<tr><td>40</td><td>1.1050 3301</td><td>0.9049 5034</td><td>42.0132 0405</td><td>38.0198 6336</td><td>0.0238 0204</td><td>0.0263 0204</td><td>40</td></tr>
<tr><td>41</td><td>1.1077 9559</td><td>0.9026 9361</td><td>43.1182 3706</td><td>38.9225 5697</td><td>0.0231 9204</td><td>0.0256 9204</td><td>41</td></tr>
<tr><td>42</td><td>1.1105 6508</td><td>0.9004 4250</td><td>44.2260 3265</td><td>39.8229 9947</td><td>0.0226 1112</td><td>0.0251 1112</td><td>42</td></tr>
<tr><td>43</td><td>1.1133 4149</td><td>0.8981 9701</td><td>45.3365 9774</td><td>40.7211 9648</td><td>0.0220 5724</td><td>0.0245 5724</td><td>43</td></tr>
<tr><td>44</td><td>1.1161 2485</td><td>0.8959 5712</td><td>46.4499 3923</td><td>41.6171 5359</td><td>0.0215 2855</td><td>0.0240 2855</td><td>44</td></tr>
<tr><td>45</td><td>1.1189 1516</td><td>0.8937 2281</td><td>47.5660 6408</td><td>42.5108 7640</td><td>0.0210 2339</td><td>0.0235 2339</td><td>45</td></tr>
<tr><td>46</td><td>1.1217 1245</td><td>0.8914 9407</td><td>48.6849 7924</td><td>43.4023 7047</td><td>0.0205 4022</td><td>0.0230 4022</td><td>46</td></tr>
<tr><td>47</td><td>1.1245 1673</td><td>0.8892 7090</td><td>49.8066 9169</td><td>44.2916 4137</td><td>0.0200 7762</td><td>0.0225 7762</td><td>47</td></tr>
<tr><td>48</td><td>1.1273 2802</td><td>0.8870 5326</td><td>50.9312 0842</td><td>45.1786 9463</td><td>0.0196 3433</td><td>0.0221 3433</td><td>48</td></tr>
<tr><td>49</td><td>1.1301 4634</td><td>0.8848 4116</td><td>52.0585 3644</td><td>46.0635 3580</td><td>0.0192 0915</td><td>0.0217 0915</td><td>49</td></tr>
<tr><td>50</td><td>1.1329 7171</td><td>0.8826 3457</td><td>53.1886 8278</td><td>46.9461 7037</td><td>0.0188 0099</td><td>0.0213 0099</td><td>50</td></tr>
</tbody>
</table>

Rate ⅓%	E Compound Amount	F Present Value	G Amount of Annuity	H Present Value of Annuity	I Sinking Fund	J Amortization	
n	$(1 + i)^n$	$(1 + i)^{-n}$	$S_{\overline{n}|i}$	$A_{\overline{n}|i}$	$1/S_{\overline{n}|i}$	$1/A_{\overline{n}|i}$	n
1	1.0033 3333	0.9966 7774	1.0000 0000	0.9966 7744	1.0000 0000	1.0033 3333	1
2	1.0066 7778	0.9933 6652	2.0033 3333	1.9900 4426	0.4991 6805	0.5025 0139	2
3	1.0100 3337	0.9900 6630	3.0100 1111	2.9801 1056	0.3322 2469	0.3355 5802	3
4	1.0134 0015	0.9867 7704	4.0200 4448	3.9668 8760	0.2487 5347	0.2520 8680	4
5	1.0167 7815	0.9834 9871	5.0334 4463	4.9503 8631	0.1986 7110	0.2020 0444	5
6	1.0201 6741	0.9802 3127	6.0502 2278	5.9306 1759	0.1652 8317	0.1686 1650	6
7	1.0235 6797	0.9769 7469	7.0703 9019	6.9075 9228	0.1414 3491	0.1447 6824	7
8	1.0269 7986	0.9737 2893	8.0939 5816	7.8813 2121	0.1235 4895	0.1268 8228	8
9	1.0304 0313	0.9704 9395	9.1209 3802	8.8518 1516	0.1096 3785	0.1129 7118	9
10	1.0338 3780	0.9672 6972	10.1513 4114	9.8190 8487	0.0985 0915	0.1018 4248	10
11	1.0372 8393	0.9640 5620	11.1851 7895	10.7831 4107	0.0894 0402	0.0927 3736	11
12	1.0407 4154	0.9608 5335	12.2224 6288	11.7439 9442	0.0818 1657	0.0851 4990	12
13	1.0442 1068	0.9576 6115	13.2632 0442	12.7016 5557	0.0753 9656	0.0787 2989	13
14	1.0476 9138	0.9544 7955	14.3074 1510	13.6561 3512	0.0698 9383	0.0732 2716	14
15	1.0511 8369	0.9513 0852	15.3551 0648	14.6074 4364	0.0651 2491	0.0684 5825	15
16	1.0546 8763	0.9481 4803	16.4062 9017	15.5555 9167	0.0609 5223	0.0642 8557	16
17	1.0582 0326	0.9449 9803	17.4609 7781	16.5005 8970	0.0572 7056	0.0606 0389	17
18	1.0617 3060	0.9418 5851	18.5191 8107	17.4424 4821	0.0539 9807	0.0573 3140	18
19	1.0652 6971	0.9387 2941	19.5809 1167	18.3811 7762	0.0510 7015	0.0544 0348	19
20	1.0688 2060	0.9356 1071	20.6461 8137	19.3167 8832	0.0484 3511	0.0517 6844	20
21	1.0723 8334	0.9325 0236	21.7150 0198	20.2492 9069	0.0460 5111	0.0493 8445	21
22	1.0759 5795	0.9294 0435	22.7873 8532	21.1786 9504	0.0438 8393	0.0472 1726	22
23	1.0795 4448	0.9263 1663	23.8633 4327	22.1050 1167	0.0419 0528	0.0452 3861	23
24	1.0831 4296	0.9232 3916	24.9428 8775	23.0282 5083	0.0400 9159	0.0434 2492	24
25	1.0867 5344	0.9201 7192	26.0260 3071	23.9484 2275	0.0384 2307	0.0417 5640	25
26	1.0903 7595	0.9171 1487	27.1127 8414	24.8655 3763	0.0368 8297	0.0402 1630	26
27	1.0940 1053	0.9140 6798	28.2031 6009	25.7796 0561	0.0354 5702	0.0387 9035	27
28	1.0976 5724	0.9110 3121	29.2971 7062	26.6906 3682	0.0341 3299	0.0374 6632	28
29	1.1013 1609	0.9080 0453	30.3948 2786	27.5986 4135	0.0329 0033	0.0362 3367	29
30	1.1049 8715	0.9049 8790	31.4961 4395	28.5036 2925	0.0317 4992	0.0350 8325	30
31	1.1086 7044	0.9019 8130	32.6011 3110	29.4056 1055	0.0306 7378	0.0340 0712	31
32	1.1123 6601	0.8989 8468	33.7098 0154	30.3045 9523	0.0296 6496	0.0329 9830	32
33	1.1160 7389	0.8959 9802	34.8221 6754	31.2005 9325	0.0287 1734	0.0320 5067	33
34	1.1197 9414	0.8930 2128	35.9382 4143	32.0936 1454	0.0278 2551	0.0311 5885	34
35	1.1235 2679	0.8900 5444	37.0580 3557	32.9836 6898	0.0269 8470	0.0303 1803	35
36	1.1272 7187	0.8870 9745	38.1815 6236	33.8707 6642	0.0261 9065	0.0295 2399	36
37	1.1310 2945	0.8841 5028	39.3088 3423	34.7549 1670	0.0254 3957	0.0287 7291	37
38	1.1347 9955	0.8812 1290	40.4398 6368	35.6361 2960	0.0247 2808	0.0280 6141	38
39	1.1385 8221	0.8782 8528	41.5746 6322	36.5144 1488	0.0240 5311	0.0273 8644	39
40	1.1423 7748	0.8753 6739	42.7132 4543	37.3897 8228	0.0234 1194	0.0267 4527	40
41	1.1461 8541	0.8724 5920	43.8556 2292	38.2622 4147	0.0228 0209	0.0261 3543	41
42	1.1500 0603	0.8695 6066	45.0018 0833	39.1318 0213	0.0222 2133	0.0255 5466	42
43	1.1538 3938	0.8666 7175	46.1518 1436	39.9984 7389	0.0216 6762	0.0250 0095	43
44	1.1576 8551	0.8637 9245	47.3056 5374	40.8622 6633	0.0211 3912	0.0244 7246	44
45	1.1615 4446	0.8609 2270	48.4633 3925	41.7231 8903	0.0206 3415	0.0239 6749	45
46	1.1654 1628	0.8580 6249	49.6248 8371	42.5812 5153	0.0201 5118	0.0234 8451	46
47	1.1693 0100	0.8552 1179	50.7902 9999	43.4364 6332	0.0196 8880	0.0230 2213	47
48	1.1731 9867	0.8523 7055	51.9596 0099	44.2888 3387	0.0192 4572	0.0225 7905	48
49	1.1771 0933	0.8495 3876	53.1327 9966	45.1383 7263	0.0188 2077	0.0221 5410	49
50	1.1810 3303	0.8467 1637	54.3099 0899	45.9850 8900	0.0184 1285	0.0217 4618	50

Rate ½%	E Compound Amount	F Present Value	G Amount of Annuity	H Present Value of Annuity	I Sinking Fund	J Amortization	
n	$(1 + i)^n$	$(1 + i)^{-n}$	$S_{\overline{n}|i}$	$A_{\overline{n}|i}$	$1/S_{\overline{n}|i}$	$1/A_{\overline{n}|i}$	n
1	1.0050 0000	0.9950 2488	1.0000 0000	0.9950 2488	1.0000 0000	1.0050 0000	1
2	1.0100 2500	0.9900 7450	2.0050 0000	1.9850 9938	0.4987 5312	0.5037 5312	2
3	1.0150 7513	0.9851 4876	3.0150 2500	2.9702 4814	0.3316 7221	0.3366 7221	3
4	1.0201 5050	0.9802 4752	4.0301 0013	3.9504 9566	0.2481 3279	0.2531 3279	4
5	1.0252 5125	0.9753 7067	5.0502 5063	4.9258 6633	0.1980 0998	0.2030 0997	5
6	1.0303 7751	0.9705 1808	6.0755 0188	5.8963 8441	0.1645 9546	0.1695 9546	6
7	1.0355 2940	0.9656 8963	7.1058 7939	6.8620 7404	0.1407 2854	0.1457 2854	7
8	1.0407 0704	0.9608 8520	8.1414 0879	7.8229 5924	0.1228 2886	0.1278 2886	8
9	1.0459 1058	0.9561 0468	9.1821 1583	8.7790 6392	0.1089 0736	0.1139 0736	9
10	1.0511 4013	0.9513 4794	10.2280 2641	9.7304 1186	0.0977 7057	0.1027 7057	10
11	1.0563 9583	0.9466 1487	11.2791 6654	10.6770 2673	0.0886 5903	0.0936 5903	11
12	1.0616 7781	0.9419 0534	12.3355 6237	11.6189 3207	0.0810 6643	0.0860 6643	12
13	1.0669 8620	0.9372 1924	13.3972 4018	12.5561 5131	0.0746 4224	0.0796 4224	13
14	1.0723 2113	0.9325 5646	14.4642 2639	13.4887 0777	0.0691 3609	0.0741 3609	14
15	1.0776 8274	0.9279 1688	15.5365 4752	14.4166 2465	0.0643 6436	0.0693 6436	15
16	1.0830 7115	0.9233 0037	16.6142 3026	15.3399 2502	0.0601 8937	0.0651 8937	16
17	1.0884 8651	0.9187 0684	17.6973 0141	16.2586 3186	0.0565 0579	0.0615 0579	17
18	1.0939 2894	0.9141 3616	18.7857 8791	17.1727 6802	0.0532 3173	0.0582 3173	18
19	1.0993 9858	0.9095 8822	19.8797 1685	18.0823 5624	0.0503 0253	0.0553 0253	19
20	1.1048 9558	0.9050 6290	20.9791 1544	18.9874 1915	0.0476 6645	0.0526 6645	20
21	1.1104 2006	0.9005 6010	22.0840 1101	19.8879 7925	0.0452 8163	0.0502 8163	21
22	1.1159 7216	0.8960 7971	23.1944 3107	20.7840 5896	0.0431 1380	0.0481 1380	22
23	1.1215 5202	0.8916 2160	24.3104 0322	21.6756 8055	0.0411 3465	0.0461 3465	23
24	1.1271 5978	0.8871 8567	25.4319 5524	22.5628 6622	0.0393 2061	0.0443 2061	24
25	1.1327 9558	0.8827 7181	26.5591 1502	23.4456 3803	0.0376 5186	0.0426 5186	25
26	1.1384 5955	0.8783 7991	27.6919 1059	24.3240 1794	0.0361 1163	0.0411 1163	26
27	1.1441 5185	0.8740 0986	28.8303 7015	25.1980 2780	0.0346 8565	0.0396 8565	27
28	1.1498 7261	0.8696 6155	29.9745 2200	26.0676 8936	0.0333 6167	0.0383 6167	28
29	1.1556 2197	0.8653 3488	31.1243 9461	26.9330 2423	0.0321 2914	0.0371 2914	29
30	1.1614 0008	0.8610 2973	32.2800 1658	27.7940 5397	0.0309 7892	0.0359 7892	30
31	1.1672 0708	0.8567 4600	33.4414 1666	28.6507 9997	0.0299 0304	0.0349 0304	31
32	1.1730 4312	0.8524 8358	34.6086 2375	29.5032 8355	0.0288 9453	0.0338 9453	32
33	1.1789 0833	0.8482 4237	35.7816 6686	30.3515 2592	0.0279 4727	0.0329 4727	33
34	1.1848 0288	0.8440 2226	36.9605 7520	31.1955 4818	0.0270 5586	0.0320 5586	34
35	1.1907 2689	0.8398 2314	38.1453 7807	32.0353 7132	0.0262 1550	0.0312 1550	35
36	1.1966 8052	0.8356 4492	39.3361 0496	32.8710 1624	0.0254 2194	0.0304 2194	36
37	1.2026 6393	0.8314 8748	40.5327 8549	33.7025 0372	0.0246 7139	0.0296 7139	37
38	1.2086 7725	0.8273 5073	41.7354 4942	34.5298 5445	0.0239 6045	0.0289 6045	38
39	1.2147 2063	0.8232 3455	42.9441 2666	35.3530 8900	0.0232 8607	0.0282 8607	39
40	1.2207 9424	0.8191 3886	44.1588 4730	36.1722 2786	0.0226 4552	0.0276 4552	40
41	1.2268 9821	0.8150 6354	45.3796 4153	36.9872 9141	0.0220 3631	0.0270 3631	41
42	1.2330 3270	0.8110 0850	46.6065 3974	37.7982 9991	0.0214 5622	0.0264 5622	42
43	1.2391 9786	0.8069 7363	47.8395 7244	38.6052 7354	0.0209 0320	0.0259 0320	43
44	1.2453 9385	0.8029 5884	49.0787 7030	39.4082 3238	0.0203 7541	0.0253 7541	44
45	1.2516 2082	0.7989 6402	50.3241 6415	40.2071 9640	0.0198 7117	0.0248 7117	45
46	1.2578 7892	0.7949 8907	51.5757 8497	41.0021 8547	0.0193 8894	0.0243 8894	46
47	1.2641 6832	0.7910 3390	52.8336 6390	41.7932 1937	0.0189 2733	0.0239 2733	47
48	1.2704 8916	0.7870 9841	54.0978 3222	42.5803 1778	0.0184 8503	0.0234 8503	48
49	1.2768 4161	0.7831 8250	55.3683 2138	43.3635 0028	0.0180 6087	0.0230 6087	49
50	1.2832 2581	0.7792 8607	56.6451 6299	44.1427 8635	0.0176 5376	0.0226 5376	50

Rate ¾%	E Compound Amount	F Present Value	G Amount of Annuity	H Present Value of Annuity	I Sinking Fund	J Amortization	
n	$(1 + i)^n$	$(1 + i)^{-n}$	$S_{\overline{n}|i}$	$A_{\overline{n}|i}$	$1/S_{\overline{n}|i}$	$1/A_{\overline{n}|i}$	n
1	1.0075 0000	0.9925 5583	1.0000 0000	0.9925 5583	1.0000 0000	1.0075 0000	1
2	1.0150 5625	0.9851 6708	2.0075 0000	1.9777 2291	0.4981 3201	0.5056 3201	2
3	1.0226 6917	0.9778 3333	3.0225 5625	2.9555 5624	0.3308 4579	0.3383 4579	3
4	1.0303 3919	0.9705 5417	4.0452 2542	3.9261 1041	0.2472 0501	0.2547 0501	4
5	1.0380 6673	0.9633 2920	5.0755 6461	4.8894 3961	0.1970 2242	0.2045 2242	5
6	1.0458 5224	0.9561 5802	6.1136 3135	5.8455 9763	0.1635 6891	0.1710 6891	6
7	1.0536 9613	0.9490 4022	7.1594 8358	6.7946 3785	0.1396 7488	0.1471 7488	7
8	1.0615 9885	0.9419 7540	8.2131 7971	7.7366 1325	0.1217 5552	0.1292 5552	8
9	1.0695 6084	0.9349 6318	9.2747 7856	8.6715 7642	0.1078 1929	0.1153 1929	9
10	1.0775 8255	0.9280 0315	10.3443 3940	9.5995 7958	0.0966 7123	0.1041 7123	10
11	1.0856 6441	0.9210 9494	11.4219 2194	10.5206 7452	0.0875 5094	0.0950 5094	11
12	1.0938 0690	0.9142 3815	12.5075 8636	11.4349 1267	0.0799 5148	0.0874 5148	12
13	1.1020 1045	0.9074 3241	13.6013 9325	12.3423 4508	0.0735 2188	0.0810 2188	13
14	1.1102 7553	0.9006 7733	14.7034 0370	13.2430 2242	0.0680 1146	0.0755 1146	14
15	1.1186 0259	0.8939 7254	15.8136 7923	14.1369 9495	0.0632 3639	0.0707 3639	15
16	1.1269 9211	0.8873 1766	16.9322 8183	15.0243 1261	0.0590 5879	0.0665 5879	16
17	1.1354 4455	0.8807 1231	18.0592 7394	15.9050 2492	0.0553 7321	0.0628 7321	17
18	1.1439 6039	0.8741 5614	19.1947 1849	16.7791 8107	0.0520 9766	0.0595 9766	18
19	1.1525 4009	0.8676 4878	20.3386 7888	17.6468 2984	0.0491 6740	0.0566 6740	19
20	1.1611 8414	0.8611 8985	21.4912 1897	18.5080 1969	0.0465 3063	0.0540 3063	20
21	1.1698 9302	0.8547 7901	22.6524 0312	19.3627 9870	0.0441 4543	0.0516 4543	21
22	1.1786 6722	0.8484 1589	23.8222 9614	20.2112 1459	0.0419 7748	0.0494 7748	22
23	1.1875 0723	0.8421 0014	25.0009 6336	21.0533 1473	0.0399 9846	0.0474 9846	23
24	1.1964 1353	0.8358 3140	26.1884 7059	21.8891 4614	0.0381 8474	0.0456 8474	24
25	1.2053 8663	0.8296 0933	27.3848 8412	22.7187 5547	0.0365 1650	0.0440 1650	25
26	1.2144 2703	0.8234 3358	28.5902 7075	23.5421 8905	0.0349 7693	0.0424 7693	26
27	1.2235 3523	0.8173 0380	29.8046 9778	24.3594 9286	0.0335 5176	0.0410 5176	27
28	1.2327 1175	0.8112 1966	31.0282 3301	25.1707 1251	0.0322 2871	0.0397 2871	28
29	1.2419 5709	0.8051 8080	32.2609 4476	25.9758 9331	0.0309 9723	0.0384 9723	29
30	1.2512 7176	0.7991 8690	33.5029 0184	26.7750 8021	0.0298 4816	0.0373 4816	30
31	1.2606 5630	0.7932 3762	34.7541 7361	27.5683 1783	0.0287 7352	0.0362 7352	31
32	1.2701 1122	0.7873 3262	36.0148 2991	28.3556 5045	0.0277 6634	0.0352 6634	32
33	1.2796 3706	0.7814 7158	37.2849 4113	29.1371 2203	0.0268 2048	0.0343 2048	33
34	1.2892 3434	0.7756 5418	38.5645 7819	29.9127 7621	0.0259 3053	0.0334 3053	34
35	1.2989 0359	0.7698 8008	39.8538 1253	30.6826 5629	0.0250 9170	0.0325 9170	35
36	1.3086 4537	0.7641 4896	41.1527 1612	31.4468 0525	0.0242 9973	0.0317 9973	36
37	1.3184 6021	0.7584 6051	42.4613 6149	32.2052 6576	0.0235 5082	0.0310 5082	37
38	1.3283 4866	0.7528 1440	43.7798 2170	32.9580 8016	0.0228 4157	0.0303 4157	38
39	1.3383 1128	0.7472 1032	45.1081 7037	33.7052 9048	0.0221 6893	0.0296 6893	39
40	1.3483 4861	0.7416 4796	46.4464 8164	34.4469 3844	0.0215 3016	0.0290 3016	40
41	1.3584 6123	0.7361 2701	47.7948 3026	35.1830 6545	0.0209 2277	0.0284 2276	41
42	1.3686 4969	0.7306 4716	49.1532 9148	35.9137 1260	0.0203 4452	0.0278 4452	42
43	1.3789 1456	0.7252 0809	50.5219 4117	36.6389 2070	0.0197 9338	0.0272 9338	43
44	1.3892 5642	0.7198 0952	51.9008 5573	37.3587 3022	0.0192 6751	0.0267 6751	44
45	1.3996 7584	0.7144 5114	53.2901 1215	38.0731 8136	0.0187 6521	0.0262 6521	45
46	1.4101 7341	0.7091 3264	54.6897 8799	38.7823 1401	0.0182 8495	0.0257 8495	46
47	1.4207 4971	0.7038 5374	56.0999 6140	39.4861 6775	0.0178 2532	0.0253 2532	47
48	1.4314 0533	0.6986 1414	57.5207 1111	40.1847 8189	0.0173 8504	0.0248 8504	48
49	1.4421 4087	0.6934 1353	58.9521 1644	40.8781 9542	0.0169 6292	0.0244 6292	49
50	1.4529 5693	0.6882 5165	60.3942 5732	41.5664 4707	0.0165 5787	0.0240 5787	50

Rate 1%	E Compound Amount	F Present Value	G Amount of Annuity	H Present Value of Annuity	I Sinking Fund	J Amortization	
n	$(1 + i)^n$	$(1 + i)^{-n}$	$S_{\overline{n}|i}$	$A_{\overline{n}|i}$	$1/S_{\overline{n}|i}$	$1/A_{\overline{n}|i}$	n
1	1.0100 0000	0.9900 9901	1.0000 0000	0.9900 9901	1.0000 0000	1.0100 0000	1
2	1.0201 0000	0.9802 9605	2.0100 0000	1.9703 9506	0.4975 1244	0.5075 1244	2
3	1.0303 0100	0.9705 9015	3.0301 0000	2.9409 8521	0.3300 2211	0.3400 2211	3
4	1.0406 0401	0.9609 8034	4.0604 0100	3.9019 6555	0.2462 8109	0.2562 8109	4
5	1.0510 1005	0.9514 6569	5.1010 0501	4.8534 3124	0.1960 3980	0.2060 3980	5
6	1.0615 2015	0.9420 4524	6.1520 1506	5.7954 7647	0.1625 4837	0.1725 4837	6
7	1.0721 3535	0.9327 1805	7.2135 3521	6.7281 9453	0.1386 2828	0.1486 2828	7
8	1.0828 5671	0.9234 8322	8.2856 7056	7.6516 7775	0.1206 9029	0.1306 9029	8
9	1.0936 8527	0.9143 3982	9.3685 2727	8.5660 1758	0.1067 4036	0.1167 4036	9
10	1.1046 2213	0.9052 8695	10.4622 1254	9.4713 0453	0.0955 8208	0.1055 8208	10
11	1.1156 6835	0.8963 2372	11.5668 3467	10.3676 2825	0.0864 5408	0.0964 5408	11
12	1.1268 2503	0.8874 4923	12.6825 0301	11.2550 7747	0.0788 4879	0.0888 4879	12
13	1.1380 9328	0.8786 6260	13.8093 2804	12.1337 4007	0.0724 1482	0.0824 1482	13
14	1.1494 7421	0.8699 6297	14.9474 2132	13.0037 0304	0.0669 0117	0.0769 0117	14
15	1.1609 6896	0.8613 4947	16.0968 9554	13.8650 5252	0.0621 2378	0.0721 2378	15
16	1.1725 7864	0.8528 2126	17.2578 6449	14.7178 7378	0.0579 4460	0.0679 4460	16
17	1.1843 0443	0.8443 7749	18.4304 4314	15.5622 5127	0.0542 5806	0.0642 5806	17
18	1.1961 4748	0.8360 1731	19.6147 4757	16.3982 6858	0.0509 8205	0.0609 8205	18
19	1.2081 0895	0.8277 3992	20.8108 9504	17.2260 0850	0.0480 5175	0.0580 5175	19
20	1.2201 9004	0.8195 4447	22.0190 0399	18.0455 5297	0.0454 1531	0.0554 1531	20
21	1.2323 9194	0.8114 3017	23.2391 9403	18.8569 8313	0.0430 3075	0.0530 3075	21
22	1.2447 1586	0.8033 9621	24.4715 8598	19.6603 7934	0.0408 6372	0.0508 6372	22
23	1.2571 6302	0.7954 4179	25.7163 0183	20.4558 2113	0.0388 8584	0.0488 8584	23
24	1.2697 3465	0.7875 6613	26.9734 6485	21.2433 8726	0.0370 7347	0.0470 7347	24
25	1.2824 3200	0.7797 6844	28.2431 9950	22.0231 5570	0.0354 0675	0.0454 0675	25
26	1.2952 5631	0.7720 4796	29.5256 3150	22.7952 0366	0.0338 6888	0.0438 6888	26
27	1.3082 0888	0.7644 0392	30.8208 8781	23.5596 0759	0.0324 4553	0.0424 4553	27
28	1.3212 9097	0.7568 3557	32.1290 9669	24.3164 4316	0.0311 2444	0.0411 2444	28
29	1.3345 0388	0.7493 4215	33.4503 8766	25.0657 8530	0.0298 9502	0.0398 9502	29
30	1.3478 4892	0.7419 2292	34.7848 9153	25.8077 0822	0.0287 4811	0.0387 4811	30
31	1.3613 2740	0.7345 7715	36.1327 4045	26.5422 8537	0.0276 7573	0.0376 7573	31
32	1.3749 4068	0.7273 0411	37.4940 6785	27.2695 8947	0.0266 7089	0.0366 7089	32
33	1.3886 9009	0.7201 0307	38.8690 0853	27.9896 9255	0.0257 2744	0.0357 2744	33
34	1.4025 7699	0.7129 7334	40.2576 9862	28.7026 6589	0.0248 3997	0.0348 3997	34
35	1.4166 0276	0.7059 1420	41.6602 7560	29.4085 8009	0.0240 0368	0.0340 0368	35
36	1.4307 6878	0.6989 2495	43.0768 7836	30.1075 0504	0.0232 1431	0.0332 1431	36
37	1.4450 7647	0.6920 0490	44.5076 4714	30.7995 0994	0.0224 6805	0.0324 6805	37
38	1.4595 2724	0.6851 5337	45.9527 2361	31.4846 6330	0.0217 6150	0.0317 6150	38
39	1.4741 2251	0.6783 6967	47.4122 5085	32.1630 3298	0.0210 9160	0.0310 9160	39
40	1.4888 6373	0.6716 5314	48.8863 7336	32.8346 8611	0.0204 5560	0.0304 5560	40
41	1.5037 5237	0.6650 0311	50.3752 3709	33.4996 8922	0.0198 5102	0.0298 5102	41
42	1.5187 8989	0.6584 1892	51.8789 8946	34.1581 0814	0.0192 7563	0.0292 7563	42
43	1.5339 7779	0.6518 9992	53.3977 7936	34.8100 0806	0.0187 2737	0.0287 2737	43
44	1.5493 1757	0.6454 4546	54.9317 5715	35.4554 5352	0.0182 0441	0.0282 0441	44
45	1.5648 1075	0.6390 5492	56.4810 7472	36.0945 0844	0.0177 0505	0.0277 0505	45
46	1.5804 5885	0.6327 2764	58.0458 8547	36.7272 3608	0.0172 2775	0.0272 2775	46
47	1.5962 6344	0.6264 6301	59.6263 4432	37.3536 9909	0.0167 7111	0.0267 7111	47
48	1.6122 2608	0.6202 6041	61.2226 0777	37.9739 5949	0.0163 3384	0.0263 3384	48
49	1.6283 4834	0.6141 1921	62.8348 3385	38.5880 7871	0.0159 1474	0.0259 1474	49
50	1.6446 3182	0.6080 3882	64.4631 8218	39.1961 1753	0.0155 1273	0.0255 1273	50

Rate 1¼%	E Compound Amount	F Present Value	G Amount of Annuity	H Present Value of Annuity	I Sinking Fund	J Amortization	
n	$(1+i)^n$	$(1+i)^{-n}$	$S_{\overline{n}|i}$	$A_{\overline{n}|i}$	$1/S_{\overline{n}|i}$	$1/A_{\overline{n}|i}$	n
1	1.0125 0000	0.9876 5432	1.0000 0000	0.9876 5432	1.0000 0000	1.0125 0000	1
2	1.0251 5625	0.9754 6106	2.0125 0000	1.9631 1538	0.4968 9441	0.5093 9441	2
3	1.0379 7070	0.9634 1833	3.0376 5625	2.9265 3371	0.3292 0117	0.3417 0117	3
4	1.0509 4534	0.9515 2428	4.0756 2695	3.8780 5798	0.2453 6102	0.2578 6102	4
5	1.0640 8215	0.9397 7706	5.1265 7229	4.8178 3504	0.1950 6211	0.2075 6211	5
6	1.0773 8318	0.9281 7488	6.1906 5444	5.7460 0992	0.1615 3381	0.1740 3381	6
7	1.0908 5047	0.9167 1593	7.2680 3762	6.6627 2585	0.1375 8872	0.1500 8872	7
8	1.1044 8610	0.9053 9845	8.3588 8809	7.5681 2429	0.1196 3314	0.1321 3314	8
9	1.1182 9218	0.8942 2069	9.4633 7420	8.4623 4498	0.1056 7055	0.1181 7055	9
10	1.1322 7083	0.8831 8093	10.5816 6637	9.3455 2591	0.0945 0307	0.1070 0307	10
11	1.1464 2422	0.8722 7746	11.7139 3720	10.2178 0337	0.0853 6839	0.9078 6839	11
12	1.1607 5452	0.8615 0860	12.8603 6142	11.0793 1197	0.0777 5831	0.0902 5831	12
13	1.1752 6395	0.8508 7269	14.0211 1594	11.9301 8466	0.0713 2100	0.0838 2100	13
14	1.1899 5475	0.8403 6809	15.1963 7988	12.7705 5275	0.0658 0515	0.0783 0515	14
15	1.2048 2918	0.8299 9318	16.3863 3463	13.6005 4592	0.0610 2646	0.0735 2646	15
16	1.2198 8955	0.8197 4635	17.5911 6382	14.4202 9227	0.0568 4672	0.0693 4672	16
17	1.2351 3817	0.8096 2602	18.8110 5336	15.2299 1829	0.0531 6023	0.0656 6023	17
18	1.2505 7739	0.7996 3064	20.0461 9153	16.0295 4893	0.0498 8479	0.0623 8479	18
19	1.2662 0961	0.7897 5866	21.2967 6893	16.8193 0759	0.0469 5548	0.0594 5548	19
20	1.2820 3723	0.7800 0855	22.5629 7854	17.5993 1613	0.0443 2039	0.0568 2039	20
21	1.2980 6270	0.7703 7881	23.8450 1577	18.3696 9495	0.0419 3749	0.0544 3749	21
22	1.3142 8848	0.7608 6796	25.1430 7847	19.1305 6291	0.0397 7238	0.0522 7238	22
23	1.3307 1709	0.7514 7453	26.4573 6695	19.8820 3744	0.0377 9666	0.0502 9666	23
24	1.3473 5105	0.7421 9707	27.7880 8403	20.6242 3451	0.0359 8665	0.0484 8665	24
25	1.3641 9294	0.7330 3414	29.1354 3508	21.3572 6865	0.0343 2247	0.0468 2247	25
26	1.3812 4535	0.7239 8434	30.4996 2802	22.0812 5299	0.0327 8729	0.0452 8729	26
27	1.3985 1092	0.7150 4626	31.8808 7337	22.7962 9925	0.0313 6677	0.0438 6677	27
28	1.4159 9230	0.7062 1853	33.2793 8429	23.5025 1778	0.0300 4863	0.0425 4863	28
29	1.4336 9221	0.6974 9978	34.6953 7659	24.2000 1756	0.0288 2228	0.0413 2228	29
30	1.4516 1336	0.6888 8867	36.1290 6880	24.8889 0623	0.0276 7854	0.0401 7854	30
31	1.4697 5853	0.6803 8387	37.5806 8216	25.5692 9010	0.0266 0942	0.0391 0942	31
32	1.4881 3051	0.6719 8407	39.0504 4069	26.2412 7418	0.0256 0791	0.0381 0791	32
33	1.5067 3214	0.6636 8797	40.5385 7120	26.9049 6215	0.0246 6787	0.0371 6786	33
34	1.5255 6629	0.6554 9429	42.0453 0334	27.5604 5644	0.0237 8387	0.0362 8387	34
35	1.5446 3587	0.6474 0177	43.5708 6963	28.2078 5822	0.0229 5111	0.0354 5111	35
36	1.5639 4382	0.6394 0916	45.1155 0550	28.8472 6737	0.0221 6533	0.0346 6533	36
37	1.5834 9312	0.6315 1522	46.6794 4932	29.4787 8259	0.0214 2270	0.0339 2270	37
38	1.6032 8678	0.6237 1873	48.2629 4243	30.1025 0133	0.0207 1983	0.0332 1983	38
39	1.6233 2787	0.6160 1850	49.8662 2921	30.7185 1983	0.0200 5365	0.0325 5365	39
40	1.6436 1946	0.6084 1334	51.4895 5708	31.3269 3316	0.0194 2141	0.0319 2141	40
41	1.6641 6471	0.6009 0206	53.1331 7654	31.9278 3522	0.0188 2063	0.0313 2063	41
42	1.6849 6677	0.5934 8352	54.7973 4125	32.5213 1874	0.0182 4906	0.0307 4906	42
43	1.7060 2885	0.5861 5656	56.4823 0801	33.1074 7530	0.0177 0466	0.0302 0466	43
44	1.7273 5421	0.5789 2006	58.1883 3687	33.6863 9536	0.0171 8557	0.0296 8557	44
45	1.7489 4614	0.5717 7290	59.9156 9108	34.2581 6825	0.0166 9012	0.0291 9012	45
46	1.7708 0797	0.5647 1397	61.6646 3721	34.8228 8222	0.0162 1675	0.0287 1675	46
47	1.7929 4306	0.5577 4219	63.4354 4518	35.3806 2442	0.0157 6406	0.0282 6406	47
48	1.8153 5485	0.5508 5649	65.2283 8824	35.9314 8091	0.0153 3075	0.0278 3075	48
49	1.8380 4679	0.5440 5579	67.0437 4310	36.4755 3670	0.0149 1564	0.0274 1563	49
50	1.8610 2237	0.5373 3905	68.8817 8989	37.0128 7575	0.0145 1763	0.0270 1763	50

Rate 1½%	E Compound Amount	F Present Value	G Amount of Annuity	H Present Value of Annuity	I Sinking Fund	J Amortization	
n	$(1 + i)^n$	$(1 + i)^{-n}$	$S_{\overline{n}|i}$	$A_{\overline{n}|i}$	$1/S_{\overline{n}|i}$	$1/A_{\overline{n}|i}$	n
1	1.0150 0000	0.9852 2167	1.0000 0000	0.9852 2167	1.0000 0000	1.0150 0000	1
2	1.0302 2500	0.9706 6175	2.0150 0000	1.9558 8342	0.4962 7792	0.5112 7792	2
3	1.0456 7838	0.9563 1699	3.0452 2500	2.9122 0042	0.3283 8296	0.3433 8296	3
4	1.0613 6355	0.9421 8423	4.0909 0338	3.8543 8465	0.2444 4479	0.2594 4479	4
5	1.0772 8400	0.9282 6033	5.1522 6693	4.7826 4497	0.1940 8932	0.2090 8932	5
6	1.0934 4326	0.9145 4219	6.2295 5093	5.6971 8717	0.1605 2521	0.1755 2521	6
7	1.1098 4491	0.9010 2679	7.3229 9419	6.5982 1396	0.1365 5616	0.1515 5616	7
8	1.1264 9259	0.8877 1112	8.4328 3911	7.4859 2508	0.1185 8402	0.1335 8402	8
9	1.1433 8998	0.8745 9224	9.5593 3169	8.3605 1732	0.1046 0982	0.1196 0982	9
10	1.1605 4083	0.8616 6723	10.7027 2167	9.2221 8455	0.0934 3418	0.1084 3418	10
11	1.1779 4894	0.8489 3323	11.8632 6249	10.0711 1779	0.0842 9384	0.0992 9384	11
12	1.1956 1817	0.8363 8742	13.0412 1143	10.9075 0521	0.0766 7999	0.0916 7999	12
13	1.2135 5244	0.8240 2702	14.2368 2960	11.7315 3222	0.0702 4036	0.0852 4036	13
14	1.2317 5573	0.8118 4928	15.4503 8205	12.5433 8150	0.0647 2332	0.0797 2332	14
15	1.2502 3207	0.7998 5150	16.6821 3778	13.3432 3301	0.0599 4436	0.0749 4436	15
16	1.2689 8555	0.7880 3104	17.9323 6984	14.1312 6405	0.0557 6508	0.0707 6508	16
17	1.2880 2033	0.7763 8526	19.2013 5539	14.9076 4931	0.0520 7966	0.0670 7966	17
18	1.3073 4064	0.7649 1159	20.4893 7572	15.6725 6089	0.0488 0578	0.0638 0578	18
19	1.3269 5075	0.7536 0747	21.7967 1636	16.4261 6837	0.0458 7847	0.0608 7847	19
20	1.3468 5501	0.7424 7042	23.1236 6710	17.1686 3879	0.0432 4574	0.0582 4574	20
21	1.3670 5783	0.7314 9795	24.4705 2211	17.9001 3673	0.0408 6550	0.0558 6550	21
22	1.3875 6370	0.7206 8763	25.8375 7994	18.6208 2437	0.0387 0332	0.0537 0332	22
23	1.4083 7715	0.7100 3708	27.2251 4364	19.3308 6145	0.0367 3075	0.0517 3075	23
24	1.4295 0281	0.6995 4392	28.6335 2080	20.0304 0537	0.0349 2410	0.0499 2410	24
25	1.4509 4535	0.6892 0583	30.0630 2361	20.7196 1120	0.0332 6345	0.0482 6345	25
26	1.4727 0953	0.6790 2052	31.5139 6896	21.3986 3172	0.0317 3196	0.0467 3196	26
27	1.4948 0018	0.6689 8574	32.9866 7850	22.0676 1746	0.0303 1527	0.0453 1527	27
28	1.5172 2218	0.6590 9925	34.4814 7867	22.7267 1671	0.0290 0108	0.0440 0108	28
29	1.5399 8051	0.6493 5887	35.9987 0085	23.3760 7558	0.0277 7878	0.0427 7878	29
30	1.5630 8022	0.6397 6243	37.5386 8137	24.0158 3801	0.0266 3919	0.0416 3919	30
31	1.5865 2642	0.6303 0781	39.1017 6159	24.6461 4582	0.0255 7430	0.0405 7430	31
32	1.6103 2432	0.6209 9292	40.6882 8801	25.2671 3874	0.0245 7710	0.0395 7710	32
33	1.6344 7918	0.6118 1568	42.2986 1233	25.8789 5442	0.0236 4144	0.0386 4144	33
34	1.6589 9637	0.6027 7407	43.9330 9152	26.4817 2849	0.0227 6189	0.0377 6189	34
35	1.6838 8132	0.5938 6608	45.5920 8789	27.0755 9458	0.0219 3363	0.0369 3363	35
36	1.7091 3954	0.5850 8974	47.2759 6921	27.6606 8431	0.0211 5240	0.0361 5240	36
37	1.7347 7663	0.5764 4309	48.9851 0874	28.2371 2740	0.0204 1437	0.0354 1437	37
38	1.7607 9828	0.5679 2423	50.7198 8538	28.8050 5163	0.0197 1613	0.0347 1613	38
39	1.7872 1025	0.5595 3126	52.4806 8366	29.3645 8288	0.0190 5463	0.0340 5463	39
40	1.8140 1841	0.5512 6232	54.2678 9391	29.9158 4520	0.0184 2710	0.0334 2710	40
41	1.8412 2868	0.5431 1559	56.0819 1232	30.4589 6079	0.0178 3106	0.0328 3106	41
42	1.8688 4712	0.5350 8925	57.9231 4100	30.9940 5004	0.0172 6426	0.0322 6426	42
43	1.8968 7982	0.5271 8153	59.7919 8812	31.5212 3157	0.0167 2465	0.0317 2465	43
44	1.9253 3302	0.5193 9067	61.6888 6794	32.0406 2223	0.0162 1038	0.0312 1038	44
45	1.9542 1301	0.5117 1494	63.6142 0096	32.5523 3718	0.0157 1976	0.0307 1976	45
46	1.9835 2621	0.5041 5265	65.5684 1398	33.0564 8983	0.0152 5125	0.0302 5125	46
47	2.0132 7910	0.4967 0212	67.5519 4018	33.5531 9195	0.0148 0342	0.0298 0342	47
48	2.0434 7829	0.4893 6170	69.5652 1929	34.0425 5365	0.0143 7500	0.0293 7500	48
49	2.0741 3046	0.4821 2975	71.6086 9758	34.5246 8339	0.0139 6478	0.0289 6478	49
50	2.1052 4242	0.4750 0468	73.6828 2804	34.9996 8807	0.0135 7168	0.0285 7168	50

Rate 1¾%	E Compound Amount	F Present Value	G Amount of Annuity	H Present Value of Annuity	I Sinking Fund	J Amortization	
n	$(1 + i)^n$	$(1 + i)^{-n}$	$S_{\overline{n}|i}$	$A_{\overline{n}|i}$	$1/S_{\overline{n}|i}$	$1/A_{\overline{n}|i}$	n
1	1.0175 0000	0.9828 0098	1.0000 0000	0.9828 0098	1.0000 0000	1.0175 0000	1
2	1.0353 0625	0.9658 9777	2.0175 0000	1.9486 9875	0.4956 6295	0.5131 6295	2
3	1.0534 2411	0.9492 8528	3.0528 0625	2.8979 8403	0.3275 6746	0.3450 6746	3
4	1.0718 5903	0.9329 5851	4.1062 3036	3.8309 4254	0.2435 3237	0.2610 3237	4
5	1.0906 1656	0.9169 1254	5.1780 8939	4.7478 5508	0.1931 2142	0.2106 2142	5
6	1.1097 0235	0.9011 4254	6.2687 0596	5.6489 9762	0.1595 2256	0.1770 2256	6
7	1.1291 2215	0.8856 4378	7.3784 0831	6.5346 4139	0.1355 3059	0.1530 3059	7
8	1.1488 8178	0.8704 1157	8.5075 3045	7.4050 5297	0.1175 4292	0.1350 4292	8
9	1.1689 8721	0.8554 4135	9.6564 1224	8.2604 9432	0.1035 5813	0.1210 5813	9
10	1.1894 4449	0.8407 2860	10.8253 9945	9.1012 2291	0.0923 7534	0.1098 7534	10
11	1.2102 5977	0.8262 6889	12.0148 4394	9.9274 9181	0.0832 3038	0.1007 3038	11
12	1.2314 3931	0.8120 5788	13.2251 0371	10.7395 4969	0.0756 1378	0.0931 1377	12
13	1.2529 8950	0.7980 9128	14.4565 4303	11.5376 4097	0.0691 7283	0.0866 7283	13
14	1.2749 1682	0.7843 6490	15.7095 3253	12.3220 0587	0.0636 5562	0.0811 5562	14
15	1.2972 2786	0.7708 7459	16.9844 4935	13.0928 8046	0.0588 7739	0.0763 7739	15
16	1.3199 2935	0.7576 1631	18.2816 7721	13.8504 9677	0.0546 9958	0.0721 9958	16
17	1.3430 2811	0.7445 8605	19.6016 0656	14.5950 8282	0.0510 1623	0.0685 1623	17
18	1.3665 3111	0.7317 7990	20.9446 3468	15.3268 6272	0.0477 4492	0.0652 4492	18
19	1.3904 4540	0.7191 9401	22.3111 6578	16.0460 5673	0.0448 2061	0.0623 2061	19
20	1.4147 7820	0.7068 2458	23.7016 1119	16.7528 8130	0.0421 9122	0.0596 9122	20
21	1.4395 3681	0.6946 6789	25.1163 8938	17.4475 4919	0.0398 1464	0.0573 1464	21
22	1.4647 2871	0.6827 2028	26.5559 2620	18.1302 6948	0.0376 5638	0.0551 5638	22
23	1.4903 6146	0.6709 7817	28.0206 5490	18.8012 4764	0.0356 8796	0.0531 8796	23
24	1.5164 4279	0.6594 3800	29.5110 1637	19.4606 8565	0.0338 8565	0.0513 8565	24
25	1.5429 8054	0.6480 9632	31.0274 5915	20.1087 8196	0.0322 2952	0.0497 2952	25
26	1.5699 8269	0.6369 4970	32.5704 3969	20.7457 3166	0.0307 0269	0.0482 0269	26
27	1.5974 5739	0.6259 9479	34.1404 2238	21.3717 2644	0.0292 9079	0.0467 9079	27
28	1.6254 1290	0.6152 2829	35.7378 7977	21.9869 5474	0.0279 8151	0.0454 8151	28
29	1.6538 5762	0.6046 4697	37.3632 9267	22.5916 0171	0.0267 6424	0.0442 6424	29
30	1.6828 0013	0.5942 4764	39.0171 5029	23.1858 4934	0.0256 2975	0.0431 2975	30
31	1.7122 4913	0.5840 2716	40.6999 5042	23.7698 7650	0.0245 7005	0.0420 7005	31
32	1.7422 1349	0.5739 8247	42.4121 9955	24.3438 5897	0.0235 7812	0.0410 7812	32
33	1.7727 0223	0.5641 1053	44.1544 1305	24.9079 6951	0.0226 4779	0.0401 4779	33
34	1.8037 2452	0.5544 0839	45.9271 1527	25.4623 7789	0.0217 7363	0.0392 7363	34
35	1.8352 8970	0.5448 7311	47.7308 3979	26.0072 5100	0.0209 5082	0.0384 5082	35
36	1.8674 0727	0.5355 0183	49.5661 2949	26.5427 5283	0.0201 7507	0.0376 7507	36
37	1.9000 8689	0.5262 9172	51.4335 3675	27.0690 4455	0.0194 4257	0.0369 4257	37
38	1.9333 3841	0.5172 4002	53.3336 2365	27.5862 8457	0.0187 4990	0.0362 4990	38
39	1.9671 7184	0.5083 4400	55.2669 6206	28.0946 2857	0.0180 9399	0.0355 9399	39
40	2.0015 9734	0.4996 0098	57.2341 3390	28.5942 2955	0.0174 7209	0.0349 7209	40
41	2.0366 2530	0.4910 0834	59.2357 3124	29.0852 3789	0.0168 8170	0.0343 8170	41
42	2.0722 6624	0.4825 6348	61.2723 5654	29.5678 0135	0.0163 2057	0.0338 2057	42
43	2.1085 3090	0.4742 6386	63.3446 2278	30.0420 6522	0.0157 8666	0.0332 8666	43
44	2.1454 3019	0.4661 0699	65.4531 5367	30.5081 7221	0.0152 7810	0.0327 7810	44
45	2.1829 7522	0.4580 9040	67.5985 8386	30.9662 6261	0.0147 9321	0.0322 9321	45
46	2.2211 7728	0.4502 1170	69.7815 5908	31.4164 7431	0.0143 3043	0.0318 3043	46
47	2.2600 4789	0.4424 6850	72.0027 3637	31.8589 4281	0.0138 8836	0.0313 8836	47
48	2.2995 9872	0.4348 5848	74.2627 8425	32.2938 0129	0.0134 6570	0.0309 6569	48
49	2.3398 4170	0.4273 7934	76.5623 8298	32.7211 8063	0.0130 6124	0.0305 6124	49
50	2.3807 8893	0.4200 2883	78.9022 2468	33.1412 0946	0.0126 7391	0.0301 7391	50

Rate 2%	E Compound Amount	F Present Value	G Amount of Annuity	H Present Value of Annuity	I Sinking Fund	J Amortization	
n	$(1 + i)^n$	$(1 + i)^{-n}$	$S_{\overline{n}|i}$	$A_{\overline{n}|i}$	$1/S_{\overline{n}|i}$	$1/A_{\overline{n}|i}$	n
1	1.0200 0000	0.9803 9216	1.0000 0000	0.9803 9216	1.0000 0000	1.0200 0000	1
2	1.0404 0000	0.9611 6878	2.0200 0000	1.9415 6094	0.4950 4951	0.5150 4950	2
3	1.0612 0800	0.9423 2233	3.0604 0000	2.8838 8327	0.3267 5467	0.3467 5467	3
4	1.0824 3216	0.9238 4543	4.1216 0800	3.8077 2870	0.2426 2375	0.2626 2375	4
5	1.1040 8080	0.9057 3081	5.2040 4016	4.7134 5951	0.1921 5839	0.2121 5839	5
6	1.1261 6242	0.8879 7138	6.3081 2096	5.6014 3089	0.1585 2581	0.1785 2581	6
7	1.1486 8567	0.8705 6018	7.4342 8338	6.4719 9107	0.1345 1196	0.1545 1196	7
8	1.1716 5938	0.8534 9037	8.5829 6905	7.3254 8144	0.1165 0980	0.1365 0980	8
9	1.1950 9257	0.8367 5527	9.7546 2843	8.1622 3671	0.1025 1544	0.1225 1544	9
10	1.2189 9442	0.8203 4830	10.9497 2100	8.9825 8501	0.0913 2653	0.1113 2653	10
11	1.2433 7431	0.8042 6304	12.1687 1542	9.7868 4805	0.0821 7794	0.1021 7794	11
12	1.2682 4179	0.7884 9318	13.4120 8973	10.5753 4122	0.0745 5960	0.0945 5960	12
13	1.2936 0663	0.7730 3253	14.6803 3152	11.3483 7375	0.0681 1835	0.0881 1835	13
14	1.3194 7876	0.7578 7502	15.9739 3815	12.1062 4877	0.0626 0197	0.0826 0197	14
15	1.3458 6834	0.7430 1473	17.2934 1692	12.8492 6350	0.0578 2547	0.0778 2547	15
16	1.3727 8571	0.7284 4581	18.6392 8525	13.5777 0931	0.0536 5013	0.0736 5013	16
17	1.4002 4142	0.7141 6256	20.0120 7096	14.2918 7188	0.0499 6984	0.0699 6984	17
18	1.4282 4625	0.7001 5937	21.4123 1238	14.9920 3125	0.0467 0210	0.0667 0210	18
19	1.4568 1117	0.6864 3076	22.8405 5863	15.6784 6201	0.0437 8177	0.0637 8177	19
20	1.4859 4740	0.6729 7133	24.2973 6980	16.3514 3334	0.0411 5672	0.0611 5672	20
21	1.5156 6634	0.6597 7582	25.7833 1719	17.0112 0916	0.0387 8477	0.0587 8477	21
22	1.5459 7967	0.6468 3904	27.2989 8354	17.6580 4820	0.0366 3140	0.0566 3140	22
23	1.5768 9926	0.6341 5592	28.8449 6321	18.2922 0412	0.0346 6810	0.0546 6810	23
24	1.6084 3725	0.6217 2149	30.4218 6247	18.9139 2560	0.0328 7110	0.0528 7110	24
25	1.6406 0599	0.6095 3087	32.0302 9972	19.5234 5647	0.0312 2044	0.0512 2044	25
26	1.6734 1811	0.5975 7928	33.6709 0572	20.1210 3576	0.0296 9923	0.0496 9923	26
27	1.7068 8648	0.5858 6204	35.3443 2383	20.7068 9780	0.0282 9309	0.0482 9309	27
28	1.7410 2421	0.5743 7455	37.0512 1031	21.2812 7236	0.0269 8967	0.0469 8967	28
29	1.7758 4469	0.5631 1231	38.7922 3451	21.8443 8466	0.0257 7836	0.0457 7836	29
30	1.8113 6158	0.5520 7089	40.5680 7921	22.3964 5555	0.0246 4992	0.0446 4992	30
31	1.8475 8882	0.5412 4597	42.3794 4079	22.9377 0152	0.0235 9635	0.0435 9635	31
32	1.8845 4059	0.5306 3330	44.2270 2961	23.4683 3482	0.0226 1061	0.0426 1061	32
33	1.9222 3140	0.5202 2873	46.1115 7020	23.9885 6355	0.0216 8653	0.0416 8653	33
34	1.9606 7603	0.5100 2817	48.0338 0160	24.4985 9172	0.0208 1867	0.0408 1867	34
35	1.9998 8955	0.5000 2761	49.9944 7763	24.9986 1933	0.0200 0221	0.0400 0221	35
36	2.0398 8734	0.4902 2315	51.9943 6719	25.4888 4248	0.0192 3285	0.0392 3285	36
37	2.0806 8509	0.4806 1093	54.0342 5453	25.9694 5341	0.0185 0678	0.0385 0678	37
38	2.1222 9879	0.4711 8719	56.1149 3962	26.4406 4060	0.0178 2057	0.0378 2057	38
39	2.1647 4477	0.4619 4822	58.2372 3841	26.9025 8883	0.0171 7114	0.0371 7114	39
40	2.2080 3966	0.4528 9042	60.4019 8318	27.3554 7924	0.0165 5575	0.0365 5575	40
41	2.2522 0046	0.4440 1021	62.6100 2284	27.7994 8945	0.0159 7188	0.0359 7188	41
42	2.2972 4447	0.4353 0413	64.8622 2330	28.2347 9358	0.0154 1729	0.0354 1729	42
43	2.3431 8936	0.4267 6875	67.1594 6777	28.6615 6233	0.0148 8993	0.0348 8993	43
44	2.3900 5314	0.4184 0074	69.5026 5712	29.0799 6307	0.0143 8794	0.0343 8794	44
45	2.4378 5421	0.4101 9680	71.8927 1027	29.4901 5987	0.0139 0962	0.0339 0962	45
46	2.4866 1129	0.4021 5373	74.3305 6447	29.8923 1360	0.0134 5342	0.0334 5342	46
47	2.5363 4352	0.3942 6836	76.8171 7576	30.2865 8196	0.0130 1792	0.0330 1792	47
48	2.5870 7039	0.3865 3761	79.3535 1927	30.6731 1957	0.0126 0184	0.0326 0184	48
49	2.6388 1179	0.3789 5844	81.9405 8966	31.0520 7801	0.0122 0396	0.0322 0396	49
50	2.6915 8803	0.3715 2788	84.5794 0145	31.4236 0589	0.0118 2321	0.0318 2321	50

Rate 2¼%	E Compound Amount	F Present Value	G Amount of Annuity	H Present Value of Annuity	I Sinking Fund	J Amortization	
n	$(1 + i)^n$	$(1 + i)^{-n}$	$S_{\overline{n}|i}$	$A_{\overline{n}|i}$	$1/S_{\overline{n}|i}$	$1/A_{\overline{n}|i}$	n
1	1.0225 0000	0.9779 9511	1.0000 0000	0.9779 9511	1.0000 0000	1.0225 0000	1
2	1.0455 0625	0.9564 7444	2.0225 0000	1.9344 6955	0.4944 3758	0.5169 3758	2
3	1.0690 3014	0.9354 2732	3.0680 0625	2.8698 9687	0.3259 4458	0.3484 4458	3
4	1.0930 8332	0.9148 4335	4.1370 3639	3.7847 4021	0.2417 1893	0.2642 1893	4
5	1.1176 7769	0.8947 1232	5.2301 1971	4.6794 5253	0.1912 0021	0.2137 0021	5
6	1.1428 2544	0.8750 2427	6.3477 9740	5.5544 7680	0.1575 3496	0.1800 3496	6
7	1.1685 3901	0.8557 6946	7.4906 2284	6.4102 4626	0.1335 0025	0.1560 0025	7
8	1.1948 3114	0.8369 3835	8.6591 6186	7.2471 8461	0.1154 8462	0.1379 8462	8
9	1.2217 1484	0.8185 2161	9.8539 9300	8.0657 0622	0.1014 8170	0.1239 8170	9
10	1.2492 0343	0.8005 1013	11.0757 0784	8.8662 1635	0.0902 8768	0.1127 8768	10
11	1.2773 1050	0.7828 9499	12.3249 1127	9.6491 1134	0.0811 3649	0.1036 3649	11
12	1.3060 4999	0.7656 6748	13.6022 2177	10.4147 7882	0.0735 1740	0.0960 1740	12
13	1.3354 3611	0.7488 1905	14.9082 7176	11.1635 9787	0.0670 7686	0.0895 7686	13
14	1.3654 8343	0.7323 4137	16.2437 0788	11.8959 3924	0.0615 6230	0.0840 6230	14
15	1.3962 0680	0.7162 2628	17.6091 9130	12.6121 6551	0.0567 8853	0.0792 8852	15
16	1.4276 2146	0.7004 6580	19.0053 9811	13.3126 3131	0.0526 1663	0.0751 1663	16
17	1.4597 4294	0.6850 5212	20.4330 1957	13.9976 8343	0.0489 4039	0.0714 4039	17
18	1.4925 8716	0.6699 7763	21.8927 6251	14.6676 6106	0.0456 7720	0.0681 7720	18
19	1.5261 7037	0.6552 3484	23.3853 4966	15.3228 9590	0.0427 6182	0.0652 6182	19
20	1.5605 0920	0.6408 1647	24.9115 2003	15.9637 1237	0.0401 4207	0.0626 4207	20
21	1.5956 2066	0.6267 1538	26.4720 2923	16.5904 2775	0.0377 7572	0.0602 7572	21
22	1.6315 2212	0.6129 2457	28.0676 4989	17.2033 5232	0.0356 2821	0.0581 2821	22
23	1.6682 3137	0.5994 3724	29.6991 7201	17.8027 8955	0.0336 7097	0.0561 7097	23
24	1.7057 6658	0.5862 4668	31.3674 0338	18.3890 3624	0.0318 8023	0.0543 8023	24
25	1.7441 4632	0.5733 4639	33.0731 6996	18.9623 8263	0.0302 3599	0.0527 3599	25
26	1.7833 8962	0.5607 2997	34.8173 1628	19.5231 1260	0.0287 2134	0.0512 2134	26
27	1.8235 1588	0.5483 9117	36.6007 0590	20.0715 0376	0.0273 2188	0.0498 2188	27
28	1.8645 4499	0.5363 2388	38.4242 2178	20.6078 2764	0.0260 2525	0.0485 2525	28
29	1.9064 9725	0.5245 2213	40.2887 6677	21.1323 4877	0.0248 2081	0.0473 2081	29
30	1.9493 9344	0.5129 8008	42.1952 6402	21.6453 2985	0.0236 9934	0.0461 9934	30
31	1.9932 5479	0.5016 9201	44.1446 5746	22.1470 2186	0.0226 5280	0.0451 5280	31
32	2.0381 0303	0.4906 5233	46.1379 1226	22.6376 7419	0.0216 7415	0.0441 7415	32
33	2.0839 6034	0.4798 5558	48.1760 1528	23.1175 2977	0.0207 5722	0.0432 5722	33
34	2.1308 4945	0.4692 9641	50.2599 7563	23.5868 2618	0.0198 9655	0.0423 9655	34
35	2.1787 9356	0.4589 6960	52.3908 2508	24.0457 9577	0.0190 8731	0.0415 8731	35
36	2.2278 1642	0.4488 7002	54.5696 1864	24.4946 6579	0.0183 2522	0.0408 2522	36
37	2.2779 4229	0.4389 9268	56.7974 3506	24.9336 5848	0.0176 0643	0.0401 0643	37
38	2.3291 9599	0.4293 3270	59.0753 7735	25.3629 9118	0.0169 2753	0.0394 2753	38
39	2.3816 0290	0.4198 8528	61.4045 7334	25.7828 7646	0.0162 8543	0.0387 8543	39
40	2.4351 8897	0.4106 4575	63.7861 7624	26.1935 2221	0.0156 7738	0.0381 7738	40
41	2.4899 8072	0.4016 0954	66.2213 6521	26.5951 3174	0.0151 0087	0.0376 0087	41
42	2.5460 0528	0.3927 7216	68.7113 4592	26.9879 0390	0.0145 5364	0.0370 5364	42
43	2.6032 9040	0.3841 2925	71.2573 5121	27.3720 3316	0.0140 3364	0.0365 3364	43
44	2.6618 6444	0.3756 7653	73.8606 4161	27.7477 0969	0.0135 3901	0.0360 3901	44
45	2.7217 5639	0.3674 0981	76.5225 0605	28.1151 1950	0.0130 6805	0.0355 6805	45
46	2.7829 9590	0.3593 2500	79.2442 6243	28.4744 4450	0.0126 1921	0.0351 1921	46
47	2.8456 1331	0.3514 1809	82.0272 5834	28.8258 6259	0.0121 9107	0.0346 9107	47
48	2.9096 3961	0.3436 8518	84.8728 7165	29.1695 4777	0.0117 8233	0.0342 8233	48
49	2.9751 0650	0.3361 2242	87.7825 1126	29.5056 7019	0.0113 9179	0.0338 9179	49
50	3.0420 4640	0.3287 2608	90.7576 1776	29.8343 9627	0.0110 1836	0.0335 1836	50

Rate 2½%	E Compound Amount	F Present Value	G Amount of Annuity	H Present Value of Annuity	I Sinking Fund	J Amortization	
n	$(1+i)^n$	$(1+i)^{-n}$	$S_{\overline{n}|i}$	$A_{\overline{n}|i}$	$1/S_{\overline{n}|i}$	$1/A_{\overline{n}|i}$	n
1	1.0250 0000	0.9756 0976	1.0000 0000	0.9756 0976	1.0000 0000	1.0250 0000	1
2	1.0506 2500	0.9518 1440	2.0250 0000	1.9274 2415	0.4938 2716	0.5188 2716	2
3	1.0768 9063	0.9285 9941	3.0756 2500	2.8560 2356	0.3251 3717	0.3501 3717	3
4	1.1038 1289	0.9059 5064	4.1525 1563	3.7619 7421	0.2408 1788	0.2658 1788	4
5	1.1314 0821	0.8838 5429	5.2563 2852	4.6458 2850	0.1902 4686	0.2152 4686	5
6	1.1596 9342	0.8622 9687	6.3877 3673	5.5081 2536	0.1565 4997	0.1815 4997	6
7	1.1886 8575	0.8412 6524	7.5474 3015	6.3493 9060	0.1324 9543	0.1574 9543	7
8	1.2184 0290	0.8207 4657	8.7361 1590	7.1701 3717	0.1144 6735	0.1394 6735	8
9	1.2488 6297	0.8007 2836	9.9545 1880	7.9708 6553	0.1004 5689	0.1254 5689	9
10	1.2800 8454	0.7811 9840	11.2033 8177	8.7520 6393	0.0892 5876	0.1142 5876	10
11	1.3120 8666	0.7621 4478	12.4834 6631	9.5142 0871	0.0801 0596	0.1051 0596	11
12	1.3448 8882	0.7435 5589	13.7955 5297	10.2577 6460	0.0724 8713	0.0974 8713	12
13	1.3785 1104	0.7254 2038	15.1404 4179	10.9831 8497	0.0660 4827	0.0910 4827	13
14	1.4129 7382	0.7077 2720	16.5189 5284	11.6909 1217	0.0605 3652	0.0855 3652	14
15	1.4482 9817	0.6904 6556	17.9319 2666	12.3813 7773	0.0557 6646	0.0807 6646	15
16	1.4845 0562	0.6736 2493	19.3802 2483	13.0550 0266	0.0515 9899	0.0765 9899	16
17	1.5216 1826	0.6571 9506	20.8647 3045	13.7121 9772	0.0479 2777	0.0729 2777	17
18	1.5596 5872	0.6411 6591	22.3863 4871	14.3533 6363	0.0446 7008	0.0696 7008	18
19	1.5986 5019	0.6255 2772	23.9460 0743	14.9788 9134	0.0417 6062	0.0667 6062	19
20	1.6386 1644	0.6102 7094	25.5446 5761	15.5891 6229	0.0391 4713	0.0641 4713	20
21	1.6795 8185	0.5953 8629	27.1832 7405	16.1845 4857	0.0367 8733	0.0617 8733	21
22	1.7215 7140	0.5808 6467	28.8628 5590	16.7654 1324	0.0346 4661	0.0596 4661	22
23	1.7646 1068	0.5666 9724	30.5844 2730	17.3321 1048	0.0326 9638	0.0576 9638	23
24	1.8087 2595	0.5528 7535	32.3490 3798	17.8849 8583	0.0309 1282	0.0559 1282	24
25	1.8539 4410	0.5393 9059	34.1577 6393	18.4243 7642	0.0292 7592	0.0542 7592	25
26	1.9002 9270	0.5262 3472	36.0117 0803	18.9506 1114	0.0277 6875	0.0527 6875	26
27	1.9478 0002	0.5133 9973	37.9120 0073	19.4640 1087	0.0263 7687	0.0513 7687	27
28	1.9964 9502	0.5008 7778	39.8598 0075	19.9648 8866	0.0250 8793	0.0500 8793	28
29	2.0464 0739	0.4886 6125	41.8562 9577	20.4535 4991	0.0238 9127	0.0488 9127	29
30	2.0975 6758	0.4767 4269	43.9027 0316	20.9302 9259	0.0227 7764	0.0477 7764	30
31	2.1500 0677	0.4651 1481	46.0002 7074	21.3954 0741	0.0217 3900	0.0467 3900	31
32	2.2037 5694	0.4537 7055	48.1502 7751	21.8491 7796	0.0207 6831	0.0457 6831	32
33	2.2588 5086	0.4427 0298	50.3540 3445	22.2918 8094	0.0198 5938	0.0448 5938	33
34	2.3153 2213	0.4319 0534	52.6128 8531	22.7237 8628	0.0190 0675	0.0440 0675	34
35	2.3732 0519	0.4213 7107	54.9282 0744	23.1451 5734	0.0182 0558	0.0432 0558	35
36	2.4325 3532	0.4110 9372	57.3014 1263	23.5562 5107	0.0174 5158	0.0424 5158	36
37	2.4933 4870	0.4010 6705	59.7339 4794	23.9573 1812	0.0167 4090	0.0417 4090	37
38	2.5556 8242	0.3912 8492	62.2272 9664	24.3486 0304	0.0160 7012	0.0410 7012	38
39	2.6195 7448	0.3817 4139	64.7829 7906	24.7303 4443	0.0154 3615	0.0404 3615	39
40	2.6850 6384	0.3724 3062	67.4025 5354	25.1027 7505	0.0148 3623	0.0398 3623	40
41	2.7521 9043	0.3633 4695	70.0876 1737	25.4661 2200	0.0142 6786	0.0392 6786	41
42	2.8209 9520	0.3544 8483	72.8398 0781	25.8206 0683	0.0137 2876	0.0387 2876	42
43	2.8915 2008	0.3458 3886	75.6608 0300	26.1664 4569	0.0132 1688	0.0382 1688	43
44	2.9638 0808	0.3374 0376	78.5523 2308	26.5038 4945	0.0127 3037	0.0377 3037	44
45	3.0379 0328	0.3291 7440	81.5161 3116	26.8330 2386	0.0122 6751	0.0372 6751	45
46	3.1138 5086	0.3211 4576	84.5540 3443	27.1541 6962	0.0118 2676	0.0368 2676	46
47	3.1916 9713	0.3133 1294	87.6678 8530	27.4674 8255	0.0114 0669	0.0364 0669	47
48	3.2714 8956	0.3056 7116	90.8595 8243	27.7731 5371	0.0110 0599	0.0360 0599	48
49	3.3532 7680	0.2982 1576	94.1310 7199	28.0713 6947	0.0106 2348	0.0356 2348	49
50	3.4371 0872	0.2909 4221	97.4843 4879	28.3623 1168	0.0102 5806	0.0352 5806	50

Rate 2¾%	E Compound Amount	F Present Value	G Amount of Annuity	H Present Value of Annuity	I Sinking Fund	J Amortization	
n	$(1+i)^n$	$(1+i)^{-n}$	$S_{\overline{n}|i}$	$A_{\overline{n}|i}$	$1/S_{\overline{n}|i}$	$1/A_{\overline{n}|i}$	n
1	1.0275 0000	0.9732 3601	1.0000 0000	0.9732 3601	1.0000 0000	1.0275 0000	1
2	1.0557 5625	0.9471 8833	2.0275 0000	1.9204 2434	0.4932 1825	0.5207 1825	2
3	1.0847 8955	0.9218 3779	3.0832 5625	2.8422 6213	0.3243 3243	0.3518 3243	3
4	1.1146 2126	0.8971 6573	4.1680 4580	3.7394 2787	0.2399 2059	0.2674 2059	4
5	1.1452 7334	0.8731 5400	5.2826 6706	4.6125 8186	0.1892 9832	0.2167 9832	5
6	1.1767 6836	0.8497 8491	6.4279 4040	5.4623 6678	0.1555 7083	0.1830 7083	6
7	1.2091 2949	0.8270 4128	7.6047 0876	6.2894 0806	0.1314 9748	0.1589 9747	7
8	1.2423 8055	0.8049 0635	8.8138 3825	7.0943 1441	0.1134 5795	0.1409 5795	8
9	1.2765 4602	0.7833 6385	10.0562 1880	7.8776 7826	0.0994 4095	0.1269 4095	9
10	1.3116 5103	0.7623 9791	11.3327 6482	8.6400 7616	0.0882 3972	0.1157 3972	10
11	1.3477 2144	0.7419 9310	12.6444 1585	9.3820 6926	0.0790 8629	0.1065 8629	11
12	1.3847 8378	0.7221 3440	13.9921 3729	10.1042 0366	0.0714 6871	0.0989 6871	12
13	1.4228 6533	0.7028 0720	15.3769 2107	10.8070 1086	0.0650 3252	0.0925 3252	13
14	1.4619 9413	0.6839 9728	16.7997 8639	11.4910 0814	0.0595 2457	0.0870 2457	14
15	1.5021 9896	0.6656 9078	18.2617 8052	12.1566 9892	0.0547 5917	0.0822 5917	15
16	1.5435 0944	0.6478 7424	19.7639 7948	12.8045 7315	0.0505 9710	0.0780 9710	16
17	1.5859 5595	0.6305 3454	21.3074 8892	13.4351 0769	0.0469 3186	0.0744 3186	17
18	1.6295 6973	0.6136 5892	22.8934 4487	14.0487 6661	0.0436 8063	0.0711 8063	18
19	1.6743 8290	0.5972 3496	24.5230 1460	14.6460 0157	0.0407 7802	0.0682 7802	19
20	1.7204 2843	0.5812 5057	26.1973 9750	15.2272 5213	0.0381 7173	0.0656 7173	20
21	1.7677 4021	0.5656 9398	27.9178 2593	15.7929 4612	0.0358 1941	0.0633 1941	21
22	1.8163 5307	0.5505 5375	29.6855 6615	16.3434 9987	0.0336 8640	0.0611 8640	22
23	1.8663 0278	0.5358 1874	31.5019 1921	16.8793 1861	0.0317 4410	0.0592 4410	23
24	1.9176 2610	0.5214 7809	33.3682 2199	17.4007 9670	0.0299 6863	0.0574 6863	24
25	1.9703 6082	0.5075 2126	35.2858 4810	17.9083 1795	0.0283 3997	0.0558 3997	25
26	2.0245 4575	0.4939 3796	37.2562 0892	18.4022 5592	0.0268 4116	0.0543 4116	26
27	2.0802 2075	0.4807 1821	39.2807 5467	18.8829 7413	0.0254 5776	0.0529 5776	27
28	2.1374 2682	0.4678 5227	41.3609 7542	19.3508 2640	0.0241 7738	0.0516 7738	28
29	2.1962 0606	0.4553 3068	43.4984 0224	19.8061 5708	0.0229 8935	0.0504 8935	29
30	2.2566 0173	0.4431 4421	45.6946 0830	20.2493 0130	0.0218 8442	0.0493 8442	30
31	2.3186 5828	0.4312 8391	47.9512 1003	20.6805 8520	0.0208 5453	0.0483 5453	31
32	2.3824 2138	0.4197 4103	50.2698 6831	21.1003 2623	0.0198 9263	0.0473 9263	32
33	2.4479 3797	0.4085 0708	52.6522 8969	21.5088 3332	0.0189 9253	0.0464 9253	33
34	2.5152 5626	0.3975 7380	55.1002 2765	21.9064 0712	0.0181 4875	0.0456 4875	34
35	2.5844 2581	0.3869 3314	57.6154 8391	22.2933 4026	0.0173 5645	0.0448 5645	35
36	2.6554 9752	0.3765 7727	60.1999 0972	22.6699 1753	0.0166 1132	0.0441 1132	36
37	2.7285 2370	0.3664 9856	62.8554 0724	23.0364 1609	0.0159 0953	0.0434 0953	37
38	2.8035 5810	0.3566 8959	65.5839 3094	23.3931 0568	0.0152 4764	0.0427 4764	38
39	2.8806 5595	0.3471 4316	68.3874 8904	23.7402 4884	0.0146 2256	0.0421 2256	39
40	2.9598 7399	0.3378 5222	71.2681 4499	24.0781 0106	0.0140 3151	0.0415 3151	40
41	3.0412 7052	0.3288 0995	74.2280 1898	24.4069 1101	0.0134 7200	0.0409 7200	41
42	3.1249 0546	0.3200 0968	77.2692 8950	24.7269 2069	0.0129 4175	0.0404 4175	42
43	3.2108 4036	0.3114 4495	80.3941 9496	25.0383 6563	0.0124 3871	0.0399 3871	43
44	3.2991 3847	0.3031 0944	83.6050 3532	25.3414 7507	0.0119 6100	0.0394 6100	44
45	3.3898 6478	0.2949 9702	86.9041 7379	25.6364 7209	0.0115 0693	0.0390 0693	45
46	3.4830 8606	0.2871 0172	90.2940 3857	25.9235 7381	0.0110 7493	0.0385 7493	46
47	3.5788 7093	0.2794 1773	93.7771 2463	26.2029 9154	0.0106 6358	0.0381 6358	47
48	3.6772 8988	0.2719 3940	97.3559 9556	26.4749 3094	0.0102 7158	0.0377 7158	48
49	3.7784 1535	0.2646 6122	101.0332 8544	26.7395 9215	0.0098 9773	0.0373 9773	49
50	3.8823 2177	0.2575 7783	104.8117 0079	26.9971 6998	0.0095 4092	0.0370 4092	50

Rate 3%	E Compound Amount	F Present Value	G Amount of Annuity	H Present Value of Annuity	I Sinking Fund	J Amortization	
n	$(1+i)^n$	$(1+i)^{-n}$	$S_{\overline{n}\rvert i}$	$A_{\overline{n}\rvert i}$	$1/S_{\overline{n}\rvert i}$	$1/A_{\overline{n}\rvert i}$	n
1	1.0300 0000	0.9708 7379	1.0000 0000	0.9708 7379	1.0000 0000	1.0300 0000	1
2	1.0609 0000	0.9425 9591	2.0300 0000	1.9134 6970	0.4926 1084	0.5226 1084	2
3	1.0927 2700	0.9151 4166	3.0909 0000	2.8286 1135	0.3235 3036	0.3535 3036	3
4	1.1255 0881	0.8884 8705	4.1836 2700	3.7170 9840	0.2390 2705	0.2690 2705	4
5	1.1592 7407	0.8626 0878	5.3091 3581	4.5797 0719	0.1883 5457	0.2183 5457	5
6	1.1940 5230	0.8374 8426	6.4684 0988	5.4171 9144	0.1545 9750	0.1845 9750	6
7	1.2298 7387	0.8130 9151	7.6624 6218	6.2302 8296	0.1305 0635	0.1605 0635	7
8	1.2667 7008·	0.7894 0923	8.8923 3605	7.0196 9219	0.1124 5639	0.1424 5639	8
9	1.3047 7318	0.7664 1673	10.1591 0613	7.7861 0892	0.0984 3386	0.1284 3386	9
10	1.3439 1638	0.7440 9391	11.4638 7931	8.5302 0284	0.0872 3051	0.1172 3051	10
11	1.3842 3387	0.7224 2128	12.8077 9569	9.2526 2411	0.0780 7745	0.1080 7745	11
12	1.4257 6089	0.7013 7988	14.1920 2956	9.9540 0399	0.0704 6209	0.1004 6209	12
13	1.4685 3371	0.6809 5134	15.6177 9045	10.6349 5533	0.0640 2954	0.0940 2954	13
14	1.5125 8972	0.6611 1781	17.0863 2416	11.2960 7314	0.0585 2634	0.0885 2634	14
15	1.5579 6742	0.6418 6195	18.5989 1389	11.9379 3509	0.0537 6658	0.0837 6658	15
16	1.6047 0644	0.6231 6694	20.1568 8130	12.5611 0203	0.0496 1085	0.0796 1085	16
17	1.6528 4763	0.6050 1645	21.7615 8774	13.1661 1847	0.0459 5253	0.0759 5253	17
18	1.7024 3306	0.5873 9461	23.4144 3537	13.7535 1308	0.0427 0870	0.0727 0870	18
19	1.7535 0605	0.5702 8603	25.1168 6844	14.3237 9911	0.0398 1388	0.0698 1388	19
20	1.8061 1123	0.5536 7575	26.8703 7449	14.8774 7486	0.0372 1571	0.0672 1571	20
21	1.8602 9457	0.5375 4928	28.6764 8572	15.4150 2414	0.0348 7178	0.0648 7178	21
22	1.9161 0341	0.5218 9250	30.5367 8030	15.9369 1664	0.0327 4739	0.0627 4739	22
23	1.9735 8651	0.5066 9175	32.4528 8370	16.4436 0839	0.0308 1390	0.0608 1390	23
24	2.0327 9411	0.4919 3374	34.4264 7022	16.9355 4212	0.0290 4742	0.0590 4742	24
25	2.0937 7793	0.4776 0557	36.4592 6432	17.4131 4769	0.0274 2787	0.0574 2787	25
26	2.1565 9127	0.4636 9473	38.5530 4225	17.8768 4242	0.0259 3829	0.0559 3829	26
27	2.2212 8901	0.4501 8906	40.7096 3352	18.3270 3147	0.0245 6421	0.0545 6421	27
28	2.2879 2768	0.4370 7675	42.9309 2252	18.7641 0823	0.0232 9323	0.0532 9323	28
29	2.3565 6551	0.4243 4636	45.2188 5020	19.1884 5459	0.0221 1467	0.0521 1467	29
30	2.4272 6247	0.4119 8676	47.5754 1571	19.6004 4135	0.0210 1926	0.0510 1926	30
31	2.5000 8035	0.3999 8715	50.0026 7818	20.0004 2849	0.0199 9893	0.0499 9893	31
32	2.5750 8276	0.3883 3703	52.5027 5852	20.3887 6553	0.0190 4662	0.0490 4662	32
33	2.6523 3524	0.3770 2625	55.0778 4128	20.7657 9178	0.0181 5612	0.0481 5612	33
34	2.7319 0530	0.3660 4490	57.7301 7652	21.1318 3668	0.0173 2196	0.0473 2196	34
35	2.8138 6245	0.3553 8340	60.4620 8181	21.4872 2007	0.0165 3929	0.0465 3929	35
36	2.8982 7833	0.3450 3243	63.2759 4427	21.8322 5250	0.0158 0379	0.0458 0379	36
37	2.9852 2668	0.3349 8294	66.1742 2259	22.1672 3544	0.0151 1162	0.0451 1162	37
38	3.0747 8348	0.3252 2615	69.1594 4927	22.4924 6159	0.0144 5934	0.0444 5934	38
39	3.1670 2698	0.3157 5355	72.2342 3275	22.8082 1513	0.0138 4385	0.0438 4385	39
40	3.2620 3779	0.3065 5684	75.4012 5973	23.1147 7197	0.0132 6238	0.0432 6238	40
41	3.3598 9893	0.2976 2800	78.6632 9753	23.4123 9997	0.0127 1241	0.0427 1241	41
42	3.4606 9589	0.2889 5922	82.0231 9645	23.7013 5920	0.0121 9167	0.0421 9167	42
43	3.5645 1677	0.2805 4294	85.4838 9234	23.9819 0213	0.0116 9811	0.0416 9811	43
44	3.6714 5227	0.2723 7178	89.0484 0911	24.2542 7392	0.0112 2985	0.0412 2985	44
45	3.7815 9584	0.2644 3862	92.7198 6139	24.5187 1254	0.0107 8518	0.0407 8518	45
46	3.8950 4372	0.2567 3653	96.5014 5723	24.7754 4907	0.0103 6254	0.0403 6254	46
47	4.0118 9503	0.2492 5876	100.3965 0095	25.0247 0783	0.0099 6051	0.0399 6051	47
48	4.1322 5188	0.2419 9880	104.4083 9598	25.2667 0664	0.0095 7777	0.0395 7777	48
49	4.2562 1944	0.2349 5029	108.5406 4785	25.5016 5693	0.0092 1314	0.0392 1314	49
50	4.3839 0602	0.2281 0708	112.7968 6729	25.7297 6401	0.0088 6549	0.0388 6549	50

Rate 3½%	E Compound Amount	F Present Value	G Amount of Annuity	H Present Value of Annuity	I Sinking Fund	J Amortization	
n	$(1+i)^n$	$(1+i)^{-n}$	$S_{\overline{n}\rvert i}$	$A_{\overline{n}\rvert i}$	$1/S_{\overline{n}\rvert i}$	$1/A_{\overline{n}\rvert i}$	n
1	1.0350 0000	0.9661 8357	1.0000 0000	0.9661 8357	1.0000 0000	1.0350 0000	1
2	1.0712 2500	0.9335 1070	2.0350 0000	1.8996 9428	0.4914 0049	0.5264 0049	2
3	1.1087 1788	0.9019 4271	3.1062 2500	2.8016 3698	0.3219 3418	0.3569 3418	3
4	1.1475 2300	0.8714 4223	4.2149 4288	3.6730 7921	0.2372 5114	0.2722 5114	4
5	1.1876 8631	0.8419 7317	5.3624 6588	4.5150 5238	0.1864 8137	0.2214 8137	5
6	1.2292 5533	0.8135 0064	6.5501 5218	5.3285 5302	0.1526 6821	0.1876 6821	6
7	1.2722 7926	0.7859 9096	7.7794 0751	6.1145 4398	0.1285 4449	0.1635 4449	7
8	1.3168 0904	0.7594 1156	9.0516 8677	6.8739 5554	0.1104 7665	0.1454 7665	8
9	1.3628 9735	0.7337 3097	10.3684 9581	7.6076 8651	0.0964 4601	0.1314 4601	9
10	1.4105 9876	0.7089 1881	11.7313 9316	8.3166 0532	0.0852 4137	0.1202 4137	10
11	1.4599 6972	0.6849 4571	13.1419 9192	9.0015 5104	0.0760 9197	0.1110 9197	11
12	1.5110 6866	0.6617 8330	14.6019 6164	9.6633 3433	0.0684 8395	0.1034 8395	12
13	1.5639 5606	0.6394 0415	16.1130 3030	10.3027 3849	0.0620 6157	0.0970 6157	13
14	1.6186 9452	0.6177 8179	17.6769 8636	10.9205 2028	0.0565 7073	0.0915 7073	14
15	1.6753 4883	0.5968 9062	19.2956 8088	11.5174 1090	0.0518 2507	0.0868 2507	15
16	1.7339 8604	0.5767 0591	20.9710 2971	12.0941 1681	0.0476 8483	0.0826 8483	16
17	1.7946 7555	0.5572 0378	22.7050 1575	12.6513 2059	0.0440 4313	0.0790 4313	17
18	1.8574 8920	0.5383 6114	24.4996 9130	13.1896 8173	0.0408 1684	0.0758 1684	18
19	1.9225 0132	0.5201 5569	26.3571 8050	13.7098 3742	0.0379 4033	0.0729 4033	19
20	1.9897 8886	0.5025 6588	28.2796 8181	14.2124 0330	0.0353 6108	0.0703 6108	20
21	2.0594 3147	0.4855 7090	30.2694 7068	14.6979 7420	0.0330 3659	0.0680 3659	21
22	2.1315 1158	0.4691 5063	32.3289 0215	15.1671 2484	0.0309 3207	0.0659 3207	22
23	2.2061 1448	0.4532 8563	34.4604 1373	15.6204 1047	0.0290 1880	0.0640 1880	23
24	2.2833 2849	0.4379 5713	36.6665 2821	16.0583 6760	0.0272 7283	0.0622 7283	24
25	2.3632 4498	0.4231 4699	38.9498 5669	16.4815 1459	0.0256 7404	0.0606 7404	25
26	2.4459 5856	0.4088 3767	41.3131 0168	16.8903 5226	0.0242 0540	0.0592 0540	26
27	2.5315 6711	0.3950 1224	43.7590 6024	17.2853 6451	0.0228 5241	0.0578 5241	27
28	2.6201 7196	0.3816 5434	46.2906 2734	17.6670 1885	0.0216 0265	0.0566 0265	28
29	2.7118 7798	0.3687 4815	48.9107 9930	18.0357 6700	0.0204 4538	0.0554 4538	29
30	2.8067 9370	0.3562 7841	51.6226 7728	18.3920 4541	0.0193 7133	0.0543 7133	30
31	2.9050 3148	0.3442 3035	54.4294 7098	18.7362 7576	0.0183 7240	0.0533 7240	31
32	3.0067 0759	0.3325 8971	57.3345 0247	19.0688 6547	0.0174 4150	0.0524 4150	32
33	3.1119 4235	0.3213 4271	60.3412 1005	19.3902 0818	0.0165 7242	0.0515 7242	33
34	3.2208 6033	0.3104 7605	63.4531 5240	19.7006 8423	0.0157 5966	0.0507 5966	34
35	3.3335 9045	0.2999 7686	66.6740 1274	20.0006 6110	0.0149 9835	0.0499 9835	35
36	3.4502 6611	0.2898 3272	70.0076 0318	20.2904 9381	0.0142 8416	0.0492 8416	36
37	3.5710 2543	0.2800 3161	73.4578 6930	20.5705 2542	0.0136 1325	0.0486 1325	37
38	3.6960 1132	0.2705 6194	77.0288 9472	20.8410 8736	0.0129 8214	0.0479 8214	38
39	3.8253 7171	0.2614 1250	80.7249 0604	21.1024 9987	0.0123 8775	0.0473 8775	39
40	3.9592 5972	0.2525 7247	84.5502 7775	21.3550 7234	0.0118 2728	0.0468 2728	40
41	4.0978 3381	0.2440 3137	88.5095 3747	21.5991 0371	0.0112 9822	0.0462 9822	41
42	4.2412 5799	0.2357 7910	92.6073 7128	21.8348 8281	0.0107 9828	0.0457 9828	42
43	4.3897 0202	0.2278 0590	96.8486 2928	22.0626 8870	0.0103 2539	0.0453 2539	43
44	4.5433 4160	0.2201 0231	101.2383 3130	22.2827 9102	0.0098 7768	0.0448 7768	44
45	4.7023 5855	0.2126 5924	105.7816 7290	22.4954 5026	0.0094 5343	0.0444 5343	45
46	4.8669 4110	0.2054 6787	110.4840 3145	22.7009 1813	0.0090 5108	0.0440 5108	46
47	5.0372 8404	0.1985 1968	115.3509 7255	22.8994 3780	0.0086 6919	0.0436 6919	47
48	5.2135 8898	0.1918 0645	120.3882 5659	23.0912 4425	0.0083 0646	0.0433 0646	48
49	5.3960 6459	0.1853 2024	125.6018 4557	23.2765 6450	0.0079 6167	0.0429 6167	49
50	5.5849 2686	0.1790 5337	130.9979 1016	23.4556 1787	0.0076 3371	0.0426 3371	50

Rate 4%	E Compound Amount	F Present Value	G Amount of Annuity	H Present Value of Annuity	I Sinking Fund	J Amortization	
n	$(1+i)^n$	$(1+i)^{-n}$	$S_{\overline{n}|i}$	$A_{\overline{n}|i}$	$1/S_{\overline{n}|i}$	$1/A_{\overline{n}|i}$	n
1	1.0400 0000	0.9615 3846	1.0000 0000	0.9615 3846	1.0000 0000	1.0400 0000	1
2	1.0816 0000	0.9245 5621	2.0400 0000	1.8860 9467	0.4901 9608	0.5301 9608	2
3	1.1248 6400	0.8889 9636	3.1216 0000	2.7750 9103	0.3203 4854	0.3603 4854	3
4	1.1698 5856	0.8548 0419	4.2464 6400	3.6298 9522	0.2354 9005	0.2754 9005	4
5	1.2166 5290	0.8219 2711	5.4163 2256	4.4518 2233	0.1846 2711	0.2246 2711	5
6	1.2653 1902	0.7903 1453	6.6329 7546	5.2421 3686	0.1507 6190	0.1907 6190	6
7	1.3159 3178	0.7599 1781	7.8982 9448	6.0020 5467	0.1266 0961	0.1666 0961	7
8	1.3685 6905	0.7306 9021	9.2142 2626	6.7327 4487	0.1085 2783	0.1485 2783	8
9	1.4233 1181	0.7025 8674	10.5827 9531	7.4353 3161	0.0944 9299	0.1344 9299	9
10	1.4802 4428	0.6755 6417	12.0061 0712	8.1108 9578	0.0832 9094	0.1232 9094	10
11	1.5394 5406	0.6495 8093	13.4863 5141	8.7604 7671	0.0741 4904	0.1141 4904	11
12	1.6010 3222	0.6245 9705	15.0258 0546	9.3850 7376	0.0665 5217	0.1065 5217	12
13	1.6650 7351	0.6005 7409	16.6268 3768	9.9856 4785	0.0601 4373	0.1001 4373	13
14	1.7316 7645	0.5774 7508	18.2919 1119	10.5631 2293	0.0546 6897	0.0946 6897	14
15	1.8009 4351	0.5552 6450	20.0235 8764	11.1183 8743	0.0499 4110	0.0899 4110	15
16	1.8729 8125	0.5339 0818	21.8245 3114	11.6522 9561	0.0458 2000	0.0858 2000	16
17	1.9479 0050	0.5133 7325	23.6975 1239	12.1656 6885	0.0421 9852	0.0821 9852	17
18	2.0258 1652	0.4936 2812	25.6454 1288	12.6592 9697	0.0389 9333	0.0789 9333	18
19	2.1068 4918	0.4746 4242	27.6712 2940	13.1339 3940	0.0361 3862	0.0761 3862	19
20	2.1911 2314	0.4563 8695	29.7780 7858	13.5903 2634	0.0335 8175	0.0735 8175	20
21	2.2787 6807	0.4388 3360	31.9692 0172	14.0291 5995	0.0312 8011	0.0712 8011	21
22	2.3699 1879	0.4219 5539	34.2479 6979	14.4511 1533	0.0291 9881	0.0691 9881	22
23	2.4647 1554	0.4057 2633	36.6178 8858	14.8568 4167	0.0273 0906	0.0673 0906	23
24	2.5633 0416	0.3901 2147	39.0826 0412	15.2469 6314	0.0255 8683	0.0655 8683	24
25	2.6658 3633	0.3751 1680	41.6459 0829	15.6220 7994	0.0240 1196	0.0640 1196	25
26	2.7724 6978	0.3606 8923	44.3117 4462	15.9827 6918	0.0225 6738	0.0625 6738	26
27	2.8833 6858	0.3468 1657	47.0842 1440	16.3295 8575	0.0212 3854	0.0612 3854	27
28	2.9987 0332	0.3334 7747	49.9675 8298	16.6630 6322	0.0200 1298	0.0600 1298	28
29	3.1186 5145	0.3206 5141	52.9662 8630	16.9837 1463	0.0188 7993	0.0588 7993	29
30	3.2433 9751	0.3083 1867	56.0849 3775	17.2920 3330	0.0178 3010	0.0578 3010	30
31	3.3731 3341	0.2964 6026	59.3283 3526	17.5884 9356	0.0168 5535	0.0568 5535	31
32	3.5080 5875	0.2850 5794	62.7014 6867	17.8735 5150	0.0159 4859	0.0559 4859	32
33	3.6483 8110	0.2740 9417	66.2095 2742	18.1476 4567	0.0151 0357	0.0551 0357	33
34	3.7943 1634	0.2635 5209	69.8579 0851	18.4111 9776	0.0143 1477	0.0543 1477	34
35	3.9460 8899	0.2534 1547	73.6522 2486	18.6646 1323	0.0135 7732	0.0535 7732	35
36	4.1039 3255	0.2436 6872	77.5983 1385	18.9082 8195	0.0128 8688	0.0528 8688	36
37	4.2680 8986	0.2342 9685	81.7022 4640	19.1425 7880	0.0122 3957	0.0522 3957	37
38	4.4388 1345	0.2252 8543	85.9703 3626	19.3678 6423	0.0116 3192	0.0516 3192	38
39	4.6163 6599	0.2166 2061	90.4091 4971	19.5844 8484	0.0110 6083	0.0510 6083	39
40	4.8010 2063	0.2082 8904	95.0255 1570	19.7927 7388	0.0105 2349	0.0505 2349	40
41	4.9930 6145	0.2002 7793	99.8265 3633	19.9930 5181	0.0100 1738	0.0500 1738	41
42	5.1927 8391	0.1925 7493	104.8195 9778	20.1856 2674	0.0095 4020	0.0495 4020	42
43	5.4004 9527	0.1851 6820	110.0123 8169	20.3707 9494	0.0090 8989	0.0490 8990	43
44	5.6165 1508	0.1780 4635	115.4128 7696	20.5488 4129	0.0086 6454	0.0486 6454	44
45	5.8411 7568	0.1711 9841	121.0293 9204	20.7200 3970	0.0082 6246	0.0482 6246	45
46	6.0748 2271	0.1646 1386	126.8705 6772	20.8846 5356	0.0078 8205	0.0478 8205	46
47	6.3178 1562	0.1582 8256	132.9453 9043	21.0429 3612	0.0075 2189	0.0475 2189	47
48	6.5705 2824	0.1521 9476	139.2632 0604	21.1951 3088	0.0071 8065	0.0471 8065	48
49	6.8333 4937	0.1463 4112	145.8337 3429	21.3414 7200	0.0068 5712	0.0468 5712	49
50	7.1066 8335	0.1407 1262	152.6670 8366	21.4821 8462	0.0065 5020	0.0465 5020	50

Rate 4½%	E Compound Amount	F Present Value	G Amount of Annuity	H Present Value of Annuity	I Sinking Fund	J Amortization	
n	$(1 + i)^n$	$(1 + i)^{-n}$	$S_{\overline{n}\mid i}$	$A_{\overline{n}\mid i}$	$1/S_{\overline{n}\mid i}$	$1/A_{\overline{n}\mid i}$	n
1	1.0450 0000	0.9569 3780	1.0000 0000	0.9569 3780	1.0000 0000	1.0450 0000	1
2	1.0920 2500	0.9157 2995	2.0450 0000	1.8726 6775	0.4889 9756	0.5339 9756	2
3	1.1411 6613	0.8762 9660	3.1370 2500	2.7489 6435	0.3187 7336	0.3637 7336	3
4	1.1925 1860	0.8385 6134	4.2781 9113	3.5875 2570	0.2337 4365	0.2787 4365	4
5	1.2461 8194	0.8024 5105	5.4707 0973	4.3899 7674	0.1827 9164	0.2277 9164	5
6	1.3022 6012	0.7678 9574	6.7168 9166	5.1578 7248	0.1488 7839	0.1938 7839	6
7	1.3608 6183	0.7348 2846	8.0191 5179	5.8927 0094	0.1247 0147	0.1697 0147	7
8	1.4221 0061	0.7031 8513	9.3800 1362	6.5958 8607	0.1066 0965	0.1516 0965	8
9	1.4860 9514	0.6729 0443	10.8021 1423	7.2687 9050	0.0925 7447	0.1375 7447	9
10	1.5529 6942	0.6439 2768	12.2882 0937	7.9127 1818	0.0813 7882	0.1263 7882	10
11	1.6228 5305	0.6161 9874	13.8411 7879	8.5289 1692	0.0722 4818	0.1172 4818	11
12	1.6958 8143	0.5896 6386	15.4640 3184	9.1185 8078	0.0646 6619	0.1096 6619	12
13	1.7721 9610	0.5642 7164	17.1599 1327	9.6828 5242	0.0582 7535	0.1032 7535	13
14	1.8519 4492	0.5399 7286	18.9321 0937	10.2228 2528	0.0537 2032	0.0978 2032	14
15	1.9352 8244	0.5167 2044	20.7840 5429	10.7395 4573	0.0481 1381	0.0931 1381	15
16	2.0223 7015	0.4944 6932	22.7193 3673	11.2340 1505	0.0440 1537	0.0890 1537	16
17	2.1133 7681	0.4731 7639	24.7417 0689	11.7071 9143	0.0404 1758	0.0854 1758	17
18	2.2084 7877	0.4528 0037	26.8550 8370	12.1599 9180	0.0372 3690	0.0822 3690	18
19	2.3078 6031	0.4333 0179	29.0635 6246	12.5932 9359	0.0344 0734	0.0794 0734	19
20	2.4117 1402	0.4146 4286	31.3714 2277	13.0079 3645	0.0318 7614	0.0768 7614	20
21	2.5202 4116	0.3967 8743	33.7831 3680	13.4047 2388	0.0296 0057	0.0746 0057	21
22	2.6336 5201	0.3797 0089	36.3033 7795	13.7844 2476	0.0275 4565	0.0725 4565	22
23	2.7521 6635	0.3633 5013	38.9370 2996	14.1477 7489	0.0256 8249	0.0706 8249	23
24	2.8760 1383	0.3477 0347	41.6891 9631	14.4954 7837	0.0239 8703	0.0689 8703	24
25	3.0054 3446	0.3327 3060	44.5652 1015	14.8282 0896	0.0224 3903	0.0674 3903	25
26	3.1406 7901	0.3184 0248	47.5706 4460	15.1466 1145	0.0210 2137	0.0660 2137	26
27	3.2820 0956	0.3046 9137	50.7113 2361	15.4513 0282	0.0197 1946	0.0647 1946	27
28	3.4296 9999	0.2915 7069	53.9933 3317	15.7428 7351	0.0185 2081	0.0635 2081	28
29	3.5840 3649	0.2790 1502	57.4230 3316	16.0218 8853	0.0174 1461	0.0624 1461	29
30	3.7453 1813	0.2670 0002	61.0070 6966	16.2888 8854	0.0163 9154	0.0613 9154	30
31	3.9138 5745	0.2555 0241	64.7523 8779	16.5443 9095	0.0154 4345	0.0604 4345	31
32	4.0899 8104	0.2444 9991	68.6662 4524	16.7888 9086	0.0145 6320	0.0595 6320	32
33	4.2740 3018	0.2339 7121	72.7562 2628	17.0228 6207	0.0137 4453	0.0587 4453	33
34	4.4663 6154	0.2238 9589	77.0302 5646	17.2467 5796	0.0129 8191	0.0579 8191	34
35	4.6673 4781	0.2142 5444	81.4966 1800	17.4610 1240	0.0122 7045	0.0572 7045	35
36	4.8773 7846	0.2050 2817	86.1639 6581	17.6660 4058	0.0116 0578	0.0566 0578	36
37	5.0968 6049	0.1961 9921	91.0413 4427	17.8622 3979	0.0109 8402	0.0559 8402	37
38	5.3262 1921	0.1877 5044	96.1382 0476	18.0499 9023	0.0104 0169	0.0554 0169	38
39	5.5658 9908	0.1796 6549	101.4644 2398	18.2296 5572	0.0098 5567	0.0548 5567	39
40	5.8163 6454	0.1719 2870	107.0303 2306	18.4015 8442	0.0093 4315	0.0543 4315	40
41	6.0781 0094	0.1645 2507	112.8466 8760	18.5661 0949	0.0088 6158	0.0538 6158	41
42	6.3516 1548	0.1574 4026	118.9247 8854	18.7235 4975	0.0084 0868	0.0534 0868	42
43	6.6374 3818	0.1506 6054	125.2764 0402	18.8742 1029	0.0079 8235	0.0529 8235	43
44	6.9361 2290	0.1441 7276	131.9138 4220	19.0183 8305	0.0075 8071	0.0525 8071	44
45	7.2482 4843	0.1379 6437	138.8499 6510	19.1563 4742	0.0072 0202	0.0522 0202	45
46	7.5744 1961	0.1320 2332	146.0982 1353	19.2883 7074	0.0068 4471	0.0518 4471	46
47	7.9152 6849	0.1263 3810	153.6726 3314	19.4147 0884	0.0065 0734	0.0515 0734	47
48	8.2714 5557	0.1208 9771	161.5879 0163	19.5356 0654	0.0061 8858	0.0511 8858	48
49	8.6436 7107	0.1156 9158	169.8593 5720	19.6512 9813	0.0058 8722	0.0508 8722	49
50	9.0326 3627	0.1107 0965	178.5030 2828	19.7620 0778	0.0056 0215	0.0506 0215	50

Rate 5%	E Compound Amount	F Present Value	G Amount of Annuity	H Present Value of Annuity	I Sinking Fund	J Amortization	
n	$(1+i)^n$	$(1+i)^{-n}$	$S_{\overline{n}\rceil i}$	$A_{\overline{n}\rceil i}$	$1/S_{\overline{n}\rceil i}$	$1/A_{\overline{n}\rceil i}$	n
1	1.0500 0000	0.9523 8095	1.0000 0000	0.9523 8095	1.0000 0000	1.0500 0000	1
2	1.1025 0000	0.9070 2948	2.0500 0000	1.8594 1043	0.4878 0488	0.5378 0488	2
3	1.1576 2500	0.8638 3760	3.1525 0000	2.7232 4803	0.3172 0856	0.3672 0856	3
4	1.2155 0625	0.8227 0247	4.3101 2500	3.5459 5050	0.2320 1183	0.2820 1183	4
5	1.2762 8156	0.7835 2617	5.5256 3125	4.3294 7667	0.1809 7480	0.2309 7480	5
6	1.3400 9564	0.7462 1540	6.8019 1281	5.0756 9207	0.1470 1747	0.1970 1747	6
7	1.4071 0042	0.7106 8133	8.1420 0845	5.7863 7340	0.1228 1982	0.1728 1982	7
8	1.4774 5544	0.6768 3936	9.5491 0888	6.4632 1276	0.1047 2181	0.1547 2181	8
9	1.5513 2822	0.6446 0892	11.0265 6432	7.1078 2168	0.0906 9008	0.1406 9008	9
10	1.6288 9463	0.6139 1325	12.5778 9254	7.7217 3493	0.0795 0458	0.1295 0458	10
11	1.7103 3936	0.5846 7929	14.2067 8716	8.3064 1422	0.0703 8889	0.1203 8889	11
12	1.7958 5633	0.5568 3742	15.9171 2652	8.8632 5164	0.0628 2541	0.1128 2541	12
13	1.8856 4914	0.5303 2135	17.7129 8285	9.3935 7299	0.0564 5577	0.1064 5577	13
14	1.9799 3160	0.5050 6795	19.5986 3199	9.8986 4094	0.0510 2397	0.1010 2397	14
15	2.0789 2818	0.4810 1710	21.5785 6359	10.3796 5804	0.0463 4229	0.0963 4229	15
16	2.1828 7459	0.4581 1152	23.6574 9177	10.8377 6956	0.0422 6991	0.0922 6991	16
17	2.2920 1832	0.4362 9669	25.8403 6636	11.2740 6625	0.0386 9914	0.0886 9914	17
18	2.4066 1923	0.4155 2065	28.1323 8467	11.6895 8690	0.0355 4622	0.0855 4622	18
19	2.5269 5020	0.3957 3396	30.5390 0391	12.0853 2086	0.0327 4501	0.0827 4501	19
20	2.6532 9771	0.3768 8948	33.0659 5410	12.4622 1034	0.0302 4259	0.0802 4259	20
21	2.7859 6259	0.3589 4236	35.7192 5181	12.8211 5271	0.0279 9611	0.0779 9611	21
22	2.9252 6072	0.3418 4987	38.5052 1440	13.1630 0258	0.0259 7051	0.0759 7051	22
23	3.0715 2376	0.3255 7131	41.4304 7512	13.4885 7388	0.0241 3682	0.0741 3682	23
24	3.2250 9994	0.3100 6791	44.5019 9887	13.7986 4179	0.0224 7090	0.0724 7090	24
25	3.3863 5494	0.2953 0277	47.7270 9882	14.0939 4457	0.0209 5246	0.0709 5246	25
26	3.5556 7269	0.2812 4073	51.1134 5376	14.3751 8530	0.0195 6432	0.0695 6432	26
27	3.7334 5632	0.2678 4832	54.6691 2645	14.6430 3362	0.0182 9186	0.0682 9186	27
28	3.9201 2914	0.2550 9364	58.4025 8277	14.8981 2726	0.0171 2253	0.0671 2253	28
29	4.1161 3560	0.2429 4632	62.3227 1191	15.1410 7358	0.0160 4551	0.0660 4551	29
30	4.3219 4238	0.2313 7745	66.4388 4750	15.3724 5103	0.0150 5144	0.0650 5144	30
31	4.5380 3949	0.2203 5947	70.7607 8988	15.5928 1050	0.0141 3212	0.0641 3212	31
32	4.7649 4147	0.2098 6617	75.2988 2937	15.8026 7667	0.0132 8042	0.0632 8042	32
33	5.0031 8854	0.1998 7254	80.0637 7084	16.0025 4921	0.0124 9004	0.0624 9004	33
34	5.2533 4797	0.1903 5480	85.0669 5938	16.1929 0401	0.0117 5545	0.0617 5545	34
35	5.5160 1537	0.1812 9029	90.3203 0735	16.3741 9429	0.0110 7171	0.0610 7171	35
36	5.7918 1614	0.1726 5741	95.8363 2272	16.5468 5171	0.0104 3446	0.0604 3446	36
37	6.0814 0694	0.1644 3563	101.6281 3886	16.7112 8734	0.0098 3979	0.0598 3979	37
38	6.3854 7729	0.1566 0536	107.7095 4580	16.8678 9271	0.0092 8423	0.0592 8423	38
39	6.7047 5115	0.1491 4797	114.0950 2309	17.0170 4067	0.0087 6462	0.0587 6462	39
40	7.0399 8871	0.1420 4568	120.7997 7424	17.1590 8635	0.0082 7816	0.0582 7816	40
41	7.3919 8815	0.1352 8160	127.8397 6295	17.2943 6796	0.0078 2229	0.0578 2229	41
42	7.7615 8756	0.1288 3962	135.2317 5110	17.4232 0758	0.0073 9471	0.0573 9471	42
43	8.1496 6693	0.1227 0440	142.9933 3866	17.5459 1198	0.0069 9333	0.0569 9333	43
44	8.5571 5028	0.1168 6133	151.1430 0559	17.6627 7331	0.0066 1625	0.0566 1625	44
45	8.9850 0779	0.1112 9651	159.7001 5587	17.7740 6982	0.0062 6173	0.0562 6173	45
46	9.4342 5818	0.1059 9668	168.6851 6366	17.8800 6650	0.0059 2820	0.0559 2820	46
47	9.9059 7109	0.1009 4921	178.1194 2185	17.9810 1571	0.0056 1421	0.0556 1421	47
48	10.4012 6965	0.0961 4211	188.0253 9294	18.0771 5782	0.0053 1843	0.0553 1843	48
49	10.9213 3313	0.0915 6391	198.4266 6259	18.1687 2173	0.0050 3965	0.0550 3965	49
50	11.4673 9979	0.0872 0373	209.3479 9572	18.2559 2546	0.0047 7674	0.0547 7674	50

Rate 6%	E Compound Amount	F Present Value	G Amount of Annuity	H Present Value of Annuity	I Sinking Fund	J Amortization	
n	$(1 + i)^n$	$(1 + i)^{-n}$	$S_{\overline{n}|i}$	$A_{\overline{n}|i}$	$1/S_{\overline{n}|i}$	$1/A_{\overline{n}|i}$	n
1	1.0600 0000	0.9433 9623	1.0000 0000	0.9433 9623	1.0000 0000	1.0600 0000	1
2	1.1236 0000	0.8899 9644	2.0600 0000	1.8333 9267	0.4854 3689	0.5454 3689	2
3	1.1910 1600	0.8396 1928	3.1836 0000	2.6730 1195	0.3141 0981	0.3741 0981	3
4	1.2624 7696	0.7920 9366	4.3746 1600	3.4651 0561	0.2285 9149	0.2885 9149	4
5	1.3382 2558	0.7472 5817	5.6370 9296	4.2123 6379	0.1773 9640	0.2373 9640	5
6	1.4185 1911	0.7049 6054	6.9753 1854	4.9173 2433	0.1433 6263	0.2033 6263	6
7	1.5036 3026	0.6650 5711	8.3938 3765	5.5823 8144	0.1191 3502	0.1791 3502	7
8	1.5938 4807	0.6274 1237	9.8974 6791	6.2097 9381	0.1010 3594	0.1610 3594	8
9	1.6894 7896	0.5918 9846	11.4913 1598	6.8016 9227	0.0870 2224	0.1470 2224	9
10	1.7908 4770	0.5583 9478	13.1807 9494	7.3600 8705	0.0758 6796	0.1358 6796	10
11	1.8982 9856	0.5267 8753	14.9716 4264	7.8868 7458	0.0667 9294	0.1267 9294	11
12	2.0121 9647	0.4969 6936	16.8699 4120	8.3838 4394	0.0592 7703	0.1192 7703	12
13	2.1329 2826	0.4688 3902	18.8821 3767	8.8526 8296	0.0529 6011	0.1129 6011	13
14	2.2609 0396	0.4423 0096	21.0150 6593	9.2949 8393	0.0475 8491	0.1075 8491	14
15	2.3965 5819	0.4172 6506	23.2759 6988	9.7122 4899	0.0429 6276	0.1029 6276	15
16	2.5403 5168	0.3936 4628	25.6725 2808	10.1058 9527	0.0389 5214	0.0989 5214	16
17	2.6927 7279	0.3713 6442	28.2128 7976	10.4772 5969	0.0354 4480	0.0954 4480	17
18	2.8543 3915	0.3503 4379	30.9056 5255	10.8276 0348	0.0323 5654	0.0923 5654	18
19	3.0255 9950	0.3305 1301	33.7599 9170	11.1581 1649	0.0296 2086	0.0896 2086	19
20	3.2071 3547	0.3118 0473	36.7855 9120	11.4699 2122	0.0271 8456	0.0871 8456	20
21	3.3995 6360	0.2941 5540	39.9927 2668	11.7640 7662	0.0250 0455	0.0850 0455	21
22	3.6035 3742	0.2775 0510	43.3922 9028	12.0415 8172	0.0230 4557	0.0830 4557	22
23	3.8197 4966	0.2617 9726	46.9958 2769	12.3033 7898	0.0212 7848	0.0812 7848	23
24	4.0489 3464	0.2469 7855	50.8155 7735	12.5503 5753	0.0196 7901	0.0796 7900	24
25	4.2918 7072	0.2329 9863	54.8645 1200	12.7833 5616	0.0182 2672	0.0782 2672	25
26	4.5493 8296	0.2198 1003	59.1563 8272	13.0031 6619	0.0169 0435	0.0769 0435	26
27	4.8223 4594	0.2073 6795	63.7057 6568	13.2105 3414	0.0156 9717	0.0756 9717	27
28	5.1116 8670	0.1956 3014	68.5281 1162	13.4061 6428	0.0145 9255	0.0745 9255	28
29	5.4183 8790	0.1845 5674	73.6397 9832	13.5907 2102	0.0135 7961	0.0735 7961	29
30	5.7434 9117	0.1741 1013	79.0581 8622	13.7648 3115	0.0126 4891	0.0726 4891	30
31	6.0881 0064	0.1642 5484	84.8016 7739	13.9290 8599	0.0117 9222	0.0717 9222	31
32	6.4533 8668	0.1549 5740	90.8897 7803	14.0840 4339	0.0110 0234	0.0710 0234	32
33	6.8405 8988	0.1461 8622	97.3431 6471	14.2302 2961	0.0102 7294	0.0702 7293	33
34	7.2510 2528	0.1379 1153	104.1837 5460	14.3681 4114	0.0095 9843	0.0695 9843	34
35	7.6860 8679	0.1301 0522	111.4347 7987	14.4982 4636	0.0089 7386	0.0689 7386	35
36	8.1472 5200	0.1227 4077	119.1208 6666	14.6209 8713	0.0083 9483	0.0683 9483	36
37	8.6360 8712	0.1157 9318	127.2681 1866	14.7367 8031	0.0078 5743	0.0678 5743	37
38	9.1542 5235	0.1092 3885	135.9042 0578	14.8460 1916	0.0073 5812	0.0673 5812	38
39	9.7035 0749	0.1030 5552	145.0584 5813	14.9490 7468	0.0068 9377	0.0668 9377	39
40	10.2857 1794	0.0972 2219	154.7619 6562	15.0462 9687	0.0064 6154	0.0664 6154	40
41	10.9028 6101	0.0917 1905	165.0476 8356	15.1380 1592	0.0060 5886	0.0660 5886	41
42	11.5570 3267	0.0865 2740	175.9505 4457	15.2245 4332	0.0056 8342	0.0656 8342	42
43	12.2504 5463	0.0816 2962	187.5075 7724	15.3061 7294	0.0053 3312	0.0653 3312	43
44	12.9854 8191	0.0770 0908	199.7580 3188	15.3831 8202	0.0050 0606	0.0650 0606	44
45	13.7646 1083	0.0726 5007	212.7435 1379	15.4558 3209	0.0047 0050	0.0647 0050	45
46	14.5904 8748	0.0685 3781	226.5081 2462	15.5243 6990	0.0044 1485	0.0644 1485	46
47	15.4659 1673	0.0646 5831	241.0986 1210	15.5890 2821	0.0041 4768	0.0641 4768	47
48	16.3938 7173	0.0609 9840	256.5645 2882	15.6500 2661	0.0038 9765	0.0638 9765	48
49	17.3775 0403	0.0575 4566	272.9584 0055	15.7075 7227	0.0036 6356	0.0636 6356	49
50	18.4201 5427	0.0542 8836	290.3359 0458	15.7618 6064	0.0034 4429	0.0634 4429	50

Rate 7%	E Compound Amount	F Present Value	G Amount of Annuity	H Present Value of Annuity	I Sinking Fund	J Amortization	
n	$(1 + i)^n$	$(1 + i)^{-n}$	$S_{\overline{n}|i}$	$A_{\overline{n}|i}$	$1/S_{\overline{n}|i}$	$1/A_{\overline{n}|i}$	n
1	1.0700 0000	0.9345 7944	1.0000 0000	0.9345 7944	1.0000 0000	1.0700 0000	1
2	1.1449 0000	0.8734 3873	2.0700 0000	1.8080 1817	0.4830 9179	0.5530 9179	2
3	1.2250 4300	0.8162 9788	3.2149 0000	2.6243 1604	0.3110 5167	0.3810 5167	3
4	1.3107 9601	0.7628 9521	4.4399 4300	3.3872 1126	0.2252 2812	0.2952 2812	4
5	1.4025 5173	0.7129 8618	5.7507 3901	4.1001 9744	0.1738 9069	0.2438 9069	5
6	1.5007 3035	0.6663 4222	7.1532 9074	4.7665 3966	0.1397 9580	0.2097 9580	6
7	1.6057 8148	0.6227 4974	8.6540 2109	5.3892 8940	0.1155 5322	0.1855 5322	7
8	1.7181 8618	0.5820 0910	10.2598 0257	5.9712 9851	0.0974 6776	0.1674 6776	8
9	1.8384 5921	0.5439 3374	11.9779 8875	6.5152 3225	0.0834 8647	0.1534 8647	9
10	1.9671 5136	0.5083 4929	13.8164 4796	7.0235 8154	0.0723 7750	0.1423 7750	10
11	2.1048 5195	0.4750 9280	15.7835 9932	7.4986 7434	0.0633 5690	0.1333 5690	11
12	2.2521 9159	0.4440 1196	17.8884 5127	7.9426 8630	0.0559 0199	0.1259 0199	12
13	2.4098 4500	0.4149 6445	20.1406 4286	8.3576 5074	0.0496 5085	0.1196 5085	13
14	2.5785 3415	0.3878 1724	22.5504 8786	8.7454 6799	0.0443 4494	0.1143 4494	14
15	2.7590 3154	0.3624 4602	25.1290 2201	9.1079 1401	0.0397 9462	0.1097 9462	15
16	2.9521 6375	0.3387 3460	27.8880 5355	9.4466 4860	0.0358 5765	0.1058 5765	16
17	3.1588 1521	0.3165 7439	30.8402 1730	9.7632 2299	0.0324 2519	0.1024 2519	17
18	3.3799 3228	0.2958 6392	33.9990 3251	10.0590 8691	0.0294 1260	0.0994 1260	18
19	3.6165 2754	0.2765 0833	37.3789 6479	10.3355 9524	0.0267 5301	0.0967 5301	19
20	3.8696 8446	0.2584 1900	40.9954 9232	10.5940 1425	0.0243 9293	0.0943 9293	20
21	4.1405 6237	0.2415 1309	44.8651 7678	10.8355 2733	0.0222 8900	0.0922 8900	21
22	4.4304 0174	0.2257 1317	49.0057 3916	11.0612 4050	0.0204 0577	0.0904 0577	22
23	4.7405 2986	0.2109 4688	53.4361 4090	11.2721 8738	0.0187 1393	0.0887 1393	23
24	5.0723 6695	0.1971 4662	58.1766 7076	11.4693 3400	0.0171 8902	0.0871 8902	24
25	5.4274 3264	0.1842 4918	63.2490 3772	11.6535 8318	0.0158 1052	0.0858 1052	25
26	5.8073 5292	0.1721 9549	68.6764 7036	11.8257 7867	0.0145 6103	0.0845 6103	26
27	6.2138 6763	0.1609 3037	74.4838 2328	11.9867 0904	0.0134 2573	0.0834 2573	27
28	6.6488 3836	0.1504 0221	80.6976 9091	12.1371 1125	0.0123 9193	0.0823 9193	28
29	7.1142 5705	0.1405 6282	87.3465 2927	12.2776 7407	0.0114 4865	0.0814 4865	29
30	7.6122 5504	0.1313 6712	94.4607 8632	12.4090 4118	0.0105 8640	0.0805 8640	30
31	8.1451 1290	0.1227 7301	102.0730 4137	12.5318 1419	0.0097 9691	0.0797 9691	31
32	8.7152 7080	0.1147 4113	110.2181 5426	12.6465 5532	0.0090 7292	0.0790 7292	32
33	9.3253 3975	0.1072 3470	118.9334 2506	12.7537 9002	0.0084 0807	0.0784 0807	33
34	9.9781 1354	0.1002 1934	128.2587 6481	12.8540 0936	0.0077 9674	0.0777 9674	34
35	10.6765 8148	0.0936 6294	138.2368 7835	12.9476 7230	0.0072 3396	0.0772 3396	35
36	11.4239 4219	0.0875 3546	148.9134 5984	13.0352 0776	0.0067 1531	0.0767 1531	36
37	12.2236 1814	0.0818 0884	160.3374 0202	13.1170 1660	0.0062 3685	0.0762 3685	37
38	13.0792 7141	0.0764 5686	172.5610 2017	13.1934 7345	0.0057 9505	0.0757 9505	38
39	13.9948 2041	0.0714 5501	185.6402 9158	13.2649 2846	0.0053 8676	0.0753 8676	39
40	14.9744 5784	0.0667 8038	199.6351 1199	13.3317 0884	0.0050 0914	0.0750 0914	40
41	16.0226 6989	0.0624 1157	214.6095 6983	13.3941 2041	0.0046 5962	0.0746 5962	41
42	17.1442 5678	0.0583 2857	230.6322 3972	13.4524 4898	0.0043 3591	0.0743 3591	42
43	18.3443 5475	0.0545 1268	247.7764 9650	13.5069 6167	0.0040 3590	0.0740 3590	43
44	19.6284 5959	0.0509 4643	266.1208 5125	13.5579 0810	0.0037 5769	0.0737 5769	44
45	21.0024 5176	0.0476 1349	285.7493 1084	13.6055 2159	0.0034 9957	0.0734 9957	45
46	22.4726 2338	0.0444 9859	306.7517 6260	13.6500 2018	0.0032 5997	0.0732 5996	46
47	24.0457 0702	0.0415 8747	329.2243 8598	13.6916 0764	0.0030 3744	0.0730 3744	47
48	25.7289 0651	0.0388 6679	353.2700 9300	13.7304 7443	0.0028 3070	0.0728 3070	48
49	27.5299 2997	0.0363 2410	378.9989 9951	13.7667 9853	0.0026 3853	0.0726 3853	49
50	29.4570 2506	0.0339 4776	406.5289 2947	13.8007 4629	0.0024 5985	0.0724 5985	50

Rate 8%	E Compound Amount	F Present Value	G Amount of Annuity	H Present Value of Annuity	I Sinking Fund	J Amortization	
n	$(1 + i)^n$	$(1 + i)^{-n}$	$S_{\overline{n}\rceil i}$	$A_{\overline{n}\rceil i}$	$1/S_{\overline{n}\rceil i}$	$1/A_{\overline{n}\rceil i}$	n
1	1.0800 0000	0.9259 2593	1.0000 0000	0.9259 2593	1.0000 0000	1.0800 0000	1
2	1.1664 0000	0.8573 3882	2.0800 0000	1.7832 6475	0.4807 6923	0.5607 6923	2
3	1.2597 1200	0.7938 3224	3.2464 0000	2.5770 9699	0.3080 3351	0.3880 3351	3
4	1.3604 8896	0.7350 2985	4.5061 1200	3.3121 2684	0.2219 2080	0.3019 2080	4
5	1.4693 2808	0.6805 8320	5.8666 0096	3.9927 1004	0.1704 5645	0.2504 5645	5
6	1.5868 7432	0.6301 6963	7.3359 2904	4.6228 7966	0.1363 1539	0.2163 1539	6
7	1.7138 2427	0.5834 9040	8.9228 0336	5.2063 7006	0.1120 7240	0.1920 7240	7
8	1.8509 3021	0.5402 6888	10.6366 2763	5.7466 3894	0.0940 1476	0.1740 1476	8
9	1.9990 0463	0.5002 4897	12.4875 5784	6.2468 8791	0.0800 7971	0.1600 7971	9
10	2.1589 2500	0.4631 9349	14.4865 6247	6.7100 8140	0.0690 2949	0.1490 2949	10
11	2.3316 3900	0.4288 8286	16.6454 8746	7.1389 6426	0.0600 7634	0.1400 7634	11
12	2.5181 7012	0.3971 1376	18.9771 2646	7.5360 7802	0.0526 9502	0.1326 9502	12
13	2.7196 2373	0.3676 9792	21.4952 9658	7.9037 7594	0.0465 2181	0.1265 2181	13
14	2.9371 9362	0.3404 6104	24.2149 2030	8.2442 3698	0.0412 9685	0.1212 9685	14
15	3.1721 6911	0.3152 4170	27.1521 1393	8.5594 7869	0.0368 2954	0.1168 2954	15
16	3.4259 4264	0.2918 9047	30.3242 8304	8.8513 6916	0.0329 7687	0.1129 7687	16
17	3.7000 1805	0.2702 6895	33.7502 2569	9.1216 3811	0.0296 2943	0.1096 2943	17
18	3.9960 1950	0.2502 4903	37.4502 4374	9.3718 8714	0.0267 0210	0.1067 0210	18
19	4.3157 0106	0.2317 1206	41.4462 6324	9.6035 9920	0.0241 2763	0.1041 2763	19
20	4.6609 5714	0.2145 4821	45.7619 6430	9.8181 4741	0.0218 5221	0.1018 5221	20
21	5.0338 3372	0.1986 5575	50.4229 2144	10.0168 0316	0.0198 3225	0.0998 3225	21
22	5.4365 4041	0.1839 4051	55.4567 5516	10.2007 4366	0.0180 3207	0.0980 3207	22
23	5.8714 6365	0.1703 1528	60.8932 9557	10.3710 5895	0.0164 2217	0.0964 2217	23
24	6.3411 8074	0.1576 9934	66.7647 5922	10.5287 5828	0.0149 7796	0.0949 7796	24
25	6.8484 7520	0.1460 1790	73.1059 3995	10.6747 7619	0.0136 7878	0.0936 7878	25
26	7.3963 5321	0.1352 0176	79.9544 1515	10.8099 7795	0.0125 0713	0.0925 0713	26
27	7.9880 6147	0.1251 8682	87.3507 6836	10.9351 6477	0.0114 4810	0.0914 4810	27
28	8.6271 0639	0.1159 1372	95.3388 2983	11.0510 7849	0.0104 8891	0.0904 8891	28
29	9.3172 7490	0.1073 2752	103.9659 3622	11.1584 0601	0.0096 1854	0.0896 1854	29
30	10.0626 5689	0.0993 7733	113.2832 1111	11.2577 8334	0.0088 2743	0.0888 2743	30
31	10.8676 6944	0.0920 1605	123.3458 6800	11.3497 9939	0.0081 0728	0.0881 0728	31
32	11.7370 8300	0.0852 0005	134.2135 3744	11.4349 9944	0.0074 5081	0.0874 5081	32
33	12.6760 4964	0.0788 8893	145.9506 2044	11.5138 8837	0.0068 5163	0.0868 5163	33
34	13.6901 3361	0.0730 4531	158.6266 7007	11.5869 3367	0.0063 0411	0.0863 0411	34
35	14.7853 4429	0.0676 3454	172.3168 0368	11.6545 6822	0.0058 0326	0.0858 0326	35
36	15.9681 7184	0.0626 2458	187.1021 4797	11.7171 9279	0.0053 4467	0.0853 4467	36
37	17.2456 2558	0.0579 8572	203.0703 1981	11.7751 7851	0.0049 2440	0.0849 2440	37
38	18.6252 7563	0.0536 9048	220.3159 4540	11.8288 6899	0.0045 3894	0.0845 3894	38
39	20.1152 9768	0.0497 1341	238.9412 2103	11.8785 8240	0.0041 8513	0.0841 8513	39
40	21.7245 2150	0.0460 3093	259.0565 1871	11.9246 1333	0.0038 6016	0.0838 6016	40
41	23.4624 8322	0.0426 2123	280.7810 4021	11.9672 3457	0.0035 6149	0.0835 6149	41
42	25.3394 8187	0.0394 6411	304.2435 2342	12.0066 9867	0.0032 8684	0.0832 8684	42
43	27.3666 4042	0.0365 4084	329.5830 0530	12.0432 3951	0.0030 3414	0.0830 3414	43
44	29.5559 7166	0.0338 3411	356.9496 4572	12.0770 7362	0.0028 0152	0.0828 0152	44
45	31.9204 4939	0.0313 2788	386.5056 1738	12.1084 0150	0.0025 8728	0.0825 8728	45
46	34.4740 8534	0.0290 0730	418.4260 6677	12.1374 0880	0.0023 8991	0.0823 8991	46
47	37.2320 1217	0.0268 5861	452.9001 5211	12.1642 6741	0.0022 0799	0.0822 0799	47
48	40.2105 7314	0.0248 6908	490.1321 6428	12.1891 3649	0.0020 4027	0.0820 4027	48
49	43.4274 1899	0.0230 2693	530.3427 3742	12.2121 6341	0.0018 8557	0.0818 8557	49
50	46.9016 1251	0.0213 2123	573.7701 5642	12.2334 8464	0.0017 4286	0.0817 4286	50

Appendix K
Annual Percentage Rate (APR) Table

NUMBER OF PAYMENTS	ANNUAL PERCENTAGE RATE															
	6.00%	6.25%	6.50%	6.75%	7.00%	7.25%	7.50%	7.75%	8.00%	8.25%	8.50%	8.75%	9.00%	9.25%	9.50%	9.75%
	(FINANCE CHARGE PER $100 OF AMOUNT FINANCED)															
1	0.50	0.52	0.54	0.56	0.58	0.60	0.62	0.65	0.67	0.69	0.71	0.73	0.75	0.77	0.79	0.81
2	0.75	0.78	0.81	0.84	0.88	0.91	0.94	0.97	1.00	1.03	1.06	1.10	1.13	1.16	1.19	1.22
3	1.00	1.04	1.09	1.13	1.17	1.21	1.25	1.29	1.34	1.38	1.42	1.46	1.50	1.55	1.59	1.63
4	1.25	1.31	1.36	1.41	1.46	1.51	1.57	1.62	1.67	1.72	1.78	1.83	1.88	1.93	1.99	2.04
5	1.50	1.57	1.63	1.69	1.76	1.82	1.88	1.95	2.01	2.07	2.13	2.20	2.26	2.32	2.39	2.45
6	1.76	1.83	1.90	1.98	2.05	2.13	2.20	2.27	2.35	2.42	2.49	2.57	2.64	2.72	2.79	2.86
7	2.01	2.09	2.18	2.26	2.35	2.43	2.52	2.60	2.68	2.77	2.85	2.94	3.02	3.11	3.19	3.28
8	2.26	2.36	2.45	2.55	2.64	2.74	2.83	2.93	3.02	3.12	3.21	3.31	3.40	3.50	3.60	3.69
9	2.52	2.62	2.73	2.83	2.94	3.05	3.15	3.26	3.36	3.47	3.57	3.68	3.79	3.89	4.00	4.11
10	2.77	2.89	3.00	3.12	3.24	3.35	3.47	3.59	3.70	3.82	3.94	4.05	4.17	4.29	4.41	4.52
11	3.02	3.15	3.28	3.41	3.53	3.66	3.79	3.92	4.04	4.17	4.30	4.43	4.56	4.68	4.81	4.94
12	3.28	3.42	3.56	3.69	3.83	3.97	4.11	4.25	4.39	4.52	4.66	4.80	4.94	5.08	5.22	5.36
13	3.53	3.68	3.83	3.98	4.13	4.28	4.43	4.58	4.73	4.88	5.03	5.18	5.33	5.48	5.63	5.78
14	3.79	3.95	4.11	4.27	4.43	4.59	4.75	4.91	5.07	5.23	5.39	5.55	5.72	5.88	6.04	6.20
15	4.05	4.22	4.39	4.56	4.73	4.90	5.07	5.24	5.42	5.59	5.76	5.93	6.10	6.28	6.45	6.62
16	4.30	4.48	4.67	4.85	5.03	5.21	5.40	5.58	5.76	5.94	6.13	6.31	6.49	6.68	6.86	7.05
17	4.56	4.75	4.95	5.14	5.33	5.52	5.72	5.91	6.11	6.30	6.49	6.69	6.88	7.08	7.27	7.47
18	4.82	5.02	5.22	5.43	5.63	5.84	6.04	6.25	6.45	6.66	6.86	7.07	7.28	7.48	7.69	7.90
19	5.07	5.29	5.50	5.72	5.94	6.15	6.37	6.58	6.80	7.02	7.23	7.45	7.67	7.89	8.10	8.32
20	5.33	5.56	5.78	6.01	6.24	6.46	6.69	6.92	7.15	7.38	7.60	7.83	8.06	8.29	8.52	8.75
21	5.59	5.83	6.07	6.30	6.54	6.78	7.02	7.26	7.50	7.74	7.97	8.21	8.46	8.70	8.94	9.18
22	5.85	6.10	6.35	6.60	6.84	7.09	7.34	7.59	7.84	8.10	8.35	8.60	8.85	9.10	9.36	9.61
23	6.11	6.37	6.63	6.89	7.15	7.41	7.67	7.93	8.19	8.46	8.72	8.98	9.25	9.51	9.77	10.04
24	6.37	6.64	6.91	7.18	7.45	7.73	8.00	8.27	8.55	8.82	9.09	9.37	9.64	9.92	10.19	10.47
25	6.63	6.91	7.19	7.48	7.76	8.04	8.33	8.61	8.90	9.18	9.47	9.75	10.04	10.33	10.62	10.90
26	6.89	7.18	7.48	7.77	8.07	8.36	8.66	8.95	9.25	9.55	9.84	10.14	10.44	10.74	11.04	11.34
27	7.15	7.46	7.76	8.07	8.37	8.68	8.99	9.29	9.60	9.91	10.22	10.53	10.84	11.15	11.46	11.77
28	7.41	7.73	8.05	8.36	8.68	9.00	9.32	9.64	9.96	10.28	10.60	10.92	11.24	11.56	11.89	12.21
29	7.67	8.00	8.33	8.66	8.99	9.32	9.65	9.98	10.31	10.64	10.97	11.31	11.64	11.98	12.31	12.65
30	7.94	8.28	8.61	8.96	9.30	9.64	9.98	10.32	10.66	11.01	11.35	11.70	12.04	12.39	12.74	13.09

31	8.20	8.55	8.90	9.25	9.60	9.96	10.31	10.67	11.02	11.38	11.73	12.09	12.45	12.81	13.17	13.53	
32	8.46	8.82	9.19	9.55	9.91	10.28	10.64	11.01	11.38	11.74	12.11	12.48	12.85	13.22	13.59	13.97	
33	8.73	9.10	9.47	9.85	10.22	10.60	10.98	11.36	11.73	12.11	12.49	12.88	13.26	13.64	14.02	14.41	
34	8.99	9.37	9.76	10.15	10.53	10.92	11.31	11.70	12.09	12.48	12.88	13.27	13.66	14.06	14.45	14.85	
35	9.25	9.65	10.05	10.45	10.85	11.25	11.65	12.05	12.45	12.85	13.26	13.66	14.07	14.48	14.89	15.29	
36	9.52	9.93	10.34	10.75	11.16	11.57	11.98	12.40	12.81	13.23	13.64	14.06	14.48	14.90	15.32	15.74	
37	9.78	10.20	10.63	11.05	11.47	11.89	12.32	12.74	13.17	13.60	14.03	14.46	14.89	15.32	15.75	16.19	
38	10.05	10.48	10.91	11.35	11.78	12.22	12.66	13.09	13.53	13.97	14.41	14.85	15.30	15.74	16.19	16.63	
39	10.32	10.76	11.20	11.65	12.10	12.54	12.99	13.44	13.89	14.35	14.80	15.25	15.71	16.17	16.62	17.08	
40	10.58	11.04	11.49	11.95	12.41	12.87	13.33	13.79	14.26	14.72	15.19	15.65	16.12	16.59	17.06	17.53	
41	10.85	11.32	11.78	12.25	12.72	13.20	13.67	14.14	14.62	15.10	15.57	16.05	16.53	17.01	17.50	17.98	
42	11.12	11.60	12.08	12.56	13.04	13.52	14.01	14.50	14.98	15.47	15.96	16.45	16.95	17.44	17.94	18.43	
43	11.38	11.87	12.37	12.86	13.36	13.85	14.35	14.85	15.35	15.85	16.35	16.86	17.36	17.87	18.38	18.89	
44	11.65	12.15	12.66	13.16	13.67	14.18	14.69	15.20	15.71	16.23	16.74	17.26	17.78	18.30	18.82	19.34	
45	11.92	12.44	12.95	13.47	13.99	14.51	15.03	15.55	16.08	16.61	17.13	17.66	18.19	18.73	19.26	19.79	
46	12.19	12.72	13.24	13.77	14.31	14.84	15.37	15.91	16.45	16.99	17.53	18.07	18.61	19.16	19.70	20.25	
47	12.46	13.00	13.54	14.08	14.62	15.17	15.72	16.26	16.81	17.37	17.92	18.47	19.03	19.59	20.15	20.71	
48	12.73	13.28	13.83	14.39	14.94	15.50	16.06	16.62	17.18	17.75	18.31	18.88	19.45	20.02	20.59	21.16	
49	13.00	13.56	14.13	14.69	15.26	15.83	16.40	16.98	17.55	18.13	18.71	19.29	19.87	20.45	21.04	21.62	
50	13.27	13.84	14.42	15.00	15.58	16.16	16.75	17.33	17.92	18.51	19.10	19.69	20.29	20.89	21.48	22.08	
51	13.54	14.13	14.72	15.31	15.90	16.50	17.09	17.69	18.29	18.89	19.50	20.10	20.71	21.32	21.93	22.55	
52	13.81	14.41	15.01	15.62	16.22	16.83	17.44	18.05	18.66	19.28	19.89	20.51	21.13	21.76	22.38	23.01	
53	14.08	14.69	15.31	15.92	16.54	17.16	17.78	18.41	19.03	19.66	20.29	20.92	21.56	22.19	22.83	23.47	
54	14.36	14.98	15.61	16.23	16.86	17.50	18.13	18.77	19.41	20.05	20.69	21.34	21.98	22.63	23.28	23.94	
55	14.63	15.26	15.90	16.54	17.19	17.83	18.48	19.13	19.78	20.43	21.09	21.75	22.41	23.07	23.73	24.40	
56	14.90	15.55	16.20	16.85	17.51	18.17	18.83	19.49	20.15	20.82	21.49	22.16	22.83	23.51	24.19	24.87	
57	15.17	15.84	16.50	17.17	17.83	18.50	19.18	19.85	20.53	21.21	21.89	22.58	23.26	23.95	24.64	25.34	
58	15.45	16.12	16.80	17.48	18.16	18.84	19.53	20.21	20.91	21.60	22.29	22.99	23.69	24.39	25.10	25.80	
59	15.72	16.41	17.10	17.79	18.48	19.18	19.88	20.58	21.28	21.99	22.70	23.41	24.12	24.84	25.55	26.27	
60	16.00	16.70	17.40	18.10	18.81	19.52	20.23	20.94	21.66	22.38	23.10	23.82	24.55	25.28	26.01	26.75	

NUMBER OF PAYMENTS	ANNUAL PERCENTAGE RATE															
	10.00%	10.25%	10.50%	10.75%	11.00%	11.25%	11.50%	11.75%	12.00%	12.25%	12.50%	12.75%	13.00%	13.25%	13.50%	13.75%
	(FINANCE CHARGE PER $100 OF AMOUNT FINANCED)															
1	0.83	0.85	0.87	0.90	0.92	0.94	0.96	0.98	1.00	1.02	1.04	1.06	1.08	1.10	1.12	1.15
2	1.25	1.28	1.31	1.35	1.38	1.41	1.44	1.47	1.50	1.53	1.57	1.60	1.63	1.66	1.69	1.72
3	1.67	1.71	1.76	1.80	1.84	1.88	1.92	1.96	2.01	2.05	2.09	2.13	2.17	2.22	2.26	2.30
4	2.09	2.14	2.20	2.25	2.30	2.35	2.41	2.46	2.51	2.57	2.62	2.67	2.72	2.78	2.83	2.88
5	2.51	2.58	2.64	2.70	2.77	2.83	2.89	2.96	3.02	3.08	3.15	3.21	3.27	3.34	3.40	3.46
6	2.94	3.01	3.08	3.16	3.23	3.31	3.38	3.45	3.53	3.60	3.68	3.75	3.83	3.90	3.97	4.05
7	3.36	3.45	3.53	3.62	3.70	3.78	3.87	3.95	4.04	4.12	4.21	4.29	4.38	4.47	4.55	4.64
8	3.79	3.88	3.98	4.07	4.17	4.26	4.36	4.46	4.55	4.65	4.74	4.84	4.94	5.03	5.13	5.22
9	4.21	4.32	4.43	4.53	4.64	4.75	4.85	4.96	5.07	5.17	5.28	5.39	5.49	5.60	5.71	5.82
10	4.64	4.76	4.88	4.99	5.11	5.23	5.35	5.46	5.58	5.70	5.82	5.94	6.05	6.17	6.29	6.41
11	5.07	5.20	5.33	5.45	5.58	5.71	5.84	5.97	6.10	6.23	6.36	6.49	6.62	6.75	6.88	7.01
12	5.50	5.64	5.78	5.92	6.06	6.20	6.34	6.48	6.62	6.76	6.90	7.04	7.18	7.32	7.46	7.60
13	5.93	6.08	6.23	6.38	6.53	6.68	6.84	6.99	7.14	7.29	7.44	7.59	7.75	7.90	8.05	8.20
14	6.36	6.52	6.69	6.85	7.01	7.17	7.34	7.50	7.66	7.82	7.99	8.15	8.31	8.48	8.64	8.81
15	6.80	6.97	7.14	7.32	7.49	7.66	7.84	8.01	8.19	8.36	8.53	8.71	8.88	9.06	9.23	9.41
16	7.23	7.41	7.60	7.78	7.97	8.15	8.34	8.53	8.71	8.90	9.08	9.27	9.46	9.64	9.83	10.02
17	7.67	7.86	8.06	8.25	8.45	8.65	8.84	9.04	9.24	9.44	9.63	9.83	10.03	10.23	10.43	10.63
18	8.10	8.31	8.52	8.73	8.93	9.14	9.35	9.56	9.77	9.98	10.19	10.40	10.61	10.82	11.03	11.24
19	8.54	8.76	8.98	9.20	9.42	9.64	9.86	10.08	10.30	10.52	10.74	10.96	11.18	11.41	11.63	11.85
20	8.98	9.21	9.44	9.67	9.90	10.13	10.37	10.60	10.83	11.06	11.30	11.53	11.76	12.00	12.23	12.46
21	9.42	9.66	9.90	10.15	10.39	10.63	10.88	11.12	11.36	11.61	11.85	12.10	12.34	12.59	12.84	13.08
22	9.86	10.12	10.37	10.62	10.88	11.13	11.39	11.64	11.90	12.16	12.41	12.67	12.93	13.19	13.44	13.70
23	10.30	10.57	10.84	11.10	11.37	11.63	11.90	12.17	12.44	12.71	12.97	13.24	13.51	13.78	14.05	14.32
24	10.75	11.02	11.30	11.58	11.86	12.14	12.42	12.70	12.98	13.26	13.54	13.82	14.10	14.38	14.66	14.95
25	11.19	11.48	11.77	12.06	12.35	12.64	12.93	13.22	13.52	13.81	14.10	14.40	14.69	14.98	15.28	15.57
26	11.64	11.94	12.24	12.54	12.85	13.15	13.45	13.75	14.06	14.36	14.67	14.97	15.28	15.59	15.89	16.20
27	12.09	12.40	12.71	13.03	13.34	13.66	13.97	14.29	14.60	14.92	15.24	15.56	15.87	16.19	16.51	16.83
28	12.53	12.86	13.18	13.51	13.84	14.16	14.49	14.82	15.15	15.48	15.81	16.14	16.47	16.80	17.13	17.46
29	12.98	13.32	13.66	14.00	14.33	14.67	15.01	15.35	15.70	16.04	16.38	16.72	17.07	17.41	17.75	18.10
30	13.43	13.78	14.13	14.48	14.83	15.19	15.54	15.89	16.24	16.60	16.95	17.31	17.66	18.02	18.38	18.74

31	13.89	14.25	14.61	14.97	15.33	15.70	16.06	16.43	16.79	17.16	17.53	17.90	18.27	18.63	19.00	19.38
32	14.34	14.71	15.09	15.46	15.84	16.21	16.59	16.97	17.35	17.73	18.11	18.49	18.87	19.25	19.63	20.02
33	14.79	15.18	15.57	15.95	16.34	16.73	17.12	17.51	17.90	18.29	18.69	19.08	19.47	19.87	20.26	20.66
34	15.25	15.65	16.05	16.44	16.85	17.25	17.65	18.05	18.46	18.86	19.27	19.67	20.08	20.49	20.90	21.31
35	15.70	16.11	16.53	16.94	17.35	17.77	18.18	18.60	19.01	19.43	19.85	20.27	20.69	21.11	21.53	21.95
36	16.16	16.58	17.01	17.43	17.86	18.29	18.71	19.14	19.57	20.00	20.43	20.87	21.30	21.73	22.17	22.60
37	16.62	17.06	17.49	17.93	18.37	18.81	19.25	19.69	20.13	20.58	21.02	21.46	21.91	22.36	22.81	23.25
38	17.08	17.53	17.98	18.43	18.88	19.33	19.78	20.24	20.69	21.15	21.61	22.07	22.52	22.99	23.45	23.91
39	17.54	18.00	18.46	18.93	19.39	19.86	20.32	20.79	21.26	21.73	22.20	22.67	23.14	23.61	24.09	24.56
40	18.00	18.48	18.95	19.43	19.90	20.38	20.86	21.34	21.82	22.30	22.79	23.27	23.76	24.25	24.73	25.22
41	18.47	18.95	19.44	19.93	20.42	20.91	21.40	21.89	22.39	22.88	23.38	23.88	24.38	24.88	25.38	25.88
42	18.93	19.43	19.93	20.43	20.93	21.44	21.94	22.45	22.96	23.47	23.98	24.49	25.00	25.51	26.03	26.55
43	19.40	19.91	20.42	20.94	21.45	21.97	22.49	23.01	23.53	24.05	24.57	25.10	25.62	26.15	26.68	27.21
44	19.86	20.39	20.91	21.44	21.97	22.50	23.03	23.57	24.10	24.64	25.17	25.71	26.25	26.79	27.33	27.88
45	20.33	20.87	21.41	21.95	22.49	23.03	23.58	24.12	24.67	25.22	25.77	26.32	26.88	27.43	27.99	28.55
46	20.80	21.35	21.90	22.46	23.01	23.57	24.13	24.69	25.25	25.81	26.37	26.94	27.51	28.08	28.65	29.22
47	21.27	21.83	22.40	22.97	23.53	24.10	24.68	25.25	25.82	26.40	26.98	27.56	28.14	28.72	29.31	29.89
48	21.74	22.32	22.90	23.48	24.06	24.64	25.23	25.81	26.40	26.99	27.58	28.18	28.77	29.37	29.97	30.57
49	22.21	22.80	23.39	23.99	24.58	25.18	25.78	26.38	26.98	27.59	28.19	28.80	29.41	30.02	30.63	31.24
50	22.69	23.29	23.89	24.50	25.11	25.72	26.33	26.95	27.56	28.18	28.80	29.42	30.04	30.67	31.29	31.92
51	23.16	23.78	24.40	25.02	25.64	26.26	26.89	27.52	28.15	28.78	29.41	30.05	30.68	31.32	31.96	32.60
52	23.64	24.27	24.90	25.53	26.17	26.81	27.45	28.09	28.73	29.38	30.02	30.67	31.32	31.98	32.63	33.29
53	24.11	24.76	25.40	26.05	26.70	27.35	28.00	28.66	29.32	29.98	30.64	31.30	31.97	32.63	33.30	33.97
54	24.59	25.25	25.91	26.57	27.23	27.90	28.56	29.23	29.91	30.58	31.25	31.93	32.61	33.29	33.98	34.66
55	25.07	25.74	26.41	27.09	27.77	28.44	29.13	29.81	30.50	31.18	31.87	32.56	33.26	33.95	34.65	35.35
56	25.55	26.23	26.92	27.61	28.30	28.99	29.69	30.39	31.09	31.79	32.49	33.20	33.91	34.62	35.33	36.04
57	26.03	26.73	27.43	28.13	28.84	29.54	30.25	30.97	31.68	32.39	33.11	33.83	34.56	35.28	36.01	36.74
58	26.51	27.23	27.94	28.66	29.37	30.10	30.82	31.55	32.27	33.00	33.74	34.47	35.21	35.95	36.69	37.43
59	27.00	27.72	28.45	29.18	29.91	30.65	31.39	32.13	32.87	33.61	34.36	35.11	35.86	36.62	37.37	38.13
60	27.48	28.22	28.96	29.71	30.45	31.20	31.96	32.71	33.47	34.23	34.99	35.75	36.52	37.29	38.06	38.83

NUMBER OF PAYMENTS	ANNUAL PERCENTAGE RATE															
	14.00%	14.25%	14.50%	14.75%	15.00%	15.25%	15.50%	15.75%	16.00%	16.25%	16.50%	16.75%	17.00%	17.25%	17.50%	17.75%
	(FINANCE CHARGE PER $100 OF AMOUNT FINANCED)															
1	1.17	1.19	1.21	1.23	1.25	1.27	1.29	1.31	1.33	1.35	1.37	1.40	1.42	1.44	1.46	1.48
2	1.75	1.78	1.82	1.85	1.88	1.91	1.94	1.97	2.00	2.04	2.07	2.10	2.13	2.16	2.19	2.22
3	2.34	2.38	2.43	2.47	2.51	2.55	2.59	2.64	2.68	2.72	2.76	2.80	2.85	2.89	2.93	2.97
4	2.93	2.99	3.04	3.09	3.14	3.20	3.25	3.30	3.36	3.41	3.46	3.51	3.57	3.62	3.67	3.73
5	3.53	3.59	3.65	3.72	3.78	3.84	3.91	3.97	4.04	4.10	4.16	4.23	4.29	4.35	4.42	4.48
6	4.12	4.20	4.27	4.35	4.42	4.49	4.57	4.64	4.72	4.79	4.87	4.94	5.02	5.09	5.17	5.24
7	4.72	4.81	4.89	4.98	5.06	5.15	5.23	5.32	5.40	5.49	5.58	5.66	5.75	5.83	5.92	6.00
8	5.32	5.42	5.51	5.61	5.71	5.80	5.90	6.00	6.09	6.19	6.29	6.38	6.48	6.58	6.67	6.77
9	5.92	6.03	6.14	6.25	6.35	6.46	6.57	6.68	6.78	6.89	7.00	7.11	7.22	7.32	7.43	7.54
10	6.53	6.65	6.77	6.88	7.00	7.12	7.24	7.36	7.48	7.60	7.72	7.84	7.96	8.08	8.19	8.31
11	7.14	7.27	7.40	7.53	7.66	7.79	7.92	8.05	8.18	8.31	8.44	8.57	8.70	8.83	8.96	9.09
12	7.74	7.89	8.03	8.17	8.31	8.45	8.59	8.74	8.88	9.02	9.16	9.30	9.45	9.59	9.73	9.87
13	8.36	8.51	8.66	8.81	8.97	9.12	9.27	9.43	9.58	9.73	9.89	10.04	10.20	10.35	10.50	10.66
14	8.97	9.13	9.30	9.46	9.63	9.79	9.96	10.12	10.29	10.45	10.62	10.78	10.95	11.11	11.28	11.45
15	9.59	9.76	9.94	10.11	10.29	10.47	10.64	10.82	11.00	11.17	11.35	11.53	11.71	11.88	12.06	12.24
16	10.20	10.39	10.58	10.77	10.95	11.14	11.33	11.52	11.71	11.90	12.09	12.28	12.46	12.65	12.84	13.03
17	10.82	11.02	11.22	11.42	11.62	11.82	12.02	12.22	12.42	12.62	12.83	13.03	13.23	13.43	13.63	13.83
18	11.45	11.66	11.87	12.08	12.29	12.50	12.72	12.93	13.14	13.35	13.57	13.78	13.99	14.21	14.42	14.64
19	12.07	12.30	12.52	12.74	12.97	13.19	13.41	13.64	13.86	14.09	14.31	14.54	14.76	14.99	15.22	15.44
20	12.70	12.93	13.17	13.41	13.64	13.88	14.11	14.35	14.59	14.82	15.06	15.30	15.54	15.77	16.01	16.25
21	13.33	13.58	13.82	14.07	14.32	14.57	14.82	15.06	15.31	15.56	15.81	16.06	16.31	16.56	16.81	17.07
22	13.96	14.22	14.48	14.74	15.00	15.26	15.52	15.78	16.04	16.30	16.57	16.83	17.09	17.36	17.62	17.88
23	14.59	14.87	15.14	15.41	15.68	15.96	16.23	16.50	16.78	17.05	17.32	17.60	17.88	18.15	18.43	18.70
24	15.23	15.51	15.80	16.08	16.37	16.65	16.94	17.22	17.51	17.80	18.09	18.37	18.66	18.95	19.24	19.53
25	15.87	16.17	16.46	16.76	17.06	17.35	17.65	17.95	18.25	18.55	18.85	19.15	19.45	19.75	20.05	20.36
26	16.51	16.82	17.13	17.44	17.75	18.06	18.37	18.68	18.99	19.30	19.62	19.93	20.24	20.56	20.87	21.19
27	17.15	17.47	17.80	18.12	18.44	18.76	19.09	19.41	19.74	20.06	20.39	20.71	21.04	21.37	21.69	22.02
28	17.80	18.13	18.47	18.80	19.14	19.47	19.81	20.15	20.48	20.82	21.16	21.50	21.84	22.18	22.52	22.86
29	18.45	18.79	19.14	19.49	19.83	20.18	20.53	20.89	21.23	21.58	21.94	22.29	22.64	22.99	23.35	23.70
30	19.10	19.45	19.81	20.17	20.54	20.90	21.26	21.62	21.99	22.35	22.72	23.08	23.45	23.81	24.18	24.55

31	19.75	20.12	20.49	20.87	21.24	21.61	21.99	22.37	22.74	23.12	23.50	23.88	24.26	24.64	25.02	25.40
32	20.40	20.79	21.17	21.56	21.95	22.33	22.72	23.11	23.50	23.89	24.28	24.68	25.07	25.46	25.86	26.25
33	21.06	21.46	21.85	22.25	22.65	23.06	23.46	23.86	24.26	24.67	25.07	25.48	25.88	26.29	26.70	27.11
34	21.72	22.13	22.54	22.95	23.37	23.78	24.19	24.61	25.03	25.44	25.86	26.28	26.70	27.12	27.54	27.97
35	22.38	22.80	23.23	23.65	24.08	24.51	24.94	25.36	25.79	26.23	26.66	27.09	27.52	27.96	28.39	28.83
36	23.04	23.48	23.92	24.35	24.80	25.24	25.68	26.12	26.57	27.01	27.46	27.90	28.35	28.80	29.25	29.70
37	23.70	24.16	24.61	25.06	25.51	25.97	26.42	26.88	27.34	27.80	28.26	28.72	29.18	29.64	30.10	30.57
38	24.37	24.84	25.30	25.77	26.24	26.70	27.17	27.64	28.11	28.59	29.06	29.53	30.01	30.49	30.96	31.44
39	25.04	25.52	26.00	26.48	26.96	27.44	27.92	28.41	28.89	29.38	29.87	30.36	30.85	31.34	31.83	32.32
40	25.71	26.20	26.70	27.19	27.69	28.18	28.68	29.18	29.68	30.18	30.68	31.18	31.68	32.19	32.69	33.20
41	26.39	26.89	27.40	27.91	28.41	28.92	29.44	29.95	30.46	30.97	31.49	32.01	32.52	33.04	33.56	34.08
42	27.06	27.58	28.10	28.62	29.15	29.67	30.19	30.72	31.25	31.78	32.31	32.84	33.37	33.90	34.44	34.97
43	27.74	28.27	28.81	29.34	29.88	30.42	30.96	31.50	32.04	32.58	33.13	33.67	34.22	34.76	35.31	35.86
44	28.42	28.97	29.52	30.07	30.62	31.17	31.72	32.28	32.83	33.39	33.95	34.51	35.07	35.63	36.19	36.76
45	29.11	29.67	30.23	30.79	31.36	31.92	32.49	33.06	33.63	34.20	34.77	35.35	35.92	36.50	37.08	37.66
46	29.79	30.36	30.94	31.52	32.10	32.68	33.26	33.84	34.43	35.01	35.60	36.19	36.78	37.37	37.96	38.56
47	30.48	31.07	31.66	32.25	32.84	33.44	34.03	34.63	35.23	35.83	36.43	37.04	37.64	38.25	38.86	39.46
48	31.17	31.77	32.37	32.98	33.59	34.20	34.81	35.42	36.03	36.65	37.27	37.88	38.50	39.13	39.75	40.37
49	31.86	32.48	33.09	33.71	34.34	34.96	35.59	36.21	36.84	37.47	38.10	38.74	39.37	40.01	40.65	41.29
50	32.55	33.18	33.82	34.45	35.09	35.73	36.37	37.01	37.65	38.30	38.94	39.59	40.24	40.89	41.55	42.20
51	33.25	33.89	34.54	35.19	35.84	36.49	37.15	37.81	38.46	39.12	39.79	40.45	41.11	41.78	42.45	43.12
52	33.95	34.61	35.27	35.93	36.60	37.27	37.94	38.61	39.28	39.96	40.63	41.31	41.99	42.67	43.36	44.04
53	34.65	35.32	36.00	36.68	37.36	38.04	38.72	39.41	40.10	40.79	41.48	42.17	42.87	43.57	44.27	44.97
54	35.35	36.04	36.73	37.42	38.12	38.82	39.52	40.22	40.92	41.63	42.33	43.04	43.75	44.47	45.18	45.90
55	36.05	36.76	37.46	38.17	38.88	39.60	40.31	41.03	41.74	42.47	43.19	43.91	44.64	45.37	46.10	46.83
56	36.76	37.48	38.20	38.92	39.65	40.38	41.11	41.84	42.57	43.31	44.05	44.79	45.53	46.27	47.02	47.77
57	37.47	38.20	38.94	39.68	40.42	41.16	41.91	42.65	43.40	44.15	44.91	45.66	46.42	47.18	47.94	48.71
58	38.18	38.93	39.68	40.43	41.19	41.95	42.71	43.47	44.23	45.00	45.77	46.54	47.32	48.09	48.87	49.65
59	38.89	39.66	40.42	41.19	41.96	42.74	43.51	44.29	45.07	45.85	46.64	47.42	48.21	49.01	49.80	50.60
60	39.61	40.39	41.17	41.95	42.74	43.53	44.32	45.11	45.91	46.71	47.51	48.31	49.12	49.92	50.73	51.55

(FINANCE CHARGE PER $100 OF AMOUNT FINANCED)

NUMBER OF PAYMENTS	18.00%	18.25%	18.50%	18.75%	19.00%	19.25%	19.50%	19.75%	20.00%	20.25%	20.50%	20.75%	21.00%	21.25%	21.50%	21.75%
1	1.50	1.52	1.54	1.56	1.58	1.60	1.62	1.65	1.67	1.69	1.71	1.73	1.75	1.77	1.79	1.81
2	2.26	2.29	2.32	2.35	2.38	2.41	2.44	2.48	2.51	2.54	2.57	2.60	2.63	2.66	2.70	2.73
3	3.01	3.06	3.10	3.14	3.18	3.23	3.27	3.31	3.35	3.39	3.44	3.48	3.52	3.56	3.60	3.65
4	3.78	3.83	3.88	3.94	3.99	4.04	4.10	4.15	4.20	4.25	4.31	4.36	4.41	4.47	4.52	4.57
5	4.54	4.61	4.67	4.74	4.80	4.86	4.93	4.99	5.06	5.12	5.18	5.25	5.31	5.37	5.44	5.50
6	5.32	5.39	5.46	5.54	5.61	5.69	5.76	5.84	5.91	5.99	6.06	6.14	6.21	6.29	6.36	6.44
7	6.09	6.18	6.26	6.35	6.43	6.52	6.60	6.69	6.78	6.86	6.95	7.04	7.12	7.21	7.29	7.38
8	6.87	6.96	7.06	7.16	7.26	7.35	7.45	7.55	7.64	7.74	7.84	7.94	8.03	8.13	8.23	8.33
9	7.65	7.76	7.87	7.97	8.08	8.19	8.30	8.41	8.52	8.63	8.73	8.84	8.95	9.06	9.17	9.28
10	8.43	8.55	8.67	8.79	8.91	9.03	9.15	9.27	9.39	9.51	9.63	9.75	9.88	10.00	10.12	10.24
11	9.22	9.35	9.49	9.62	9.75	9.88	10.01	10.14	10.28	10.41	10.54	10.67	10.80	10.94	11.07	11.20
12	10.02	10.16	10.30	10.44	10.59	10.73	10.87	11.02	11.16	11.31	11.45	11.59	11.74	11.88	12.02	12.17
13	10.81	10.97	11.12	11.28	11.43	11.59	11.74	11.90	12.05	12.21	12.36	12.52	12.67	12.83	12.99	13.14
14	11.61	11.78	11.95	12.11	12.28	12.45	12.61	12.78	12.95	13.11	13.28	13.45	13.62	13.79	13.95	14.12
15	12.42	12.59	12.77	12.95	13.13	13.31	13.49	13.67	13.85	14.03	14.21	14.39	14.57	14.75	14.93	15.11
16	13.22	13.41	13.60	13.80	13.99	14.18	14.37	14.56	14.75	14.94	15.13	15.33	15.52	15.71	15.90	16.10
17	14.04	14.24	14.44	14.64	14.85	15.05	15.25	15.46	15.66	15.86	16.07	16.27	16.48	16.68	16.89	17.09
18	14.85	15.07	15.28	15.49	15.71	15.93	16.14	16.36	16.57	16.79	17.01	17.22	17.44	17.66	17.88	18.09
19	15.67	15.90	16.12	16.35	16.58	16.81	17.03	17.26	17.49	17.72	17.95	18.18	18.41	18.64	18.87	19.10
20	16.49	16.73	16.97	17.21	17.45	17.69	17.93	18.17	18.41	18.66	18.90	19.14	19.38	19.63	19.87	20.11
21	17.32	17.57	17.82	18.07	18.33	18.58	18.83	19.09	19.34	19.60	19.85	20.11	20.36	20.62	20.87	21.13
22	18.15	18.41	18.68	18.94	19.21	19.47	19.74	20.01	20.27	20.54	20.81	21.08	21.34	21.61	21.88	22.15
23	18.98	19.26	19.54	19.81	20.09	20.37	20.65	20.93	21.21	21.49	21.77	22.05	22.33	22.61	22.90	23.18
24	19.82	20.11	20.40	20.69	20.98	21.27	21.56	21.86	22.15	22.44	22.74	23.03	23.33	23.62	23.92	24.21
25	20.66	20.96	21.27	21.57	21.87	22.18	22.48	22.79	23.10	23.40	23.71	24.02	24.32	24.63	24.94	25.25
26	21.50	21.82	22.14	22.45	22.77	23.09	23.41	23.73	24.04	24.36	24.68	25.01	25.33	25.65	25.97	26.29
27	22.35	22.68	23.01	23.34	23.67	24.00	24.33	24.67	25.00	25.33	25.67	26.00	26.34	26.67	27.01	27.34
28	23.20	23.55	23.89	24.23	24.58	24.92	25.27	25.61	25.96	26.30	26.65	27.00	27.35	27.70	28.05	28.40
29	24.06	24.41	24.77	25.13	25.49	25.84	26.20	26.56	26.92	27.28	27.64	28.00	28.37	28.73	29.09	29.46
30	24.92	25.29	25.66	26.03	26.40	26.77	27.14	27.52	27.89	28.26	28.64	29.01	29.39	29.77	30.14	30.52

31	25.78	26.16	26.55	26.93	27.32	27.70	28.09	28.47	28.86	29.25	29.64	30.03	30.42	30.81	31.20	31.59
32	26.65	27.04	27.44	27.84	28.24	28.64	29.04	29.44	29.84	30.24	30.64	31.05	31.45	31.85	32.26	32.67
33	27.52	27.93	28.34	28.75	29.16	29.57	29.99	30.40	30.82	31.23	31.65	32.07	32.49	32.91	33.33	33.75
34	28.39	28.81	29.24	29.66	30.09	30.52	30.95	31.37	31.80	32.23	32.67	33.10	33.53	33.96	34.40	34.83
35	29.27	29.71	30.14	30.58	31.02	31.47	31.91	32.35	32.79	33.24	33.68	34.13	34.58	35.03	35.47	35.92
36	30.15	30.60	31.05	31.51	31.96	32.42	32.87	33.33	33.79	34.25	34.71	35.17	35.63	36.09	36.56	37.02
37	31.03	31.50	31.97	32.43	32.90	33.37	33.84	34.32	34.79	35.26	35.74	36.21	36.69	37.16	37.64	38.12
38	31.92	32.40	32.88	33.37	33.85	34.33	34.82	35.30	35.79	36.28	36.77	37.26	37.75	38.24	38.73	39.23
39	32.81	33.31	33.80	34.30	34.80	35.30	35.80	36.30	36.80	37.30	37.81	38.31	38.82	39.32	39.83	40.34
40	33.71	34.22	34.73	35.24	35.75	36.26	36.78	37.29	37.81	38.33	38.85	39.37	39.89	40.41	40.93	41.46
41	34.61	35.13	35.66	36.18	36.71	37.24	37.77	38.30	38.83	39.36	39.89	40.43	40.96	41.50	42.04	42.58
42	35.51	36.05	36.59	37.13	37.67	38.21	38.76	39.30	39.85	40.40	40.95	41.50	42.05	42.60	43.15	43.71
43	36.42	36.97	37.52	38.08	38.63	39.19	39.75	40.31	40.87	41.44	42.00	42.57	43.13	43.70	44.27	44.84
44	37.33	37.89	38.46	39.03	39.60	40.18	40.75	41.33	41.90	42.48	43.06	43.64	44.22	44.81	45.39	45.98
45	38.24	38.82	39.41	39.99	40.58	41.17	41.75	42.35	42.94	43.53	44.13	44.72	45.32	45.92	46.52	47.12
46	39.16	39.75	40.35	40.95	41.55	42.16	42.76	43.37	43.98	44.58	45.20	45.81	46.42	47.03	47.65	48.27
47	40.08	40.69	41.30	41.92	42.54	43.15	43.77	44.40	45.02	45.64	46.27	46.90	47.53	48.16	48.79	49.42
48	41.00	41.63	42.26	42.89	43.52	44.15	44.79	45.43	46.07	46.71	47.35	47.99	48.64	49.28	49.93	50.58
49	41.93	42.57	43.22	43.86	44.51	45.16	45.81	46.46	47.12	47.77	48.43	49.09	49.75	50.41	51.08	51.74
50	42.86	43.52	44.18	44.84	45.50	46.17	46.83	47.50	48.17	48.84	49.52	50.19	50.87	51.55	52.23	52.91
51	43.79	44.47	45.14	45.82	46.50	47.18	47.86	48.55	49.23	49.92	50.61	51.30	51.99	52.69	53.38	54.08
52	44.73	45.42	46.11	46.80	47.50	48.20	48.89	49.59	50.30	51.00	51.71	52.41	53.12	53.83	54.55	55.26
53	45.67	46.38	47.08	47.79	48.50	49.22	49.93	50.65	51.37	52.09	52.81	53.53	54.26	54.98	55.71	56.44
54	46.62	47.34	48.06	48.79	49.51	50.24	50.97	51.70	52.44	53.17	53.91	54.65	55.39	56.14	56.88	57.63
55	47.57	48.30	49.04	49.78	50.52	51.27	52.02	52.76	53.52	54.27	55.02	55.78	56.54	57.30	58.06	58.82
56	48.52	49.27	50.03	50.78	51.54	52.30	53.06	53.83	54.60	55.37	56.14	56.91	57.68	58.46	59.24	60.02
57	49.47	50.24	51.01	51.79	52.56	53.34	54.12	54.90	55.68	56.47	57.25	58.04	58.84	59.63	60.43	61.22
58	50.43	51.22	52.00	52.79	53.58	54.38	55.17	55.97	56.77	57.57	58.38	59.18	59.99	60.80	61.62	62.43
59	51.39	52.20	53.00	53.80	54.61	55.42	56.23	57.05	57.87	58.68	59.51	60.33	61.15	61.98	62.81	63.64
60	52.36	53.18	54.00	54.82	55.64	56.47	57.30	58.13	58.96	59.80	60.64	61.48	62.32	63.17	64.01	64.86

NUMBER OF PAYMENTS	ANNUAL PERCENTAGE RATE														
	22.00%	22.25%	22.50%	22.75%	23.00%	23.25%	23.50%	23.75%	24.00%	24.25%	24.50%	24.75%	25.00%	25.25%	25.50%	25.75%
	(FINANCE CHARGE PER $100 OF AMOUNT FINANCED)														
1	1.83	1.85	1.87	1.90	1.92	1.94	1.96	1.98	2.00	2.02	2.04	2.06	2.08	2.10	2.12	2.15
2	2.76	2.79	2.82	2.85	2.88	2.92	2.95	2.98	3.01	3.04	3.07	3.10	3.14	3.17	3.20	3.23
3	3.69	3.73	3.77	3.82	3.86	3.90	3.94	3.98	4.03	4.07	4.11	4.15	4.20	4.24	4.28	4.32
4	4.62	4.68	4.73	4.78	4.84	4.89	4.94	5.00	5.05	5.10	5.16	5.21	5.26	5.32	5.37	5.42
5	5.57	5.63	5.69	5.76	5.82	5.89	5.95	6.02	6.08	6.14	6.21	6.27	6.34	6.40	6.46	6.53
6	6.51	6.59	6.66	6.74	6.81	6.89	6.96	7.04	7.12	7.19	7.27	7.34	7.42	7.49	7.57	7.64
7	7.47	7.55	7.64	7.73	7.81	7.90	7.99	8.07	8.16	8.24	8.33	8.42	8.51	8.59	8.68	8.77
8	8.42	8.52	8.62	8.72	8.82	8.91	9.01	9.11	9.21	9.31	9.40	9.50	9.60	9.70	9.80	9.90
9	9.39	9.50	9.61	9.72	9.83	9.94	10.04	10.15	10.26	10.37	10.48	10.59	10.70	10.81	10.92	11.03
10	10.36	10.48	10.60	10.72	10.84	10.96	11.08	11.21	11.33	11.45	11.57	11.69	11.81	11.93	12.06	12.18
11	11.33	11.47	11.60	11.73	11.86	12.00	12.13	12.26	12.40	12.53	12.66	12.80	12.93	13.06	13.20	13.33
12	12.31	12.46	12.60	12.75	12.89	13.04	13.18	13.33	13.47	13.62	13.76	13.91	14.05	14.20	14.34	14.49
13	13.30	13.46	13.61	13.77	13.93	14.08	14.24	14.40	14.55	14.71	14.87	15.03	15.18	15.34	15.50	15.66
14	14.29	14.46	14.63	14.80	14.97	15.13	15.30	15.47	15.64	15.81	15.98	16.15	16.32	16.49	16.66	16.83
15	15.29	15.47	15.65	15.83	16.01	16.19	16.37	16.56	16.74	16.92	17.10	17.28	17.47	17.65	17.83	18.02
16	16.29	16.48	16.68	16.87	17.06	17.26	17.45	17.65	17.84	18.03	18.23	18.42	18.62	18.81	19.01	19.21
17	17.30	17.50	17.71	17.92	18.12	18.33	18.53	18.74	18.95	19.16	19.36	19.57	19.78	19.99	20.20	20.40
18	18.31	18.53	18.75	18.97	19.19	19.41	19.62	19.84	20.06	20.28	20.50	20.72	20.95	21.17	21.39	21.61
19	19.33	19.56	19.79	20.02	20.26	20.49	20.72	20.95	21.19	21.42	21.65	21.89	22.12	22.35	22.59	22.82
20	20.35	20.60	20.84	21.09	21.33	21.58	21.82	22.07	22.31	22.56	22.81	23.05	23.30	23.55	23.79	24.04
21	21.38	21.64	21.90	22.16	22.41	22.67	22.93	23.19	23.45	23.71	23.97	24.23	24.49	24.75	25.01	25.27
22	22.42	22.69	22.96	23.23	23.50	23.77	24.04	24.32	24.59	24.86	25.13	25.41	25.68	25.96	26.23	26.50
23	23.46	23.74	24.03	24.31	24.60	24.88	25.17	25.45	25.74	26.02	26.31	26.60	26.88	27.17	27.46	27.75
24	24.51	24.80	25.10	25.40	25.70	25.99	26.29	26.59	26.89	27.19	27.49	27.79	28.09	28.39	28.69	29.00
25	25.56	25.87	26.18	26.49	26.80	27.11	27.43	27.74	28.05	28.36	28.68	28.99	29.31	29.62	29.94	30.25
26	26.62	26.94	27.26	27.59	27.91	28.24	28.56	28.89	29.22	29.55	29.87	30.20	30.53	30.86	31.19	31.52
27	27.68	28.02	28.35	28.69	29.03	29.37	29.71	30.05	30.39	30.73	31.07	31.42	31.76	32.10	32.45	32.79
28	28.75	29.10	29.45	29.80	30.15	30.51	30.86	31.22	31.57	31.93	32.28	32.64	33.00	33.35	33.71	34.07
29	29.82	30.19	30.55	30.92	31.28	31.65	32.02	32.39	32.76	33.13	33.50	33.87	34.24	34.61	34.98	35.36
30	30.90	31.28	31.66	32.04	32.42	32.80	33.18	33.57	33.95	34.33	34.72	35.10	35.49	35.88	36.26	36.65

31	31.98	32.38	32.77	33.17	33.56	33.96	34.35	34.75	35.15	35.55	35.95	36.35	36.75	37.15	37.55	37.95
32	33.07	33.48	33.89	34.30	34.71	35.12	35.53	35.94	36.35	36.77	37.18	37.60	38.01	38.43	38.84	39.26
33	34.17	34.59	35.01	35.44	35.86	36.29	36.71	37.14	37.57	37.99	38.42	38.85	39.28	39.71	40.14	40.58
34	35.27	35.71	36.14	36.58	37.02	37.46	37.90	38.34	38.78	39.23	39.67	40.11	40.56	41.01	41.45	41.90
35	36.37	36.83	37.28	37.73	38.18	38.64	39.09	39.55	40.01	40.47	40.92	41.38	41.84	42.31	42.77	43.23
36	37.49	37.95	38.42	38.89	39.35	39.82	40.29	40.77	41.24	41.71	42.19	42.66	43.14	43.61	44.09	44.57
37	38.60	39.08	39.56	40.05	40.53	41.02	41.50	41.99	42.48	42.96	43.45	43.94	44.43	44.93	45.42	45.91
38	39.72	40.22	40.72	41.21	41.71	42.21	42.71	43.22	43.72	44.22	44.73	45.23	45.74	46.25	46.75	47.26
39	40.85	41.36	41.87	42.39	42.90	43.42	43.93	44.45	44.97	45.49	46.01	46.53	47.05	47.57	48.10	48.62
40	41.98	42.51	43.04	43.56	44.09	44.62	45.16	45.69	46.22	46.76	47.29	47.83	48.37	48.91	49.45	49.99
41	43.12	43.66	44.20	44.75	45.29	45.84	46.39	46.94	47.48	48.04	48.59	49.14	49.69	50.25	50.80	51.36
42	44.26	44.82	45.38	45.94	46.50	47.06	47.62	48.19	48.75	49.32	49.89	50.46	51.03	51.60	52.17	52.74
43	45.41	45.98	46.56	47.13	47.71	48.29	48.87	49.45	50.03	50.61	51.19	51.78	52.36	52.95	53.54	54.13
44	46.56	47.15	47.74	48.33	48.93	49.52	50.11	50.71	51.31	51.91	52.51	53.11	53.71	54.31	54.92	55.52
45	47.72	48.33	48.93	49.54	50.15	50.76	51.37	51.98	52.59	53.21	53.82	54.44	55.06	55.68	56.30	56.92
46	48.89	49.51	50.13	50.75	51.37	52.00	52.63	53.26	53.89	54.52	55.15	55.78	56.42	57.05	57.69	58.33
47	50.06	50.69	51.33	51.97	52.61	53.25	53.89	54.54	55.18	55.83	56.48	57.13	57.78	58.44	59.09	59.75
48	51.23	51.88	52.54	53.19	53.85	54.51	55.16	55.83	56.49	57.15	57.82	58.49	59.15	59.82	60.50	61.17
49	52.41	53.08	53.75	54.42	55.09	55.77	56.44	57.12	57.80	58.48	59.16	59.85	60.53	61.22	61.91	62.60
50	53.59	54.28	54.96	55.65	56.34	57.03	57.73	58.42	59.12	59.81	60.51	61.21	61.92	62.62	63.33	64.03
51	54.78	55.48	56.19	56.89	57.60	58.30	59.01	59.73	60.44	61.15	61.87	62.59	63.31	64.03	64.75	65.47
52	55.98	56.69	57.41	58.13	58.86	59.58	60.31	61.04	61.77	62.50	63.23	63.97	64.70	65.44	66.18	66.92
53	57.18	57.91	58.65	59.38	60.12	60.87	61.61	62.35	63.10	63.85	64.60	65.35	66.11	66.86	67.62	68.38
54	58.38	59.13	59.88	60.64	61.40	62.16	62.92	63.68	64.44	65.21	65.98	66.75	67.52	68.29	69.07	69.84
55	59.59	60.36	61.13	61.90	62.67	63.45	64.23	65.01	65.79	66.57	67.36	68.14	68.93	69.72	70.52	71.31
56	60.80	61.59	62.38	63.17	63.96	64.75	65.54	66.34	67.14	67.94	68.74	69.55	70.36	71.16	71.97	72.79
57	62.02	62.83	63.63	64.44	65.25	66.06	66.87	67.68	68.50	69.32	70.14	70.96	71.78	72.61	73.44	74.27
58	63.25	64.07	64.89	65.71	66.54	67.37	68.20	69.03	69.86	70.70	71.54	72.38	73.22	74.06	74.91	75.76
59	64.48	65.32	66.15	67.00	67.84	68.68	69.53	70.38	71.23	72.09	72.94	73.80	74.66	75.52	76.39	77.25
60	65.71	66.57	67.42	68.28	69.14	70.01	70.87	71.74	72.61	73.48	74.35	75.23	76.11	76.99	77.87	78.76

NUMBER OF PAYMENTS	ANNUAL PERCENTAGE RATE															
	26.00%	26.25%	26.50%	26.75%	27.00%	27.25%	27.50%	27.75%	28.00%	28.25%	28.50%	28.75%	29.00%	29.25%	29.50%	29.75%
	(FINANCE CHARGE PER $100 OF AMOUNT FINANCED)															
1	2.17	2.19	2.21	2.23	2.25	2.27	2.29	2.31	2.33	2.35	2.37	2.40	2.42	2.44	2.46	2.48
2	3.26	3.29	3.32	3.36	3.39	3.42	3.45	3.48	3.51	3.54	3.58	3.61	3.64	3.67	3.70	3.73
3	4.36	4.41	4.45	4.49	4.53	4.58	4.62	4.66	4.70	4.74	4.79	4.83	4.87	4.91	4.96	5.00
4	5.47	5.53	5.58	5.63	5.69	5.74	5.79	5.85	5.90	5.95	6.01	6.06	6.11	6.17	6.22	6.27
5	6.59	6.66	6.72	6.79	6.85	6.91	6.98	7.04	7.11	7.17	7.24	7.30	7.37	7.43	7.49	7.56
6	7.72	7.79	7.87	7.95	8.02	8.10	8.17	8.25	8.32	8.40	8.48	8.55	8.63	8.70	8.78	8.85
7	8.85	8.94	9.03	9.11	9.20	9.29	9.37	9.46	9.55	9.64	9.72	9.81	9.90	9.98	10.07	10.16
8	9.99	10.09	10.19	10.29	10.39	10.49	10.58	10.68	10.78	10.88	10.98	11.08	11.18	11.28	11.38	11.47
9	11.14	11.25	11.36	11.47	11.58	11.69	11.80	11.91	12.03	12.14	12.25	12.36	12.47	12.58	12.69	12.80
10	12.30	12.42	12.54	12.67	12.79	12.91	13.03	13.15	13.28	13.40	13.52	13.64	13.77	13.89	14.01	14.14
11	13.46	13.60	13.73	13.87	14.00	14.13	14.27	14.40	14.54	14.67	14.81	14.94	15.08	15.21	15.35	15.48
12	14.64	14.78	14.93	15.07	15.22	15.37	15.51	15.66	15.81	15.95	16.10	16.25	16.40	16.54	16.69	16.84
13	15.82	15.97	16.13	16.29	16.45	16.61	16.77	16.93	17.09	17.24	17.40	17.56	17.72	17.88	18.04	18.20
14	17.00	17.17	17.35	17.52	17.69	17.86	18.03	18.20	18.37	18.54	18.72	18.89	19.06	19.23	19.41	19.58
15	18.20	18.38	18.57	18.75	18.93	19.12	19.30	19.48	19.67	19.85	20.04	20.22	20.41	20.59	20.78	20.96
16	19.40	19.60	19.79	19.99	20.19	20.38	20.58	20.78	20.97	21.17	21.37	21.57	21.76	21.96	22.16	22.36
17	20.61	20.82	21.03	21.24	21.45	21.66	21.87	22.08	22.29	22.50	22.71	22.92	23.13	23.34	23.55	23.77
18	21.83	22.05	22.27	22.50	22.72	22.94	23.16	23.39	23.61	23.83	24.06	24.28	24.51	24.73	24.96	25.18
19	23.06	23.29	23.53	23.76	24.00	24.23	24.47	24.71	24.94	25.18	25.42	25.65	25.89	26.13	26.37	26.61
20	24.29	24.54	24.79	25.04	25.28	25.53	25.78	26.03	26.28	26.53	26.78	27.04	27.29	27.54	27.79	28.04
21	25.53	25.79	26.05	26.32	26.58	26.84	27.11	27.37	27.63	27.90	28.16	28.43	28.69	28.96	29.22	29.49
22	26.78	27.05	27.33	27.61	27.88	28.16	28.44	28.71	28.99	29.27	29.55	29.82	30.10	30.38	30.66	30.94
23	28.04	28.32	28.61	28.90	29.19	29.48	29.77	30.07	30.36	30.65	30.94	31.23	31.53	31.82	32.11	32.41
24	29.30	29.60	29.90	30.21	30.51	30.82	31.12	31.43	31.73	32.04	32.34	32.65	32.96	33.27	33.57	33.88
25	30.57	30.89	31.20	31.52	31.84	32.16	32.48	32.80	33.12	33.44	33.76	34.08	34.40	34.72	35.04	35.37
26	31.85	32.18	32.51	32.84	33.18	33.51	33.84	34.18	34.51	34.84	35.18	35.51	35.85	36.19	36.52	36.86
27	33.14	33.48	33.83	34.17	34.52	34.87	35.21	35.56	35.91	36.26	36.61	36.96	37.31	37.66	38.01	38.36
28	34.43	34.79	35.15	35.51	35.87	36.23	36.59	36.96	37.32	37.68	38.05	38.41	38.78	39.15	39.51	39.88
29	35.73	36.10	36.48	36.85	37.23	37.61	37.98	38.36	38.74	39.12	39.50	39.88	40.26	40.64	41.02	41.40
30	37.04	37.43	37.82	38.21	38.60	38.99	39.38	39.77	40.17	40.56	40.95	41.35	41.75	42.14	42.54	42.94

31	38.35	38.76	39.16	39.57	39.97	40.38	40.79	41.19	41.60	42.01	42.42	42.83	43.24	43.65	44.06	44.48
32	39.68	40.10	40.52	40.94	41.36	41.78	42.20	42.62	43.05	43.47	43.90	44.32	44.75	45.17	45.60	46.03
33	41.01	41.44	41.88	42.31	42.75	43.19	43.62	44.06	44.50	44.94	45.38	45.82	46.26	46.70	47.15	47.59
34	42.35	42.80	43.25	43.70	44.15	44.60	45.05	45.51	45.96	46.42	46.87	47.33	47.79	48.24	48.70	49.16
35	43.69	44.16	44.62	45.09	45.56	46.02	46.49	46.96	47.43	47.90	48.37	48.85	49.32	49.79	50.27	50.74
36	45.05	45.53	46.01	46.49	46.97	47.45	47.94	48.42	48.91	49.40	49.88	50.37	50.86	51.35	51.84	52.33
37	46.41	46.90	47.40	47.90	48.39	48.89	49.39	49.89	50.40	50.90	51.40	51.91	52.41	52.92	53.42	53.93
38	47.77	48.29	48.80	49.31	49.82	50.34	50.86	51.37	51.89	52.41	52.93	53.45	53.97	54.49	55.02	55.54
39	49.15	49.68	50.20	50.73	51.26	51.79	52.33	52.86	53.39	53.93	54.46	55.00	55.54	56.08	56.62	57.16
40	50.53	51.07	51.62	52.16	52.71	53.26	53.81	54.35	54.90	55.46	56.01	56.56	57.12	57.67	58.23	58.79
41	51.92	52.48	53.04	53.60	54.16	54.73	55.29	55.86	56.42	56.99	57.56	58.13	58.70	59.28	59.85	60.42
42	53.32	53.89	54.47	55.05	55.63	56.21	56.79	57.37	57.95	58.54	59.12	59.71	60.30	60.89	61.48	62.07
43	54.72	55.31	55.90	56.50	57.09	57.69	58.29	58.89	59.49	60.09	60.69	61.30	61.90	62.51	63.11	63.72
44	56.13	56.74	57.35	57.96	58.57	59.19	59.80	60.42	61.03	61.65	62.27	62.89	63.51	64.14	64.76	65.39
45	57.55	58.17	58.80	59.43	60.06	60.69	61.32	61.95	62.59	63.22	63.86	64.50	65.13	65.77	66.42	67.06
46	58.97	59.61	60.26	60.90	61.55	62.20	62.84	63.49	64.15	64.80	65.45	66.11	66.76	67.42	68.08	68.74
47	60.40	61.06	61.72	62.38	63.05	63.71	64.38	65.05	65.71	66.38	67.06	67.73	68.40	69.08	69.75	70.43
48	61.84	62.52	63.20	63.87	64.56	65.24	65.92	66.60	67.29	67.98	68.67	69.36	70.05	70.74	71.44	72.13
49	63.29	63.98	64.68	65.37	66.07	66.77	67.47	68.17	68.87	69.58	70.29	70.99	71.70	72.41	73.13	73.84
50	64.74	65.45	66.16	66.88	67.59	68.31	69.03	69.75	70.47	71.19	71.91	72.64	73.37	74.10	74.83	75.56
51	66.20	66.93	67.66	68.39	69.12	69.86	70.59	71.33	72.07	72.81	73.55	74.29	75.04	75.78	76.53	77.28
52	67.67	68.41	69.16	69.91	70.66	71.41	72.16	72.92	73.67	74.43	75.19	75.95	76.72	77.48	78.25	79.02
53	69.14	69.90	70.67	71.43	72.20	72.97	73.74	74.52	75.29	76.07	76.85	77.62	78.41	79.19	79.97	80.76
54	70.62	71.40	72.18	72.97	73.75	74.54	75.33	76.12	76.91	77.71	78.50	79.30	80.10	80.90	81.71	82.51
55	72.11	72.91	73.71	74.51	75.31	76.12	76.92	77.73	78.55	79.36	80.17	80.99	81.81	82.63	83.45	84.27
56	73.60	74.42	75.24	76.06	76.88	77.70	78.53	79.35	80.18	81.02	81.85	82.68	83.52	84.36	85.20	86.04
57	75.10	75.94	76.77	77.61	78.45	79.29	80.14	80.98	81.83	82.68	83.53	84.39	85.24	86.10	86.96	87.82
58	76.61	77.46	78.32	79.17	80.03	80.89	81.75	82.62	83.48	84.35	85.22	86.10	86.97	87.85	88.72	89.60
59	78.12	78.99	79.87	80.74	81.62	82.50	83.38	84.26	85.15	86.03	86.92	87.81	88.71	89.60	90.50	91.40
60	79.64	80.53	81.42	82.32	83.21	84.11	85.01	85.91	86.81	87.72	88.63	89.54	90.45	91.37	92.28	93.20

ANNUAL PERCENTAGE RATE

NUMBER OF PAYMENTS	30.00%	30.25%	30.50%	30.75%	31.00%	31.25%	31.50%	31.75%	32.00%	32.25%	32.50%	32.75%	33.00%	33.25%	33.50%	33.75%
					(FINANCE CHARGE PER $100 OF AMOUNT FINANCED)											
1	2.50	2.52	2.54	2.56	2.58	2.60	2.62	2.65	2.67	2.69	2.71	2.73	2.75	2.77	2.79	2.81
2	3.77	3.80	3.83	3.86	3.89	3.92	3.95	3.99	4.02	4.05	4.08	4.11	4.14	4.18	4.21	4.24
3	5.04	5.08	5.13	5.17	5.21	5.25	5.30	5.34	5.38	5.42	5.46	5.51	5.55	5.59	5.63	5.68
4	6.33	6.38	6.43	6.49	6.54	6.59	6.65	6.70	6.75	6.81	6.86	6.91	6.97	7.02	7.08	7.13
5	7.62	7.69	7.75	7.82	7.88	7.95	8.01	8.08	8.14	8.20	8.27	8.33	8.40	8.46	8.53	8.59
6	8.93	9.01	9.08	9.16	9.23	9.31	9.39	9.46	9.54	9.61	9.69	9.77	9.84	9.92	9.99	10.07
7	10.25	10.33	10.42	10.51	10.60	10.68	10.77	10.86	10.95	11.03	11.12	11.21	11.30	11.39	11.47	11.56
8	11.57	11.67	11.77	11.87	11.97	12.07	12.17	12.27	12.37	12.47	12.57	12.67	12.77	12.87	12.97	13.07
9	12.91	13.02	13.13	13.24	13.36	13.47	13.58	13.69	13.80	13.91	14.02	14.14	14.25	14.36	14.47	14.58
10	14.26	14.38	14.50	14.63	14.75	14.87	15.00	15.12	15.24	15.37	15.49	15.62	15.74	15.86	15.99	16.11
11	15.62	15.75	15.89	16.02	16.16	16.29	16.43	16.56	16.70	16.84	16.97	17.11	17.24	17.38	17.52	17.65
12	16.98	17.13	17.28	17.43	17.58	17.72	17.87	18.02	18.17	18.32	18.47	18.61	18.76	18.91	19.06	19.21
13	18.36	18.52	18.68	18.84	19.00	19.16	19.33	19.49	19.65	19.81	19.97	20.13	20.29	20.45	20.62	20.78
14	19.75	19.92	20.10	20.27	20.44	20.62	20.79	20.96	21.14	21.31	21.49	21.66	21.83	22.01	22.18	22.36
15	21.15	21.34	21.52	21.71	21.89	22.08	22.27	22.45	22.64	22.83	23.01	23.20	23.39	23.58	23.76	23.95
16	22.56	22.76	22.96	23.16	23.35	23.55	23.75	23.95	24.15	24.35	24.55	24.75	24.96	25.16	25.36	25.56
17	23.98	24.19	24.40	24.61	24.83	25.04	25.25	25.47	25.68	25.89	26.11	26.32	26.53	26.75	26.96	27.18
18	25.41	25.63	25.86	26.08	26.31	26.54	26.76	26.99	27.22	27.44	27.67	27.90	28.13	28.35	28.58	28.81
19	26.85	27.08	27.32	27.56	27.80	28.04	28.28	28.52	28.76	29.00	29.25	29.49	29.73	29.97	30.21	30.45
20	28.29	28.55	28.80	29.05	29.31	29.56	29.81	30.07	30.32	30.58	30.83	31.09	31.34	31.60	31.86	32.11
21	29.75	30.02	30.29	30.55	30.82	31.09	31.36	31.62	31.89	32.16	32.43	32.70	32.97	33.24	33.51	33.78
22	31.22	31.50	31.78	32.06	32.35	32.63	32.91	33.19	33.48	33.76	34.04	34.33	34.61	34.89	35.18	35.46
23	32.70	33.00	33.29	33.59	33.88	34.18	34.48	34.77	35.07	35.37	35.66	35.96	36.26	36.56	36.86	37.16
24	34.19	34.50	34.81	35.12	35.43	35.74	36.05	36.36	36.67	36.99	37.30	37.61	37.92	38.24	38.55	38.87
25	35.69	36.01	36.34	36.66	36.99	37.31	37.64	37.96	38.29	38.62	38.94	39.27	39.60	39.93	40.26	40.59
26	37.20	37.54	37.88	38.21	38.55	38.89	39.23	39.58	39.92	40.26	40.60	40.94	41.29	41.63	41.97	42.32
27	38.72	39.07	39.42	39.78	40.13	40.49	40.84	41.20	41.56	41.91	42.27	42.63	42.99	43.34	43.70	44.06
28	40.25	40.61	40.98	41.35	41.72	42.09	42.46	42.83	43.20	43.58	43.95	44.32	44.70	45.07	45.45	45.82
29	41.78	42.17	42.55	42.94	43.32	43.71	44.09	44.48	44.87	45.25	45.64	46.03	46.42	46.81	47.20	47.59
30	43.33	43.73	44.13	44.53	44.93	45.33	45.73	46.13	46.54	46.94	47.34	47.75	48.15	48.56	48.96	49.37

31	44.89	45.30	45.72	46.13	46.55	46.97	47.38	47.80	48.22	48.64	49.06	49.48	49.90	50.32	50.74	51.17
32	46.46	46.89	47.32	47.75	48.18	48.61	49.05	49.48	49.91	50.35	50.78	51.22	51.66	52.09	52.53	52.97
33	48.04	48.48	48.93	49.37	49.82	50.27	50.72	51.17	51.62	52.07	52.52	52.97	53.43	53.88	54.33	54.79
34	49.62	50.08	50.55	51.01	51.47	51.94	52.40	52.87	53.33	53.80	54.27	54.74	55.21	55.68	56.15	56.62
35	51.22	51.70	52.17	52.65	53.13	53.61	54.09	54.58	55.06	55.54	56.03	56.51	57.00	57.48	57.97	58.46
36	52.83	53.32	53.81	54.31	54.80	55.30	55.80	56.30	56.80	57.30	57.80	58.30	58.80	59.30	59.81	60.31
37	54.44	54.95	55.46	55.97	56.49	57.00	57.51	58.03	58.54	59.06	59.58	60.10	60.62	61.14	61.66	62.18
38	56.07	56.59	57.12	57.65	58.18	58.71	59.24	59.77	60.30	60.84	61.37	61.90	62.44	62.98	63.52	64.06
39	57.70	58.24	58.79	59.33	59.88	60.42	60.97	61.52	62.07	62.62	63.17	63.72	64.28	64.83	65.39	65.94
40	59.34	59.90	60.47	61.03	61.59	62.15	62.72	63.28	63.85	64.42	64.99	65.56	66.13	66.70	67.27	67.84
41	61.00	61.57	62.15	62.73	63.31	63.89	64.47	65.06	65.64	66.22	66.81	67.40	67.99	68.57	69.16	69.76
42	62.66	63.25	63.85	64.44	65.04	65.64	66.24	66.84	67.44	68.04	68.65	69.25	69.86	70.46	71.07	71.68
43	64.33	64.94	65.56	66.17	66.78	67.40	68.01	68.63	69.25	69.87	70.49	71.11	71.74	72.36	72.99	73.61
44	66.01	66.64	67.27	67.90	68.53	69.17	69.80	70.43	71.07	71.71	72.35	72.99	73.63	74.27	74.91	75.56
45	67.70	68.35	69.00	69.64	70.29	70.94	71.60	72.25	72.90	73.56	74.21	74.87	75.53	76.19	76.85	77.52
46	69.40	70.07	70.73	71.40	72.06	72.73	73.40	74.07	74.74	75.42	76.09	76.77	77.44	78.12	78.80	79.48
47	71.11	71.79	72.47	73.16	73.84	74.53	75.22	75.90	76.60	77.29	77.98	78.67	79.37	80.07	80.76	81.46
48	72.83	73.53	74.23	74.93	75.63	76.34	77.04	77.75	78.46	79.17	79.88	80.59	81.30	82.02	82.74	83.45
49	74.55	75.27	75.99	76.71	77.43	78.15	78.88	79.60	80.33	81.06	81.79	82.52	83.25	83.98	84.72	85.45
50	76.29	77.02	77.76	78.50	79.24	79.98	80.72	81.46	82.21	82.96	83.70	84.45	85.20	85.96	86.71	87.47
51	78.03	78.79	79.54	80.30	81.06	81.81	82.58	83.34	84.10	84.87	85.63	86.40	87.17	87.94	88.71	89.49
52	79.79	80.56	81.33	82.11	82.88	83.66	84.44	85.22	86.00	86.79	87.57	88.36	89.15	89.94	90.73	91.52
53	81.55	82.34	83.13	83.92	84.72	85.51	86.31	87.11	87.91	88.72	89.52	90.33	91.13	91.94	92.75	93.57
54	83.32	84.13	84.94	85.75	86.56	87.38	88.19	89.01	89.83	90.66	91.48	92.30	93.13	93.96	94.79	95.62
55	85.10	85.93	86.75	87.58	88.42	89.25	90.09	90.92	91.76	92.60	93.45	94.29	95.14	95.99	96.83	97.69
56	86.89	87.73	88.58	89.43	90.28	91.13	91.99	92.84	93.70	94.56	95.43	96.29	97.15	98.02	98.89	99.76
57	88.68	89.55	90.41	91.28	92.15	93.02	93.90	94.77	95.65	96.53	97.41	98.30	99.18	100.07	100.96	101.85
58	90.49	91.37	92.26	93.14	94.03	94.92	95.82	96.71	97.61	98.51	99.41	100.31	101.22	102.12	103.03	103.94
59	92.30	93.20	94.11	95.01	95.92	96.83	97.75	98.66	99.58	100.50	101.42	102.34	103.26	104.19	105.12	106.05
60	94.12	95.04	95.97	96.89	97.82	98.75	99.68	100.62	101.56	102.49	103.43	104.38	105.32	106.27	107.21	108.16

Appendix L
Answers to the Odd-Numbered Problems

LEARNING UNIT 1.1

1. eighteen
3. four thousand, seventy-three
5. one hundred seventy thousand, six hundred
7. thirty-nine million, forty thousand, three hundred twenty-seven
9. three hundredths
11. one hundred twenty-two and five tenths
13. nine and three hundred sixty-three hundred thousandths
15. five and two hundred sixty-three millionths
17. 825
19. 7,200
21. 48,203
23. 123.456
25. 401.00034
27. 13,240.065
29. 3; 7; thirty-seven hundredths
31. 4; 6; 0; 3; 8; forty-six and thirty-eight thousandths
33. 5; 8; 8; 7; 1; 2; 3; five-hundred eighty-eight and seven thousand one hundred twenty-three ten-thousandths.

LEARNING UNIT 1.2

1. 26,490; 26,500; 26,000
3. 7,140; 7,100; 7,000
5. 1,860; 1,900; 2,000
7. 327,000; 330,000; 300,000
9. 150,000; 150,000; 100,000
11. 79,000,000
13. 3,000,000
15. 77; 76.8; 76.83
17. 9; 9.4; 9.44
19. 5; 5.4; 5.43
21. .39; .394
23. 13.65; 13.653

LEARNING UNIT 1.3

1. 15,079
3. 2,054
5. 190
7. 2,255
9. 1,660; 2,210; 1,222; 5,092
11. 1,192; 2,080; 2,030; 5,302
13. 141
15. 187
17. 4,686
19. 12,512
21. 33,835
23. 101,893
25. 314
27. 8,291
29. 10,564

31.	$401
33.	$1,485
35.	$1,411
37.	$6,688
39.	2,139
41.	3,522
43.	1,333
45.	$2,722
47.	$3,454; $3,691; $3,838; $3,614; $3,243; $17,840
49.	$81
51.	$1,456

LEARNING UNIT 1.4

1. 154,070
3. 182,736
5. 1,091,350
7. 2,515,030
9. 19,559,162
11. 29,130,387
13. 44,367,600
15. 269,992,260
17. 16,273
19. 489,069
21. 113; 2
23. 60; 16
25. 17; 54
27. 42; 302
29. 80; 172
31. 54
33. 78
35. 789
37. 327
39. 672
41. $108; $132; $145; $532; $917
43. $6

LEARNING UNIT 1.5

1. 30.23
3. 21.94
5. 184.24
7. $2,319.54
9. 2,016.44
11. $85.66
13. .86
15. 2.99
17. 337.11
19. 1.22
21. $35.18
23. $47.95
25. $660.69

LEARNING UNIT 1.6

1. 4.7
3. .75
5. 129.2
7. 1.75
9. 286.69
11. 41.48
13. 149.61
15. $128.19
17. .01
19. 3,720
21. 960
23. 36
25. 144
27. 96,300
29. 1,340
31. 16,500
33. 477.5
35. 55,200
37. 1,580
39. 4.59
41. 14.654
43. 16.8
45. 3.68
47. .768
49. .62
51. $6.40

53. 3.249
55. $1.71
57. .0546
59. $5,162.48
61. $142.08
63. $1,126.88
65. $2.88

LEARNING UNIT 2.1

1. $\frac{3}{5}$
3. $\frac{3}{5}$
5. $\frac{3}{4}$
7. $\frac{18}{53}$
9. $\frac{5}{13}$
11. $\frac{9}{16}$
13. $\frac{11}{18}$
15. $\frac{7}{12}$
17. 15
19. 49
21. 65
23. 102
25. 66
27. 348
29. 18
31. 38
33. 32

LEARNING UNIT 2.2

1. $2\frac{1}{2}$
3. $6\frac{1}{6}$
5. $17\frac{1}{4}$
7. $3\frac{7}{30}$
9. $\frac{13}{2}$
11. $\frac{51}{8}$
13. $\frac{59}{12}$

15. $\frac{293}{20}$
17. .6
19. .833
21. .563
23. 26.725
25. $\frac{7}{10}$
27. $\frac{13}{20}$
29. $18\frac{1}{40}$
31. $3\frac{1}{4}$

LEARNING UNIT 2.3

1. $1\frac{1}{2}$
3. $30\frac{19}{20}$
5. $7\frac{17}{72}$
7. $\frac{1}{2}$
9. $26\frac{1}{20}$
11. $2\frac{1}{90}$
13. $1\frac{83}{90}$
15. $\frac{23}{180}$
17. $7\frac{29}{30}$
19. $78\frac{1}{6}$
21. $163\frac{37}{40}$

LEARNING UNIT 2.4

1. $\frac{2}{9}$
3. $\frac{5}{21}$
5. $36\frac{1}{6}$
7. $45\frac{13}{15}$
9. $\frac{1}{108}$
11. $\frac{10}{11}$
13. $\frac{3}{4}$

15. $\frac{37}{76}$

17. $3\frac{1}{4}$

19. $1\frac{29}{394}$

21. $58

23. Rust 18,480; Smith 13,860; Towns 23,100

25. $113\frac{7}{16}$

LEARNING UNIT 3.1

1. .03
3. .36
5. .273
7. .1406
9. .135
11. .2625
13. .005
15. 1.97
17. .9632
19. 2.737
21. 4%
23. 520%
25. 2.2%
27. 900%
29. $33\frac{1}{3}$%
31. 20%
33. 42.06%
35. 525%
37. 3700%
39. 1326%
41. $\frac{1}{10}$
43. $\frac{2}{175}$
45. $2\frac{81}{500}$
47. $\frac{4}{25}$
49. $\frac{3}{400}$
51. $\frac{1}{4}$
53. $\frac{1}{500}$
55. $\frac{9}{400}$

57. $\frac{1}{2}$
59. $\frac{1}{200}$
61. $33\frac{1}{3}$%
63. 20%
65. 1710%
67. 87.5%
69. 570%
71. 262.5%
73. 106.25%
75. 75%
77. 1820%
79. 12.5%
81. .5, 50%
83. .20, 20%
85. $2\frac{9}{20}$, 245%
87. 2.75, 275%
89. $\frac{31}{200}$, .155
91. $5
93. $60
95. $100

LEARNING UNIT 3.2

1. 14
3. 9
5. $\frac{2}{7}$
7. 7
9. 5
11. 20
13. $1\frac{2}{5}$
15. $\frac{1}{6}$
17. $3\frac{1}{2}$
19. 2

LEARNING UNIT 3.3

1. 14.4
3. .035
5. 25%

7. 250
9. 100
11. 6
13. 20%
15. 1,200
17. $210,000
19. 95
21. $110; $99
23. $750
25. $1,562.70
27. $156
29. $800
31. $7,500
33. 17.54%
35. $2,457.14
37. 48.72%
39. $350,000

LEARNING UNIT 4.1

1. 57%; $51.30
3. 76%; $494
5. $66\frac{2}{3}$%; $624
7. 68%; $24.64
9. $87\frac{1}{2}$%; $42.42
11. 60%; $115.44
13. 56.7%; $111.13
15. 57.6%; $65.72
17. 28%
19. 43.3%
21. 45.85%
23. 30%, 10%
25. 25%, 20%
27. $209.97
29. $179.17; $193.96
31. $140.11; $137.89
33. $272.16
35. Specialty Wholesale Company; $1.25

LEARNING UNIT 4.2

1. $370.99
3. $595.02
5. $946.34
7. $790.39
9. $85.62
11. $189.23
13. October 12; November 1
15. May 10; May 25
17. March 31; June 19
19. $3.40; $173.70
21. $24; $586
23. $9.60; $310.40
25. $9.24; $452.76
27. $153.06; $169.34
29. $434.34; $483.76
31. $180.41; $219.46
33. $7.63; $7.48
35. December 23
37. November 17; October 23; $274; $268.52
39. $237.80
41. July 26; August 15
43. Yes; 20 days; $4.85
45. $154.64; $172.36

LEARNING UNIT 5.1

1. $205.00
3. $190.00
5. $123.00
7. $114.00
9. $82.00
11. $76.00
13. $14.85
15. $10.10
17. $20.41
19. $14.93

21. $6.64
23. $7.35
25. $5.43; 46.02%
27. $3.82; 35.05%
29. $3.90; 25.00%
31. $19.80
33. $26.54
35. $22.16
37. $10.73
39. $4.98
41. $7.00
43. $5.43; 31.51%
45. $3.82; 25.95%
47. $3.90; 20%
49. $13.87
51. 42.76%
53. $5.47
55. $30.40
57. $28
59. 43.75%
61. $15.38

LEARNING UNIT 5.2

1.	$1.86	9.	$.14
3.	$2.11	11.	$5.56
5.	$61.89	13.	$9.73
7.	167.44	15.	$.60

LEARNING UNIT 5.3

1. $5, $33\frac{1}{3}$%
3. $6, $16\frac{2}{3}$%
5. $20, 50%
7. $4, 40%
9. $12, $37\frac{1}{2}$%
11. $.05, 25%
13. $4, 25%
15. $5, 100%

17. $7, 50%
19. $2, 40%
21. $30
23. $10
25. $9
27. $50
29. $15, $37\frac{1}{2}$%
31. $50, $66\frac{2}{3}$%
33. $97.62, $27.33
35. $71.43

LEARNING UNIT 6.1

1. $1,250
3. $340.00
5. $701.54
7. $312.80
9. $282.00
11. $240.00
13. $204.80
15. $94.40
17. $351.00
19. $1,213.60
21. $1,396.88
23. $321.64
25. $1,575.00
27. $259.99
29. $399.75

LEARNING UNIT 6.2

1. $26.90
3. $55.50
5. $16.80
7. $18.64
9. $25.32
11. $10.30
13. $256.12
15. $195.12
17. $180.11

19. $235.22
21. $196.01
23. $297.96
25. $225.85
27. $209.36
29. $235.20
31. $30.00
33. $30.19
35. $56.70
37. $85.84
39. $66.49
41. $200.63
43. $2,210.82
45. $1,104.62
47. $1,932.76

LEARNING UNIT 7.1

1. $4,000; $1,000
3. $18,500; $2,312.50
5. $21,789; $3,631.50
7. 4
9. 11
11. 10
13. $300
15. $1,047.62
17. $1,263.64
19.

Year	Cost	Depreciation Expense	Accumulated Depreciation	Book Value
0	$8,300	$ —0—	$ —0—	$8,300
1	8,300	1,500	1,500	6,800
2	8,300	1,500	3,000	5,300
3	8,300	1,500	4,500	3,800
4	8,300	1,500	6,000	2,300
5	8,300	1,500	7,500	800

21. $122.60
23. $160
25. $9,474.70
27. $20.48; 10%; $816.62

LEARNING UNIT 7.2

1. $6,000; $.60; $805.20
3. $63,000; $1.26; $6,737.22
5. $182,245; $2.87;
   $5,866.28
7. $50,000; $.50; $1,083
9. $157,500; $.63;
   $24,640.56
11. $8,625; $.069; $1,815.18
13. $15,600
15. $304.75; $438.84

LEARNING UNIT 7.3

1. $\frac{1}{2}$ (SYD = 6)

3. $\frac{2}{7}$ (SYD = 21).

5. $\frac{1}{5}$ (SYD = 45)

7. $\frac{3}{40}$ (SYD = 120)

9. $367.11; $1,384.89
11. $234; $618

13.

Year	Cost	Depreciation Fraction	Depreciation Expense	Accumulated Depreciation	Book Value
0	$9,474.70		$ —0—	$ —0—	$9,474.70
1	9,474.70	$\frac{4}{10}$	3,389.88	3,389.88	6,084.82
2	9,474.70	$\frac{3}{10}$	2,542.41	5,932.29	3,542.41
3	9,474.70	$\frac{2}{10}$	1,694.94	7,627.23	1,847.47
4	9,474.70	$\frac{1}{10}$	847.47	8,474.70	1,000.00

15.

Year	Cost	Depreciation Fraction	Depreciation Expense	Accumulated Depreciation	Book Value
0	$71,340		$ —0—	$ —0—	$71,340.00
1	71,340	$\frac{5}{15}$	16,113.33	16,113.33	55,226.67
2	71,340	$\frac{4}{15}$	12,890.67	29,004.00	42,336.00
3	71,340	$\frac{3}{15}$	9,668.00	38,672.00	32,668.00
4	71,340	$\frac{2}{15}$	6,445.33	45,117.33	26,222.67
5	71,340	$\frac{1}{15}$	3,222.67	48,340.00	23,000.00

1. 50%
3. $33\frac{1}{3}$%
5. 20%
7. 8%
9. $438; $1,314
11. $340.80; $511.20

13.

Year	Cost	Depreciation Rate	Depreciation Expense	Accumulated Depreciation	Book Value
0	$9,474.70		$ —0—	$ —0—	$9,474.70
1	9,474.70	50%	4,737.35	4,737.35	4,737.35
2	9,474.70	50%	2,368.68	7,106.03	2,368.67
3	9,474.70	50%	1,184.34	8,290.37	1,184.33
4	9,474.70	50%	184.33	8,474.70	1,000.00

15.

Year	Cost	Depreciation Rate	Depreciation Expense	Accumulated Depreciation	Book Value
0	$71,340		$ —0—	$ —0—	$71,340.00
1	71,340	40%	28,536.00	28,536.00	42,804.00
2	71,340	40%	17,121.60	45,657.60	25,682.40
3	71,340	40%	2,682.40	48,340.00	23,000.00
4	71,340	40%	—0—	48,340.00	23,000.00
5	71,340	40%	—0—	48,340.00	23,000.00

1. $276
3. $288
5. $745
7. $710
9. $1,769
11. $1,552
13. $350.00
15. $330.00
17. $364.00
19. $239.60
21. $45.00
23. (a) 36, (b) $153.58, (c) $55.51
25. $2,552.04

1. $301,244
3. $492,178
5. $167,265
7. $78,000
9. $218,026
11. $609,373
13. $362,544, $360,544
15. $990,505, $93,761
17. $41,481, $355,701
19. $333,967
21. $1,102
23. $25,244
25. $446,421.91

LEARNING UNIT 9.1

1. 53.91
   15.30
   16.43
   2.04
   2.22
   2.00
   .41
   .38
   92.70
   7.30
3. $ 4,300   2.29%
   (3,000)   (3.41)
   3,000   7.69
   2,300   16.20
   50   2.33
   1,100   21.57
   (100)   (16.67)
   (100)   (14.29)
   (350)   (28.00)
   2,900   1.92
   1,400   3.78

LEARNING UNIT 9.2

1. 2.55:1
3. 1.71:1
5. 20.62%
7. (a)   1.04:1   (19-1)
        .875:1   (19-2)
   (b)   acid test ratio
9. 2
11. 12%

LEARNING UNIT 9.3

1. $948.90
3. $8,216.37

LEARNING UNIT 10.1

1. $15,700 each

3. Spears, $24,600
   Tison, $36,900
   Young, $24,600
5. Jones, $22,380
   Miles, $11,190
   Moody, $33,570
7. Pool, $7,020
   Wagner, $3,060
   Weems, $1,080
9. Guy, $20,400
   Nail, $21,040
   Ross, $21,360
11. a. $11,500 each
    b. $9,200, $13,800
    c. $9,200, $13,800
    d. $13,000, $10,000

LEARNING UNIT 10.2

1. $2.13
3. $5 pf, $1 common
5. $7 pf, $7 common
7. $8 pf, $3 common
9. $100,000 pf, $207,000 common
11. $43,600, $109,000
13. $73,250 common
15. $1,260,000 pf, $1,512,000 common
17. a. $1.14
    b. $4.80 pf, $.44 common
19. a. $544,000 common
    b. $285,000 pf
       $259,000 common
    c. $160,000 pf
       $324,000 common
       $60,000 cum pf

LEARNING UNIT 11.1

1. $18.00
3. $128.89

5. $733.33
7. $108.50
9. $48.33
11. $25.88
13. $15.85
15. $38.00
17. $44.38
19. $733.56
21. $195.96
23. $65.75
25. $37.07
27. $26.00 ordinary
    $25.64 exact
    $.36 difference
29. $240.83 ordinary
    $237.53 exact
    $3.30 difference
31. $12,789.40
33. $7
35. $355.07
37. $3,972.50

LEARNING UNIT 11.2

1. $4,000.00
3. $960.00
5. $8,340.00
7. 12%
9. 3%
11. 9.3%
13. 36 days
15. 45 days
17. 15 days
19. 180 days
21. $20,000.00
23. $36,000.00
25. 90 days

LEARNING UNIT 11.3

1. August 8, 1979
3. July 7, 1980
5. March 6, 1981
7. May 18, 1981
9. February 12, 1980
11. $59.18, $2,940.82
13. $17.20, $1,362.80
15. $94.03, $1,205.97
17. $798.90, $11,201.10
19. $13.17, $749.83
21. May 5, 1979, $2,026.30
23. March 7, 1980, $966.12
25. December 14, 1981, $2,217.39
27. June 30, 1980, $4,351.03
29. June 27, 1981, $1,260.21
31. $58.89, $4,998.64
33. $45.59, $3,217.53
35. $46.86, $8,002.46
37. $53.16, $2,800.35
39. $84.46, $12,004.31

LEARNING UNIT 12.1

1. $146.88
3. $744.41
5. $2,258.89
7. $1,325.38, $125.38
9. $8,308.59, $2,108.59
11. $27,891.51, $10,591.51
13. $5,161.01, $1,861.01
15. $135,849.63, $73,849.63
17. $6,743.37
19. (a) $7,319.34,
    (b) $1,319.34

LEARNING UNIT 12.2

1. 18%
3. 9%
5. 6%
7. $7\frac{1}{4}$ yr. or 7 yr. and 3 months
9. 3 years
11. $3\frac{1}{3}$ years or 3 years 4 mo.

13. $4\frac{3}{4}$ yr. or 4 yr. 9 mo.

15. $3\frac{1}{2}\%$, 7%

LEARNING UNIT 12.3

1. $1,849.11
3. $3,248.23
5. $4,728.95
7. $1,228.63
9. $10,338.74
11. $20,046.15
13. $16,861.54
15. (a) $3,132.32,
    (b) $2,114.60,
    (c) $7,158.01
17. $22,819.35
19. $18,621.53

LEARNING UNIT 12.4

1. $5,187.90
3. $11,977.99
5. $20,220.77
7. $4,018.48
9. $5,029.62
11. $6,423.69
13. $40,281.29
15. 20
17. $37,625.96
19. $39,676.76

LEARNING UNIT 12.5

1. $2,159.17
3. $2,268.19
5. $409.79
7. $1,485.17
9. $1,126.65, $2,973.60
11. $342.12, $6,367.92
13. $1,518.83, $5,623.40
15. $680.39, $3,505.96
17. $1,297.87
19. $7,009.77

21. $839.33
23. $2,112.68
25. $146.22, $5,848.80,
    $1,848.80
27. $521.69, $15,650.70,
    $1,150.70
29. $1,972.08, $11,832.48,
    $2,432.48
31. $11,548.74, $57,743.70,
    $7,743.70
33. $5,261.75
35. (a) $16,555.75
    (b) $337,770.00
    (c) $662,230.00
37. (a) $159.00
    (b) $724.00

LEARNING UNIT 13.1

1. 13.00%
3. 15.50%
5. 16.00%
7. 10.75%
9. 17.00%
11. 21.50%
13. 30.50%
15. 17.25%
17. 28.00%
19. 24.25%
21. 28.50%
23. 20.50%
25. a. 15.75%
    b. 17.50%
    c. 9.75%
    d. 14.25%
    e. 14.50%

LEARNING UNIT 13.2

1. $166.14, 12%
3. $136.00, 18%
5. $78.70, 21%
7. $65.30, 21%

9. $85.55, 18%
11. $160.19
13. $160.89
15. $88.98
17. $378.75
19. $557.95
21. $2.40

LEARNING UNIT 14.1

1. $30.625
3. $32.125
5. $104.125
7. $17.875
9. $14.875
11. $45.75
13. $1.40
15. $1.96
17. $.64
19. $.44
21. $.96
23. 13, 6.4%
25. 17, 4.8%
27. 18, 4.5%
29. 11, 7.6%
31. $45.875
33. $.86
35. .02, 2.3%

LEARNING UNIT 14.2

1. $980, $107.50
3. $870, $30
5. $837.50, $73.75
7. $935, $50
9. $795, $61
11. $730, $45
13. discount
15. 8.6%
17. 9%
19. 61.5%
21. $980
23. $1,033.44

25. $750, 5.3%, $20
27. $975

LEARNING UNIT 15.1

1. $6,360
3. $3,350
5. $2,990
7. $3,700; $1,850
9. $2,160; $1,296
11. $3,360; $1,848
13. 6%
15. 5.5%
17. 5%
19. $92,000
21. $108,000
23. $196,000
25. $3,157
27. $45,000
29. $52,127.66
31. $28,571

LEARNING UNIT 15.2

1. $333.90; $458.90
3. $260.40; $410.40
5. $319.20; $544.20
7. $650
9. $590
11. $1,980
13. 4; $1,280
15. $515

LEARNING UNIT 15.3

1. $32,500; $471.25
3. $4,800; $228
5. $71,250; $997.50
7. $62,400; $686.40
9. $48,000; $466.56
11. $27,600; $368.46
13. $54,000; $345.06
15. $57,000; $498.18

17. $2,166.75
19. $642.79

LEARNING UNIT 15.4

1. $17,700
3. $18,300
5. 4%
7. 3.5%

LEARNING UNIT 16.1

1. $20,000; $4,000
3. $20,000; $8,000
5. $7,000; $25,000
7. $71
9. $68
11. $103.68
13. $105
15. $42
17. $47
19. $25
21. $54
23. $169
25. $511.82
27. $118.37
29. $428
31. $837
33. $186.96

LEARNING UNIT 16.2

1. $81
3. $260.11
5. $386.60
7. $653.40
9. $195; $37.05
11. $241.86; $154.79
13. $144.90; $31.88
15. $23,000
17. $18,000
19. $4,401.41
21. $39,187.57

23. $178.20
25. $21,153.84

LEARNING UNIT 16.3

1. $14.30
3. $37.24
5. $2.37
7. $2.88; $288
9. $21.42; $535.50
11. $25.91; $259.10
13. $33.07; $496.05
15. $28.80; $14.69; $7.49; $2.59
17. $214.20; $109.24; $55.69; $19.28
19. $8.10
21. $1,955

LEARNING UNIT 17.1

1. $33.48
3. $244.13
5. $117.05
7. $90.75
9. $353.72
11. $144.48
13. $33.60
15. $133.06
17. $267.90
19. $462.17
21. $294.64
23. $500

LEARNING UNIT 17.2

1. 4,690
3. 23,214
5. $66.80, 14,191
7. $429.00, 43,006
9. $736.00
11. $666.00
13. $1,025.00

LEARNING UNIT 18.1

1. (a) 238.25, (b) 240,
   (c) 246
3. (a) $13,000, (b) $11,000,
   (c) b
5. 89
7. (a) 20.57, (b) 21, (c) 23

LEARNING UNIT 18.2

1. (a) 89.58, (b) 66.67,
   (c) 0–49
3. (a) 75.3, (b) 76.11,
   (c) 70–79 and 80–89
5. (a) 87,845, (b) 93, 306,
   (c) 70–129

LEARNING UNIT 18.3

1. Dollars in Thousands — Comparison of Sales and Cost of Goods Sold

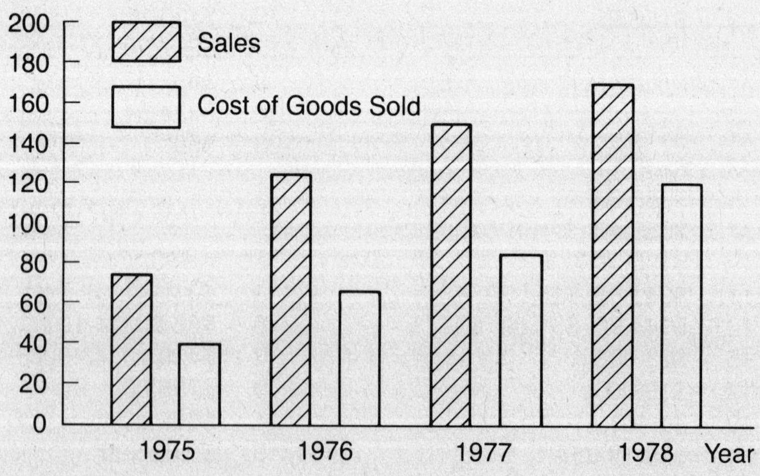

3.

Employee Turnover
80
70
60
50
40
30
20
10
0
1973
'74
'75
'76
'77
'78
Year

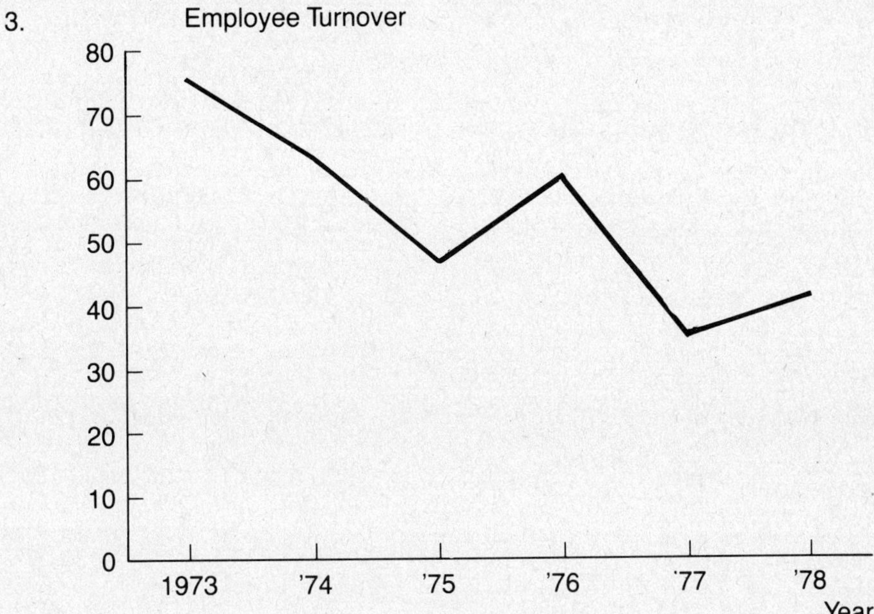

5.

The Budget Dollar
of the Federal Government
(Receipts, where
$ comes from)
38¢
28¢
9¢
12¢
13¢

The Budget Dollar
of the Federal Government
(Expenditures, where
$ goes)
37¢
24¢
8¢
14¢
17¢

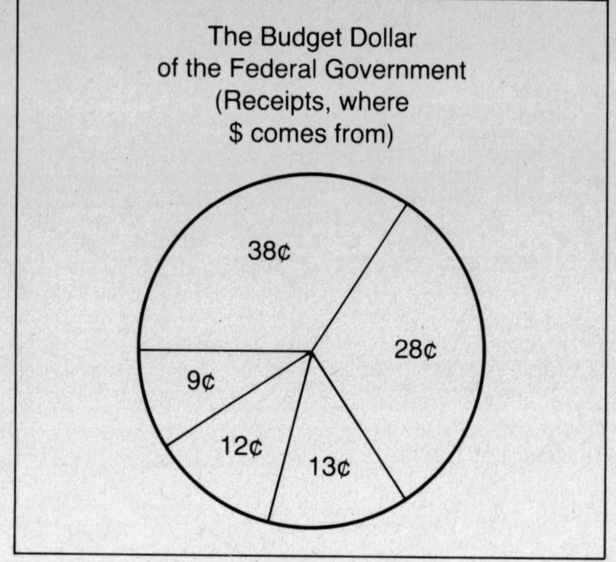

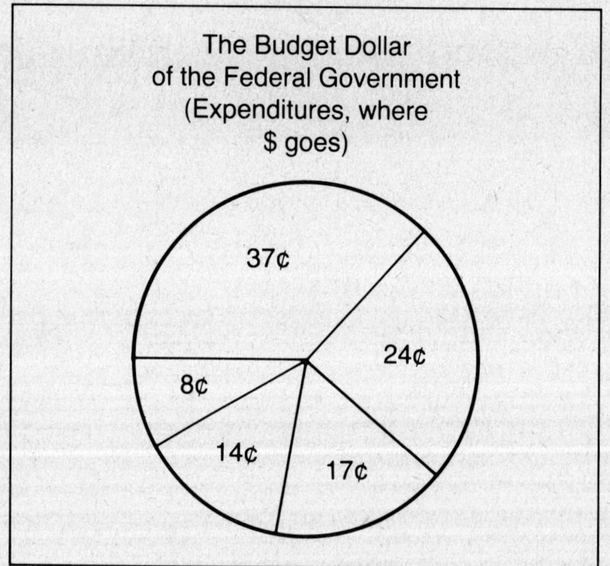

Appendix M
Answers to the Chapter Self-Evaluations

CHAPTER 1

1. 124,357
2. six and five thousand four ten-thousandths
3. 133.16; 548.3; 4.224
4. 362,628
5. 1,346
6. 14,943
7. $106,254
8. $188,876
9. 197.12
10. 209.54
11. 152.11
12. 14.5
13. $159.85

CHAPTER 2

1. $\frac{2}{3}$
2. 9
3. 9
4. $9\frac{3}{4}$
5. $\frac{29}{4}$
6. .25
7. $\frac{3}{4}$
8. $1\frac{7}{24}$
9. $\frac{5}{12}$
10. $\frac{1}{3}$
11. $2\frac{10}{27}$
12. $185\frac{5}{8}$
13. 112

CHAPTER 3

1. .29
2. 35.5%
3. $\frac{1}{4}$
4. 320%
5. $3.60
6. 25%
7. $1,200
8. 20%
9. $13.28
10. 2%
11. $2,600
12. $66,667
13. 4
14. 17
15. $20.00

CHAPTER 4

1. $473.77
2. $34.60
3. Yes
4. Yes
5. 64.8%; $106.27
6. 76.5%; $156.52
7. $6.55; $321.05
8. $2.90; $141.86
9. $6.40; $160.10
10. $24.30; $796.10
11. $459.18; $432.42

CHAPTER 5

1. $45
2. $28

3. $13
4. $12
5. $33.33
6. $50
7. $.43
8. $3.61
9. $5 or 20%
10. $5 or $33\frac{1}{3}$%

CHAPTER 6

1. $1,885
2. $738.46
3. $312.00
4. $354.75
5. $256.00
6. $956.00
7. $1,910.11
8. (a) $58.10, (b) $19.31
9. $61.30

CHAPTER 7

1. $593.13
2. $1,160
3. $1,054.44
4. $1,386.25
5. $6.73

CHAPTER 8

1. (a) $93.00, (b) $105.00
   (c) $77.00, (d) $94.50
2. (a) $110.40, (b) $114.00,
   (c) $110.40
3. $45,175.65
4. $132,485

CHAPTER 9

1. 65.04
   34.96
   9.08

   25.88
2. $34,000, 79.07%
   $21,000, 10.88%
   $55,000, 23.31%
   ($12,000), (46.15%)
   $8,000, 6.84%
   ($4,000), (2,80%)
   $59,000, 63.44%
   $55,000, 23.31%
3. (a) 5.5:1
   (b) 4.43:1
   (c) 1.71:1
   (d) 76.7%
   (e) 6.38
4. $3,539.43

CHAPTER 10

1. $19,890, $19890
2. $17,000, $18,200,
   $20,800
3. $30,540, $18,324
4. $16,670, $18,670,
   $15,670
5. $36,000, $200,000
6. $18,000, $33,000
7. $5, $7, $.75

CHAPTER 11

1. $33.00
2. $60.00
3. (a) 9%
   (b) $2,500
   (c) $32.40
   (d) 12%
4. (a) July 16
   (b) February 9
5. $3,635.12
6. (a) September 5
   (b) $7,138.08
7. $2,697.08

CHAPTER 12

1. $98.18
2. $3,163.48
3. $4,997.90
4. 11%
5. 23
6. $1,382.21
7. $8,083.50
8. $13,388.62
9. $11,504.14
10. $5,287.67
11. $n = 26$
12. (a) $3,150.46
    (b) $151,222.08
    (c) $98,777.92
13. (a) $348.39
    (b) $2,722.72
    (c) $16,722.72

CHAPTER 13

1. 16.50%
2. 15.00%
3. 32.25%
4. 25.50%
5. $149.49, 16%
6. $472.77

CHAPTER 14

1. 11.625
2. 1.25
3. 18
4. 5.5%
5. $1,145.00
6. $31.25
7. $928.75

CHAPTER 15

1. $3,384
2. $930
3. 5.5%
4. $162,400
5. $56,375
6. $60,531.91
7. $368.75
8. $805
9. 5
10. $1,394.02
11. $3,243
12. $425

CHAPTER 16

1. $355.60
2. $874.20
3. $16,250
4. $36.99
5. $228.67
6. $18,532

CHAPTER 17

1. $384.38
2. $17.82
3. $508.93
4. 16.524
5. $11.60 combined

CHAPTER 18

1. (a) 77.83
   (b) 79.5
   (c) 71 and 82
2. (a) 14.41
   (b) 14.29
   (c) 11-15

3.

Men
Women
Elementary
Secondary
College
Secondary
Elementary
College

4.

100%
80%
60%
40%
20%
30%
70%
35%
65%
45%
55%
42%
58%
Women
Men
1950
1960
1970
1975

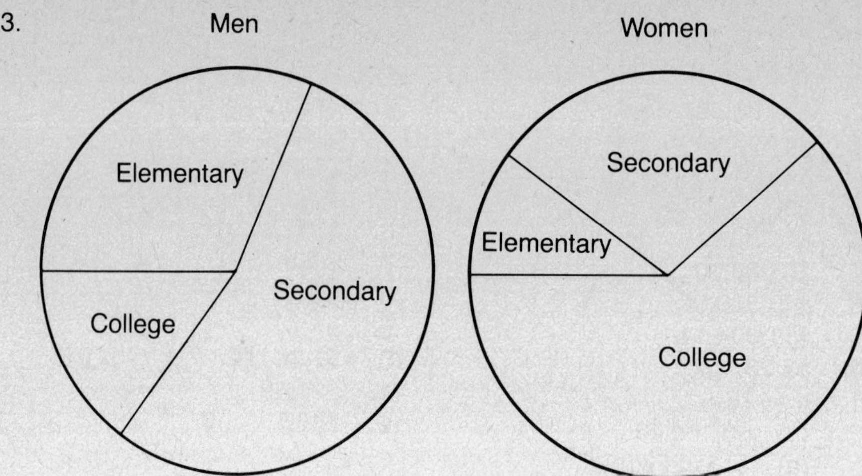

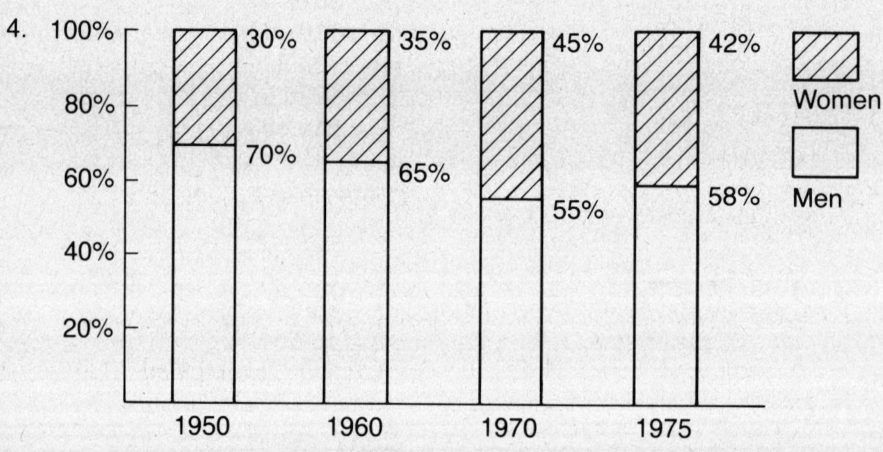

Index

Commission
    graduated, 127, 128
    real estate, 325–26, 327, 332
    sales, 127–28
    split, 325–26
    stock, 309
Common stock, 230, 231, 310, 316
Comprehensive insurance, 345,
    347–51
Compound interest, 265–77
    annuity, 280–83, 285–87
    period, 267–68
    present value, 273, 276–77
    tables, 268–69
Corporation
    investment in, 307–10, 313–16
    as ownership form, 221, 229–30
Cost
    and depreciation, 157, 163, 166,
        170–71
    and inventory, 185–88
    as markon base, 99
    in trade pricing, 95–103
Credit
    consumer, 293–303
    installment, 293–98
    open-end, 293, 300–303
    rating, 314
    trade, 81–86, 241
Cumulative stock, 233
Current assets, 156
Current ratio, 206, 208

Decimal number
    fraction equivalent, 37–38,
        52–53
    net equivalent of percent, 77
    operations with, 19–24
    percent equivalent, 52–54, 61,
        75, 77
    positional value of, 6, 52–53
    rounding of, 9

Deductible clause, 347–48, 350
Denominator, 31, 55
    lowest common, 39–40
Depreciation, 155–74
    accelerated, 165–74
    double-declining balance,
        171–72, 173, 174
    schedules, 159, 168, 172, 173
    straight-line, 157–59, 172–73
    sum of the years' digits, 165–68,
        173, 174
    units-of-production, 162–63,
        172–73
Disclosure statement, 296–97,
    302–303
Discount
    bank, 254–61
    bond price, 314
    cash, 81–86
    chain, 76–78
    series, 76–78
    single, 74–76, 78
    trade, 74–78
Dividend
    in division, 16
    stock, 230–33, 308, 309, 310
Division
    decimal numbers, 22–24
    equations, 59
    fractions, 44, 45–46
    ways to indicate, 17
    whole numbers, 16–17
Divisor, 16
    greatest common, 32–33
Double-declining balance, 170–72,
    173, 174

Earnings per share, 309–10
Earnings record, employee. *See*
    Payroll, register
Endowment life insurance, 361